Advertising Empire

RACE AND VISUAL CULTURE IN IMPERIAL GERMANY

David Ciarlo

HARVARD UNIVERSITY PRESS
Cambridge, Massachusetts
London, England
2011

Printed in the United States of America

Library of Congress Cataloging-in-Publication Data

Ciarlo, David.
Advertising empire : race and visual culture in imperial Germany / David Ciarlo.
p. cm.
Includes bibliographical references and index.
ISBN 978-0-674-05006-8 (alk. paper)
1. Advertising—Social aspects—Germany—History. I. Title.
HF5813.G4C53 2010
659.10943'09034—dc22 2010012449

To my parents,
Dorothy and Jim

CONTENTS

ILLUSTRATIONS

Color Plates

Following page 212

Plate

ACKNOWLEDGMENTS

This book has been a long journey in the making, with many unexpected turns along the way. The idea of studying the culture of colonialism came to me in 1995, while living in Zimbabwe. On a short trip to the coastal town of Swakopmund, in Namibia, I was struck by the enormous jetty that leads out to sea—and to nothingness. It is a stark testament to the failed attempt by German colonizers to remake the very landscape. And yet, the intensity with which the German tourists there scoured the town for traces of Germanness was equally striking; it pointed to something else at work, something powerful. I resolved to figure out what it was. This book is not the answer to that question, but it is the answer to a different question stumbled across along the way. Several years later, in the old state library on Unter den Linden in Berlin, I chanced across an eighty-five-year-old booklet with an odd-sounding title, *Warenzeichen Humor:* it was a picture booklet of advertisements, some funny, some horrific. The six-digit number under each picture piqued my curiosity, and I went in search of a main registry. The rest was history—in all of its messiness. This book has taken many twists and turns, and I would like to give heartfelt thanks to all who have helped along the way.

Rudy Koshar's support has been instrumental from the very beginning, and I want to thank him especially for his insight, his advice, and his ongoing belief in the project. Laird Boswell offered great counsel at an early stage, not only about the project, but also about how to be a historian. Suzanne Desan has been a guiding light, both for her lively spirit and her vibrant intellect. (One seemingly innocuous question from her caused me first to rethink, then to rework the entire book from the ground up.) Long ago, Maura O'Connor first opened my eyes to the wonderful possibilities of approaching history in new ways, and this inspired me to take risks; while they do not always pan out, I am always glad to have made the attempt, and I thank her for the courage.

Erik Jensen has seen this evolve from the beginning and has generously shared boundless energy, good advice, and an infectious optimism. Chris Capozzola, a colleague without peer, read a chapter at a crucial moment and, when asked, offered sagacious advice on virtually everything. Jonathan Zatlin, Devin Pendas, Tim Brown, and Alison Frank generously shared insights and inspiration. Harriet Ritvo closely read a chapter; more important, she has been a wonderful role model offering all-around good mentorship (though I have not always listened properly). My heartfelt thanks to John Dower for his gems of wisdom and, particularly, for timely words of encouragement. Conversations with Cynthia Milton remind me anew why I entered academia in the first place. Barbara and Willi Höfer generously shared their home and their knowledge of Berlin. And Beth Kun brought a talented designer's eye to the images; far more important, though, was her unswerving moral support at a most difficult stage.

A Fulbright fellowship at the very beginning made the research for this book possible, and while this project was still germinating, the generous input of Wolfgang Wippermann and Albert Wirz in Berlin helped enormously. Stefan Negelmann, at the Deutsches Historisches Museum, allowed me to rummage around in the collections haphazardly, for which I am grateful. And the entire staff of the Museum Europäischer Kulturen was also very helpful. At the project's midpoint, Patricia Flaherty pored through every page of a draft with careful pen; her suggestions have made me into a far better writer. Heather Hughes offered calm guidance through the labyrinthine process of image permissions. With the end in sight, the Deans' Fund at the Massachusetts Institute of Technology helped with the reproduction of images, and I especially owe the History Department of Harvard University, collectively, an enormous debt of gratitude. Most important, I am lucky to have Kathleen McDermott as my editor. Her advice is sage, her eye keen, and her patience seemingly infinite. (Sorry to have tested the last.) I am indebted to her professional acuity.

Finally, to my sister, Catherine, and my brother-in-law, Erik, who have given me a home away from home over a decade of travels: I am lucky to have you both. And to my parents, Dorothy and James, who have always supported me in every way; I can only say: thank you.

Advertising Empire

INTRODUCTION

> The larger, more eye-catching, obtrusive, and exotic the advertisement, the less the likelihood that it deals with a real and solid business.
>
> —Rudolf Cronau, in Germany's first advertising handbook, 1887

In 1911 a Düsseldorf cigar retailer by the name of Eduard Palm registered a trademark with the German Imperial Patent Office (see Plate 1). Originally designed as a poster by the renowned graphic artist Julius Klinger, the new profession of advertising in Germany heralded it as a masterpiece of form and color. It was also lauded as a clever use of humor, for it plays upon a verbal joke, namely the similarity of the retailer's last name to the tropical tree (*Palme* in German). The glowering, smoking African figure almost adds a visual exclamation mark to the textual wordplay. The figurine might also seem to incorporate the brand name, a sort of virtual spokesperson not entirely unlike famous predecessors such as the Quaker man of Quaker Oats (first appearing in ads in the 1880s) or the Michelin Man (1898). Though it never became as famous as other German commercial icons such as the pale, slender white woman of Persil (laundry soap) or the black serving moor of Sarotti (chocolate), it remained in use for more than eighty years in Berlin, Düsseldorf, Frankfurt am Main, and many other German cities. In the late 1990s a larger tobacco consortium purchased the fourteen stores of the Eduard Palm chain, and the brand disappeared from Germany and from German history.[1]

Scholars have looked at this image, and other images like it, from two entirely different vantage points. The first is to see it as an aesthetic triumph, and correspondingly as a model of advertising acumen. The Palm image is indeed an exemplary work of graphic design: a minimalist palm tree arcs through and over the firm name, culminating in a verdant cluster that compositionally balances the lopsidedness of the first capital *P*. Looping gray smoke rings, the largest in the optical center of the poster, lead the eye incrementally back to the red *O* of the figure's lips—and thence to the cigar. We then realize that the palm tree itself bows under the weight of the glaring, yet innocuous homunculus. Finally, the product itself, "cigars," appears in knock-out type underneath, subtle as an afterthought. This is a beautiful example of the *Sachplakat* (Object Poster), a commercial style that arose in Berlin and Munich after 1905 that used bold, aestheticized design to convey a vivid advertising message with minimal text. The Object Poster came as a reaction to the more ornate predecessors of *Jugendstil* and Art Nouveau, its simpler mode deemed more suited to the hectic pace of the modern city. This New Objectivity has aptly been termed the German Modern.[2] Whether one traces the genesis of this new design style back to the genius of individual artists, or to the evolution of professional advertising as a new communicative mode of capitalism, or to the acumen of the modern entrepreneur adopting new techniques of branding (all three origins have been averred), the emergence of the Object Poster definitively established Germany as a world leader of graphic design.[3]

A second stance from which to look at this image is to zero in more critically on the precarious position of the black figure itself. Given the violent history of European colonialism and racism in the nineteenth century, this view is less rosy. Caricatures of black figures appear in the advertising of most nations that were colonial powers (and many that were not) and are seen to reflect a Europe-wide popular culture defined by a diffuse sense of racial identity if not an active racism.[4] Advertisements in the vein of Eduard Palm's are often seen as reflective of the political economy of European colonialism. The presence of black figures in British and American tobacco ads, for instance, are seen as a legacy of tobacco plantation slavery, or even as a literal referent to the racial hierarchies around 1900 that still suffused the economies in the colonies that produced tobacco.[5] The presence of the black figure might also be seen as a reflection of the popularity of the "science" of race over the nineteenth century or, less sinisterly, as a reflection of a broad fascination with an exotic "Other."[6] Germany came belatedly to imperialism just as it came belatedly to national unification; an advertisement like that of Eduard Palm might be said to merely reflect its new role as colonizer.[7]

We are left with the same logo used to illustrate two very different historical phenomena—the rise of modern advertising culture and the subjugation of colonized peoples. It is one argument of this book that the two phenomena are, in fact, closely intertwined. The Eduard Palm logo is indeed a sign of Germany's advancing commercial modernity, exemplifying a new modern commercial aesthetic that would attain full fruition in the modern consumer and artistic flowering of the Weimar Republic. Yet it is simultaneously the mark of the power of the colonizer, reflecting a narcissistic interest in the exotic and a casualness with racism that was instrumental to Germany's often brutal projection of rule overseas. Modernity, however defined, so often seems to possess a Janus face.

Yet neither angle of approach, whether seeing the Eduard Palm design as innovative and modern or as racially insensitive and anachronistic, appreciates the full cultural landscape in which it sits. First and foremost, this image was never, at any point, just a single illustration. It was one droplet in a visual cascade. It appeared as chromolithographs lining the street and plastered onto walls of train stations. It was painted onto store display windows and laminated onto porcelain storefront signs. It circulated, as a black-and-white insert, in newspapers and tabloids seen by readers numbering in the millions. It rolled through the city on the sides of new electric delivery trucks; it was carried back into the home as a chromolithographed cigar tin; and as a package-sealing stamp, it was collected and doted over by adults and children alike. More important, tens of thousands of designs, many of them cut from the same cloth, were mass-reproduced by thousands of other firms and circulated in similar ways—a veritable tide of visuality washing through the urban landscape.

Four decades earlier, at the founding of the German nation, there was no such pictorial ocean. Though chromolithography traces as far back as the 1830s, five-color printing for such a trifle as a throwaway poster or advertising stamp before the 1880s was economically impracticable. In the 1860s lithographs were found in expensive journals and books and were purchased to hang as art above the mantelpiece. Technological innovations, such as the rotary press, offset printing on tins, and, eventually, offset printing on paper, would all make image reproduction cheaper and more readily available. Far more important, however, was a fundamental transformation in the economic, social, and cultural priorities of Germans. In 1870 the desire to pay for thousands or millions of images to be circulated among the public to stimulate sales might have been technologically possible, but it was commercially risky, socially unacceptable, and culturally peculiar. By 1911 it was ordinary.[8] On the eve of the First World War, the stirrings of a mass consumer society had already profoundly altered not only the tenor of economic life but the cultural landscape as well.

The German nation had also changed in other ways. In 1887 the first advertising handbook appeared in Germany; just three years earlier, however, Germany had staked a claim to colonial dominion over territory in West and South-West Africa (now Namibia). A small but vocal minority of Germans looked to colonialism as the solution to all of Germany's social problems, but they were quickly disappointed; despite a brief surge of interest (buoyed largely by the press), the German public seemed, at least to the die-hard colonial "enthusiasts," to largely ignore Germany's colonies. The German public could engage with themes of colonialism outside of these enthusiasts' purview, as we will see; but as a topic of politics and in the public sphere, Germany's colonies often took a back seat to other pressing issues of the day. In 1904, however, this all changed when Germany's ostensible subjects, the Herero, rose in armed revolt. Germans waged a colonial war in South-West Africa but with extreme brutality, using genocidal rhetoric and genocidal tactics. The appearance of Eduard Palm's glowering native on the heels of this colonial warfare and genocide might seem, on the face of it, odd—controversial or even confrontational. As this book will show, however, there was nothing unusual at all about Klinger's design or Eduard Palm's use of it; countless such figures were appearing then, all increasingly similar to each other. It is the task of this book to explain why, though German physical rule of its colonies swung through phases of apathy, brutality, and reform, commercial imagery of the colonies followed a more linear historical trajectory. Visuality, we will see, answered to its own logic—a logic that revolved around the dynamics of commercialized pictorial power.

The history of commercial visuality in Germany is a fascinating one. Advertising's empire was built, in part, on the advertising *of* empire. The notion of adorning a product with an illustration, of fusing commerce with image, first emerged in Germany, curiously enough, intertwined with elements that many have termed colonial, using the broadest sense of the word. Pioneers of German commercial culture looked overseas, at exotic lands, at exotic peoples, at the commercial cultures of other colonizing nations, and (eventually) at their "own" colonies. Yet advertising in Germany was not only an observer, importer, and imitator; it would soon carve out its own dominion. It would build its *own* "empire" in Germany and beyond. The empire of advertising is an enormous realm; its domain can be mapped in countless ways. This book traces it by focusing on a single thread, the growing hegemony of a single visual construction of race. In Germany advertising generated a new vision of race that not only overshadowed earlier ideological constructions, but also pointed to and even produced a new social identity. Benedict Anderson famously described nations as imagined communities.[9] This book explores one of the diverse processes by which identity, racial and national both, were not just imagined, but materially imaged. In color.

The larger arc of the visual commercial culture of race is foreshadowed here in four images. The first is a so-called Tobacco Moor *(Tabakmohr)* from the second half of the nineteenth century (Figure I.1). The second, from 1900, is a trademark for cigarettes that references a famous Shakespearean play (Figure I.2). A soap advertisement from 1905 is the third; its illustration plays upon an old German adage about the futility of trying to "wash a moor white" (Figure I.3). Finally, we come to the Sarotti Moor, the brand of a leading Berlin chocolate manufacturer in the second decade of the twentieth century (Figure I.4). At first glance, all of these images might seem broadly similar: each is an illustration used in some sort of mercantile setting, and each falls under the same descriptive rubric—"the moor"—a term denoting blackness and which holds a long history and a dense web of associations.[10] Any superficial similarities, however, obscure the profound distinctions between them.

Seen side by side, these images immediately reveal a host of differences in style, artistic technique, and quality of reproduction. The gulf that separates them, however, is far wider even than any point-by-point comparison of the pictures would indicate. For the crucial aspects of each image are those *not* seen: the historical backdrop; the images' commercial and cultural functions; and their potential viewing audiences. The Tobacco Moor (Figure I.1) was a traditional icon, carved into a cliché block that could stamp the image onto the wrapping of tobacco packages. (This particular one was actually registered as an early trademark in 1875 by a small

Figure I.1 Tobacco label featuring a Tobacco Moor (*Tabakmohr*) from before 1875, by Ubbo & Petersen of Norden. *Source: Warenzeichenblatt des Kaiserliches Patentamts* (hereafter WZB) (1896): 383, reg. no. 14896.

tobacconist in the town of Norden, but was likely used for centuries, unchanged, before that.) The image's clarity in reproduction is poor, and it therefore relies upon long-standing allegorical markers—an old-style pipe and tobacco-leaf skirt (native), a barrelhead (trade), and a topcoat (European)—to be recognizable. Only a few local customers would have seen it, stamped (perhaps) onto a parcel tucked under their arm on the way home from the tobacconist.

The trademark for Othello cigarettes around 1900 (Figure I.2), on the other hand, was a different thing entirely: a professionally crafted engraving that made use of more sophisticated design techniques, it was suitable for reproduction in quantity in a newspaper's advertising section. Fashioned for a short-lived brand of cigarettes produced by a midsized Dresden manufacturer at the turn of the century, it is an inside joke: to use Othello, "the Moor of Venice," in a tobacco ad is a riff on the venerable Tobacco Moor (above), but now cleverly updated for a more cosmopolitan clientele.[11] Whether all viewers would have caught the looping reference to Dutch tobacco culture via English literature remains an

Figure I.2 Othello "Moor" cigarette advertisement, 1900, by A. M. Eckstein & Söhne of Dresden. *Source:* WZB (1900): 162, reg. no. 41840.

open question. There is no doubt, however, that the physical reach of the image—reproduced in newspapers—is of an entirely different scale than that of its predecessor. It not only denoted the merchants' wares, but underwrote a new economy of print media; for this image (and others like it) subsidized newspapers, thereby lowering subscription prices, which increased circulations and extended the physical and social reach of the image itself.

The figures in the 1905 soap advertisement by the Georg Schicht company in Außig, on the other hand, stands at an even denser tangle of

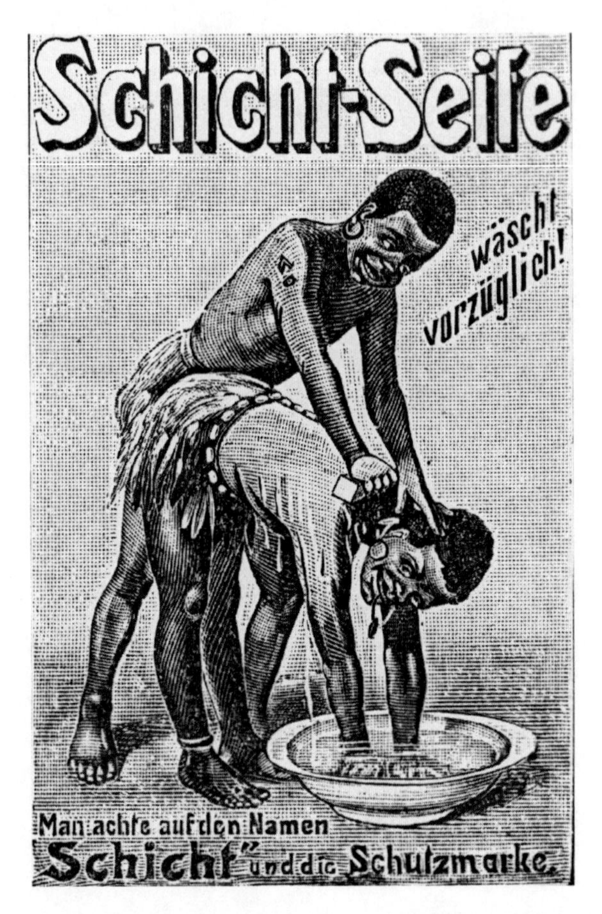

Figure I.3 Soap advertisement from 1905, by Georg Schicht, Außig (Austria). *Source:* WZB (1905): 675, reg. no. 77688.

visual threads (Figure I.3). Schicht is an Austrian firm, but it crafted this advertisement for the German soap market.[12] The graphic artist has skillfully staged a scene that makes multiple references, and produced it as an intaglio for mass reproduction in tabloids or humor magazines—new media that had circulations in the hundreds of thousands. The scene taps into the centuries-old parable concerning the futility "of attempting to wash a moor white": these two African boys, no matter how hard they scrub, will never be able to wash their blackness away. The classic parable would be known to a wide range of German viewers. Far more important, it would have been paraded before their eyes much more recently, in a mass of soap advertisements crafted after the 1890s.[13] On a more immediate level, this ad is derivative of a different source—one of the most famous American logos, the Gold Dust Twins of the Fairbanks Company of Chicago, which featured two black American children scrubbing each other in a washtub. In 1901 Fairbanks had registered the logo for use in Germany; the Schicht firm promptly plagiarized it—cashing in on the Gold Dust Twins cachet but moving the tableau to Africa to absolve themselves of copyright infringement. At the same time, Schicht was also borrowing from two decades of British advertising by Pears and Sunlight that used colonial natives to sell soap as a "civilizing" commodity.[14] (Note, for instance, how the bare feet of the African natives are drawn as if reflecting sunlight, which subtly serves to call attention to the fact that the poor Africans have no shoes.) Last, the image taps into the topicality of Germany's own colonial project in Africa—a project that had, as of 1905, taken a turn toward extreme violence. An American theme, pirated by an Austrian firm, given a classical overlay from a Greco-Roman parable that provided the pattern for a British ad, but transported to Africa in order to "Germanize" it—this vignette was truly transnational.

The last image, that of the Sarotti Moor (Figure I.4), mass-produced a stereotype in both the figurative and the literal senses of the word. Crafted by the master designer Julius Gipkens and trademarked in 1919, the Sarotti Moor was reproduced in literally endless variations, as a poster, as an ad insert, as cardboard wrapping, as a chromolithographed tin box, as a newspaper insert, and even as a collectible figurine. As one of the most widely recognized commercial icons in German history, the image has been seen by well over 200 million people, to estimate conservatively, and likely ten times that number. Sarotti's image was crafted for a new kind of viewer, the German consumer. This stereotype was in no way original; it was wholly in line with virtually every other depiction of black figures in mass consumer culture after 1910, drawing upon a fixed template of graphic conventions that pushed products ranging from shirt collars to accordions. Gipkens simply drew his figure the way all black figures were being drawn. Indeed, its key pictorial elements—the bright red lips, rounded head, and indeterminate maturity—had become so ubiquitous by the second decade of the twentieth century that they bore the interpretive weight of the image; they had become obligatory.[15]

One might reasonably ask what an African native or orientalized black figure has to do with cigars manufactured in Cuba, with soap

Figure I.4 1925 version of the Sarotti Moor drawn by Jarosy. *Source: Die Annonce* 1 (1925).

manufactured in Austria, or with chocolate manufactured in Germany. These images did not reflect the origins of the products—they were in no meaningful way reflections of actual trade relations, colonial or otherwise, as we will see. In fact, the widening gulf between the tangible reality of a good and the "aura" forged by its representation—*pace* Walter Benjamin—is a hallmark of modern consumer society.[16] In Germany that gulf emerges at the fin de siècle, even before the highly polished "surfaces" of Weimar.[17]

A more pointed and historically precise way to phrase the question would be to ask: why should these natives, or these black figures with enormous red lips, oversized eyes and ears, and bumpy heads, be reasonably expected to inspire a German viewer—a German viewer of 1900, but *not* earlier—to purchase the product? This is a complicated question, but the crux of the matter. Consumer society did not arise mechanistically out of some abstract principle of supply-and-demand economics; it was learned. This book therefore pursues two different avenues. The first is to trace how images in general, and how illustrations of blacks in particular, came to be seen as not only legitimate for commercial use, but as necessary for commercial success. The second is to see how such illustrations might have "worked"; though the complexities of reception can never truly be escaped, commercial imagery itself, as a corpus, provides clues to its own interpretation.

In Germany both the motifs of visual advertising and the initial conviction that those motifs would "work" came initially from an overseas gaze. German visual advertising was constructed transnationally; it emerged by looking at the "modernity" of America or Britain. And some of its practices emerged by gazing at the "savagery" of Africa. The circulation of these overseas visions was guided by a multiplicity of cooperating and countervailing forces in Germany, ranging from organized politics to new media to new commercial enterprises and practices. As we will see, vignettes such as those for Schicht's soap and Palm's tobacco were initially connected with a particular sort of overseas gaze—namely one loosely bound up with the German colonial project, in the broad sense.[18] Themes such as overseas exoticism, obsession with imperial Britain, fascination with primitives, and delineations of racial difference were all also found in more expressly political German colonialism. In Germany a number of institutions of colonialism, such as the German state (particularly the Colonial Section of the Foreign Office), pressure groups (such as the German Colonial Society), and academic institutions (such as Berlin's Museum for Ethnology), generated or circulated their own representations that dealt with Germany's overseas colonial effort. Over time, however, commercial imagery became only more detached from such overt, official sources. Yet it only became all the more powerful because of this autonomy. It was able to convey fantasies of colonial rule and disseminate alluring visions of racial difference to a cross-section of Germans far beyond those who were directly engaged in, or even evinced any interest in, the prosaic realities of the German colonial empire.

The Limits of the Colonial Archive

In the world of letters, imagining "the colonial" had long played an important role. In the eighteenth century, long before there was a German empire or even a German state, German literature, drama, travel writing, and scientific texts all engaged in fantasies of colonial rule that fictively described the Germans as superior colonizers in the New World. Such fantasy even helped, it has been convincingly argued, to prophesy German nationhood itself.[19] Even after Germany first claimed actual political dominion over colonies in Africa and the Pacific in the mid-1880s, the colonies, as an abstraction, continued to offer a literary terrain in which issues of political and social crisis could be discursively worked through. In the world of text, "the Colonies" posed an imaginative space onto which new social orders, fantasies of racial superiority, or desires for gender emancipation could be projected.[20] One of the peculiarities of German colonialism after 1885, however, was the degree to which such imaginings in the world of print became organized in specific institutions—institutions that then made public claims to expertise and even exclusive dominion. And they sought to steer the public sphere and to sway popular audiences by a variety of means.

The relationship between the discursive and the coercive is the lynchpin of modern colonial history, and such "tensions of empire" had enormous social consequences for colonies and metropole alike. We have learned from historians and sociologists, for instance, how colonialist ideas and practices dramatically affected the social world through avenues such as policy debates, the dicta of scientific professions, the professional inscription of ethnographic prejudices, and even the propaganda of political activists. Constructions of ethnography held enormous ramifications for the native policies of the German colonial state, for instance, while German utopian conceptions manifested in mechanisms of rule that ran up against pragmatic practices and conflicting interests. German efforts to construct a colonial inflection of "modernity" held wide-ranging implications for colonial settlement, environmental and education policies, and anti-miscegenation laws.[21] Colonial contexts, in turn, had an impact on the social world back on the German metropole. Debates over policies in the colonies parsed the meaning of "race" as the legal determinant for citizenship in Germany.[22] Women's colonial activism reshaped publicly permissible gender roles.[23] Colonialism similarly structured scientific thought: the structures of colonial medicine, anthropology, and even planning fed into the pervasiveness of eugenicist thinking more broadly in German society, which proved so insidious in later decades.[24] Thus such disparate professional groups as lawyers, politicians, scientists, academics, and political activists developed professional practices and political ideologies that drew from colonial practice and colonialist rhetoric.

In most of these scholarly investigations of the influence of the colonial project across German society, however, the *organized* colonialists continue to occupy the most prominent place. Colonialist publishing houses churned out a vast array of publications on colonial themes for their members to purchase. These publications, including many essays written for (or planted in) mainstream media, all stem from a centralized secretariat, staffed by a fairly small group of middle-class nationalists. The "message" in these publications is thereby remarkably consistent, and they compose the bibliographic mainstay of many scholarly investigations. The colonial archive—or more precisely the *colonialists'* archive—continues to construct the central narrative of the importance of colonialism to German society and culture more broadly. There is a very real question, however, as to whether the colonial archive can ever inform us meaningfully about its own limitations and blind spots.

Commercial culture, with its diffuse points of origin, offers a new opportunity. It resists investigation through institutional or organizational lenses, but this very dispersal can offer an entry point into a broader view of society. By way of comparison, scholars have shown how British and French advertising were infused with diffusely produced images of imperial rule; the imperial roots of British commodity culture, for instance, and the centrality of blackness in advertising in jazz-age France each point to linkages between the colonial encounter on the one hand, and metropolitan advertising on the other.[25] For Germany, however, there have been few investigations of commercial culture.[26] Indeed, apart from filmic representations—cinema and photography—there has been very little investigation of colonialism and colonial themes in German visual culture more broadly.[27] Yet at the fin de siècle, far more Germans saw engraved illustrations than saw photos or films.

The relationship between commercial culture, colonization, and visuality is a complex one. As this book will demonstrate, the imagery associated with "the colonial" constituted a substantial and even formative element in German advertising as well as in other forms of mass-produced visual culture. German advertising reveals the influence of the intense nationalistic competition of *Weltpolitik,* the cooperative pan-European project of the "civilizing mission," and even the global network of scientific discovery and commercial exchange. Commercial interests inside of Germany in the 1880s and 1890s drew indiscriminately from each of these facets. Yet German mass-reproduced culture did more than just borrow; it disseminated imagery of colonialism to an audience far broader than that ever reached by any institution. Ads were seen by far more Germans than any colonialist's talk on tropical hygiene or any museum's painstaking ethnographic construction. As advertising mass-reproduced the imagery of colonialism to serve commercial ends, it increasingly veered from and then overshadowed the scientific, nationalistic, religious, and even mercantile missions of official German colonialism. Institutions, the traditional purveyors of colonial ideology, could not match the new scope of mass culture.

Advertising: From Gallery to Arcade

Over the first decade of the twentieth century, visual advertising (*Bildreklame* in German) fundamentally transformed the German landscape.[28] Though early advertising writers declared their profession to be "as old as language," scholars recognize that advertising involved a communicative revolution that took place just before the end of the nineteenth century.[29] This book will argue that the first appearance of visual advertising in the 1880s and 1890s can be seen to draw a great deal of creative inspiration and commercial acumen from visions of overseas encounters. One of the strange aspects of German advertising, however, is the degree to which these themes and tropes are *not* seen in the professional literature, and in the successive scholarship that is built upon it. Like colonialists, advertising professionals, it turns out, have their own "archive"—or rather, their own museum. From the first, advertising professionals struggled to legitimize their place in German society. They accomplished this, in part, by emphasizing the aesthetic worth of their endeavor. As early as the mid-1890s, with advertising still barely reputable, museum curators such as

Justus Brinckmann began to hold up the very best, most exquisitely crafted advertising posters as not only a model for inspiration but as examples of popular art.[30] Brinckmann, the pioneering curator of Hamburg's Museum of Arts and Crafts (Museum für Kunst und Gewerbe, which opened in 1877), made no bones about his desire to use the collecting capacity of his museum to give designers something to aspire to, and thereby elevate the work of the profession as a whole.[31] Meanwhile, private collectors, such as the dentist Hans Sachs, built up their own assortment of the best, most artistic posters, which became the core collections for institutions like the Deutsches Historisches Museum.[32]

This tradition of focusing on the artistic poster spread beyond the walls of the museum through publications, such as J. L. Sponsel's *Das Moderne Plakat*, and particularly the new design magazines, such as the *Monograph of German Advertising-Artists* (published by a sort of virtual museum) and the lavishly illustrated *Das Plakat*.[33] The rich, beautiful, full-color illustrations of *Das Plakat* are a pleasure to behold, and have made it the centerpiece of art-historical investigations, which follow its concern to introduce "art" into "commerce."[34] Yet the beautiful posters that made it into the attentions of museum curators (such as Brinckmann), and into museum collections and the pages of design journals, were carefully selected at every step of the way. The Object Poster is indeed an icon of modern design, but it is also an artifact of selective self-promotion—a claim to artistic merit by poster promoters and advertising writers with their own professional agendas. In the chapters that follow, the illustrations are every bit as powerful and inventive as the more familiar Object Poster, but they are also very different from those typically seen in the canon of German design.

Seeing Germany: A Method of Visual History

Did advertising images merely echo widespread public perceptions, or did the creators of these images produce perceptions with their advertising? Is advertising a cultural mirror, or were advertisers the puppet masters of the popular mind? Some version of this conundrum has structured investigations of advertising from the very earliest days. Two divergent approaches have tended to dominate: the first, which sees advertisers as manipulators, often takes as a starting point the Frankfurt School's notion of a "culture industry."[35] The second, which sees advertising as a cultural product, might instead look more to either semiology or cultural studies, where advertisements can be decoded for their reflection of gender norms and imperial ideologies.[36]

The quandary is not only a problem for advertising. The relationship between image and interpretation has haunted broader theoretical ruminations from the very first coalescence of art history as an academic field, and it remains a thorny crux of contemporary studies of visual culture.[37] The theoretical dilemma is ultimately irresolvable, yet to some degree it is artificial. Most theoretical reflections on the manipulative capacity of images, or alternately, about the innumerable ways images can be interpreted, seem to postulate or presuppose—even if quite subtly—an observer face to face with an image. That is, a discrete individual, faced with a discrete individual image. Thus formulated, the act of interpretation becomes framed by an arbitrarily determined origin—an origin that overtly or subtly incorporates the intentions behind the initial production of the image—and an arbitrary ending point—the moment when the viewer first sees the image and reacts. Both observer and image are thereby each extracted from their historical milieu—the very milieu that informed both the production of the image *and* the consciousness of the observer.[38] Advertising images, in particular, need to be seen less as a laboratory test tube, held up to the light, and more as a pattern in a downpour. Other theoretical stances, on the other hand, particularly in some of the new approaches of visual culture, go a bit too far in the other direction. They treat images as so fluid as to be infinitely portable, or always open to multiplicity of interpretation—an ocean in which viewers can see what they will.[39] Each of these leads to its own flavor of decontextualization, and both lose sight of overarching structures of power (of all varieties, political, economic, social disciplinary, visual) that contain and channel imagery.

Here is where historians can offer something new to the debate. When the analysis shifts away from such an imagined juxtaposition of a single (autonomous) observer and a single (extracted) image, and looks instead at larger patterns of imagery over time, the dilemma over the precise relationship between any individual image and any individual's consciousness fades in significance. Viewing imagery collectively and coherently, as a corpus over time, allows us to see the existence of patterns—of ways of crafting *and* of seeing imagery—that are mutually reinforcing. Oftentimes imagery that doesn't make sense—where we today do not understand the joke or fail to see the associative connection—offers some of the best opportunities to see reception at work, for it points to visual patterns no longer in evidence. And this, in turn, gives us a window into how people used to "see." Overall, some patterns of imagery can be recognized ultimately as so pervasive, this book argues, that they collectively constitute a visual hegemony—a codification of representation so ubiquitous that those seeking to craft a representation need to deploy it to be easily understood. In simpler terms, a broad, historical survey of visuality might be able to tell us something about *how* people saw, and even how they interpreted those images, merely by showing and analyzing *what* they saw, over and over and over again.

Additionally, viewing these visual hegemonies historically allows us to chart the discrete operations of power—whether political, social, cultural, or (as I will describe) visual power—at work in constructing, maintaining, and reshaping such hegemonies. Visual patterns were never permanently fixed. My emphasis throughout this book centers on the historical dynamism of visuality—on the way that patterns of imagery shifted, and on the political, commercial, and cultural forces that produced such shifts. In some cases I also suggest moments in which the reverse might have occurred—where social or political power could be produced by visual hegemonies. Just as social practices generate images, images generate social practices. Moreover, visual hegemonies themselves are historical, and therefore transitory—undermined by external and internal forces, as the epilogue will suggest. My methodology of visuality in the pages that follow is to approach each image with an eye toward its pictorial lineage, the historical context in which it circulates, and the image's power—both within the frame of the image and outside of that frame, in the scope of its reproduction.

At the core of this analysis lies a comprehensive visual archive, namely the collection of trademark registration rolls of the Imperial Patent Office *(Warenzeichenblatt des Kaiserliches Patentamt)*. The extensive registers of text and illustrations in the trademark registration rolls provide a great deal more than a simple list of brand names. Businesses of every type, from every region of Germany, rather cleverly registered their pictorial advertisements in addition to their trademarks and slogans in the often futile effort to protect them from being appropriated or stolen outright.[40] One advertiser from 1918 likened an advertisement to a child, and waxed poetically that, just as the name of the newborn child is proudly noted in the register of the Civil Registry Office *(Standesamt)*, so the word or image of the ad is proudly noted in the trademark rolls of the Patent Office *(Patentamt)*.[41] A methodical examination of these registration rolls from 1894 into the mid-1920s yielded a very large pool of images by which to trace the patterns of visual mass marketing.[42] Other comprehensive collections of visual sources complement my use of the trademark registration rolls.[43] The physical collections of the Deutsche Historisches Museum in Berlin, moreover, have been especially useful, as well as those of the Museum Europäischer Kulturen and the Übersemuseum in Bremen. To map the connections (and disconnections) of this imagery to professional circles, the professional advertising journals and handbooks published before 1918 have been scoured; so too the records of the German Colonial Society in the Bundesarchiv and a thorough sample of the vast array of publications by colonial enthusiasts.

Balancing visual sources against one another reveals insights that might not otherwise be recognized: trademark registrations, compared against posters or against advertising stamps, shows the subtle alterations made to illustrations when recrafted for a different medium. When Julius Klinger's poster designs were adapted for use as an advertising stamp, for instance, the printers cut away all unnecessary detail, leaving—and thereby revealing—what the printers themselves saw as the design's most meaningful or essential elements. Second, trademarks offer a more even-handed survey of advertising imagery. On the one hand, museum collections generally contain posters originally chosen primarily for their artistic merit—and so for their uniqueness rather then their typicality. They are therefore hardly representative of what was actually seen. On the other hand, the giant national brands that have survived to this day, such as Odol, Nivea, Persil, or Sarotti, often link their imagery teleologically to their economic success by way of highlighting the originality of their brand.[44] Yet these companies were but a sliver of the vast, transitory world of commercial imagery at the fin de siècle. The vast majority of trademarked illustrations in the registration rolls were produced by scattered small businesses and were as fleeting as the businesses that crafted them.[45] Moreover, these giant brands, as we will see, were in no way original; they were in fact highly derivative of broader trends.

Historians need to take visuality seriously as a dense source material in its own right, not merely as an "illustration"—a reflection—of economic power or of political ideology. Nor should they be used by scholars as illustrations of observations or insights gleaned from textual sources.[46] Indeed, visual history can also tell us a great deal about non-visual history. The decentralized production of trademark registrations can usefully set the colonial enthusiasts' claims to what is (and is not) public opinion or popular appeal into sharper relief. In a similar vein, visual trademarks reveal that advertising writers (publishing in trade journals and handbooks) are equally self-aggrandizing; their rhetorical claims to striking originality, or their larger assertions about the usefulness of tasteful decorum, can similarly be evaluated against actual practice. Overall, my research suggests that colonialists were less popular than they claimed, and advertisers less original than they claimed. The visual field requires its own history. By 1914 visual imagery was not only omnipresent but was generated by dispersed producers. This does not mean it was diverse; imitation, not originality, was the rule for advertising. Indeed, imitation was one of the primary building blocks of hegemony.

What these visual sources do not allow access to, however, are the voices of the subaltern. Sander Gilman memorably described German cultural and literary appropriations of blackness as "independent of any external reality"—in other words, as "blackness without blacks."[47] But pioneering work by scholars in Germany and the United States has begun to erode this conception. The history of the Afro-German experience from the 1920s, and even some of the lost stories of the small African and African American communities in Germany in the imperial period, are being recovered.[48] The recuperation of this history is an uphill struggle, for Germany has been consistently defined as an ethnically monolithic nation, despite centuries at the crossroads of multicultural exchange and geographic migration.[49] Unfortunately, in the long-overdue effort to recapture the multiethnic history of Germany, this book will be of little help. As the epigraph that opened this chapter (by Rudolph Cronau) suggests, commercial visuality is not about the social reality that lays unseen, beneath the surface. It is about the surface—about how highly visible constructions obscured social complexity in powerful ways. Afro-Germans, like Africans and African Americans, could all interpret racial imagery in very different ways, of course (just as white Germans could), and even appropriate it. In one sterling example, a poster image (from the firm Adolph Friedländer), designed as an eroticized, exoticized orientalism for a white male audience, made its way to central Africa, where it was appropriated and reinterpreted as religious iconography by devotees of the indigenous cult of Mami Wata, and from there made fantastic journeys further still, to Cuba and beyond.[50] But such appropriations are difficult to see. The investigation of the larger patterns of commercial imagery—and the ways that such patterns structured the visual field as a whole—leaves little room for the recuperation of important but unseen social and cultural histories. This does not mean that visual power structures are invariably repressive or offensive; the link between the racialization that this book describes and the racism of everyday discrimination is neither axiomatic nor simple.

Envisioning German Modernity

After the fin de siècle, the emerging forces of commercial mass culture offered a new, more powerful vision of Germany's future by explicitly illustrating a new comprehensive identity for Germans. By the First World War, advertising appeared on every conceivable surface. Indeed, one of the most important dynamics of commercial imagery, as this book will show, was its ubiquity; collectively, it formed a "consumer imaginary." Within this consumer imaginary, both colonial power and the racial otherness of Africans offered touchstones around which sectors of German society could orient their engagement with modernity. Much has been written about Germany's relationship to the "modern."[51] And there were, of course, many touchstones for modernity in Germany—from notions of *Heimat* and landscape, to gendered visions of consumerism or of domesticity, to the cult of *Technik*, just to name three. Local sensibilities of community in Hamburg or the Rhineland provided the motor for innovative developments in artistic education, urban planning, or landscape preservation—which a modernizing state could dismiss as obstructionist.[52] Debates about the place of women in the domestic sphere, in the public sphere, in the workforce, or as mothers to the nation could articulate and contest the very meaning of modernity.[53] And the cult of technological progress could run up against fears about the unnerving pace of modern life.[54] The German consumer imaginary of the early twentieth century included a constellation of visions, and many of these visions touched on such areas. Depictions of idealized motherhood or of romanticized childhood circulated alongside those of eroticized femininity or of avant-garde fashion; landmarks of local culture circulated alongside more national visions that invoked a fetishized technology or a masculinized militarism. Each of these multifaceted visions has its own unique historical trajectory up through the fin de siècle. Collectively, they all reflected, contributed to, and remade identities of nation, region, social class, gender, and race.

As they did so, these visions played off each other. One of the single most ubiquitous commercial tropes in Germany at the fin de siècle, for instance, was of a happy, slightly chubby white child with bright eyes, clutching either a chocolate bar or his mother's skirt, or imitating an adult (dressed in a naval uniform, for instance) (see Figure I.5). Some of these pleasant images of cherubic childhood stretch all the way back to religious iconography of Italian Renaissance painters. Yet they also amplified other images circulating in the consumer imaginary—namely, those of childlike black racial figures, such as the one in the Palm advertisement that opens this book. Indeed, such images of whiteness depended upon the juxtaposition of contrasting images for their potency. (In a similar way, images of eroticized femininity were sharpened by images of domestic motherhood.) To extract any single pictorial thread—in my case, the thread of "race"—from this unfolding visual tapestry of consumer imagery may be as methodologically perilous as it is a practical necessity. Focusing on race alone, for instance, overlooks the ways in which gendered visions and racial visions mutually constructed each other. (Indeed, a second book could easily be written on that very interaction alone.) Among the most persistent and powerful visions in the German consumer imaginary, however, were those that engaged with the interaction of colonial rule and racial differentiation. Within the larger course of German history, marked by extreme violence, these racial visions were particularly salient. They have also proven particularly persistent.

Advertising Empire: Race and Visual Culture in Imperial Germany consists of two parts, with the fin de siècle as a rough line between them. Chapters 1–3 offer a history of visuality and map the origins of mass-produced commercial imagery before the turn of the twentieth century. Chapter 1 offers a panorama of the origins of commodity culture. As intellectuals such as Walter Benjamin have suggested, commodities first came to be invested with larger meanings partly through the great exhibition, which arrayed products into artful presentations that both exalted the product

Figure I.5. Enameled poster for Seelig's candied corn-coffee (an ersatz coffee). *Source:* Andreas Maurer and Klaus Pressmann, eds., *Email-Reklame-Schilder* (Zürich: Museum für Gestaltung Zürich Kunstgewerbemuseum, 1986), 29.

and infused it with an aura of significance. In the Bremen exhibition of 1890, the first grand exhibition in Germany, goods were integrated into a painted panorama of exotic lands and an ethnography of curious fetishes. But why, and who held the paintbrush? Such practices of display stood at the conflux of diverse impulses, ranging from pecuniary interest, to educational legitimacy, to political imperative, which came together on the common ground of the exhibition space. The tensions between these different interests came out six years later, in Berlin's great Industrial Exhibition of 1896, where enrapturing entertainments, gripping spectacles, and consumable pleasures (an emphasis on the panorama's vivid color, if you will) were segregated from the colonialist exhibitors (a focus on the ethnographic detail).

Chapter 2 turns to the "impressions" of other peoples—that is, the habit of producing and reproducing, in the world of print, a distant land in the form of a human figure. Clichés (in the literal sense) of exotic foreigners appear as far back as the voyages of discovery in the fifteenth century, but in the 1880s, such engraved exotics were supplanted by a colorful new embodiment, the profit-driven "people show" *(Völkerschau).* These performances of live natives were among the earliest commercial spectacles of the exotic; but just as important, their visual promotion introduced new visual styles to the German public sphere. Sensational spectacles in the 1880s gave way to planographic panopticism in the 1890s. From there it was but one step to chromolithographed savagery. Together, these visual styles created a template for German commercial culture.

Chapter 3 describes the emergence of the masters of the modern exotic, from erudite amateurs to the professionalized experts of advertising and of colonialism. The very earliest German advertisers looked overseas for inspiration and, more important, as a means by which to establish their credentials in the German social landscape; they staked their status (professional and social) on mastering the new, modern methods developed in such nations as Britain and the United States. Professional colonialists, meanwhile, wrapped themselves in the flag and needed no further legitimation, but their rhetoric of populism, I argue, is belied by a vision more pedantic than popular. These three chapters collectively show some of the impulses, forces, and contradictions behind the emergence of commercial visuality as a new social practice.

The second half of the book presents a visual history. Turning primarily to visual sources more than any other, it sketches broad patterns of imagery in advertising and packaging across different products and media, and traces how these patterns shifted over the first decade of the new century. Such shifts can be seen at the confluence of events, opportunities, and unseen forces, from the refraction of thrilling news in the new mass media, to lingering strands of colonialist ideology, to professional habits of iconological imitation, to the dynamics internal to advertising itself as a mass-produced visual form.

Chapter 4 focuses on the new prevalence of the motif of the African native in advertising and packaging around 1900. The salience and the "visual momentum" of this figure drew from a number of contexts and historical confluences, from the packaging of the exotic to the commodification of colonial warfare. But the growing popularity of the African native as a motif also flowed from the possibilities inherent in commercial visuality and the cultural and visual dynamic inherent to mass replication. While the first half of the chapter focuses on themes, the second half introduces several new shades to the pictorialization of colonial "rule"—a gauge that included both conceptual and visual components. Commercial imagery offered a "visual logic" of colonialism, but it also offered tactics at the optical level, which could unerringly guide the interpretation of the image.

Chapters 5 and 6 turn to the racialization of black figures in German visual culture. Chapter 5 traces the patterns of racial depictions back to such unrecognized origins as the American minstrel show, which crossed the Atlantic in the 1880s to surface in German advertising in the 1890s, and in particular to minstrelsy's attendant promotional posters. American products such as toothpaste were also imported directly into Germany wrapped in racial imagery. Germans then repackaged their own commodities with an eye on the export market. Finally, traditional forms seen as "German," such as caricature, were appropriated for commercial purposes, and in the process were redrawn. Chapter 6 maps the expanding empire (in the figurative sense) of a racialized consumer imagery at the midpoint of the first decade of the twentieth century. A growing hegemony of racial depiction can be seen in relation to Germany's genocidal war against the Herero in South-West Africa after 1904. But it also flowed from the internal mechanics and dynamics of visual mass culture, which involved imitation, exaggeration, distance recognition, and visual impact. By 1914 a coherent vision of racial difference was stereotypified and broadcast to virtually every person in Germany, with important implications for German national, racial, and consumer identity. The conclusion traces the import of racial hegemony in the lead-up to the First World War, with a quick glimpse into the Weimar Republic to spotlight two of the ways that this racial hegemony could be either playfully subverted or used as a bludgeon.

1

EXOTIC PANORAMAS AND LOCAL COLOR

Commercial Exhibitions and Colonial Expositions

In his unfinished work on the Paris shopping arcades, the essayist and philosopher Walter Benjamin glimpsed the origins of modern advertising in the pleasures of the great exhibitions of the late nineteenth century, where amusements were sold en masse and commodities were laid out before the eyes of strolling spectators. He wrote, "The business of pleasure [in the exhibition] refines and multiplies the varieties of the reactive behavior of the masses. In this way it prepares them to be worked upon by advertising. The connection between this industry and the world exhibitions is thus well-founded."[1] Today we can immediately sense the parallel: wandering through a contemporary shopping mall, with its stylish window displays and clamoring distractions, can seem in the same moment like a trade show and an amusement park—and also seem, in some uncanny way, to be transporting us into a three-dimensional glossy advertising flyer. Written in the 1930s, Benjamin's description resonates with an earthly physicality: "pleasures," "reactive," "the masses," "worked upon."[2] Benjamin's writings overall emerge out of a long line of materially oriented thinkers tracing back to Karl Marx. Marx, the unswerving rational materialist, had struggled a bit with the more irrational elements of political economy. A product's value should be equal to either the time, capital, and labor it took to make it, for instance, or its use-value (as with an umbrella in a downpour), and the overvaluation of a commodity—a costly Gucci umbrella in a sunny climate—did not fit well into a materialist frame. In grappling with such processes that were really more psychological than material, Marx introduced the notion of the "commodity fetish." The condescension inherent in the phrase—connoting both superstition and primitiveness—was not unintentional.[3] The notion of the commodity fetish has influenced thinking on exhibitions, and on advertising, ever since.

The word "fetish" may have been more telling than Marx ever realized. Originally from the Portuguese word for "charm," it arose out of encounters on the Guinea coast in the first wave of European colonization in the sixteenth century to describe the Africans' amulets and objects used for enchantment. "Fetish" quickly entered into the English lexicon, perhaps because of its usefulness: the word could deride the excess of idolatry, but without risking insult to legitimate objects of veneration—because, by definition, the fetish remained an attribute of another culture, a primitive culture.[4] Our sacred object cannot possibly be the same as their superstition-laden fetish. But by the nineteenth century, the word had expanded; particularly after Freud, it became synonymous with any nonrational obsession. Today the word has come full circle, with some contemporary scholars arguing that Europeans' obsession with the primitive cultures of other parts of the world itself amounted to fetishism.[5]

This book will point to a relationship that is more than just one of terminology. The fetishization of the commodity—in the broadest sense, the taproot of consumerism—was connected to the commodification of the fetish—in the sense that the "fetish" here stands as an encapsulation of an exotic, overseas culture. In Germany, the exhibition played a crucial early role in both processes, facilitating the means by which representation and commodity could be and would be more tightly bound together. The connection of commodities to broader meanings did not occur only in the misperception of the material, as Marx would have it, or solely in the mimesis (reactive behavior) per Benjamin's reflections.[6] It also took place in the realm of the eye. And in late nineteenth-century Germany the grand exhibition became one staging ground for a new visual strategy—a visual strategy that looked to distant shores for its entertaining character.

The grand exhibition of the nineteenth century was many things: a shrine to science, a marker of Europeans' progress, an arena for nationalistic competition, and even a theater of cultural diversity. The success of Britain's legendary Crystal Palace in 1851 inspired a procession of great exhibitions in Paris, Amsterdam, and other European capitals, each one larger, more costly, and better attended than the one before. These exhibitions reflected the capacity of the European industrial age. Equally important, they also helped to construct its worldview; some have seen these exhibitions as a building block of Western identity itself—an "exhibitionary complex" that drove Europeans to arrange the bewildering multiplicity of the world into discrete and comprehensible parts, and then display these parts as a way to showcase their own cultural power.[7] Yet one of the most important aspect of the grand exhibitions, often overlooked, was that they were wondrously, uniquely entertaining. They were a business of *pleasure,* and this accounts for a great deal of their prominence in European social and cultural life. As Walter Benjamin wrote: "world exhibitions are places of pilgrimage to the commodity fetish . . . [They] open up a phantasmagoria which a person enters in order to be *distracted.*[8]

In Germany the business of pleasure as part of the exhibitionary complex followed a circuitous route. None of the largest international exhibitions in the 1860s, 1870s, and 1880s were in German lands. The closest was the World's Fair in Vienna in 1873. Exhibitions in Berlin or Munich before the late nineteenth century remained smaller local or regional affairs.[9] Belated German unification factored into Germany's belated culture of grand exhibitions; with the British and French exhibitions, nationalism and a sensibility of international competition had often generated financing and public attention. Moreover, the perceived provincialism of many German territories and principalities before 1870 made them unlikely pilgrimage sites for visitors from abroad. Perhaps more important, however, was that the inflections of middle-class identity in the German states (and later, Germany), with its stress on *Bildung* (education/erudition) and correct comportment, seemed sharply at odds with the display practices beginning to emerge in the grand exhibitions of London and Paris.[10] British exhibition organizers began directing their appeals to cater to audiences outside the traditional middle classes as early as the 1870s,[11] but many articulations of German middle-class identity made such popularization less desirable. Germans' "exhibitionary complex" tended toward other sorts of venues, such as natural history museums.[12]

Up through the 1880s, then, Germans tended to be spectators (or participants) rather than organizers (or directors) of the grand exhibition. Many Germans attended the great international exhibitions in other European capitals, of course, and some German industries exhibited in these venues. Yet the most significant German spectatorship of grand exhibitions was not real but virtual. The German illustrated magazines in the 1880s, casting about for dramatic events and spectacles to unfold before the eyes of their subscribers, turned to the grand expositions in London, Paris, and other great cities. Leipzig's *Illustrirte Zeitung,* for instance, devoted a great deal of space to engraved illustrations from Amsterdam's International Colonial Exhibition of 1883.[13] Most Germans, seeing the grand exhibitions only on the printed page, were spectators twice removed: spectators of others' spectacles. German critics, meanwhile, viewed the Industrial Exhibitions and World's Fairs in London and Paris from positions that ranged from envy (anxiously wringing their hands over German weakness in this international "competition") to scorn for English venality and vacuity. By the 1880s, however, more Germans were calling for a grand exhibition—a World's Fair—to be staged in the newly unified nation of Germany. Some declared a grand exhibition would demonstrate to Europe and the rest of the world Germany's national industrial might and artistic talents. Others insisted more practically that such exhibitions were becoming economically necessary.[14] Ultimately, however, the pecuniary successes of British and French exhibitions pushed Germans out of their critical distance.

The Panorama of Commodities in Bremen, 1890

In 1890 *Over Land and Sea (Über Land und Meer),* an illustrated entertainment magazine with a penchant for taking its readers on imaginary journeys to exotic lands and faraway places, devoted several columns to describing the new Northwest German Commerce and Industry Exhibition, just opened in the port city of Bremen. This exhibition was the most impressive yet staged in Germany, and it would prove significant in the evolution of a German commodity fetish. In characteristically flowery prose, *Over Land and Sea* described the entryway to the exhibition's Trade Pavilion as "a meeting of intellect and fantasy for the journey to the furthest corners of the world that the visitors are about to undertake." It continued,

> Visions of the most distant lands and territories pass by the psyche *(Geiste)* of the viewer—just like in a Panorama. All the lands of the earth have their goods brought together here into this monumental museum of trade. Rich ethnographic collections teach about the cultural standing *(Kulturstand)* of the different peoples. And the artistry of the murals, many of which are pulled partway into the foreground by supplementary sculpture, enchant with their colorful images and scenic allure.

But then it returned to the commodities:

> In the midst of all this, the extraction, packaging, and stockpiling *(Verstapelung)* of all the individual commodities are shown through models and paintings. With such a stimulating imprint, the spectator will never become bored; as he strides through the rooms, alluring tropical regions morph into richly-adorned temples and houses. And he will be separated only reluctantly from this place of such pleasant and rich edification *(Belehrung)*.[15]

The secret to bringing pleasure into commodity displays became travel to exotic realms. Or virtual travel, at any rate. A visitor could stride through distant lands, according to *Over Land and Sea*'s evocative prose, just by striding from room to room. At this point, at the beginning of the 1890s, it was crucial that this vivid experience was more than just merely pleasurable; the writer insisted the exhibition was a "meeting of fantasy and *intellect*" and that the travel was not only pleasurable but richly edifying. Other leisure journals, such as the *Illustrirte Zeitung,* echoed this theme.[16] For the German middle classes in the nineteenth century, activities such as strolling through an exhibition and gazing at exhibits needed that educational element; amusement without some greater goal of self-improvement was seen as déclassé.[17] The more noble activity of self-improvement—of becoming educated about the world—legitimized the enjoyable activity of strolling through the exhibition gazing at spectacles such as exotic landscapes. Indeed, German burghers could publicly display their pursuit of edification, for a promenade through the exhibition was not just about seeing but about *being* seen. It was through the imperative for a patina of edification that German colonialism found its place in Bremen's commercial exhibition.

Bremen, a venerable Hanseatic trading town, had long been connected to distant parts of the world, second only to Hamburg as a chief import and export hub for the new German empire. It is not surprising that a port city, rather than a city from the industrial Ruhr, would bring the grand commercial exhibition to the new German nation. Port cities such as Bremen and Hamburg held close economic and cultural connections with London, the birthplace of the industrial exhibition. Moreover, as a point of exchange, port cities had not only the requisite capital to stage large-scale commercial theater but also the incentive: merchant houses could concretely benefit from greater public visibility in a way that, for instance, coal manufacturers of the Ruhr could not. Bremen's rivalry with Hamburg was also a factor. Hamburg had attempted to stage a grand exhibition the previous year, in 1889, but this was smaller and not entirely successful; and Bremen's Northwest German Commerce and Industry Exhibition would not only learn from Hamburg's mistakes, but capitalize on them—and thereby demonstrate Bremen's superiority over its maritime rival to the rest of Germany and the world.

Bremen's Northwest German Commerce and Industry Exhibition also inaugurated the first real colonial exhibition on German soil, although this fact has gone unnoticed by historians of German colonialism.[18] Bremen's connections with London probably fed into this colonial cast; London was not only the world's commercial hub, but also the showcase of the empire. In fact, London's Colonial and Indian Exhibition, just four years earlier in 1886, was a thoroughly imperially minded endeavor. It featured an opulent Indian Court of more than 100,000 square feet, displaying this "Jewel in the Crown" of the British Empire for all (including Germans) to covet. The 1880s overall saw a general escalation of colonialist displays across Western Europe. The first grand exhibition to bank primarily on colonial prestige (rather than industrial prowess) had been that of Amsterdam, staged three years prior in 1883. Paris upped the imperial ante in 1889, building artificial "colonial villages" on the exhibition grounds, which were populated with peoples brought in from Africa and Asia; it netted an enormous profit.[19] These exhibitions not only reflected an intensification of international competition in the colonial arena, but also played off of (and into) British and French media interest in colonial matters—a publicity that could generate greater ticket sales. Germany's transnational public gaze, in turn, was directed to these Dutch, British, and French colonial exhibitions by Germany's own middle-class journals, imitating British magazines in the effort to expand circulations.[20] Bremen's own foray into panoramic commercial theater and colonial "color" occurred at the tail end of this wave that began in London.

Planners of Bremen's great exhibition spared no expense. The initial sponsorship for Bremen's 1890 exhibition came from shipping magnates; the "Grosskaufmann" Christoph Papendieck was instrumental in securing guarantees of more than 300,000 marks from the "Burgher-circles" in Bremen, and Gustav Deetjen, "enthused with patriotism," donated 300,000 marks.[21] Built in the midst of a large park, the exhibition spanned more than forty hectares. The large exhibition grounds were extensively landscaped, with two central courts that facilitated promenading (and were even illuminated with that new technological wonder, the electric light). The exhibition proper consisted of four main pavilions. A Machine Hall geared to science and engineering stood next to a Hall of Art that brimmed with Renaissance and Baroque masterpieces. The Marine and High-Seas Fishing Pavilion, with a stylized ship atop its cupola, presented models of the steamers of Bremen's merchant marine alongside the warships of the new German Imperial Navy. Yet the "pearl of the exhibition" was the Trade Pavilion, in which all the wares of the world were arrayed in panoramic fashion. In it, local goods were next to those from a great distance, the familiar placed alongside the exotic, and the mundane adjacent to the most rare. The Trade Pavilion drew the most attention from commentators and visitors alike; with more than 100 major exhibitors, it showcased Bremen's status as a center of Germany's trade, and Bremen's international reach.

As with earlier exhibitions in other nations, Bremen's effort was torn between a respectable, restrained display (in this case, of the city's mercantile prowess) and the need to offer amusements and entertainments to attract admissions-paying crowds to cover the exhibition's costs.[22] And the "businesses of pleasure" (as Benjamin termed it) thrived in Bremen's exhibition grounds. Orientalist architecture, from both the near and far East, titillated the eye.[23] Among other distractions and amusements, a tethered balloon (which had proven to be a hit at Hamburg the year before)[24] took spectators up to a height of more than 600 meters, from which they could survey the exhibition grounds and the surrounding city. Castan's *Irrgarten,* a hall of mirrors, also offered an altered perspective; a paid announcement in the official guide proclaimed Castan's to be "The Sight Most Worth Seeing in the Modern Era!"[25] Such boastfulness stood out among the other more restrained announcements for restaurants and the like.

But what about edification? A looming danger had been confronted before, at a smaller Commerce and Industry Exhibition staged in Hamburg in 1889. Constructed in haste, it met with negative responses (despite financial success).[26] The visitors entirely ignored the exhibition halls themselves, one Hamburg newspaper commentator said, bristling. He bemoaned that four-fifths of Hamburg's visitors were "mere pleasure-seekers." Instead of entering the display halls to learn about Hamburg's trade, they spent their time with the spectacular amusements, from the hot-air balloon ride to the Panorama.[27] Another newspaper complained that the season-pass holders "were not looking for instruction nor inspiration, but to frequent the exhibit as a pleasant resort to relax for the duration of the summer."[28] Yet the exhibition halls were not only the raison d'être of the exhibition; they were important to legitimize the pleasure-seeking in the first place. Unfortunately, the displays in Hamburg seem to have been less than gripping. A hint as to why can be seen in the main display hall's name: it was ploddingly termed "The Exhibition Hall of Overseas Raw Materials and Half-Manufactures." At Bremen the following year, most of the official guidebooks and catalogs opened by mentioning Hamburg's earlier effort and, perhaps somewhat cattily, expressing sympathy that there had not been sufficient preparation time for Hamburg to make its displays "more interesting."[29]

How to avoid the fate of Hamburg—boredom? The chief editor of Bremen's exhibition catalog, none other than Werner Sombart, illuminated their strategy in his closing comments. Sombart, later to become one of Germany's preeminent economists and sociologists, began his career working for Bremen's Chamber of Commerce, and he wrote here:

> The leading personages [of the Commerce and Industry Exhibition] endeavored from the very first to hold at bay the danger of a boring display of product samples. A bit of the peculiar needed to be brought before the eyes of the public. Out of this stemmed the effort to pull everything possible out of every land. This all had but one aim: to lend the sample wares some "local color."[30]

Sombart's assessment of the need for "a bit of the peculiar" and for the goods to be lent some local "color" might at first glance seem to be nothing more than a strategy to make the exhibition more interesting, and thereby boost attendance and profits. But there was already plenty of stimulation on the exhibition grounds clamoring for attendees' attention, from the aerial panorama of the hot-air balloon to the titillating narcissism of the funhouse mirror. And Hamburg, the previous year—despite being profitable precisely because of such stimulations—had not been deemed successful. The organizers needed to generate the right *sort* of excitement. The "boring display of product samples" needed "a bit of the peculiar" to remain competitive. To keep up with the development of popular new entertainments in order to remain the focal point of the exhibition and thereby legitimize the whole enterprise, commodities needed to be *seen* as more than just "half-manufactures." As Sombart described, this was done by lending the wares some of the "local color" derivative of their exotic origins. But as we will see, color could come in a number of palettes.

Trade, in this exhibition, emerged as more than the actual (and rather mundane) operation of warehouses, manifests, shipping timetables, and ledger books. The *Illustrirte Zeitung* reported that the exhibits were designed to illustrate the "circumstances behind the winning of the most important commodities." Trade thereby became imbued with a competitive sensibility ("winning"), overheated evaluation ("most important"), and edification, folded into a panoramic survey of exotic places. Consumption, too, became more than simply perusing a stock of overseas raw materials and half-manufactures. The *Illustrirte Zeitung* stressed that the exhibits laid out the "climatic, ethnological, and scientific relationships" embodied within the displayed commodities. In order "to present the spectator with impressive and educational images," the magazine insisted, "artistic and practical work must go hand in hand."[31] The consumption of representation thereby became enmeshed with an edifying form of imaginative travel to distant and exotic lands. According to the official guidebook, the goal of the Trade Pavilion was "to demonstrate the dimensions and power of Bremen's trade before the visitors' very eyes," and to do so in a manner that truly "excites interest," but just as important, it was to "enrich with the knowledge of the lands of the earth in its geographic, cultural, and ethnographic peculiarities."[32]

The Trade Pavilion offered "an artistic ordering, with great wall murals to provide a backdrop of fitting landscapes—murals which offer the eye new delights and joys with every step."[33] In the central foyer, a gigantic statue of Atlas with the globe on his straining stone shoulders dominated the entryway; red lines mapped Bremen's trade routes with distant parts of the world (Figure 1.1). (Also marked in red, we learn only from other sources, were the new German protectorates in Africa and the South Seas.) Palm trees and other exotic vegetation surrounded the statue and lined the staircases. In the four corners of this central foyer stood the

Figure 1.1 Illustration of the Trade Pavilion interior. Illustrated journals often featured renditions of an exhibition's most dramatic vistas. Note how the engraver includes palm fronds and native thatched roof (lower right) to lend a hint of the exotic to the opulence. Red lines on the globe, one guidebook tells us, mapped Bremen's trade routes with distant parts of the world, while a colonialist journal asserts that Germany's colonies were also shaded red. *Source: Illustrirte Zeitung* 94 (1890): 123.

"trophies" of trade—the most important products from each of the four corners of the earth in their crates, bales, and kegs.

Like all modern exhibitionary practices, the Trade Pavilion set about arranging a complicated world into a simplified spatial order that was at the same time aesthetically pleasing. The Trade Hall's overarching organization, as the official guidebook explained, was simple: the tobacco exhibits stood in the center of the pavilion, in recognition of tobacco's central place in Bremen's economic life. The Oriental world occupied the left wing of the hall, while North America and the rest of the Occident occupied the right wing. Meanwhile, at the outermost ends of each wing lay the extremes of geography—at one end the ice- and snow-world of the northernmost lands, while emanating from the other end came "the glow from the black continent, Africa."[34] "The thinking behind this organization," one writer explained, "was to exhibit East and West each in their own rooms . . . and in each apsis of these wings lies the most extreme contrast between cold and hot."[35] We will return to the extremes below; here, it is important to recognize that not only was the world bifurcated neatly into diametrical opposites—the Orient and the Occident—but that these worlds were spatially connected by a single pivotal commodity—in this case, that of tobacco. Tobacco had seen a fantastic increase in consumption over the previous decade, much of which flowed through Bremen. But in the larger view, the commodity was presented not only conceptually as a unifier of East and West, but spatially, as its central pivot.

The tobacco display of the Trade Hall laid out 600 cases of tobacco samples, with their original packing hung from the walls. A large model of a plantation on Borneo occupied the center. Large murals, painted by Arthur Fitger, depicted picturesque scenes of Bremen, "that most important tobacco shipping harbor."[36] Fitger was an artist who had moved to Bremen in 1869 and built his fame around monumentalist portrayals of seafaring and trade. In the late 1870s, for instance, Fitger crafted enormous paintings for Bremen's Haus Seefahrt; the three at the apse of the house's main hall were huge allegorical figurations of continents: Europe, flanked by Asia and Africa.[37] Fitger even designed the promotional poster for the exhibition itself; in his classically themed composition, the figure of Roland (the traditional protector of Bremen) stands guard with sword and shield, classical mermaids at his feet. (The poster was reproduced in one of the very first book on advertising posters, J. L. Sponsel's *Das Plakat*.)[38] Fitger's paintings were dramatic. In the tobacco room of the

Trade Hall in 1890, the paintings and displays seemed to linger (according to the descriptive material) particularly on the more exotic locales, such as South America and Sumatra—this despite the fact that, as the official exhibition guidebook admitted, the largest supplier of Germany's tobacco was Kentucky.

At the fringes of the Trade Hall, and therefore spatially located at the periphery of the commodity's domain, the cold and hot regions were to stimulate with a taste of the extreme. In fact, the African section of the exhibition, at the far "hot" end of the Eastern hall, was the third-largest section in the building (after the sections devoted to tobacco and to cotton). In the African Hall, live palm trees flanked the staircases. A sculpture of a lion gazed defiantly from its perch on the central podium, around which were arrayed various colonial products from Africa: copra, palm oil, cloves, tobacco, cotton, palm nuts, ivory, animal horns and pelts, and the like (Figure 1.2). Darkest Africa, it is clear from space alone, was intended to provide much of the allure—and much of the most exotic spectacle—for the Trade Hall as a whole. Vivid, dramatic murals set the scene, while strange masks and other startling artifacts of the primitive world shocked with their bizarre difference. It was in this African section that, as the official guidebook noted, "the German colonies have found their place."

The New German Colonialism on Display

The first page of the official catalog for Bremen's Northwest German Commerce and Industry Exhibition explained why "until now, Germany has not hosted a commercial exhibition in the grand style." The catalog explained, "Enterprises like the 1886 Colonial Exhibition in London had seemed unachievable *(unauszuführbar)* for us. Moreover, it was not thought [such exhibitions] would be popular *(volkstümlich)*. No one believed that they corresponded to needs that were widespread in Germany too."[39] The catalog continued: "Only recently has the sea air wafted deeper into the German interior of the Hansa cities of Bremen and Hamburg." Some of the new appreciation of sea air—and of the grand exhibitions of overseas realms—was attributed (in good monarchical fashion) to the new emperor Wilhelm II and his love for the "life of the sea." But it then continued, "Perhaps the ever-quicker tempo of German colonial politics *(Colonialpolitik)* has contributed to the increase in our peoples' interest in the foreign.

Figure 1.2 Illustration "From the African Section: Pyramid of Elephant Tusks," engraved by E. Limmer, 1890. While the figures in the engraved illustration attend to the pile of ivory tusks, the ethnological artifacts in the foreground—animal-skull fetish and native weapons—capture the reader's eye. The firm that supplied the ivory for this display, Heinr. Ad. Meyer, operated primarily in the Congo Free State (under Belgian authority). *Source: Illustrirte Zeitung* 94, no. 2464 (1890): 308.

Colonial politics thereby *awakened* the need to become more familiar with our economic and cultural affairs with those overseas nations—nations with whom we carry out trade, or with whom we are tied to *(anknüpfen)* in colonial relations."[40]

These opening comments in the catalog reveal a number of important issues and cross-currents. The first is the mention of London's 1886

Colonial Exhibition. Historians have often written of "Germany's" envy of the British empire, but it should be recognized that any envy felt by certain groups of Germans was not of the prosaic realities of empire—the compromises, costs, negotiations, and everyday brutalities of which the German public had little knowledge—but of the *display* of empire in grand, well-crafted, artful stagings. German colonialists often rhapsodized about how someday their holdings in central Africa would come together into a new German India, for example, but the "India" they had in mind was less Calcutta (to which few had traveled) than the Indian Court in London, as imaginatively reproduced in engravings in British and German magazines. The British Empire, alongside its political and economic facets, was also a spectacle staged for its own citizenry; this spectacle was dutifully rebroadcast to Germans in the pages of such illustrated periodicals as *Over Land and Sea.*

The passage also admitted that, "until recently," it was generally thought that there was little desire for colonial pageantry within Germany. The supposed new popularity of colonialism was likened to "sea air" wafting inland from the port city to the imperial capital—which in turn implied a natural, even causal connection between seaborne trade and colonial politics. It was often claimed that colonialism naturally follows in the wake of commodity trade, perhaps as trade's second stage. In fact, such a claim precisely inverts the flow of German colonialist politics, which coalesced primarily in inland industrial cities such as Berlin and Leipzig, and only later spread to the port cities. Importantly, the exhibition catalog claimed that "colonial politics" contributed to, perhaps even awakened, popular interest in the world overseas. (The German word *Kolonialpolitik* here can mean both colonial policy overseas and the domestic political activities of a colonialist party.) As we will see over the course of this book, the "popularity" of colonialism or even of colonialist themes is a very complicated issue indeed, with different inflections and articulations of colonialism emerging in different contexts, directed at different social groups for different purposes, with different meanings and implications. Any facile linkage between colonial politics and popular interest is problematic, for it only begs the questions: Popular with whom? And in what form?

In 1890 Germany had been a colonial power for only a few years. The first official colonialist act of the German state occurred in 1884, when Chancellor Otto von Bismarck declared German "protection" over territory on the southwest African coast. Of course, this did not mean that

Germans were uninvolved in the second broad wave of European imperialism that gained momentum after the 1860s. In fact, a great many Germans participated in what is described today as the colonial project, where exploration, penetration, conversion, and commercial exploitation all operated under the patina of a cooperative ethic of scientific inquiry and civilizing paternalism. German explorers of Africa in the 1860s and 1870s, such as Gerhard Rohlfs and Eduard Schnitzer (Emin Pasha), made full use of British and French colonial networks, outposts, and military resources in their own expeditions.[41] German missionary societies, such as the Rhenish mission, worked avidly in sub-Saharan Africa from as early as the 1830s, making their way into the African interior from the British coastal colonies.[42] German naturalists and anthropologists, such as Alfred Brehm in Africa in the 1860s and Otto Finsch in the South Pacific in the late 1870s, collected botanical specimens or engaged in anthropometric work (measuring heads) under the aegis of a broader Europe-wide colonial science.[43] Even German merchants and trading companies operated quite successfully within the larger commercial network of the British imperial economy, including the Hamburg trading houses Godeffroy & Sohn (in the South Pacific), O'Swald (in Zanzibar), and especially Woermann (on the West African coast), as well as Bremen's Oloff & Sohn (also on the west African coast). Indeed, German companies came to virtually monopolize the west African trade by the late 1850s, even in the British-controlled areas.[44] In practice, then, German individuals as well as mercantile, religious, and scientific institutions played significant roles in Europe's broader penetration into non-European areas well before the 1880s. Just as important, the achievements and adventures of German explorers, missionaries, and scientists were avidly narrated in the German press. Middle-class magazines such as *Illustrirte Zeitung* or *Over Land and Sea* celebrated these men as German heroes and, in the process, parlayed these exotic adventures into higher circulations.[45] Some of them, like Brehm and Finsch, even became regular authors for these journals.[46] Germany may not have had official colonialism before 1884, but it certainly had a thriving culture of colonial engagement and colonialist heroism.[47]

Colonial politics—the impetus for Germany to acquire colonies of its own—came from several different sources. "Colonial enthusiasm" (as it came to be called) arose initially among urban academics (and to a lesser degree, members of missionary societies) in the 1870s.[48] Most date the official birth of the German colonial movement to a keen public response to Friedrich Fabri's 1879 pamphlet, *Does Germany Need Colonies?* This tract, which presented a sprawling array of arguments concerning the vital necessity of colonies for the new German nation, went through three editions in the first five years after publication.[49] On the heels of Fabri's success, a number of organizations formed (or reinvented themselves) as "commercial geography" societies.[50] The most significant new organization to emerge was the German Colonial Association (Deutscher Kolonialverein), founded in 1882 by a mixture of nobles and notables, travelers, academics, and small businessmen. Though it attracted just over 3,000 members during its first year, the Association could count more than 9,000 members by its second year, and it quickly eclipsed all of the other commercial geography societies.[51] Its avowed purpose was to "agitate" for the acquisition of colonies, and it addressed this task primarily by means of publications.

The actual spark for Germany's venture into colonial rule, however, came from a very different direction—namely, the German fortune hunters working at the periphery of the British and French territories. In 1882 a Bremen tobacco merchant, Adolf Lüderitz, sought to establish a trading branch in Lagos (in British Nigeria); after it failed in the face of British competition, Lüderitz determined in 1883 to set up a German colony at Angra Pequeña, to exclude British rivals, on the southwest African coast. He and his agents signed treaties with local leaders there that ceded a swath of territory around the port to be under German "protection." These would have remained only scraps of paper had not Chancellor Bismarck turned around and accepted this rather dubious treaty making in 1884, cabling to Britain and France that German protection now extended over this territory in southwest Africa. The politically canny Bismarck had initially viewed the demands of the colonial enthusiasts with skepticism, but in this moment he relented. Perhaps Bismarck meant to distract the German populace from domestic political and economic turmoil, or perhaps this was part of a subtle diplomatic machination against Great Britain and France.[52] Either way, Cameroon and Togo in west Africa were added to the list of German protectorates: with these two colonies, Bismarck was likely catering to the Hamburg businessman Adolph Woermann, an ardent colonialist and budding politician, whose Hamburg firm made its fortune in the west African trade.[53]

With colonial acquisition in the air—and more important, in the daily headlines of Germany's newspapers—other adventurers joined the fray. The charismatic, nationalistic fortune hunter Carl Peters founded the Society for German Colonization (Gesellschaft für deutsche Kolonisation) in Berlin in the spring of 1884 to secure capital to carve out a German empire in east Africa. He then traveled to the east African coast and began to draw up his own treaties with local leaders, placing them under German "protection."[54] In 1885 Bismarck once again ratified the claims, creating German East Africa (present-day Rwanda, Burundi, Tanzania, and sections of Mozambique). In the Pacific, meanwhile, the explorer and naturalist Otto Finsch (with Bismarck's sanction) established claims on northeastern New Guinea and the Bismarck, Marshall, Caroline, and Mariana islands. By the turn of the century, Samoa and the Chinese port city of Tsingtao (in Jiaozhou Bay) were added to the list of German colonial possessions.

Germany's plunge into official imperialism, staking claims to overseas protectorates, therefore emerged at the confluence of three very different forces: the growing colonialist clubs in German cities; the activities of a handful of German adventurers at the periphery; and the political calculations of the German chancellor. The advent of official colonialism—by which I mean both colonial policy of the state and organized colonial politics of interest groups—was suffused throughout (*pace* Fabri) by a thick rhetoric of its "national necessity." For organized German colonialists (far more than in Britain or France), the ideology of the civilizing mission or the prospect of profits in colonial economics rarely appeared without an overlay of what such projects would "mean" for Germany.

This nationalistic character pervading Germany's colonial ideology and colonial politics would have interesting ramifications. First, the organizations that agitated for colonial expansion all emerged first in inland cities such as Frankfurt, Leipzig, Düsseldorf, and especially Berlin. With the notable exception of Woermann, the venerable international trading operations in the port cities of Hamburg and Bremen were not part of the push for colonial dominion.[55] The Hanseatic trading houses had been operating quite profitably in the late nineteenth century's globalization and so were initially quite suspicious of colonialism, which smacked too much of protectionism—their anathema.[56] Berlin was the epicenter of German colonial policy and of German colonial enthusiasm both. In 1887 the German Colonial Society (Deutsche Kolonialgesellschaft), formed out of the merger of two predecessors, had its secretariat and executive board firmly ensconced in the imperial capital. The Colonial Society concerned itself primarily with internal politics rather than overseas trade;

its principal charge was to agitate for German colonial expansion.[57] The early path of German colonialism, then, complicates the claim of a simple relationship between the commercial and colonial interests at the Northwest German Commerce and Industry Exhibition. For German colonial politics emerged first as *politics*.

The winds of colonialism therefore did not "blow inland" from the port cities to the capital; instead, colonialists' demands for colonies trumpeted outward from the new center of political power, Berlin. Even after Germany claimed protectorates, the Hamburg and Bremen merchant houses remained skeptical of colonial trade—or rather, colonialist trade. The new chartered colonial companies that administered the colonial territories in German South-West and German East Africa in the 1890s were based in Berlin, and they were staffed largely by amateurish, fortune-hunting nationalists, not canny international businessmen with experience trading in foreign lands.[58]

The gulf between Hanseatic mercantile interests and Berlin's politicized colonialist politics can be seen in the very space of the Bremen exhibition. The physical layout of the Trade Hall reflected an almost complete segmentation of the two sectors—and in the different imaginative geographies they each presented. The displays of the Orient and South American sections were largely set up by trading companies or boards of trade *(Börse)*, which took charge of displaying the commodities in which they dealt. The African wing, however, was deemed "colonial" by the guidebooks and newspaper accounts. It was managed by a very different set of organizations. A handful of small German trading outfits operated in colonized Africa, although many of these operated in areas of British or French rule, like the Transvaal or Morocco.[59] Only a very few exhibits were staged by German colonial companies that held charters to operate in *German* colonial territory, however.[60] A much larger cluster of exhibits in the African Hall were set up by the missionary societies, in particular, the North German Missionary Society of Bremen. The German Colonial Society had a hand in masterminding the organization and narrative material. And finally, the most impressive displays were those by private explorers who lent their collections, curiosities, artifacts, and trophies to the exhibition for the duration. The most prominent among these was Otto Finsch, the South Seas traveler, ethnologist, phrenologist, and colonialist. Finsch's display was by far the single most touted and most commented-upon element in the whole of the Bremen exhibition.[61]

The Ethnographic Fetish

The catalog of the Trade Hall explained that "Africa—the part of the world currently in vogue, and which has commanded our tense attention unceasingly over the last few decades—does not exactly present the most favorable conditions for economic development."[62] The conservative-leaning family magazine *Daheim* went further. Describing the Oriental wing of the Trade Hall, it reported, "The luxurious display of Indian and east-Asian products *(Erzeugnisse)* are particularly noteworthy. The Orient tempts the eyes with its all-encompassing splendor." In the African section, on the other hand, "it is, to be precise, the representations *(Darstellungsweisen)*" of murals and ethnographic collections "that make this trade-hall so interesting to the visitor."[63] In short, the Orient produced luxury goods—goods that were saturated with the exoticism of the Far East. Meanwhile, Africa *itself* was exotic. The handful of German trading and colonial companies in Africa may have failed to muster impressive displays of products, but the murals and exotic artifacts on display in the African Hall—not goods, not commodities, but representations—more than compensated; they generated ample exoticism to make the African Hall the talk of the whole exhibition. The Orient as the land of luxurious exotic goods, and Africa as the land of the thrilling exotic display, would prove to be an enduring dichotomy. In 1890 the latter served to invigorate the former; entertainment magazines assured readers who had not yet gone themselves that Bremen's Trade Pavilion "was no boring warehouse."[64] The African section was no warehouse at all; it was in some ways a blank canvas.

Evocative murals decorated the entire Trade Pavilion, but the murals of the African wing were particularly dramatic, according to commentators. The "glow" from the African wing came from the red-golden hues of one of these murals, most likely a coppery African sunset. These picturesque murals included a number of landscapes by several artists—"important masters," the exhibition catalog averred. First among these was Rudolf Hellgrewe, who would later make his career as a reliable "colonial artist" and illustrator, tendering his skills in landscape painting and ethnographic drawing to the enthusiasts of the Colonial Society.[65] In 1890, however, Hellgrewe was less compartmentalized; he helped to paint the Panorama erected in Bremen's main train station, for instance, that featured a steamer entering New York's harbor. Hellgrewe's "powerful" oil painting of Cameroon in the African Hall was said to capture the hot and humid atmosphere of the tropical forest.[66] He also painted a cityscape of Zanzibar, basking in the "tranquil, colorful glow of the Orient."[67] Many of Hellgrewe's colonial paintings are still found on the art market; in the 1890s they set the stage for later German painters of romanticized African landscapes.[68]

Such artistry lent a bit of local color to the displays, but sometimes the local color was shaded with colonialist ideology. A mural by the Berlin artist Hofmann, for instance, depicted the hoisting of the German flag over the new possessions in the South Seas. Below this iconography of possession—the hoisted imperial flag—the artist worked in a "typology" of the natives, according to the catalog description. Another mural painted Mount Kamerun in impressive colors. The exhibition literature informed viewers that Mount Kamerun was the dominant mountain of West Africa, and reassured them this natural wonder was "an imposing monument to German might."[69] The distant lands of Africa were indeed brought to life through these paintings, as the exhibition guide averred. Yet the panorama was tinted with a colonialist hue.

The highlight of the African Hall—and the highlight of the whole exhibition, according to some commentators—was more physical: the ethnographic artifacts. Tools, furniture, clothing, household items, weapons, and fetishes from regions throughout Africa—from Morocco, to Togo, to the Transvaal, to the South Seas (included under "Africa" because of its colonized status)—were displayed to "illustrate the life of the natives." Rare collections were exhibited there for the very first time, particularly the enormous ethnographic collection of Otto Finsch.[70] Thus, according to Sombart, "The exhibition has in the process picked up a special ethnographic worth."[71]

The masks, spears, drums made of animal skins, wooden idols and native fetishes, earrings, nose rings, tools, and other ethnographic artifacts lent the African exhibition a thrilling air of the exotic, which extended to the whole of the Trade Pavilion and outshone the offerings of the other halls. The "primitive" artifacts visually embellished the display of products (see Figure 1.2); a pyramid of ivory tusks, for instance, was contextualized—and made all the more exotic—by the array of weapons and fetishes adjacent. The ivory at the exhibition, however, part of the display of the firm of Heinrich Ad. Meyer, came not from German East Africa, but the Belgian Congo.[72]

With the displays concerning Germany's own newly acquired African colonies, such ethnographic objects, like the murals and maps, were a necessity, for they masked the lack of actual goods. The total value of tobacco exports from all German colonies even five years after the exhibition (in 1895), for example, tallied a mere 276,903 marks. This figure may very well be inflated, but even if not, it would amount to roughly only one-third of 1 percent of German raw tobacco imports, 89.4 million marks' worth in 1895.[73] In an exhibition devoted to trade, the absence of actual commodities from Germany's own colonies could not help but be apparent. For instance, at the center of the Trade Hall, there were 600 cases of tobacco sorts and types from all over the world—and yet only two single leaves from German East Africa.[74] Even the *German Colonial News (Deutsche Kolonialzeitung),* the usually triumphalist organ of the German Colonial Society, concluded its description of Bremen's impressive tobacco display on a rueful note: "hopefully, with time, tobacco cultivation will also become productive in our [German] colonial lands."[75] In publications circulated to their supporters, colonialists dealt with the weakness of the colonial economy by focusing on the future—on the bountiful wealth that would flow from Germany's colonizing efforts some day.[76] However, while imminence can be strong tactic in rhetoric, it is a problematic display strategy. Thus the elaborate visual displays in the African section—the murals, the ethnographic objects—served to fill the void, for the German colonies in Africa, that was left by the absence of real colonial products. Even official colonialist publications hinted at this: "our possessions outside of Europe are not only shown through trade products and ethnological artifacts and the like, but brought vividly to life through vibrant images."[77]

Textual descriptions of ethnographic objects that came from the German colonies alternated between fascination and condescension. A typical description maintained that "for handicrafts, these objects without a doubt reveal a certain natural skill; but their taste *(Geschmack)* is still undeveloped" and the forms of the handicrafts are therefore "mostly grotesque and bizarre."[78] Overall, descriptors such as "grotesque" and "bizarre" appeared frequently in the exhibition catalogs, perhaps to guide the spectator as to how objects from a primitive culture should correctly be seen. The text also seems intended to intensify the dramatic aura of the objects; a whole range of items were unmistakably presented for their shock value, such as the skulls of "actual cannibals" and the hair of "cannibals" brought in from the South Seas. Such evocative or shocking descriptions—actual cannibals!—might perhaps lure visitors into the Trade Hall and away from the stimulating amusement of the hot-air balloon rides.

The so-styled bizarre or grotesque objects did more than merely shock and titillate; they also flattered. When the guidebook described the savagery of the grotesque mask as an object produced by a primitive culture or as a reflection of primitive taste, it at once asserted and certified the superiority of the civilized culture. In the large view, moreover, the inclusion of such "primitive" artifacts set the "modernity" of the other exhibit halls, whether maritime, industrial, commercial, or artistic, into sharper relief. Andrew Zimmerman has argued that ethnographic artifacts were instrumental in showcasing the carefully constructed differences between the "peoples of culture" (i.e., the colonizers) and the "peoples of nature" (i.e., the colonized) in the world of popular science.[79] In Bremen, the African Hall revealed that this contrast appeared equally in the world of commercial display. But we should not read this effect as the product of an overarching master plan. It emerged as an unintended consequence of the confluence of interests.

The catalog text that described these ethnographic objects also worked in typologies of race—namely, as cultural attributes reified as biology. The catalog described peoples of Togo—"largely heathen Negroes"—as a "mostly well-built, powerful people with dark brown skin color and with Negro-like (but not exactly hideous) facial features." The Ovaherero of Southwest Africa, on the other hand, are "a strong people with stamina." The peoples of the East African coast are deemed "rather light"; and in the interior of East Africa live the "darker conqueror-tribes" of the Somal and the Massai.[80] For several pages, the guide placed each ethnic tribe in its geographical setting and on a spectrum of skin-pigmentation. An attentive reader will notice that the darker the described skin tone, the more the text emphasizes the strength, stamina, and warlike behavior of the described group. In marked contrast, such pigmentation typologies were absent from the narratives dealing with other parts of the world, such as Asia or South America.

Was racial typology presented visually as well in the African wing? Absent photographic record of the displays, this question is difficult to answer with certainty. One hint is the plaster and wax physiognomic masks of the South Seas explorer and colonialist Dr. Otto Finsch. These masks had been made by molding plaster onto the faces of South Seas inhabitants, and the masks were publicly displayed for the first time at Bremen. Finsch had originally chosen his subjects for the clarity of their "racial" features; in practice, physiognomies showing the greatest divergence from Western

Europeans were those most sought after. Finsch's masks were intended not only to capture and preserve an authentic, scientific visuality of race, but also to display it. The masks were painted in colors that highlighted their facial topography and garnished with earrings and other "native" adornment. Finsch later tried to sell the masks to a number of museums across Germany without success. Ultimately they, or wax replications thereof, were sold to the public out of Castan's Panopticum in Berlin.[81]

We have seen that Bremen's material commerce with the new German colonies was not especially significant, particularly in 1890. Even articles in colonialist publications such as the *German Colonial News* lamented Bremen's paltry commercial connections with the German colonies—virtually nonexistent but for a handful of tiny Bremen-based companies operating in Togo.[82] Why then did Bremen construct an African Hall that wound up being—in the words of the geographer Alwin Oppel—the most significant colonial exhibition on the European continent? (Oppel even went so far as to say that its ethnographic component put Bremen's colonial displays far in front of those at the huge colonial exhibition in Amsterdam seven years before.)[83] The functional effect of the African section was to lure in visitors with exotic panoramas and bizarre fetishes. Yet there is no evidence that this was orchestrated from the top or masterminded by the larger organizers. Nor is there evidence of a coherent colonialist ideology saturating the whole of the exhibition—because the South American displays seem relatively free from it. On close perusal, the official catalog and some of Bremen's other exhibition guidebooks are a curious ideological patchwork: the African section of the official catalog, for instance, revels in the new German colonial rule in Africa, while sections on China and Latin America make no reference to colonial policy at all. Indeed, some passages in the South American section even insist instead on the necessity of free trade—a stance inimical to the very idea of a colonial economy. In fact, it seems that sections of guidebooks and exhibition newsletters were parceled out to different writers; and the responsibility for the section on Africa was evidently turned over to the colonial enthusiasts of the German Colonial Society. The evidence for this subcontracting of editorial responsibility comes from telltale signs of style and phrasing. The prose throughout most of the exhibition's guidebooks for 1890 is enumerative and informative, peppered with tidbits of entertaining travelogue, and boosterish, sometimes to the point of smugness. Whenever the heading "German Colonial" crops up, however, the prose style lurches into something else altogether, namely grandiloquent invocations of German nationalism and belabored pedantic geography—all hallmarks of German colonialist publications. One telltale sign is the declaration that Bremen's exhibition will "carry the colonial idea into ever wider circles *(weiteren Kreisen)*."[84] "Ever wider circles" was a pet phrase of Gustav Meinecke, the editor of the *German Colonial News,* and appeared in virtually every piece of prose to cross his desk, from the front matter of Colonial Society bibliographies to the minutes of the Colonial Society executive board on which he sat.

This colonization of the African Hall by such colonial enthusiasts as Meinecke did not go unnoticed. The mainstream journal *Illustrirte Zeitung* mentioned in its fourth installment on the Bremen exhibition, "The highly controversial German colonies in Africa are represented in an extremely far-reaching display, which offers to every spectator a didactic *(lehrlich)* comparison of the relative worth of the individual possessions." The liberal-leaning bourgeois magazine seemed unenthusiastic about the displays on both the political and aesthetic plane. Yet it recognized that "*Incomparably more important* are the ethnological collections out of the personal possessions of our African explorers, which lend us a view of the personal relationships, the household life, the customs and habits of the natives."[85] The popular bourgeois magazine seemed unmoved by pedantic displays of German colonialism in Africa but was a great deal more impressed with the ethnographic objects in the African Hall. So too were business interests and the nascent advertisers.

The shipping magnates of Bremen who sponsored and organized the exhibition had been committed to making it a commercial success, and this meant attracting a massive audience. The organizers needed something more alluring than a warehouse filled with row after row of goods, and the African Hall would assume the task of drawing the middle classes into the Trade Pavilion. Since Bremen's actual African trade was minimal, the African Hall had the fewest goods to display—and therefore the most space, both physical and symbolic, to build an entertaining, awe-inspiring panorama. Meanwhile, the professional colonialists of the German Colonial Society, and affiliated explorers, small traders, missionaries, and ethnographers, were the self-proclaimed experts on Africa, and they stepped up to display, describe, and fill in the local color of this "Africa."

The Bremen exhibition, then, offered a common ground—literally—for the broad interests of commerce, the professional self-promotion of scientists, and the more narrow political and cultural agenda of the colonialists. These very different groups came together in their joint pursuit of the attentions of the exhibition-going public. The organizers saw the benefit of including an exotic, enticing, and socially legitimate ethnographic component; the anthropologists and missionaries found a well-attended forum in which to display their collections; and the colonialists organized the ethnographic objects to cover the dearth of colonial commodities and to bolster their ideological program. With Werner Sombart's quip in the exhibition guidebook about the need to infuse the sample wares with "local color," one sees that this color was genuinely *local;* it emanated as much from the political, economic, and cultural interests in Germany as from the exotic lands overseas.

Spectacle in Berlin, 1896

A mere six years after Bremen's exhibition, a far larger, grander, and more fantasy-laden exhibition appeared in the imperial capital. On the first of May in 1896, the great Berlin Industrial Exhibition opened its gates. Situated in Treptower Park, on the banks of the Spree, it covered over a million square meters, contained more than 4,000 exhibits, and was the largest commercial or industrial exhibition to be staged in Germany until Hanover's Expo in the year 2000. The organizers' stated goal was to prove that Berlin was not just a large city *(Großstadt)* but a world-class city *(Weltstadt)* by showcasing its new industrial might. The famous poster promoting the exhibition illustrates this ambition graphically: a hammer clenched in a fist bursts up from beneath the ground (Figure 1.3). In "a spirit of peaceful industrial competition across the entire planet," the organizers also explicitly aimed to surpass the successful World's Fair of Paris (1889) and the World Colombian Exhibition in Chicago (1893).[86]

The staging of the Berlin Industrial Exhibition signaled a shift in the center of gravity for commercial activity in Germany away from the coastal Hanseatic trade cities. Over the last decade of the nineteenth century, Berlin's industry had grown into a driving force in the German economy, and the extent to which Berlin's exhibition dwarfed those held in Hamburg and Bremen only six years previously demonstrated this primacy in unmistakable terms. Enormous sums were spent on this exhibition, over 5 million marks, all of which the organizers expected to recoup.[87] Small

Figure 1.3 Poster for the Berlin Industrial Exhibition, 1896, by Ludwig Sütterlin. This promotional poster became famous in the new world of poster art, and was both lauded and reproduced in advertising handbooks and design journals. The drama and movement at the center of this poster helped inaugurate a new, modernist poster style. *Source:* J. L. Sponsel, *Das Moderne Plakat* (Dresden: Gerhard Kühtmann, 1897), 273.

businessmen and large manufacturers alike not only sold their wares and services directly on the exhibition grounds but were also able to promote their businesses to the largest audience that had ever gathered in German lands. The proximity of product and spectacle, moreover, changed the tenor of commodity display. The critic Georg Simmel wrote of the Berlin exhibition that "its emphasis on pleasure seeks to forge a new synthesis between surface appeal *(aüßerliche Reiz)* and the practical functions of objects by offering the most extreme escalation of aesthetic overlay."[88]

Further, the exhibition was avidly followed in all the German news and entertainment media, broadcasting the legitimacy of this new fusion of practical product and aesthetic overlay to all of Germany. The exhibition organizers emphasized that it was a showcase of production, but equally, the great Berlin exhibition stood as a beacon for a new configuration of consumption.

Berlin's Industrial Exhibition admirably demonstrated the city's industrial and commercial might. One of the largest telescopes in the world allowed visitors an unmatched view of the heavens, and Wilhelm Röntgen's first public demonstration of medical X-rays allowed a glimpse inside the human body. One could ride on such modern marvels as the hanging tramway and the new electric train that ran around the periphery. On a more overtly nationalistic note, mechanical models of armored battleships—each well over three feet long, with working cannons—fought mock naval battles on an artificial lake, to the delight of the assembled throngs.[89]

Industrial giants such as Siemens, AEG, and Borsig staged impressive displays of technological prowess. But alongside the locomotives and huge electric generators were the exhibits mounted by the emerging giants of consumer goods. AGFA, for instance, occupied a major place in both the Chemical section (Group IX) and in the separate Photography section (Group XVII). The tobacco firm Loeser & Wolff built its own tobacco museum, near the Hildebrand & Sohn chocolate factory. Gastronomic delight was melded to spectacular fantasy: for instance, Hoffmann & Tiede, manufacturing chocolate under the brand name Sarotti, built an ornate Oriental pavilion with so-called Moorish minarets on the shore of the *Karpfen-Teich;* "this sweet brand Sarotti works an unfathomable magic, particularly on the more tender parts of the visitor," raved one writer. Six years after the exhibition, Hoffmann & Tiede reincorporated as Sarotti AG, with a capital of 1.5 million marks, surpassing Cologne's venerable chocolatier, Stollwerk.[90]

As at Bremen, the huge grounds were landscaped for pleasurable strolling, with an artificial lake built adjacent to the naturally occurring one. Around the park, spectacular sights competed for the visitor's gaze. The Alpine Panorama was said to be "one of the most gripping scenes of the exhibition."[91] Carl Hagenbeck, the famed trafficker in exotic fauna (and in exotic folk as well, as we will see in the next chapter), constructed a Polar Panorama; this showed animals and people side by side in an artificial habitat and was the first of its kind.[92] The poster that promoted the Panorama, printed by Adolph Friedländer, shows a crowd of polar bears, seals, penguins, and Eskimos clustered together, with the caption "Sensation of the Exhibition!"[93] But rival claimants to the title were not lacking. An elevated moving walkway connected the exhibition proper to an amusement park. In addition to the by-now-standard tethered balloon rides, the park included a new water ride, where wheeled boats hurtled dignified exhibition-goers down a steep track into a small lake.[94] (The poster promoting the water coaster exaggerated the height of the launching tower by a factor of three and showed a bevy of attractive young women applauding the manly courage of the intrepid coaster riders.)[95] With such an array of spectacular wonders and thrilling rides, it is no surprise that the Berlin exhibition came under criticism by some for being too much of a "pleasure park."[96]

The most spectacular component of the exhibition was the Special Exhibition Cairo, an installation evoking that Egyptian city in all of its Oriental splendor. Alleys from old Cairo and streets of modern Cairo were elaborately reconstructed, and the buildings intricately decorated. This Egyptian Orient found expression in a huge reproduction of the Great Pyramid, framed by imported palm trees. (Photos of the kaiser visiting the faux pyramids circulated through Berlin's Kaiser-Panorama, a multiseat stereoscopic viewer.) A central open square in the otherwise densely packed grounds, meanwhile, provided the space for ethnographic shows *(Völkerschauen);* the exhibit featured more than 300 "exotics" from North Africa, including Berbers, Nubians, Tunisians, and Egyptians, who performed dervish whirling, sword fights, and belly dancing, and mingled freely among the spectators. The Egyptian denizens on the poster, printed by Adolph Friedländer, underline this human component of the spectacle (see Plate 2). Drawings of the architecture and of dancing dervishes featured prominently in the German illustrated magazines.[97] In short, the promotion for the Special Exhibition Cairo promised it all: imaginative travel; a claim to authenticity by reproducing not only the streets of Cairo but its denizens as well; spectacular Oriental fantasy; and displays of exotic peoples performing unusual acts. When visitors arrived at the Special Exhibition, they could purchase cotton goods, pots, and Oriental carpets on its teeming, Oriental streets—goods indelibly imprinted (and pictorially prefigured) with an exotic experience.

The first official Colonial Exhibition in Germany also took place in Berlin in 1896. Sited directly adjacent to the larger paean to industry, consumption, amusement, and exoticism, the Colonial Exhibition was one-tenth the size. The Colonial Exhibition was autonomous in all respects, from its separate organizing committee to its separate admission and promotional material (Figure 1.4). Unlike the main exhibitions, financed privately through private entrepreneurs and civic boosters, the Colonial Exhibition emerged from unprecedented collaboration between a radical-nationalist interest group (the German Colonial Society) and the German state. The Foreign Office provided 50,000 marks to fund the Colonial Exhibition, and its Colonial Section participated in all aspects of planning and production, including enlisting colonial governors to send raw materials and native peoples to Berlin for display. The Colonial Section even paid the freight.[98] Together, the Foreign Office and a specially incorporated subsidiary of the German Colonial Society sought to stage a tightly scripted glorification of German colonial efforts and successes.

Berlin's was billed as the first German Colonial Exhibition. (This not only ignored its smaller predecessor at Bremen, but also overlooked the Colonial Exhibition in Lübeck in 1895.)[99] The Colonial Office/Colonial Society joint venture in Berlin consisted of two very distinct segments. The first, located directly adjacent to the amusement park, was the Colonial Exhibit proper. With four separate exhibit buildings and a number of smaller pavilions, stands, cafés, and sundry displays, the Colonial Exhibit seems sizeable—although the entirety could fit inside the Industrial Exhibition's Hall of Industry. Its various buildings ordered and classified the German colonial project in discrete components: a Hall of Commerce included tropical agriculture, German industry for export, and missionary work; a Hall of Science presented displays on ethnology, geography, flora and fauna of the colonies, and "tropical hygiene"; and testifying to the backbone of the new German colonial order was a model military barracks and a shooting range.

Colonial science, in the forms of geography, botany, anthropology, medicine, and "race science," was a central focus of the Colonial Exhibition. This was more than a simple attempt to tap into the resonance of scientific discourse among middle-class Germans. Indeed, the overviews of geography, flora, and fauna in the Colonial Exhibition's halls reflected the central productivity of German colonialism itself; the German colonial project in the year 1896 primarily generated colonial knowledge

Figure 1.4 Promotional poster for the Colonial Exhibition of 1896 by Walter Peck. This poster appeared in Justus Brinckmann's exhibition of poster art in 1896 but did not find the renown of other designs, such as Sütterlin's Hammer poster or the poster for the Exhibition Kairo. *Source:* Courtesy of Hamburg Museum für Kunst und Gewerbe.

rather than material goods.[100] Unfortunately for the Colonial Exhibition organizers, the public display of this colonial knowledge revolved around maps and language-family charts, desiccated leaves and native headdresses. In Bremen in 1890, such objects—particularly the more spectacular ethnographic objects, such as wax face molds, cannibal hair, and bizarre fetishes—could lure in spectators. A mere six years later, however, the ante had risen dramatically. German colonial science could offer little to rival the X-ray machines, giant telescopes, sky-trams, or photographic cameras just across the pond.

The organizers of the German Colonial Society also sought to demonstrate the economic worth of the German colonies to this concentrated German public. As visitors were funneled through the various segments of the Colonial Exhibition, they were instructed on the (eventual) economic benefits of the German colonies. In clear imitation of Bremen's Trade Hall six years earlier, the center of the 1896 Colonial Hall featured a sculpture of Atlas shouldering a giant globe on which the German colonies were carved in red—though this version (funded by the colonialists) was far smaller.[101] Meanwhile, a handful of official "German colonial goods" were offered for sale on the Colonial Exhibition's grounds. To this end, an ostensibly unaffiliated commercial affiliate of the German Colonial Society, the Kolonialhaus Bruno Antelmann, sold Usambara coffee and Cameroon cocoa to the visitors at a colonialist café that took the form of a grass-roofed hut "built in the African style." It was located at the entrance to the Colonial Exhibition, arching over the path "through which every visitor must pass."[102] Coffee and cocoa were the only two consumer products as yet available in the German colonial economy, however. Indeed, the Foreign Office had participated so avidly in financing and helping organize the exhibition because it wanted to facilitate the raising of investment capital for colonial companies—companies that would, theoretically, pay tariffs that would balance the budgets of the Colonial Section of the Foreign Office. But the colonial economy in 1896 was little more developed than six years earlier. The exhibits of the small colonial companies, such as the Jaluit Company, were still outnumbered and surpassed by displays by German missionary societies and private explorers. Despite its ostensible focus on commerce, photographs reveal the Colonial Hall, for instance, to be filled primarily with ethnographic artifacts and dioramas of tropical structures, rather than consumable goods.[103]

Meanwhile, in the Industrial Exhibition directly across the lake stood the large, ornate pavilion of Hoffmann & Tiede, selling their Sarotti chocolate. Though the more scientifically minded colonial enthusiasts may have sneered at the building's wildly inauthentic, fantastic orientalist facade, they could only gaze enviously at its massive commercial success.[104] To mask the dearth of "German colonial products," the colonialist organizers pursued a rather duplicitous display strategy. In the Tropical House, most of the displayed specimens of colonial agricultural goods did *not* come from territories under German rule.[105] Even in the Colonial Hall, where German colonial companies displayed their products, most of the products came from trade with areas *outside* of the German colonial empire. The tall tower of carefully stacked ivory tusks displayed by the Hamburg ivory trader Heinrich Ad. Meyer, for instance, was quite impressive, judging by the interior photos of the Colonial Hall, but almost all of this ivory came from African lands outside of the German sphere, mainly the Belgian Congo.[106] (The same tusk display had made an appearance at Bremen six years earlier; see Figure 1.2.)

The colonialist organizers thus trod a narrow path. As the self-proclaimed arbiters of colonial knowledge, they insisted on authenticity in their displays. This prevented them from offering such goods as chocolate or coffee—both of which were "colonial goods" *(Kolonialwaren)* in popular parlance—if they stemmed from Ecuador or Sumatra, places outside the bounds of Germany's colonial empire. But products actually imported from the lands under German colonial rule were few, expensive, and in short supply. With the possible exception of cocoa, there were simply no success stories in the German colonial economy of 1896. There was certainly no colony of prodigious wealth—no German "jewel in the crown"—to occupy the pivotal place that, say, an orientalized India played in British imperial exhibitions. Exhibitors in the German Colonial Exhibit therefore fell back upon "instructional" materials; they bolstered their displays with ethnographic artifacts, tales by triumphant military officers of colonial skirmishes, and wall maps of Germany's African possessions.[107] The stated aim of these educational displays was "to awaken the urge for foreign trade." But a glance across the pond, where Hoffmann & Tiede offered succulent chocolates—crafted from Ecuadorian cocoa imported through Amsterdam but layered in orientalist fantasy—would highlight the poverty of the German colonialists' empire. As colonialists, their appeal was nationalistic and patriotic: Germany had finally become a world power by gaining colonies, and it was every German's *duty* to support this worthy endeavor. Nationalistic invocations of duty could make an effective strategy in rhetoric and in print. But as a visual strategy, it was dry stuff indeed. The colonialists' own *Official Report* confessed, "Dead collections alone are not able to attract the great masses of the people, on whom indeed, for financial reasons, the balancing of expenses and income must be reckoned."[108]

"The Materials Are *Real* . . . and So Too Are the Coloreds!"

The Colonial Exhibition's organizers did have one dramatic spectacle up their sleeve: the display of "real live natives" in their (reconstructed) natural habitat. The second section of the Colonial Exhibition was the Native Village. Three colonial villages in total were carefully built from grass and wood shipped in from Africa and the South Pacific. Togolese, Duala (from Cameroon), Swahili, Massai (from East Africa), Herero (from Southwest Africa), and New Guineans were contracted (or in other ways brought in) to populate these villages. Promotional literature for the exhibition stressed these villages' authenticity: "the materials are *real* . . . and so too are the Coloreds!" boasted one guidebook.[109] But the exhibition organizers (and particularly the chief publicist, Gustav Meinecke) were also attempting to tap into that aura of "wild savagery" that had been so successfully capitalized upon (and cultivated) by numerous impresarios of private "people shows" *(Völkerschau)* over the past decade and a half. As the following chapter will show, the impresarios of these shows had discovered in the decade before that savagery sold tickets. Colonialists, whether scientists or armchair geographers, frequently derided such popular spectacles. But here, the Colonial Exhibition's organizers wanted to use it—appropriately draped in a veneer of scientific respectability—to bolster attendance and gate receipts.

The ethnographic display of the natives was intended to lure in spectators, but it was also structured to convey colonial ideology. First, the Native Village was an implicit demonstration of imperial power: during the exhibition, order was maintained by the strict regimentation of the movements, work, and performances of the natives. Indeed, some of the showcased colonial natives were instructed by ethnologists on how to properly construct their dwellings.[110] Second, this controlled display of natives was meant in part to counteract popular perceptions of Africa as a "savage" land, which some in the Foreign Office thought was deterring German investment and prospective colonists.[111] In displaying "wild peoples" who were contained and controlled within a colonial village—and adjacent to exhibitions showcasing the latest military gear and tropical prophylactics—the colonialists strove to erode popular anxieties about the "Dark Continent" by visibly demonstrating a complete mastery over all of its known dangers. In this effort, colonialist organizers sought to steer the audience toward an anthropological gaze, with its increasingly fine-grained discriminations of racial science. In the memento book

Germany and Its Colonies in 1896: Official Report on the German Colonial Exhibition, for instance, more than forty pages were devoted to recording the anthropometry of the displayed peoples. Every colonial native taking part in the exhibition was minutely measured by the Berlin anthropologist Felix von Luschan. The width of his or her mouth, the size of his or her lips, the width and length of his or her skull, the width and length of his or her nose and ears, and scores of other bodily minutiae were recorded, printed, and sold as an important component of the book. The measured colonial subjects were identified first by number, such as "Togolese #14."[112] These measurements of face and body warranted their own chapter, and photographs of typical "natives," frontal and profile, were included in the appendix. This scientific prowess—with its capacity to define and ascribe characteristics in minute detail—was one of the most compelling commodities the colonialists could offer.

A number of scholars have commented on how the industrial power of Germany was set into the starkest relief by the primitive handicrafts of the colonial natives at work in the artificial ethnographic village. That juxtaposition must have indeed been dramatic. Another juxtaposition was also dramatic, however; the technological and commercial power of the German industrial economy, manufacturing products such as cameras and consumables such as chocolate, set into stark relief the poverty of the German colonial economy. It is not too far of a stretch to say, therefore, that while Berlin's main exhibitors infused material goods with imaginative constructions, the colonialists replaced material goods with intellectual constructions.

The Colonial Exhibition did attract more than 1 million visitors, largely drawn, it is clear, by the Native Villages and most of all by proximity to the Industrial Exhibition. Meanwhile, the Special Exhibition Cairo pulled in more than 2 million, even given an admission fee almost double that charged by the colonialists. The Industrial Exhibition itself pulled in more than 7 million attendees.[113] Even the colonial enthusiasts' official luxury guide, *Germany and Its Colonies in the Year 1896,* otherwise noted for its unflagging boosterism, practically admitted on the first page that the Colonial Exhibition had not quite been the success that was hoped for.[114]

We must resist the temptation to see the Colonial Exhibition through the eyes of its colonialist sponsors—as a powerful presentation of Germany's imperial might. The cheap and popular *Illustrated Official Guide to the Berlin Industrial Exhibition 1896* did not even include the Colonial Exhibition on its recommended tour. The Special Exhibition Cairo, on the other hand, was first on the list.[115] The Colonial Exhibition is not even visible in a massive panoramic drawing of the Berlin Industrial Exhibition that occupied two full pages of the *Illustrirte Zeitung;* it is lost in the haze toward the back of the drawing.[116] When articles in the nationally circulating illustrated family and entertainment journals, such as the *Illustrirte Zeitung, Daheim,* and *Over Land and Sea,* declared the Colonial Exhibition to be captivating, a careful look at bylines and writing styles reveals that they were written by the colonialist organizers themselves (most often Gustav Meinecke).[117] Even the ideological message of the Native Village may have been lost entirely on the masses of visitors. A "Master Plan for Quick Orientation," mass-produced by the tabloid *Berliner Lokal-Anzeiger,* summed up the whole complexity of the painfully reconstructed, authentic ethnographic villages of Duala, East Africa, and New Guinea with a single word: *Negerdorf.* Negro village.[118]

The year 1896 has been described as a turning point in the identity of Berlin, with the great Industrial Exhibition marking the transition from a great city *(Großstadt)* to a global city *(Weltstadt).* In the exhibition, however, there were on display two very different visions of what that "world" in *Weltstadt* might really mean. There was, of course, the vision of a militaristic *Weltpolitik.* The displays of naval might and of colonial mastery seen in specific corners of the Berlin Industrial Exhibition proved that Berlin was an imperial capital and, as such, was capable of projecting power into the farthest corners of the world. Another vision of "Weltstadt" also emerged in Berlin, however. As the contemporary commentator Georg Simmel observed: "so it becomes clear what is meant by a 'world city,' and that Berlin, despite everything, is one: a single city to which the whole world supplies the material of its labors, which are refashioned into all the essential forms that appear in the present cultural world *(Culturwelt).*"[119] In this vision, *Weltstadt* Berlin was a mecca for commodities, and a place that imbued those commodities with larger cultural meanings. Its role was to be not just a city of industrial production and a nexus of material goods, but a place where meanings of consumption itself were produced.

Conclusion

When we look for the origins of advertising in the first great exhibitions in Germany, we find a more complicated story than that offered by

Walter Benjamin, quoted at the beginning of this chapter. There can be no doubt that the laying out of commodities at the commercial exhibition indeed set the pattern for modern advertising, in that it provided one of the first means by which commodities became infused with larger cultural meanings that were intentionally produced. As the sociologist Georg Simmel wrote in 1896, "the banal effort to show objects in their best light" may have originated in the age-old exhortations of street vendors, but it was at the Berlin Industrial Exhibition that this effort was refined "through the collective display of objects to impart new aesthetic meanings."[120] The objects, however, were not truly "collectively" displayed; it only seemed that way because of spatial proximity. In truth, different forces were at work in different portions of the exhibition, from sellers of goods to planners and collectors of gate receipts, demonstrators of science, purveyors of grand spectacles from Chinese pagodas to faux Egyptian pyramids, hawkers of cheap thrills, and pedants of knowledge. The changing balance of these interests, and their relative weighting and dynamic interactions, had an enormous impact upon the manner and range of meanings that could infuse the commodities.

At the Northwest German Exhibition in 1890, edifying display practices stood at the confluence of commercial, exhibitionary, and political impulses, each put forth by different groups. The shipping magnates of Bremen sought to demonstrate Bremen's prominence in trade with an eye toward expanding it. They also sought to make the exhibition itself a commercial success, as measured in gate receipts. To achieve both of these goals, they needed something more alluring than tables with conventional trade goods piled atop. In the Trade Hall, mundane displays of raw materials were spiced up by integrating them with murals, dioramas, and other exotic objects to create a virtual panorama of their land of origin. Such commercial vistas were alluring, and also could be sold as educational—thereby legitimizing the cultural and visual work of the exhibition.[121] In the Trade Hall, the African wing took on much of this burden; as the section with the fewest real products to display, it had the most space (symbolic but also physical) to build a more dramatic panorama.

In Bremen's exhibition the commodity fetish of Marx emerged literally; ethnographic artifacts from Africa and the South Seas, including strange physiognomic face molds and the hair of "cannibals," infused the bales of raw tobacco or crates of tea leaves with exotic allure. The objects themselves were provided by private explorers, scientists, missionary societies, and even a few of the tiny German colonial companies, and the commercialized picture of "the exotic" gained legitimacy from its patina of ethnographic edification. Finally, the unifying textual narrative for the African Hall was written by the professionals of the new German Colonial Society. Asserting their expertise, the colonialists became the de facto middlemen between missionaries, colonial companies, and explorers on the one hand, and the Bremen chamber of commerce on the other. They commissioned wall murals, crafted display captions, and wrote whole sections of the guidebooks, and in the process sought to place the artifacts, the goods, and the imaginative visual travel all under a narrative arc extolling the patriotic advance of the German colonial cause. In the process, colonialists greatly exaggerated the economic importance of the German colonies themselves through a careful strategy of elision and spatial deception; tropical goods from the global market were grouped together with displays of the German colonies. The larger lesson of 1890 Bremen, then, is how disparate social groups, from laissez-faire tobacco importers, to missionaries and explorers, to bombastic nationalists, could come together by fulfilling one another's needs in the commercial sphere. Displaying trade goods alongside ethnographic artifacts within a colorful painted panorama helped to build and promote the very practice of commercial spectacle by infusing it with both the mantle of science and the appeal of overseas gaze.

A mere six years later, a great deal had changed, as seen on the sprawling grounds of the dramatic Berlin Industrial Exhibition. The organized colonialists had now accumulated enough financial and political capital to stage their own separate enterprise, which they termed the first German Colonial Exhibition. It has been said that the organizers of the 1896 Colonial Exhibition sought to sell ideas rather than products.[122] The truth was that they had no products to sell. Their didactic focus on the colonial sciences of geography and ethnography was as much a tactical necessity as it was an outgrowth of ideology. But just six years after Bremen, the fetishes of colonial contact—the masks, spears, shields, masks, arrows, skulls, and pots—no longer sufficed. At the adjacent Industrial Exhibition, the great pyramid of Cairo offered a spectacle far more impressive, and the orientalist chocolate fantasies of Hoffmann & Tiede (Sarotti) provided consumable goods far more tangible. Following in the footprints of Carl Hagenbeck, colonialist organizers resorted to the thrill afforded by "real live savages." But in their insistence that the *Völkerschau* be instructional, they adhered to a rigid script of "authenticity" that—as we will glimpse in the next chapter—would undermine its popular appeal.

As Walter Benjamin suggested, exhibitions were the earliest form of advertising. It was commercial exhibitors who first incorporated elements of fantasy and visual allure into their displays to lend their commodities greater appeal to mass audiences. The character of such fantasies or such spectacles, however, was not preordained. Exoticism offered a potent theme for overseas wares, whether that exoticism was incarnated as the luxury of the Orient, as virtual travel to faraway destinations, as a bit of ethnographic color, as the authority of racial science, or as the patriotism of colonialism. In the 1890s the particular variant that would ultimately emerge triumphant had yet to be resolved.

One more innovation in the field of representation in 1896 needs to be pointed out. Though the Native Village was a draw for the Colonial Exhibition, it had been largely forgotten a century later, and its very existence only recently recovered by historians.[123] In marked contrast, the Berlin Industrial Exhibition remained firmly in view—mostly through Ludwig Sütterlin's poster for the Berlin Industrial Exhibition, which remained famous over a century of graphic design (see Figure 1.3). With its forceful hammer-in-fist design bursting forth from the ground, the poster was a vivid visualization of Berlin's and Germany's industrial might. The path by which this poster rapidly worked its way into the new canon of advertising posters is revealing. In 1896 the poster featured prominently in Justus Brinckmann's art-poster exhibition, the first such in Germany. From there it was reproduced in J. L. Sponsel's book *The Modern Poster,* which served as a design handbook for early advertisers. Sütterlin's design continued to feature prominently in advertising handbooks for decades, including the influential design magazine with international reach, *Das Plakat.*[124] The forceful sense of power and movement at the center of Sütterlin's poster is said to have helped inaugurate the modernist poster style. Its place in history was ensured in part through perfect timing: a decade later it would have been merely one of countless designs, no matter how innovative. A decade earlier, however, the poster itself could never have attained the same reach. In 1896 more than 100,000 copies of the hammer poster were printed and distributed throughout Germany. Many were even sent to other European nations. The cost was more than 300,000 marks—almost three times the colonialists' *total* expenditure on their Native Village. Countless imitations, spoofs, and satires of Sütterlin's

Figure 1.5 "The New Plant-butter Margarine—of Special Character," advertisement for margarine in early 1914 by the firm of Benedikt Klein, Cöln-Ehrenfeld. Note that the packaging itself, raised high above the genuflecting Arabs and palm trees, is bedecked with illustrations of a German child. *Source:* WZB (1914): 119, reg. no. 190721.

poster testify to its impact in the visual realm.[125] For a decade after 1896 countless trademark registrations featured hands bursting up out of the ground, holding some item or commodity. Some of these transported the scene to more exotic realms (Figure 1.5). Panoramic strategies, such as the reconstructed performers of the Native Village or the reconstructed pyramid in the Special Exhibition Cairo, may have lured visitors in with promises of savage authenticity and grand spectacle. But a hundred times that number caught a glimpse of Berlin's great exhibition—and thereby formed some sort of mental image of it—*solely* through Sütterlin's Hammer poster. The future, literally, belonged to images. Sütterlin's poster, like the grand trade exhibition it promoted, helped to propagate a new visual style—a style that set the commodity into a new, powerful tableau of meaning by placing it in a larger visual field.

2

IMPRESSIONS OF OTHERS

Allegorical Clichés, Panoptic Arrays, and Popular Savagery

Bremen's Northwest German Commerce and Industry Exhibition of 1890 included living components in its dramatic panorama of Bremen's global trade. Four Burmese participated in the exhibition. An elephant was meant to accompany them from halfway around the world, but it unfortunately died en route.[1] The expensive luxury edition of Bremen's exhibition guidebook even reproduced original photographs of the four Burmese, posed together in the manner of a family portrait, as well as a photo of their reconstructed "Burmese Hut."[2] Photographs such as these are treasured by historians, for they allow a seemingly genuine glimpse into a specific instant of history. Yet for all of its timeless veracity, a photograph may not offer the best approximation of how an event was actually seen. The encounter at Bremen, for instance, was also captured in an engraving of a modeler from Burma practicing his craft under the watchful gaze of the passing public (Figure 2.1). This illustration appeared in the *Illustrirte Zeitung,* and it is certain that many more Germans saw this illustration—with its juxtapositions of work and leisure, of exotic and refined dress, of observer and observed—than saw either the Burmese themselves or the photograph.[3] In the 1890s even the reach of photographs, expensive to reproduce, remained fairly circumscribed; engraved

Figure 2.1 Illustration of a Burmese modeler, 1890, Northwest German Commerce and Industry Exhibition in Bremen (1890). *Source: Illustrirte Zeitung* no. 2464 (1890): 308.

illustrations continued to be the far most pervasive and widespread way of "seeing."[4]

It was not by chance that the non-Europeans appearing in the Hanseatic commercial exhibitions of 1889 and 1890 came into public view, or that in Berlin six years later, even the conservatively minded German Colonial Society would attempt to use African natives in its Colonial Exhibition to lure in a broader public. The 1880s had seen the dramatic growth of the phenomenon known as the *Völkerschauen*—the live shows of exotic peoples. Such shows initially entered the German public sphere under the auspices of education, to show foreign habits and folkways. But they rapidly evolved into outlandish enterprises of sensational spectacle, and by the late 1890s, of thrilling savagery. The change in the character of these shows between 1880 and 1895 has been linked to the changing character of audiences, in which a tension played out between elite and popular forms of spectatorship. But the changing character of audiences—and the popularization of the shows more broadly—arose in part out of emerging new practices of promotion, particularly the innovative use of visualization. Both the popularity of the exotic peoples show and the visual stimulation of this popularity would have significant ramifications for the emerging field of advertising.

Primitive Exotic Clichés

Germans' interest in peoples termed "exotic" was part and parcel of a larger European fascination that stretched back centuries. Exotic people were fascinating not just for their bodily difference but because they were seen as the virtual embodiment of the distant land from which they originated. As early as the fifteenth century, exotic peoples certified the authenticity of travel; they stood—literally—as proof that the newly discovered regions of the world were not merely fantastic mariners' tales. Christopher Columbus famously brought back Native Americans (Arawak) to Spain after his second voyage in 1493 as physical proof of his discovery. (Their grim fate as slaves in Spain is less frequently recounted.) Explorers in the sixteenth and seventeenth centuries carried back Inuit and Native Americans, often by force, to display in Europe.[5] James Cook brought back a Tahitian from his second voyage to the Pacific in 1774; the Tahitian was put on public display, and his tattoos were said to be particularly fascinating.

What is less recognized is the dynamic, even fraught relationship between the physical and the representational in such encounters. The corporeality of these living stand-ins for exotic lands was less important than the representation of their corporeality. This point is easily overlooked, but before the nineteenth century, few people personally saw these living representatives of distant lands. Instead, most Europeans only saw such exotics as they appeared in lithographs and paintings—artful representations *purporting* to serve the same role of authentication. For instance, the Tahitian, Omai, played a significant role in the visual record of Cook's voyages, but it was not his physical presence but his likeness in books and paintings that certified Cook's discoveries to a larger European audience.[6]

Ironically, many painted and most printed representations were often anything but authentic. When German or Dutch engravers of the sixteenth century were tasked to depict the "Hottentots" (Khoi-san) of southern Africa to illustrate travel accounts, for instance, they turned to the familiar, long-established motif of the "wild man," which derived from illustrations of John the Baptist's early life in the wilderness.[7] In fact, the travel engravings of so-called primitives from the fifteenth up through the mid-nineteenth century offer up a surprisingly similar repertoire of images. Over a 400-year span, European illustrations of peoples ranging from Patagonians to Polynesians all look remarkably similar, as the art historian Christopher Steiner points out.[8] This clichéd portrayal of primitives from the Americas to the Pacific Islands reveals an almost interchangeability among exotic figures. It had a lot to do with the preconceptions and prejudices of European travelers, of course, and this complex of preconceptions and prejudices has often been theorized as the Western "gaze."

But the uncanny resemblance, even interchangeability, of engraved primitives across time and space emerges equally from a more prosaic factor: namely, the way in which images were produced and reproduced. Not ever having seen such exotics themselves, the thousands of engravers, painters, and others engaged in the business of image-making had little choice but to copy one another's styles and motifs over different media and across different centuries. A few portraitists worked from living models, such as when Joshua Reynolds sketched and painted Omai in the 1770s, but these were exceptional cases. Most early engravers worked from the illustrations of their predecessors. If a sixteenth-century engraving of a noble savage from the New World looks like a seventeenth-century engraving of a Hottentot, which looks like an eighteenth-century engraving of a Tahitian, the engravers can perhaps be forgiven, having only these previous representations to work from.

Moreover, in some pictorial approaches, reiteration of expected motifs was entirely the point. Allegorical representation was a linchpin in the art of early modern Europe, and allegory relied upon prior familiarity.[9] Allegorical figurations were especially useful to illustrate abstract concepts, such as Fortune, Death, Science, or later, Trade; by incorporating the abstraction as a human figure, it could be given a visual presence. One particularly common allegorical convention that would later become important to the commercial world was the representation of continents as three human figures. This harks back to early medieval imagery, where the three magi from the Gospels of Matthew became associated with the three parts of the world: Europe, Africa, and the Orient.[10] (The first representations of the world as four figures—i.e., four continents—began to emerge in the 1570s.)[11] Sixteenth-century artists, engravers, and printmakers such as Theodor de Bry, Jan van der Straet (Stradanus), Philip Galle, Adriaen Collaert, Marten de Vos, and Marcus Gheeraerts the Elder set the iconographic mold for these allegorical figurations of continents.

Later artists and engravers used these established allegories to represent abstract themes, such as travel or trade, on seventeenth-century maps; this convention carried over to frontispieces for commercial treatises in the eighteenth century, and from there to mastheads for such illustrated journals as *Over Land and Sea* in the nineteenth.[12] When the Bremen artist Arthur Fitger—who painted some of the panoramic murals in the Trade Hall of 1890, and crafted its promotional poster—was commissioned to depict "trade" for the Haus Seefahrt, he crafted five allegorical figures representing the continents.[13] To glance ahead: when advertising pioneers in Britain, France, and Germany sought to represent abstract notions such as "global trade" pictorially, they initially turned to this centuries-old allegory of trade or travel as human figuration of the continents. For instance, when the Liebig Company, one of the first multinational corporations, issued chromolithographed trading cards from the 1880s, a great many of the early designs used allegorical figurations of people to show abstract concepts such as trade and global travel.[14] For the illustration to work, of course, these allegorical figures needed to be recognizable as the representation of the distant land itself, and so these early advertising cards drew on the continuity of figuration that spanned centuries of artistic tradition.

The physical processes of certain types of image reproduction also factored into the interchangeability of exotic figures. Painting could convey tremendous amounts of detail and visual texture. But inexpensive ink printing entailed different considerations. Before the widespread adoption of planographic techniques in the nineteenth century, illustrations were reproduced by an engraved block, often placed in with set type. Originally these blocks were wood; later they were copper or steel. Blocks took tremendous skill to carve, and only printed items that commanded high prices, such as luxury editions of books, could afford to commission original engravings. For lower-cost printed matter, cliché blocks were often reused from elsewhere. Copper and steel engravings in particular could be used many times, and creatively written prose could recast the role of the adapted image. The images could then appear again and again in different contexts, even crossing national borders. For instance, one of the first inexpensive illustrated journals to appear in Germany was Jakob Weber's low-quality *Pfennig-Magazin,* first published in 1833. Only the text of the *Pfennig-Magazin* was set in Germany; its images were not even secondhand, but thirdhand, for the *Pfennig-Magazin* purchased all of its woodcuts from the *Magasin Pittoresque* in Paris, which in turn had purchased them from the *Penny Magazine* in London. With images from foreign sources, the corresponding German text was "written around" whatever illustration was available.[15] Jakob Weber went on to found the *Illustrirte Zeitung* a decade later (1843); it was a higher-quality enterprise, and with a much higher price. Nonetheless, many of its engravings clearly came from British publications. The engraved cliché blocks physically crossed national borders up through the nineteenth century, and the figurative clichés of the exotic crossed with them. The very word "cliché," from the French word for the engraved metal block, came into metaphorical use in English language around the 1850s, for those preset notions used again and again.[16] Inexpensive illustrated media before the 1890s, whether engravings in illustrated magazines or (as we will see) even early chromolithographic prints, from posters to trading cards, were profoundly transnational and pan-European in ways that national historiographies have entirely overlooked.

The mechanical conditions of print served to structure the visual canon of the primitive in the mercantile world. In Europe as early as the seventeenth century, a small range of specific wares, particularly tobacco, used black allegorical figurations of New World exotics, affixing them to bales of tobacco or even to individual wrapping as a referent of authenticity (Figure 2.2). For several centuries these Tobacco Moors ("Blackamoor" in English, *Tabakmohr* in German) served as static icons to certify the tobacco's distant origins, before ultimately being reconfigured (as we will see in later chapters) by the new capabilities of print technology and the new demands of commerce. The Tobacco Moor clichés of the seventeenth and eighteenth centuries were, in a similar way to that of Columbus's or Cook's captives, supposed to verify the distance traveled, by standing in for tobacco's land of origin—the New World. These early figures of Tobacco Moors were often depicted in languid repose, harking back directly to those sixteenth-century engravings of the voyages of dis-

Figure 2.2 "Three Moors" label by Claus Soltau of Hamburg, from the eighteenth century. The quality of reproduction is so low that identification is based upon allegorical markers, such as the tobacco-leaf headdresses, pipes, feather skirts, and "dark coloring" (crosshatching). *Source:* Eduard Maria Schranka, *Tabak-Anekdoten: Ein Historisches Braunbuch* (Cologne: Jos. Feinhals, 1914), 16.

covery, like that of Philip Galle (from a drawing by Stradanus), where a passive, reclining female "America" is being discovered by Vespucci.[17] In many instances, the Tobacco Moor figure became the centerpiece of a larger engraved scene that could include a palm-lined tropical shore, a pile of cargo, a sailing ship in the background, or all of the above. By personifying the distant land, the Tobacco Moor figure also implied the prowess of the merchant, who demonstrably had the connections to get the goods. Thus Tobacco Moor scenes very indirectly referenced the systems of English, French, and Dutch colonial enterprise in the seventeenth and eighteenth centuries, for these early colonial systems facilitated the production and transport of the goods in the first place.[18]

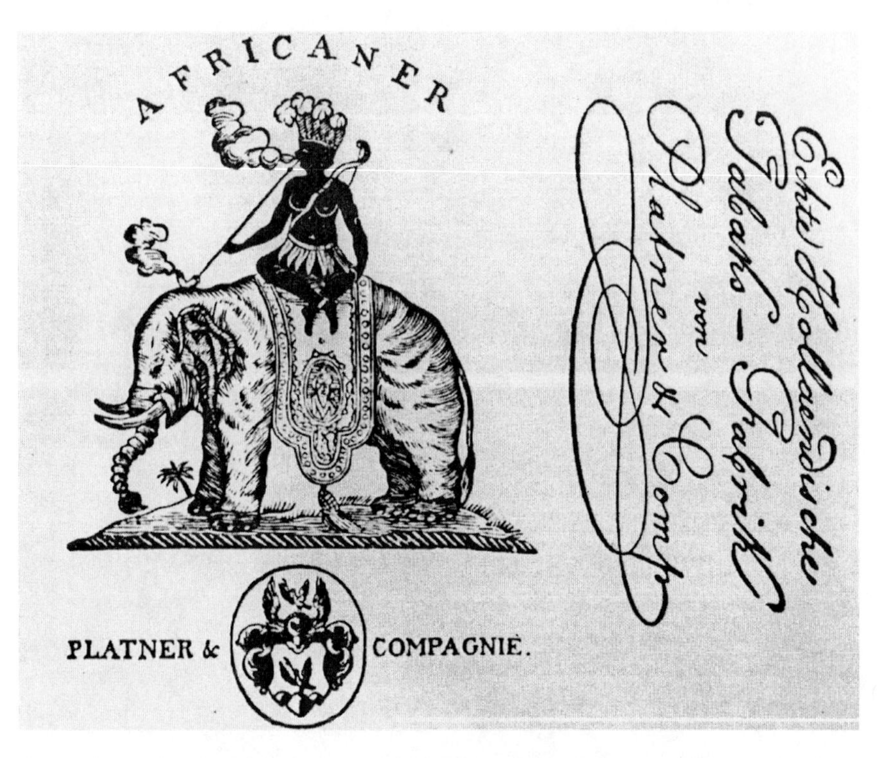

Figure 2.3 Label by the Genuine Dutch Tobacco manufacturer Platner & Co. of Nuremburg, circa 1850. This freely blends allegorical markers of the New World, Africa, and India. *Source:* Deutscher Verein für Buchwesen und Schrifttum, ed., *Alte Tabakzeichen* (Berlin: Widder Verlag, 1924), 26.

When scholars today examine these Tobacco Moor images, the question immediately turns to whether they are representations of Africans or Native Americans.[19] The figures' geographic and ethnic identity seems disturbingly fungible. Identical-looking icons, for instance, include appellations that range from "Neger" to "Indianer" to "Africaner"—appellations that today summon very different mental geographies[20] (Figure 2.3). Even the very idea of a Tobacco Moor—with "tobacco" a product of the New World, but "moor" evoking the Islamicized Orient of the Mediterranean—invites contrasting associations.[21] Indeed, with the figures themselves, contradictory allegorical markers of exoticism were often freely blended: bows and arrows were drawn alongside hookahs; palm trees were placed alongside feather headdresses; crude armadillos appeared next to blocky elephants. Even the black figure itself might be drawn with long blond hair.[22] In North America, moreover, woodcuts identical to the Tobacco Moor were used for a very different purpose—to sell slaves in American newspaper classifieds.[23] The fluidity of the race of the Tobacco Moor is sometimes attributed to "popular misconceptions."[24] But as a basic mercantile icon, there was no misconception: the figure's role was, first and foremost, to be an easily identifiable catch-all marker of exotic origin.

The interchangeability of the exotic cliché paralleled patterns in high art.[25] Though far removed from the world of classical painting, mercantile Tobacco Moor images also operated in an allegorical fashion: namely, they deployed a specific cluster of signs, whether bow or headdress, leaf or feather skirt, blackness or posture, to identify the figure, and otherwise allowed a great deal of flexibility in portrayal. This allegorical mode of identification relied upon the prior familiarity of the viewer in order to be meaningful, but in the eighteenth and early nineteenth centuries, purchasers of a luxury good such as tobacco generally came from the literate classes and could be expected to have encountered allegorical representations of New World "noble savages" in travel writing or other book engravings.[26] As long as the merchant did not seek to appeal beyond this educated clientele that shared this symbolic archive, the allegorical mode of representation remained useful—particularly since it was cheap.

Some of this mercantile dependence upon allegorical signifiers derived from the technological ramifications of its inexpensive production. For commercial images that were intended to be discarded, the high cost of the finest copper-plate engraving was not supportable. Cheap wood print blocks had a limited lifespan, however; fine detail might be achieved in small quantities, but when images were printed on a large scale, detail and quality were lost with each print. A well-known cluster of signs that together made up a familiar referent—allegory, in other words—was ideally suited for poorer quality, inexpensive print production. Viewers could recognize familiar referents—sometimes little more than inky splotches—and mentally fill in the meaning themselves. The image did not *itself* need to carry the weight of the message within its own frame; instead, the interpretive weight was borne by the familiarity of prior acquaintance.

By way of illustration, Figure 2.4 shows several from a fascinating series of four Tobacco Moor figures, all from a single tobacco importer

A

B

C

Figure 2.4 Three tobacco labels. A: Circa 1750. The motto is in Latin, French, and English. B: Circa 1830s. C: Circa 1870s, from a steel engraving *(Stahlstich)*. The motto is in Latin, French, and Dutch. *Source:* Eduard Maria Schranka, *Tabak-Anekdoten: Ein Historisches Braunbuch* (Cologne, 1914), 31–33.

spanning a century or more. In all of the icons, a few key symbols—the sun with a face, the sailing ships, the black workers, the white master-trader, and the motto, *Petum optimum Subter Solem*—remained constant for more than one hundred years. The first version from the mid-eighteenth century (Figure 2.4A) is barely perceptible; black (perhaps) figures hold up tobacco leaves to a reclining, smoking figure, which is likely a European, since the face is *not* crosshatched and the blotchy shape atop the figure might imply a hat. Ships and a sun are recognizable, though little else is. A second version, perhaps from around 1800, reveals further detail (Figure 2.4B). The black figures are recognizable as such by their color, and they wear the leaf skirts of the Tobacco Moor. The European in the image has also become recognizable by his three-cornered hat, buttoned frock coat, and high boots. A third version (not shown here), likely from the early nineteenth century, shows a greater inclusion of detail; the eyes, nose, and mouth of the European are recognizable, although the black figures remain faceless. In cheap relief printing, reproducing detail on a black face is far more difficult than on a white one. The last image, from the mid- to late nineteenth century, evinces both more detail and a new depth of field (Figure 2.4C). The bodies of the black figures, however, remain the single least developed element of the composition.[27] At a single glance, we can thus appreciate the difficulties inherent in inexpensive reproduction before the onset of the offset press, as well as the gradual innovations in technology and technique as the graven image was redesigned for greater clarity and finer detail.

The "exotic primitive" was therefore a primitive exotic—and an enduring cliché in the literal as well as figurative sense of the word. Cheap woodcuts of the Tobacco Moor drew on allegorical personifications of high art to be meaningful. This offered a highly portable cliché of exoticism and difference; though such clichés were used to mark tobacco sacks, they could equally appear in a newspaper classified for slaves or (as we will see below) to promote a Zulu show. Early modern printing woodblocks were simply reused—and they *could* be reused, meaningfully, because of the flexibility in representation based on allegorical signifiers, and because of the long-standing artistic tradition of painting primitives with broad brushstrokes. Clichés in early mercantile representation therefore emerged at the crossroads of artistic convention, allegorical interpretation, and the mechanics of print.

Inscribing the Other: The People Show and the Popular Press in the 1880s

In Germany in the 1880s, the presentation of living people rather rapidly and unexpectedly developed into a massive commercial enterprise. These *Völkerschauen,* or "people shows," were itinerant displays of "primitives" staged before increasingly large audiences throughout Germany and Europe. The premier German entertainment magazine, *Die Gartenlaube,* confided in 1884 that this "newly-reappearing display of the non-European races of men exerts a peculiar attraction on everyone."[28] Between 1880 and the First World War, well over a hundred large-scale *Völkerschauen* toured cities throughout Germany and Europe, and these were supplemented by countless smaller shows that toured through fairgrounds, zoos, and oddity museums. An array of new research has explored these displays of "exotic" or "primitive" peoples; scholars have grappled with a range of complex issues, from the relationship of the public with colonialism and the colonial project, to the changing social character of audiences and its attendant class conflicts, to the professional development of ethnography (and race science), to the construction of German or European identity itself.[29] In these sophisticated analyses, however, one important element in the new popularity of the *Völkerschau* has been largely overlooked: the novelty of its method of promotion.

Staged spectacles of supposed "savages" had been part and parcel of carnivals and fairs, displayed alongside the freakish and the monstrous in sideshows stretching all the way back to the Middle Ages. One turning point in this type of show's popularity across Europe was the success of a show of Zulus in London in the summer of 1853.[30] Just as the success of the Crystal Palace only two years earlier inspired imitators in Paris, Amsterdam, and Bremen, so too did London's Zulu show literally set the stage for later imitators. The 1853 Zulu show's success, however, was intensified by a new medium; the *Illustrated London News,* the world's first illustrated weekly newspaper, had been founded only ten years earlier in 1842, and it not only reported on the London Zulu show, but also showed it, in engraved illustrations circulated to all of England and the Continent.[31]

"Zulu" shows sprouted up all across Europe over the next two decades. Carnivals increasingly included a sideshow of one or two blacks—termed "Zulus"—shaking a spear fiercely on a ramshackle stage at a local audiences.[32] *Die Wilden,* an 1873 painting by the Berlin artist Paul Friedrich Meyerheim, depicts just such a show: a small crowd of country folk watch two African natives dance wildly on a stage, while an impresario off to the side gestures authoritatively at the "Zulu."[33] An announcement for one of these shows in the *Braunschweigische Anzeigen* of 1858 boasted of a "most curious natural oddity" consisting of two "white-born Negro girls" (albinos) displayed alongside a "wild Indian" from North America and a "wild Zulu-Kaffer" from the Cape of Good Hope.[34] The announcement even included a poor-quality woodblock cliché of a black figure: an ill-defined, inky splotch with a headdress, earring, bow and arrow, quiver, and leaf skirt. And like the Tobacco Moor of the previous century, it is difficult to say for certain whether the figure is meant to stand for the wild American Indian (because of the bow) or the wild Zulu-Negro (because of the blackness).

After 1880 these sideshows transformed, growing into elaborately staged touring productions that appeared in the fairgrounds and theaters of the largest urban centers.[35] The primary agent of this enterprise, and its most successful impresario, was Carl Hagenbeck, originally a trafficker in exotic animals from Hamburg. Facing a downturn in the exotic animal trade in 1875, Hagenbeck turned to exotic peoples; alongside a group of reindeer, Hagenbeck brought in a small family of Laplanders (Sami), displayed with all of their accoutrements and publicly performing the activities of their daily life.[36] The shift from animals to people immediately catapulted Hagenbeck to fame in Germany and throughout Europe, and it quickly became Hagenbeck's primary stock-in-trade. Over the next decade, his shows developed into well-promoted touring productions that featured "peoples of nature" from the Arctic Circle to the tropics, including Eskimos, Nubians, Hindus, Patagonians, Feuerlanders (Argentineans), Indians (Sioux), Mongols, and Singhalese (from Ceylon). Meanwhile, competitors immediately appeared, hoping to cash in on the people-show circuit: Böhle and Willardt, Charles and Henry Reich, and R. A. Cunningham all staged shows of their own, including of Laplanders, Native Americans, and Australian aboriginals.[37]

One of the reasons cited for Hagenbeck's commercial success, particularly vis-à-vis the earlier carnival shows, was his claim to authenticity. Just as authenticity (or claims to it) legitimized commercial exhibitions to the German public (as we saw in the previous chapter), so too could it legitimize performances. In the 1880s a new ethnographic component separated these shows from their disreputable carnival sideshow predecessors by purporting to be genuine; they displayed real "peoples of nature" from distant lands. Since many of Hagenbeck's shows centered on practices of daily life, whether demonstrations of cooking or primitive handicrafts, the shows could claim to be educational, and an appropriate, legitimized form of leisure.[38]

The authenticity of the performances recast the freak show as a touristic practice. Like the commercial exhibition, attending a people show was said to be the next best thing to traveling to an exotic destination.[39] As an eloquent blurb about one of Hagenbeck's competitors in 1891 attested:

> It is by means of Pinkert's Bedouin-Caravan, currently in Frankfurt, that we are transported to that fairytale land of the desert. It thereby has the advantage of being both genuine and cheap. . . . Because of it, we do not have to undertake an expensive journey. There is no need to shell out for a six-shot revolver, pith helmet, or veil . . . instead, one sits contentedly in the tram, and for 10 pennies, travels into the desert—without ever leaving the vicinity of the train station.[40]

Like the commercial exhibitions, the *Völkerschau* of the 1880s and 1890s professed to offer travel to exotic locales at prices that wide sectors of the public could afford. If you could not afford the enormous expense of a trip to South America, you could instead see Tierra del Fuego embodied in the Fuegians. Little wonder that these more authentic shows attracted larger crowds; Hagenbeck claimed that his third show, of Nubians (Sudanese) in 1877 in Breslau, had 30,000 visitors the first day; it supposedly reached 62,000 visitors in a single day at its peak. His most successful show purportedly saw more than 93,000 paying spectators in a single day.[41]

The shows' claims to authenticity were bolstered by the ties that Hagenbeck and other impresarios cultivated with the germinating field of anthropology. Anthropologists in Berlin and other German cities granted their public endorsement of these people shows, in return for access to the "natural peoples" themselves. This access was useful in an era before anthropological fieldwork was feasible or even thought necessary. In return, support of anthropologists such as Rudolf Virchow and Felix von Luschan carried legitimacy with the authorities, helping to secure police approval or the requisite permits. The Passage Panopticum in Berlin, for example, was allowed to present "scenes from a Tunisian harem" only after the police had determined that it held educational value.[42] The claim to being educational was therefore an early selling point in the *Völkerschau*—even when such claims to anthropological authenticity were less than truthful, as they often were. The mantle of "science" taken on by these shows provided cover for a popular entertainment, rooted in the carnival, to move into the leisure world of the middle classes.[43]

The educational component also facilitated the shows' coverage in the reputable middle-class press and illustrated family and entertainment weekly magazines, such as Leipzig's *Illustrirte Zeitung, Die Gartenlaube,* or *Over Land and Sea*. From their birth in the 1850s to the 1880s, these magazines were the primary purveyors of imagery to the middle classes and were the precursors of the mass media of the 1890s. The most successful was the erudite *Gartenlaube* ("the Arbor"), first published in 1853, which attained a transregional readership and the unheard-of circulation of 382,000 at its peak in 1875.[44] Each of these bourgeois journals sought to offer surveys of distant lands as a way to lace its edifying content with a bit of fascinating otherness. But it was *Gartenlaube*'s rivals, the *Illustrirte Zeitung* and particularly *Over Land and Sea,* that sought to carve out a readership with more exotic terrain. *Over Land and Sea* was first published in 1858 and took as its charge to "connect its readers to all parts of the world through image-telegrams."[45] Its masthead illustrated this allegorically: a crowned Europa in classical robes, with a book in one hand and staff of knowledge in the other, sits atop a globe. The globe, however, is carried on the straining backs of three figures representing the other continents: an Egyptian (the Orient), a feathered native (America), and a turbaned native (Africa).[46]

The dilemma was this: though all of these journals sought to include glimpses of foreign lands, travel was inordinately expensive, and they rarely had the resources to send legions of journalists and sketch artists to Africa, Asia, or South America. The *Völkerschau* therefore presented an unparalleled opportunity: they gave these magazines a means by which to report upon—and draw—authentic scenes of exotic peoples, but on the budget of local reporting. In this way, the people shows and the illustrated journals grew in symbiotic fashion. For their part, the shows gained an incalculably valuable promotional medium that spread descriptions and imagery to hundreds of thousands of potential ticket purchasers. The symbiosis was underwritten for both parties by the shows' ascribed authenticity, for the authenticity provided a veneer of edification for middle-class readers

Figure 2.5 Engraved illustration of the Singhalese (Ceylonese) *Völkerschau* at the Berlin Zoo in 1883. Note that no German spectators or Berlin landmarks are included in the illustration, which gives the impression that this scene might actually be transpiring in south Asia rather than Berlin. *Source: Illustrirte Zeitung* 81, no. 2098 (1883): 232.

and audiences, and a crucial credential for reporters and engravers. (The *Kleine Presse* in Frankfurt, for instance, reviewed an 1885 show of "Australian cannibals," admitting that the claim of human flesh-eating might sound like hokum, but assured readers the show's authenticity was certified by the renowned professor Virchow.)[47] The illustrations in these journals reflected this concern with edification and scientific veneer; they were inscribed in the detailed, painstaking style commonly found in ethnographic tomes (Figure 2.5).

The "educational" element emphasized by impresarios, authenticating anthropologists, and magazine journalists and engravers should not be taken too literally. Regardless of scientific overlay, the primary relationship between impresario and audience remained in the realm of commerce and was measured not by the intangibles of edification but in the cold calculations of gate receipts. The people shows were first and foremost show *busi-*

ness, and in show business, it was the most spectacular—the "newest sensation"—that captured the attention of the public and pulled in larger audiences.[48] To this effect, impresarios directed their efforts to create an alluring aura for the viewing public, even when this worked against the authentication they sought from ethnography.[49] As Carl Hagenbeck put it himself, describing his "Ceylon Caravan" of 1884,

> The colorful and fascinating scene of the camp; the majestic elephants (some decorated with shining gold saddle cloths and others equipped with working gear, carrying gigantic loads); the Indian magicians and jugglers; the devil-dancers with their grotesque masks; the beautiful, slender, doe-eyed Bajaderen with their dances which awaken the senses; and finally the great religious Perr-Harra-parade—all of it worked a virtually captivating magic which fell upon the audience.[50]

Popular Panoptics: Selling Sensationalism in the Wax Museums

The very spaces in which many shows were staged reveal the growing intrusion of popular spectacle into respectable edification. Though some of the larger shows by Hagenbeck in the 1880s were held in zoological gardens and other scientific establishments of the bourgeoisie, a great many were staged in venues with less respectable credentials. These were the "Panopticons" *(Panopticum),* which, coinciding chronologically with the *Völkerschau,* sprouted up across Germany in the 1880s. Castan's Panopticum was the oldest and most respectable of these establishments; molded in the vein of Madame Tussaud's wax museum, it was started in 1871 by the sculptor Louis Castan and his more mechanically inclined brother, Gustav. The Castans forged ties with scientific notables and were so successful that they established other locations in such cities as Bremen and Hamburg.[51] A few years after the Castans, Hayo Faerber opened his Hanseatic Panopticum in St. Pauli, Hamburg, in 1879; he later incorporated it as the Panopticum AG and by the 1890s was seeing more than 100,000 visitors annually.[52] By the 1880s many more sprouted up, including Süring's Universum, Umlauff's World-Museum, Eppmann's Moskauer Panoptikum in Frankfurt, Gabrieles Panopticon in Munich, Paolo's Panopticum, Otto Riedel's Panoptikum, and Willardts Panopticon.[53] All of these popular commercial museums fed from and fed into the public's desire to see for themselves the bizarre, the freakish, and the outlandish, presented in dioramas, wax displays, and live shows. The Panoptikum of Germany thus was the direct heir of P. T. Barnum's dime museum.[54]

The importance of the *Völkerschauen* to these commercial museums was clear. Most of the Panopticons had attached theaters, and they staged shows of live natives more or less continuously from the 1880s through 1900. Castan's business, in fact, was the primary venue for the earliest people shows in Berlin. Louis Castan was a personal friend of the Berlin anthropologist Rudolf Virchow, which resulted in a great deal of cooperation; Castan allowed Virchow to measure and "study" the native performers, while Virchow, in turn, certified to the authorities that Castan's business performed an educational service.[55] A competitor, the Passage Panopticum, opened its doors on the Friedrichstrasse in 1889 and strove for a more sensationalistic tone, offering more extreme and gruesome displays. It also included a thousand-seat theater.[56]

The shows of native peoples, freaks, and other oddities were also patterned by their surroundings—the permanent sculptures of wax. In the Passage Panopticum, for instance, to get to the theater, one first entered into the halls filled with the busts of renowned German aristocrats, scientists, and academics. Then came the Hall of Peoples, displaying "typical" types from Japan, Cameroon, Samoa, China, Russia, and other lands. We can catch a glimpse of what these sculptures looked like; though the Passage busts were lost, some of Castan's busts of Africans survived, housed in Berlin's Museum Europäischer Kulturen. They exaggerate cranial size and facial features; the lips are painted cherry red.[57] Moreover, on the promotional poster for Otto Riedel's Scientific Museum and Panoptikum, five busts of black racial types, including a Nubian and a Hottentot, are the centerpiece of the display room. Riedel's busts are surrounded by displays of anatomy, freaks, modern technology, mythology, and notorious crimes.[58] Even the plaster and wax masks of Otto Finsch, that had been so prominently displayed in Bremen's Hall of Commerce in the exhibition of 1890, eventually found their way to Castan's Panopticum, where they were exhibited—and apparently even sold.[59]

The next room in the Passage Panopticum staged scenes from German fairy tales (such as *Cinderella*) alongside infamous crime stories ripped from the headlines. It also held an ethnographic collection from Cameroon, "with many rare pieces, worth 35,000 Marks," and—most dramatically—the stuffed and preserved human skin of a sixteen-year-old Botokunden girl.[60] Only then—after walking through purposefully sculpted German traditionalism and sensationally carved racial otherness—would the visitor arrive at the theater to see the show. It was named the Hall of Abnormalities, and spectacles were staged every half hour, ranging from a "Real Harem out of Cairo!" (in fact they were Tunisians) to the freakishly hairy Lion-Man. For a show in 1898, a banner boasted of "35 Togo Negroes! 28 Girls—5 Men—2 Children!"[61] In short, rooms of waxen aristocrats and ethnographic objects (both human and material) exhibited the establishment's credentials, while displays such as the stuffed human skin of a West African girl offered more sensational fare to bring in customers. Nationalism, science, and popular spectacle served as backdrops for the live shows of dwarves, bearded women, snake charmers, odalisques, and last but not least, Togolese children.

The interplay between the respectable and the sensational inside the walls of the Panoptikum found its way out onto the streets—as design on chromolithographed posters. This "planographic panoptics," as I term it, similarly contrasted German notables, German traditions, and modern science against the thrill of racial deformity and criminal notoriety—but in a very condensed fashion, to fit a two-foot-by-three-foot, two-dimensional surface. Panoptikum posters generally aped the mode of the emergent mass media. The poster for Süring's Universum wax museum in the early 1890s, for instance (Plate 3) follows the layout of one of the new illustrated newspapers: the masthead promises "New, Interesting, Educational." The headlines boast of "lifesize figures!" and "newest current events!" And the text is arranged like a classified ad page, including pointing fingers to attract the eye. Around the edges are arrayed an illustrated overview of the newsworthy and the noteworthy, the bizarre and the sentimental. A mechanical professor is next to a sword-balancing acrobat. Essa the Giant Child sits alongside Princess Pauline, the Smallest Woman in the World. Little Red Riding Hood encounters the Wolf. The Seven Dwarves watch over a catatonic Snow White. A German soldier bids farewell to his family. A man and woman are roped together (a marriage ceremony? a tableau of the murderer Franz Schneider?). Meanwhile, interspersed are contrasts and aberrations: a Native American with war paint; a profile of a black boy with a misshapen cranium; two Germans distorted by funhouse mirrors; a robed African with dyed hair; an African native with inserted lip- and ear plates. At the bottom, the explorer "Cassati" [*sic*] tied to a tree.

The more sensationalistic images in the panoply, such as the African savages about to stab Gaetano Casati, or the pointed teeth and pierced lip plate of the African native, were unusual for public posters in the early 1890s.[62] Crafted by the firm of Adolph Friedländer, Süring's was only one of many in this new style, which included posters for Trabers Museum, Neumann's Museum, Paolos Panoptikum, Julius Eppmann's Moskauer Panoptikum, and Otto Riedel's Panoptikum.[63] Collectively, such posters presented a popular panoptic array that juxtaposed "natives" and "freaks" against German folklore and military heroes. What linked these diverse things together was a new, modern sensibility of spectacle.[64] The commercial ethic is paramount. Each spectacle is useful only insofar as it might trigger an emotional response in a viewer—sentimentality, curiosity, horror, disbelief—that might then propel the viewer into the establishment.

The people show and the Panoptikum were more than performances that simply catered to public curiosity. They were commercial projects, crafting a gripping view of the world and disseminating that view through innovative promotions. The enterprises of Hagenbeck and Castan, in fact, were at the very forefront of visual strategies that other commercial enterprises, particularly manufacturers, would later adopt. The successful displays of people in the 1880s, whether live or made of wax, made groundbreaking (and eye-popping) use of the most recent technological innovation: the inexpensive, vivid, full-color poster. Inexpensive chromolithography allowed new entrepreneurs of the 1880s such as Hagenbeck and Castan to not only proclaim the exotic wonder of "peoples of nature" but also to *show* it. Show business had become, quite literally, "show" business.

The vast majority of the chromolithographed show posters produced in Germany between 1880 and 1914 were the product of a single Hamburg firm, that of Adolph Friedländer (1851–1904). Friedländer had set up his small printing business in the St. Pauli district in 1872, initially printing labels for goods and products on hand presses. He moved in the rather dubious circles of showmen and carnies—he was a board member of the Society of Traveling Showmen (Vereins reisender Schausteller und Berufsgenossen) and even printed its newsletter. By the 1870s his firm was issuing posters for freak shows, circuses, panopticons, and traveling *varieté* acts and American minstrel shows.[65] The minstrel show posters, in fact, were among Friedländer's very earliest; he crafted posters for the shows of Brooks and Duncan (1873), Forrest and Harding (1875), Edwards and

Harris (1882), and Astor and Belmont (1884).[66] Friedländer's firm grew rapidly after the purchase of a rotating lithographic press in 1883, and he employed a growing number of graphic artists, the most well-known of whom was Christian Bettels. Friedländer's first posters for Carl Hagenbeck's shows began to appear in the mid-1880s. Though Friedländer was a personal friend of Hagenbeck's, he also undertook printing jobs for Hagenbeck's competition, including the ethno-sideshows of the Circus Busch and shows at the Passage Panopticum. By the mid-1880s Friedländer's chromolithographed posters were seen all over Germany. His firm had effectively injected a new visual style into the German public sphere—a style that stood out for its colorful vibrancy and startling sensationalism.[67]

It might be more accurate to say that Friedländer imported this visual style, however. The circus posters of the United States, particularly those of P. T. Barnum, served as his models, although Friedländer would refine Barnum's visual techniques. Indeed, the influence of Barnum on the development of German popularly oriented commercial culture is as extraordinary as it is unrecognized. Barnum had toured the Rhineland with General Tom Thumb in 1858, and Barnum's extensive use of loud promotions for his show made a strong impression—including on nascent German advertising.[68] Perhaps unsurprisingly, Barnum was also a pioneer in the sensationalistic exhibition of "savages"; in 1861 his American Museum showed mammoth bears, man-monkey aberrations, and—following in the footsteps of the London Zulu shows—of "Wild African Savages." These savages were allegedly Zulus, but likely costumed African-Americans. Barnum's first show dedicated entirely to savage spectacle—"real Fijian Cannibals!"—toured the United States in 1872.[69] In November of that same year, he traveled through a number of German cities on his way to the Vienna World's Fair of 1873. Barnum's first stop was Hamburg, where he purchased a boatload of live animals from Carl Hagenbeck, who thereafter became Barnum's main supplier, and even occasional business partner. In his memoirs, Hagenbeck wrote about his first meeting with the great Barnum—"the king of all showmen"—in St. Pauli in November 1872.[70] It might have been only a coincidence that, only two years after his exchange with Barnum, and on the heels of Barnum's successful Fijian cannibal show, Hagenbeck turned away from animals and toward the more lucrative showing of people. Hagenbeck himself described Barnum's enormously profitable shows as "an American amalgamation of circus, cabinet-of-curiosities, and animal arena"; and they were clearly a model for Hagenbeck, even if Hagenbeck added a large dose of anthropological/scientific authenticity to make such people shows more palatable to the conservative mores of the German middle classes.[71]

Barnum's visit to Hamburg in 1872 also coincided with the founding of Adolph Friedländer's new printing business. Even if there was no personal contact between the two men, there can be no disputing that Friedländer's approach to graphic design followed the American circus poster model.[72] A Friedländer poster for Hagenbeck's "Circus and Menagerie" from 1887, for instance, shows an array of animals, some domestic (such as horses), some exotic (such as zebras and elephants), leaping and cavorting, and performing tricks (Plate 4). The sense of movement is vivid. The show included "120 Persons . . . plus 20 Singhalese and Tamils, Natives from the Island of Ceylon. *And 2 Singhalese dwarves.*" Among the swirling array of trained animals, the Singhalese paraded by, at the bottom of the poster, in all of their exotic finery.

One key to Barnum's own successes in the United States was his vivid, aggressive promotional posters, appearing in the 1860s; twenty years later such posters were being churned out of Hamburg. A glance at Friedländer's corpus in the late 1880s reveals vivid tableaux of wild ritual dances and strange, mysterious customs. A poster for a people show staged in Umlauff's World-Museum in the 1880s, for instance, promoted "Carl Hagenbeck's 'newest' " (Plate 5).[73] This cavalcade included "Devil dancers, staff-dancers, pot-dancers, as well as a Singhalese dwarf 'Verama'—25 years old, but only 90 centimeters tall!" The poster is most striking not for its proclamations but for its use of vivid color and the way it shows the Singhalese dancers in a swirl of movement. Feet are raised off of the ground, limbs are stretched out, flowing hair shows the figures are in motion. Meanwhile, vibrant patterns and colors of dress contrast against the dark skin, which itself is drawn to gleam with reflected light. The whole composition grabs the eye and excites the senses in a collage of color and frozen movement. This type of poster differs dramatically from the sedate and static posters in the German classical style, like those for the commercial exhibitions. Friedländer's composition also diverges radically from the measured style of ethnographic illustrations in the middle-class entertainment magazines (see Figure 2.5). The show itself, as captured by a group photograph of the show's human and animal performers, seems to have been a much more prosaic affair.[74] The Singhalese show toured Europe from 1883 through 1885. In Berlin, close to 100,000 people attended the Singhalese show, from which Hagenbeck grossed approximately 32,000 marks.[75] This variant of Germans' fascination for people of exotic lands, then, was generated through an intense promotional campaign—one that reshaped exoticism in the visual sphere, replacing the languid icons of allegory or engravings of ethnography for vivid, dancing spectacle.

By the 1890s Friedländer's firm had become one of the largest poster printers in Germany: it created at least 2,000 different poster designs in the decade after 1890. As the print run for each poster usually involved 3,000 or more copies, Friedländer produced a substantial corpus of visuality before the fin de siècle.[76] At its peak, the firm printed 400 poster designs every year. Friedländer had imported his vivid style from Barnum's America in the 1880s, but by 1900 he was exporting this style, crafting posters for customers as far away as Japan, India, Australia, and even the United States.[77] The images themselves could undergo curious transoceanic and transcultural journeys: in a strange twist, one of Friedländer's more prominent chromolithographs, of a Ceylonese snake charmer, made its way to central Africa. There the orientalist image was reinterpreted by devotees of the indigenous cult of Mami Wata. From Central Africa, the image made its way across the Atlantic, where it was worked into Latino imagery of the Catholic Saint Marta in the Americas. Finally, the image ultimately became the centerpiece of artwork by a practitioner of voodoo in Haiti.[78]

Friedländer's illustrations of circuses, menageries, exotics, panopticons, and sensational shows of natives became one of the first prominent fonts of visual mass culture in late nineteenth-century Germany. The firm's corpus included less sensational work, of course. For the 1889 Commerce and Industry Exhibition in Hamburg, the firm printed the traditional and decorous official poster, even as it printed posters for Hamburg's more gripping attractions, such as Castan's *Irrgarten* and the hot-air balloon ride.[79] But the most vivid posters, especially of natives, made the greatest impression. Surviving photographs of poster plastered walls from the fin de siècle invariably show at least one poster identifiable as a Friedländer, usually a "native" of some sort. When cartoonists lampooned the growing ubiquity of advertising, they often chose to include a *Völkerschau* poster in their caricatures.[80]

Packaging the Wildly Popular

As popular phenomena, the people show and the Panoptikum had a visible impact on the early commodity culture of imperial Germany. In some cases, the connections were direct. The profitability of the people shows raised the potential for money-making opportunities beyond the stage, and this led to some of the very first examples of promotional product tie-ins to emerge in Germany. The entrepreneurial activities of Carl Hagenbeck's half-brother, John, also in the *Völkerschau* business, offers a case in point: John Hagenbeck used his contacts in Ceylon, formed while organizing a Singhalese *Völkerschau,* to purchase coconut, tea, and rubber plantations on the island.[81] Back in Germany, he then marketed tea under the brand name Hagenbeck's Ceylon Tea at least as early as 1895. Omitting his first name, of course, associated his tea brand with his increasingly legendary brother. The first advertisement for Hagenbeck's Ceylon Tea appeared as a component of the promotional poster for Carl Hagenbeck's "India" show in Berlin in 1895: the prices for John Hagenbeck's teas are printed on the show poster underneath the illustration of a dancing Indian woman in a sari bedecked with exotic jewelry.[82] The lithographer was Adolph Friedländer, whose firm increasingly drifted into advertising products by the circuitous route of product placements in show promotions.[83]

A famous advertisement for Hagenbeck's Ceylon Tea from 1899 featured a Ceylon native carrying an enormous crate of tea on his head (Figure 2.6). Designed by Ludwig Berwald, this poster became one of the very earliest exemplars for professional advertisers: it was reproduced in the earliest professional literature, including in the 1899 issue of Robert Exner's *Propaganda* and again in Johannes Lemcke's 1901 *Handbook of Advertising.*[84] The native carrying the crate serves an authenticating role; like the Tobacco Moor of a half-century earlier, the figure certifies that Hagenbeck's tea really *is* from a distant land, by incarnating that land in the body of one of its denizens. Yet Berwald's poster of 1899 differs markedly from that of the dancing Ceylonese woman of Friedländer's 1895 poster; as we will see in Chapter 4, the male figure is not just an object of a spectacle, but a performer of labor, literally lifting the brand name above himself.

The commercial opportunities presented by the *Völkerschau* extended beyond the world of showmen. As the spectacles of the shows expanded, the shows achieved tremendous recognition, and new businesses offering new products often sought to capitalize on the shows' spectacle and cultural

Figure 2.6 Poster for (John) Hagenbeck's Ceylon Tea, designed by Ludwig Berwald, 1899. *Sources: Propaganda* 2, no. 1 (1899), and Johannes Lemcke, *Handbuch der Reklame* (Berlin: Brockhaus, 1901), 113.

prominence. The Dresden Chemical Laboratory Lingner was one of the first German firms to engage in intensive, ongoing nationwide advertising campaigns, and its mouthwash Odol, appearing in 1893, was one of the very first German brand-name products.[85] One of the most prominent of Lingner's campaigns boasted that Odol was "spread to all the nations and to all peoples!" To illustrate this slogan, the Lingner firm turned to the most visible presentation of "all peoples": it crafted ads featuring "types" of peoples, and circulated them first in mass-market papers, such as the *Fliegende Blätter,*

Figure 2.7 Odol mouthwash advertisement, 1901. "Absolutely the best mouthwash in the world! Spread to all peoples!" Notice the necklace tags, which are miniature likenesses of the commodity package. *Source: Fliegende Blätter* no. 2912 (17 May 1901).

around 1900, and a decade later, in colonialist publications.[86] These figures were more ethnographically delineated than the allegorical figurations of lands or continents, but drew their pictorial style from people-show promotions: Odol's first ads were of Lapps, for instance, which corresponded to Hagenbeck's first show of native people. A close look at Odol's 1901 illustration of a representative of "Africa" (Figure 2.7) reveals an intriguing resemblance to an actual photograph of one of Hagenbeck's African performers, the Warrior-Queen Gumma, as seen in an issue of a showman's journal, *Der Kurier,* from 1896.[87] That Odol's graphic designer would draw from a photo of an ethnographic performer—perhaps the only photo of an African on hand—was not at all improbable. In fact, such stories abound. The visual traces of the *Völkerschau* had ongoing impact: a nude photograph of a "Zulu

Figure 2.8 Advertisement (by Franz Christophe) for the Berlin poster design firm Hollerbaum & Schmidt, reproduced in a professional advertising journal in 1902. *Source: Modern Reklame* 1, no. 9 (1902): 126.

Princess" who had appeared in a show in Castan's Panopticum in 1885, for instance, was used over and over again in scientific publications, reappearing in ethnographic compendia for decades.[88]

In general, when graphic designers of the 1890s were tasked to illustrate the common advertising slogan "available everywhere," some chose to playfully twist the phrase into supposedly global distribution—and then draw this global reach by showing a panoptic array of ethnic groups engaging with the product. For the emerging business of poster design, the embodiment of distant lands as peoples in a panoptic array proved doubly irresistible, for it allowed them both to illustrate a difficult concept and to demonstrate they had their finger on the popular pulse. The Berlin firm Hollerbaum and Schmidt, for instance, advertised its own services using scenes of four different peoples—Lapps, Native Americans, Japanese, and Africans—admiring their posters (Figure 2.8). This recast age-old allegorical figurations of continents into a more current symbolic representation of the four extremes of the earth: namely the Arctic, the Wild West, the Far East, and darkest Africa. But it also corresponded to the four most common types of popular shows staged in Germany: the *Völkerschauen* of Lapps, Africans, and American Indians, and the Japanese circus/magic/acrobat shows.[89]

Just as the panoptic visual array of the popular people shows spilled over into later advertising, so too did its sensibility of spectacle. The vivid scenes on Friedländer's promotional posters provided not only a pool of exotic embodiment for advertising pioneers, but also a modus operandi of pictorial style. Even more than a decade later, the packaging of Ceylon Crème chocolates, manufactured by the venerable Cologne firm of Stollwerck around 1900, duplicates all of the components of a sensational *Völkerschau* poster (Plate 6). The partial nakedness of the Ceylonese plays off the vivid, colorful splendor of their costumes. The elephants at the center of the scene are both awesome and controlled, but instead of logs carried by their trunks—showing their use as draft animals—the Stollwerck box has them carrying chocolate bars. The rich adornments on the elephants hint at princely wealth, and the spears, shields, jewelry, and musical instruments hearken to the ethnographic objects that authenticated the shows. The natives dance, play, gesture, and stride, with arms and legs outstretched in a tableau of frozen movement. The vibrancy and energy brought to life in the packaging contrasts strikingly with Stollwerck's more staid packaging from the previous decade. It clearly echoes a number of early *Völkerschau* poster illustrations from the mid-1880s (cf. Plates 4 and 5); it also draws on pictorial themes from British show posters of Ceylonese.[90] Stollwerck's graphic designer followed the techniques of Friedländer's artists, crafting a scene of intense color and vivid movement. Friedländer's Ceylon posters, in turn, drew from the promotional posters used in reprints of P. T. Barnum's memoir, including the enormously popular *The Art of Money-Getting.*[91]

In Savage Color: African *Völkerschau* Posters in the 1890s

Some poster designers took sensationalism to a new extreme, into the illustration of horrifying savagery (Plate 7). One of the most visceral, for the show "Male and Female Australian Cannibals," printed (in English) by the Berlin firm Nauck & Hartmann, depicts a gruesome scene: black cannibals, wearing feathered skirts and necklaces and large looping earrings, gnaw on human bones and hack apart the corpse of a European. A freshly killed European lies in the foreground, while in the background, two bound white men are measured for their meatiness, a third is harangued by wild dances, and a fourth thrashes vainly as he is about to be clubbed to death, cooked, and eaten. In the distant background, a ship sinks; the unfortunate whites, it is clear, are the survivors of a ship wrecked off savage shores. (This is an allusion to the wreck of the *Maria* near Cardwell in 1872.)[92] Such a graphic depiction was far beyond the pale of propriety for the German visual terrain of the mid-1880s.[93]

This poster, along with a less gruesome one for "Australian Cannibal Boomerang Throwers," shows an unusual feature for a *Völkerschau* poster from the 1880s—the graphic delineation of the performers as racially different. The black figures' features are distorted, and emphasize large, bright red lips. *Völkerschau* posters produced in Germany did not begin to deploy such racialized depictions for another twenty years (and even then only with illustrations of Africans): these Australian cannibal posters were very much ahead of their time. Like the show itself, the poster themes were an American import, as we can deduce by the English text. The basic lithographic plate or stone itself may even have been brought over the Atlantic, though the design is signed by the Berlin lithographer Alex Hönig. The yellow and green empty spaces on the poster were left blank to accommodate specific show times and locations, and could be filled in with specific information in German, as seen in several composites.[94] The German-language pamphlet for the show's German tour was printed by Franz Greven of Cologne and is no less visually gruesome, with an engraved, black-and-white version of the identical scene on its cover.[95]

The tour of Australian cannibal boomerang throwers was orchestrated by an American impresario, Robert A. Cunningham, an agent of P. T. Barnum. The supposed cannibals Cunningham brought to Europe in 1884 had toured the United States the previous year, as part of "P. T. Barnum's Last Sensation: the Ethnological Congress of Strange and Savage Tribes." The racial elements of the show, and the racialized features of the Australian cannibal poster design itself, becomes more understandable when we find that Cunningham himself, before becoming a *Völkerschau* impresario, had worked as a promoter of American minstrel shows. In 1884 and 1885, the Australian cannibal show toured Europe, including

London, Brussels, Cologne, Berlin, Dresden, and Chemnitz. In Berlin, Cunningham's show stayed over at Castan's Panopticum for three months. Three of the seven aboriginals died while in Germany.[96] The show's promotional materials minimized their humanity, presenting them simultaneously as ethnographic objects of study and (as the pamphlet described them) "truly bloodthirsty monsters."

In 1901 a report from the German Colonial Society complained that "the attraction of just observing indigenous people in their typical dress and customary jewelry surrounded by their weapons and tools, or even their native dances, is not enough to draw the spectators anymore . . . one turns to methods that are geared to titillate the masses."[97] This recognition was a decade late. In the mid-1880s and early 1890s Hagenbeck and his competitors increasingly staged shows of supposedly savage natives from Africa. Nubians (from the Sudan), Zulu, Somali, Bushmen and Hottentots (Khoi-San), Amazons (from Dahomey), Bedouin, Ashanti, Swahili, and Dinka were among the many people from various regions of the African continent brought to Europe for display. In the four years between 1885 and 1889, thirty-seven of forty-one—roughly 90 percent—of the *Völkerschau* in Germany listed by Sierra Bruckner were of peoples from the African continent. In the seventeen years prior to 1884, meanwhile, only six of twenty-four shows had been of Africans.[98]

Africans' new prominence on German stages might be seen at first as a logical outgrowth of popular interest following Germany's colonial acquisitions on that continent in the mid-1880s. However, there were few direct links between German colonialism and shows of Africans. Apart from a show of Prince Dido and other Cameroonians in 1886, and a Togo show at the Passage Panopticum in 1900, none of the shows were of Africans from areas under German colonial rule.[99] More important, the shows themselves were transnational, touring London and Paris as profitably as Berlin and Cologne. The parade of African troupes through the cities of Europe, including Germany, was part of a growing interest in Africa across Europe in the mid-1880s—an interest that was intensified by the new mass media. The expeditions of Stanley were grist for the new popular tabloids, and such media popularization fed into the "Scramble for Africa," of which Germany's leap into colonialist policy was a key component.[100]

The new prevalence of the African *Völkerschau* worked symbiotically with the new popular media. The people shows of the 1880s had been driven by a rhetoric of anthropological discovery, circulating through the bourgeois entertainment journals. In the 1890s the new illustrated mass media provided a new framework—and a new tone. The reports of colonial warfare led the headlines of the new tabloids in Britain, France, and increasingly, Germany; the impresarios of the people shows sought to capitalize on this media flurry. The stunning defeat of the British military expedition at Isandhlwana in January 1879 commanded gripping headlines throughout Europe; that same year a *Völkerschau* of so-called Zulu appeared in Berlin. In 1885 the forces of the Mahdist uprising in the Sudan besieged (and ultimately killed) General Gordon at Khartoum, which became a cause célèbre for the new mass media in London, which then spread to European papers. The impresarios were quick to seize the moment: Heinrich Möllers's Sudanese Caravan of 1885 purported to display "troops and supporters of the Mahdi." Most provocatively, when French colonial troops attacked the Kingdom of Dahomey (modern-day Benin) in 1890 and 1892, they purportedly encountered female warriors, which was avidly reported in the new papers. In the years 1890 and 1892, shows of "Dahomey Amazons" toured the European capitals.[101] The excitement of colonial warfare, in short, provided a backdrop to the stage of the *Völkerschau.* And this backdrop was not merely sensational, but *violent.* The more sedate "ethnographic" shows of Laplanders, Eskimos, and Chileans that flourished in the late 1870s and early 1880s were, by century's end, considered "too sober" to exert a lasting attraction.[102] By the 1890s Africa had arrived, and Africa was staged—and lithographed—as a land of savage warfare.

The outlines of this new illustrated popular savagery can be sketched in a brief survey of the imagery for a single show, that of the Amazons from Dahomey (Plate 8). In 1890, the very same year that shocking headlines told of French colonial troops coming under attack by female warriors of Dahomey, a Hagenbeck show featuring the Dahomey "Amazon Corps" appeared. Over several seasons, the show performed at Castan's Panopticum, Umlauff's World-Museum, and the Frankfurt Zoo, and in many other venues in Germany, before moving on to France and Britain. According to a program from 1891, the show opened with a war dance led by their fearsome warrior-queen, Gumma. The Amazons then enacted a number of military exercises and martial drills, including a sword dance.[103] The show was a remarkable success, and it spawned a number of imitators over the following decade, with shows by Albert Urbach in the

Figure 2.9 Photographic souvenir postcard from the *Völkerschau* of the Amazon Corps. "The personal guard of the King of Dahomey in West-Africa." Printed in Hamburg. *Source:* Collection of Robert Lebeck, reprinted in Hermann Pollig, ed., *Exotische Welten: Europäische Phantasien* (Stuttgart: Edition Cantz, 1987), 390.

mid-1890s and by Hood in 1899, under the title "Thirty-Three Wild Women from Dahomey."

Of course, the actual African performers, more than thirty of them, were not really from Dahomey, and neither were they former Amazons or even soldiers. Authenticity—once the entry ticket into respectable society—was becoming less of a concern. This made for an ever-growing disjunction between promotional lithograph and performed show. For instance, a photograph of the troupe from a souvenir postcard reveals a surprisingly staid scene where twenty-three West Africans of various ages, mostly women but some men and children, pose as a group for the camera (Figure 2.9). Some look stern; most look bored. A few are holding spears, but these weapons are merely accoutrements of their costume rather than deliberately held up in warlike aggression. At the center of the troupe, the Oberkriegerin (chief warrioress) Gumma, who wears a feather behind her head, appears to have a rather bemused expression on her face. And the tiniest child appears more than a bit grumpy.

Compare this tranquil pose with the poster designed by Friedländer's firm, in which a pack of wild-eyed savage warrior women, armed with muskets, knives, and cutlasses, rushes forward in the attack (Plate 8). With the glistening blades, blowing skirts, bare feet, and staring, maniacal eyes, they represent a swirling mass of brutishness that charges past the viewer. The hulking followers are undifferentiated from one another; they are uniformly masculinized with square jaws, heavy brows, and broad shoulders. Gumma herself is drawn with somewhat more feminine features—thinner, smaller in stature, a more delicate ear—and with a hint of something besides mania in her eyes. (As we will see below, she was the show's erotic focus.) Another Friedländer poster by Christian Bettels for the Amazon Corps show at Umlauff's World-Museum in Hamburg in 1890 (not pictured), though less menacing, is even more physically kinetic: it depicts a leaping Amazon with a spear battling another broad-shouldered Amazon wielding a sword. They fight over the body of a third Amazon, while others circle around.[104] The difference between Friedländer's composition of hulking and maniacal savagery (with the slightest bit of eroticism) and the photograph of the carefully arranged troupe (Figure 2.9) is striking.

Friedländer's other posters for the Amazons highlight the shows' different aspects. Some posters sketch scenes that are strictly martial. One poster from around 1890, for instance, depicts rows of black Amazons standing at parade attention, forgoing the more visceral thrill of action to emphasize the orderly regimentation of their soldierly drill; yet savagery creeps into the scene by the row of skulls, stuck on posts not so innocuously in the background.[105] Other Friedländer posters for Albert Urbach's show of "Wild Women from Dahomey" at Castan's Panopticum in 1894 also depicts martial drill; it arrays three groups of Amazons of about twenty apiece (in yellow, blue, and red costumes) marching in ordered ranks.[106] All of these posters of Amazons at military drill, however, feature one menace—namely, the chief Amazon herself, directing the marching of her she-warriors with sharp sword upraised.

A few posters tone down the trope of combat, instead offering a gesture toward the erotic. For the more respectable Castan's Panopticum, Friedländer used its premier artist, Christian Bettels (Plate 9). Note particularly the masterful play of light on the figure's bare arms and upper body. Indeed, the woman who performed as Gumma was the erotic focus of the show; a contemporary newspaper account wrote of "her gleaming brown shoulders" draped with nothing but shells and beads. And after the show, Gumma sold photos of her troupe and herself—one mark for the clothed version, or two marks for the unclothed.[107] In Bettels's somewhat eroticized poster a dagger appears in her hand, and her fist is clenched; both lend an undercurrent of danger, contradicting or perhaps escalating the erotic undertones. Bettels nonetheless approached this drawing with some sensitivity, and it differs dramatically from its more spectacular, violent competitors. As it turns out, Bettels's is the only poster of Gumma to be drawn from an actual photograph of the performer herself.[108] The text of the poster labels this show at Castan's as the *Original* Amazons, and perhaps Bettels chose to make the image in the actual likeness of the performer as a claim to authenticity in the face of competition from other troupes, such as that of Urbach.

A great deal has been written about the eroticism that underscored European perceptions of the colonial encounter, particularly in the encoding of black female bodies as sexually accessible.[109] Yet we must be wary of assuming uniformity among and between European colonizing cultures. Themes such as imperial eroticism did move freely across different cultures in Europe, but always through very specific vectors—translations of fiction, copying of engravings, itinerancy of performances—each vector with its own history. Although colonial ideologies, discourses, and motifs spread transnationally across Europe (and beyond), they were adapted and articulated locally in markedly different ways. For instance, Amazon shows toured all European capitals, such as Paris, London, and even Riga, and their promotional imagery thereby also crisscrossed national borders. The poster for J. C. Bernhardt's Amazon show in the Frankfurt Zoo in 1891, for instance, was the same as that used for the 1893 show at the Crystal Palace in London.[110] In other cases, however, posters for the Amazon shows followed local patterns in both poster design and cultural politics. French promotional posters for the 1892 Amazon shows, for instance, escalated the depictions of the Amazon's savagery dramatically: one for the Théâtre de la Porte St. Martin depicts a horde of bare-breasted maniacal savages, screaming, attacking, and gyrating and cavorting wildly in front of their cow god. Meanwhile, heroic white French colonial soldiers in their crisp white uniforms repulse a howling wave of black female savages flowing over them. Another poster for the Casino de Paris even shows a bare-breasted Dahomean holding aloft a severed African head.[111] The partial nudity of the African women is particularly striking; it is not incidental to the images, but drawn at their optical center.

In the German public sphere of the 1890s, the nudity seen on French posters would be unthinkable. In fact, black female figures overall were almost never sexualized in the overt ways common in French show culture.[112] More curiously, the female African body (as the rest of this book will implicitly show) generally appeared much more rarely in German commercial visuality, at least until the Weimar years. There are a great many reasons for this. French commercial culture was often more overtly eroticized overall. Additionally, French colonialist rhetoric of assimilation lent itself a bit more easily to erotic depictions. In Germany, meanwhile, the gendering of colonialism as a sexual relationship with Africans was politically fraught in the wake of the Carl Peters sex scandals.[113] But the most important factor may be the trajectories of specific motifs—these motifs' "momentum" in the visual realm, if you will. In German bourgeois visual culture, it was the Orient—and particularly the harem of the Near East—that had long been infused with erotic overtones.[114] In the popularly oriented people shows, meanwhile, the Pacific Islands, and especially Samoa, emerged as the primary site of ethno-colonial eroticism.[115] In the German commercial-visual landscape, the African shows' specialty was not sex, but savagery.

Over the course of the 1890s in Germany, the illustrated savagery of Amazon posters tended to increase. Yet the illustration of eroticism did not. When another incarnation of the Amazon show toured nine years later (in 1899), it did so not as drilled Amazons but as "Thirty-Three Wild Women." Despite the implicit eroticism in the show's billing, the promotional posters escalated the violence, not the sex. Adolph Friedländer's poster for Albert Urbach's "Wild Women of Dahomey" show foregrounded the violence; the Amazons charge the French with fixed bayonets, and one steps triumphantly on a French corpse (Plate 10). The mustached colonial troops, meanwhile, are steadfast in their defense and immaculate in their clean, white tropical uniforms and highly polished boots. The warrior-queen urges her Amazons forward from atop a hillock, with sword aloft and skull flag fluttering.

While some rush toward the colonial troops with their rifles shouldered—probably an echo of the show or the earlier posters of the Amazons at drill—the raised and hacking swords, the falling bodies, and the black skull waving over the scene lends the scene a menacing air. The scene poses a peril—namely, an inversion of race, gender, and even class categories—in the effort to provoke strong emotions, whether horror or fascination. And it circulated widely; a more cheaply produced, scaled-down version of this scene adorned show pamphlets, including one from Riga around 1900.

Another version (not pictured) of the same scene elevates the violence to French proportions as a chaotic wave of savage, ebony-skinned Amazons crashes into a group of white French colonial soldiers, impaling, shooting, and beating them with rifle butts.[116] The ferocity of the "Wild Women" in the poster is gripping: they are all undifferentiated, with hair uniformly frizzy—their black skin gleams with sweat. The innate barbarism of the African women in such posters, scholars have noted, plays into contemporary discourses about the proper role of women: the scenes could be read as an implicit indictment of the emerging women's movement. The racial and gender conflict, moreover, is expanded into one with class undertones as well; in some versions the warrior queen at center, as one scholar has observed, echoes Eugène Delacroix's "Liberty Leading the People." Unlike Friedlander's version (Plate 10), the more violent version of the poster had no text—a "Lagerplakat" in German parlance, preprinted for sale to whoever might need it—and so might have been produced with French purchasers in mind.[117]

For the most part, the organized enthusiasts of the German Colonial Society kept their distance from these shows. There were several notable exceptions, mostly born of financial exigency. In 1895, for instance, the Colonial Exhibition in Lübeck featured a show of "Dinka-Neger" to make ends meet; the organizers of the exhibition had initially attempted to involve Hagenbeck's company, but without success. Nonetheless, the Lübeck people show met with disapproval from some die-hard colonialists.[118] Colonial enthusiasts, who saw themselves as the "experts" in all things colonial, decried the inauthenticity of the shows. According to one colonialist writter, the Amazons from Dahomey were not the savage, bloodthirsty warrior women they were purported to be in the show's promotional material. They were instead from the Togo coast, he fumed, and had made their livelihoods as dockworkers and porters; these Amazons had been drilled in the use of weapons only recently–by some impresario in Hamburg.[119] Overall, colonialists disapproved of the sensationalism of wild dances, the vivid rituals, the staged savagery of mock battles, and the allusions to cannibalism that appealed to popular tastes. For the colonialists, a commitment to edification remained paramount, and edification required not only authenticity but a certain amount of dignified restraint.

The colonialists did construct the Native Villages in the Colonial Exhibition of 1896, as we saw in the previous chapter, and this was explicitly meant to tap into the popularity of the people shows. The colonialists justified their decision by claiming that their Native Village would "correct" the inauthenticities of the Hagenbeck-style shows. Certainly, the colonialists' Native Village was much more restrained, not just in its public performances, but in its publicity as well. The conservative magazine *Daheim,* probably parroting a Colonial Society press release, noted that in the reconstructed Native Villages "happily [the natives] are not shown like wild beasts out of sheer voyeurism *(rohe Schaulust)* as is unfortunately far too often the case by similar events. The Germans should get to know their brown and black countrymen *(Landsleute)* once from their better side."[120]

But these "encounters" of Germans with their black "countrymen," as *Daheim* optimistically phrased it, were met with growing unease in colonialist circles. Prominent members of the German Colonial Society even pressed for legislation against Germany's colonial subjects being exhibited in such shows. Some were worried about the corrupting influences of the shows or had humanitarian concerns; others were concerned that colonial subjects' familiarity with Germany itself might engender rebellion; still others scorned the shows' rowdy popular audiences.[121] This concern also reflected the German colonialists' broader cultural anxieties over "race mixing."[122] These anxieties could turn shrill; at the German Army, Marine, and Colonial Exhibition staged in Berlin in 1907, for instance, complete panic ensued when the performing Africans "escaped" from the compound to enjoy the Berlin nightlife; some conservative commentators in the press decried this as African sexuality run amok in the heart of Berlin.[123]

When crafting representations of Africans, given the complexity of colonial politics and racial politics in fin de siècle Germany, savagery seemed safer than sex. This visual convention proved enduring. We saw how the promotional poster for Süring's Universum from the 1890s (Plate 3) incarnated (in wax) a panoptic survey of subjects from the sentimental to the savage. The most prominent scene in Süring's poster is that at the bottom, of Casati, "the African Explorer, on the Martyr-Tree." The text referring to a "martyr-tree" (in the upper right quadrant) harks back to medieval accounts of Saint Sebastian's martyrdom. The words are flanked by the pointing fingers common to classified ads. In the image itself, a white European is bound to a palm tree and threatened by dancing African natives. One of the savages holds high a knife, and in the frozen tableau, one can almost see the arc of the knife as it would plunge into the viscera of the European. In fact, one *can* see this virtual arc of violence, for it is visually suggested by the blue circular border. Meanwhile, the savage holding the knife seems almost in awe of his weapon, drawing the viewer's eyes to the weapon, which hangs over Casati's head to form a sort of halo. The martyrdom here is illustrated as well as described. The focal point of the illustration is Casati's head, partially bowed, with his chiseled features conveying grim determination. His muscular neck, broad shoulders, and bare chest convey the sense of a powerful figure on the verge of breaking free of his bonds. This pictorial drama of savage African violence and determined European fortitude is the most arresting of all the vignettes on Süring's poster.

In point of fact, Major Gaetano Casati was an Italian explorer—and a rather thin and lanky one at that—who spent ten years in the southern Sudan (1879–1889), the latter part in the company of the famed German explorer Emin Pasha. In 1891, just a few years after the dramatic story of Stanley's expedition to rescue Emin Pasha dominated newspaper headlines throughout Europe, Casati published the story of his African journeys, and it appeared in Italian, German, French, and English editions.[124] *Ten Years in Equatoria* boasted more than a hundred illustrations, ranging from ethnographic photographs of black African drummers, to sketches of East African flora, to drawings that illustrated savage African rituals. Most of them, however, were lifted from other publications. Out of this array of printed images, a single scene emerged to become the icon of Casati's story: the drawing of Casati bound to the tree.[125] The actual incident that the scene illustrates was described over only a few of the book's 500 pages. The reality of the situation was fairly prosaic; Casati had been arrested on the orders of King Chua during a power struggle between local elites. Why then did the image become iconic? The violence and savagery certainly differentiated it from the reused ethnographic drawings, sketches of flora and fauna, and landscape engravings. More important, it was this illustration that was chosen to advertise the sale of Casati's book in such venues as the *Illustrirte Zeitung* (Figure 2.10).[126]

The illustration in the book itself, drawn by H. Boden, is subtly but significantly different from that on the poster for Süring's. In the book

Figure 2.10 Advertisement for Gaetano Casati's book *Ten Years in Equatoria and the Return with Emin Pasha.* The text relates that 18,000 copies were sold in the first three months. *Sources: Illustrirte Zeitung* no. 2469 (1890): 427, and *Des Deutschen Reiches Kolonial-Litteratur* [*sic*] *der letzten Zehn Jahre* (Nuremberg: J. P. Raw, 1891), 42.

illustration, the knife is far less prominent, and the tip of the African warrior's spear is similarly smaller and less visibly sharp. Perhaps most important, Boden's portrayal of a thin, tattered Casati conveys a dramatically different mood; in Boden's version of Casati, the bowed head shows not grim determination but despair and defeat. The advertisement for the book, meanwhile, offers yet a third version of the scene (Figure 2.10). This interpretation lies midway between the square-jawed resolve of Friedländer's Universum poster and the silent suffering of Boden's illustration; the visage of Casati in the advertisement is more angry than steely.

All of the illustrations of the dramatic scene—book, advertisement, poster—share the potent symbolism of a white European bound to a palm tree, facing ferocious, dancing savages. However, as the viewing audience for the illustration widened—from book purchaser, to illustrated-magazine reader, to the everyman on the street (who might be lured into the panopticum)—the visual danger posed by the savages increased. Their weapons became larger and more prominent, and correspondingly, the restrained power of the white figure was enhanced, as depicted in the bound musculature of Casati's body and in his evident resolve. As the circle of spectators widened, the scene was redrawn to heighten the violence of the conflict.

After 1905 the German coffee giant Aecht Frank issued collectible trading cards of the Herero uprising in German South-West Africa. The first card in the series shows a group of Herero looting a German homestead, the house burning in the background, and a German lying dead in a pool of blood. The centerpiece of the image is the bound captive, presumably the homesteader Gamisch (Figure 2.11). The depiction is a point-by-point transposition of Friedländer's (or Boden's) "martyrdom" of Casati into a martyrdom of a German colonist two decades later. The white captive's feet are bound in an identical way, and the savage native raises a sharp blade upright. Now, however, instead of a dagger curving down into the captive's stomach, it is an even larger blade—a bloody sword, poised to swing down on the white man's neck. And instead of natives dancing in savage glee, the rebellious colonial subjects are carrying away the valuables—oxen are being ushered off, the Herero carry bundles of loot from the burning house, and a strongbox stands empty in the foreground, as visual proof of the theft of property. In Aecht Frank's coffee advertisement of 1905, savagery has gone mainstream. In this version, however, the accompanying joy of the savage is not wild dancing but daylight robbery.

In the 1890s, however, such scenes of violence in commercial imagery lay decades in the future. As we will see in the next chapter, advertising writers in the early 1890s, who were just beginning to see their profession coalesce and all too aware of advertising's ill reputation, frequently

Figure 2.11 Collectible trading card of the Aecht Frank coffee company, after 1904. "The Herero Uprising in German West Africa: Omanbonbe Plundering the Farm of Mr. Gamisch." *Source:* author's collection.

criticized the style of the show poster as one of excess. One early professional advertising journal published an article titled "What One Is *Not* Allowed to Do (from American Praxis)," and in a not so subtle jab at Friedländer's work, the list of maxims includes: "one may not imitate the circus-style; instead, one must be more respectable and discreet!"[127] The visual tactic of vivid promotion, from spectacular savagery to panoptic array, had entered the sight of the middle classes by the 1880s and 1890s, plastered onto the walls of the city. In the world of advertising, however, it was not yet "respectable."

Conclusion

For centuries, "exotic" people stood as a bodily representation of the distant land from which they stemmed. What is less often remarked upon is the degree to which such embodiment was never actually physical, but pictorial, for the vast majority of viewers. Early figurations of exotic peoples were clichés in the most literal sense of the word, namely, preset engravings fitted into a travel narrative, dropped into a classified ad section, or stamped onto a tobacco parcel. The cheap mercantile marks of the eighteenth and early nineteenth centuries borrowed the allegorical strategies of more expensive (and more detailed) high art, not only out of cultural tradition but from technological constraint as well. When lithographic and chromolithographic technologies were refined in the second half of the nineteenth century, the possibilities for mercantile figurations expanded dramatically.

The surprising, curious explosion of the *Völkerschauen,* or shows of native people, should be reappraised in light of the first stirrings of a revolution—not a revolution in globalization, but a revolution in representation. The shows of exotic peoples were among the first truly popular entertainments based around exoticism to emerge in Germany, but this popular engagement was in part technologically virtual: chromolithography brought far more Germans a glimpse of exotic peoples than the steamship. Moreover, the shows of native people were "popular" not just in and of themselves, but as the object of sustained, energetic, innovative promotion. Once began, however, innovative promotion took on a dynamic of its own. Early on, the ethnographic component of the shows—reproduced in sketches in middle-class magazines—helped to legitimize the shows as educational in the public sphere But the chromolithographed poster facilitated a new, gripping pictorial style, which in turn fed into the very popularity of such shows in the first place. In the 1880s Adolph Friedländer papered cities with sensational illustrations of exotic peoples; in the 1890s Friedländer's posters were even more vivid and attention grabbing—and more inclined to spotlight the martial savagery of Africans. Heedless of the former restraint of the measured, legitimate ethnographic gaze, Friedländer's illustrations of savages eschewed educational purposes; they instead seized the attention of the passerby at gut level and propelled the curious and amused, the stimulated and the horrified onlooker into the show.

Recently scholars have striven to show how the performers in the *Völkerschauen* were their own agents and could put forth their own agendas.[128] On stage, certainly, "peoples of nature" were skilled performers in their own right, constructing their own personae. And when encountered off stage, they spoke European languages fluently, dressed in fine clothing, smoked cigarettes, shrewdly negotiated autograph prices, and otherwise behaved in ways to disrupt their performed and presumed identity as "primitives." In short, they were not passive victims, but active agents in their own lives.[129] The visual product of this enterprise was quite a different matter, however. The Ceylonese elephant rider, the oddly pierced African, and the Amazon rushing to attack are all perpetually frozen into a state of vibrant exoticism or chromo-savagery. We think of the power of the "live" performance, and the sway of personal presence, but in the long run, visual encounters were all the more powerful for their *two*-dimensionality. Visual corporeality reached a vastly expanded audience, and its message ran no danger of being undermined by the agency of an actual encounter.

In the 1880s Friedländer and a tiny handful of other firms were in the absolute vanguard of graphic techniques in Germany. They offered new modes of representation—representations that created new expectations in the eyes of the public as much as they catered to existing ones. The promoters of the "circus" style were among the first to fixate on the new visuality's capacity to capture public attention. One might say that it paved the way for a less erudite, less decorous, more spectacular style of public imagery. The reconfiguration of foreign bodies, from allegorical cliché to vivid exotic to chromo-savage, was one way in which the boundaries of prevailing social norms could be transgressed, and the permissibility, acceptability, or desirability of public imagery itself thereby transformed. The "interest" in African savagery (or Native American nobility, or Oriental eroticism, or South Pacific sexuality) was chromolithographed over and over again. These posters circulated a corpus of imagery of savage Africans to an extent never before seen in Germany. Most Germans in the 1890s would never personally encounter a non-European—even in a tightly scripted setting like a people show. These savage images on posters seen everywhere might very well have seemed like Africans. Collectively, they formed a template of Africa.

3

MASTERS OF THE MODERN EXOTIC

In 1887 an illustration of a rather nondescript pile of rocks with railroad tracks running alongside appeared in one of the first books on advertising to be published in Germany, Rudolf Cronau's *Das Buch der Reklame*[1] (Figure 3.1). Cronau's *The Book of Advertising* is an eclectic, wide-ranging foray into the idea and practice of advertising throughout the world and throughout the ages—a wide-spanning "cultural history" in that expansive, nineteenth-century sense of the word. It is also heavily illustrated with all manner of interesting engravings and peculiar woodcuts. Nestled into a chapter on billboards and advertising posters, this rather dull image of a slogan scratched onto a rock nonetheless seems oddly significant. Unlike most of the other illustrations in Cronau's book, this has no accompanying discussion in the text; its only description is its caption, which declares it to be an announcement *(Ankündigung)* of Pears Soap on a rock in the Sudan. And indeed, we can read the slogan painted on the rock face—"Pears Soap"—and crammed alongside, somewhat jumbled: "is the best."

Cronau attributes the woodcut to the "London News"; it is in fact from the *Illustrated London News* of 1885. In the Britain of the mid-1880s,

Figure 3.1 Engraved illustration of supposed graffiti promoting the Pears soap company, as reproduced in Rudolf Cronau's *Book of Advertising.* Note the three tiny white-robed figures at the lower left of the rocks; in the original image in the *Illustrated London News,* a number of resting black figures and camel are also visible. *Source:* Rudolf Cronau, *Das Buch der Reklame* (Ulm: Wohler'schen, 1887), part I, 27.

this small drama of an English firm's slogan scratched onto the landscape of the Sudan was particularly freighted. The year before the woodcut appeared, General Charles "Chinese" Gordon had been cut off and surrounded in Khartoum by the Mahdists; over the following months the plight of this besieged Victorian hero became a mass media event, with a highly politicized and publicized outcry to send an army to relieve the siege and save Gordon. Prime Minister William Gladstone eventually authorized a military expedition, and tabloids such as the *Illustrated London News* wrote of little else but the progress of this "war in the Soudan" throughout 1884. When the relief expedition failed to reach Gordon on time, the public outcry turned acrimonious, eventually bringing about the fall of Gladstone's government. In the midst of all this, the incident of the Pears Soap graffiti was actually based upon a press report that originated in the *Pall Mall Gazette* of 1885, saying soldiers had painted the slogan, in four-and-a-half-foot-high letters, on a rock along the railroad near Otao.[2] The report of this deed—whether real or fictional, whether a spontaneous act by soldiers, an early moment of corporate sponsorship, or a media invention—appears an attempt to rally dejected spirits by injecting a bit of humor into an otherwise grim story of military failure.

This vignette took on a much larger visibility and significance three years later, in 1887, when it reappeared as a dramatic illustrated advertisement for Pears Soap in the *Illustrated London News*, with an explication by Phil Robinson as its caption.[3] This daubing of English commodity culture into the cliffs of imperial conflict may have been unplanned (or never even happened), but the Pears company recognized an opportunity: they commissioned an advertisement to commemorate this "event"—almost three years after it supposedly occurred. More important, in the graphic overstatement that would later become characteristic of Pears' new promotional style, they crafted a stunningly powerful scene to illustrate it (Figure 3.2). The ad depicts wild-haired, half-naked dervishes who have stumbled across the slogan painted boldly on the rock, "Pears Soap is the best," and though the savages are armed with dangerous-looking spears and shields, they fall to their knees before its mysterious power, raising their arms in worship. On the off chance that the viewer might possibly miss the full weight of the imperialist overtones in the image itself, a dictum underneath forcefully declares: "The Formula of British Conquest." Clearly, by 1887, something momentous has occurred—not in faraway East Africa, but rather in the pages of the *Illustrated London News*.

The Pears company's advertisement offers nothing less than the redemption of the imperial project through domestic consumption—and particularly, through its brand name. After the deeply unsettling loss of the imperial hero Gordon, the reinscription of the vignette as a powerful tableau reaffirms the essence of British preeminence. The Pears ad includes a quotation by Phil Robinson, a well-known war correspondent who had accompanied the stymied relief expedition in 1884:

Figure 3.2 Advertisement for Pears Soap in the *Illustrated London News* of 1887. This was an unusually striking ad, even for that British tabloid. *Source: Illustrated London News* 91, no. 2520 (1887).

Even if our invasion of the Soudan has done nothing else it has in any rate left the Arab something to puzzle his fuzzy head over, for the legend "Pears' soap is the best" inscribed in huge white characters on the rock which marks the furthest point of our advance towards Berber will tax all the wits of the Dervishes of the Desert to translate.

The pessimism in the first part of Robinson's quotation ("even if our invasion . . . has done nothing else") is swept away by the latter part's affirmation of British intellectual superiority ("will tax all the wits of the Dervishes"). In the process, the Pears brand name itself becomes a condensed shorthand for British civilization. And the superiority of this civilization will transcend any momentary setback in imperial policy. In the retelling, and in the re-illustrating, a simple act of graffiti has become a boundary marker of civilization; the Pears slogan is now a high-water mark of the tide of empire, which may ebb, but like all tides, will rush in once again (someday). Drawn as a powerful scene with graphic imagery, the vignette offers a redemptive vision of the imperial project through the modern commodity.

Pears' "Formula of British Conquest" was a forerunner of a number of advertisements with imperialist (or racist) themes by British soap companies in the last years of the 1880s and into the 1890s.[4] Indeed, it is a peculiar fact that in Britain the imperial project came to be a cornerstone of soap advertising. Soap was among the first products in Britain to be mass-marketed under brand names, and the Pears Soap advertising campaign in particular was one of the first and most extensive. At the most basic level, such imperial advertising conveyed the virtues of name-brand soap to the English populace by associating it with popular themes, including nationalism and its cousin, jingo-imperialism.[5] On a deeper level, soap sat at the intersection of the domestic and the imperial; many soap ingredients, such as tropical palm oil, originally came from colonial economies before being processed in the metropole and distributed into British homes. Finally, soap advertising itself, as a manifestation of cultural preoccupations, reveals the mutual interdependency of a notion of domesticity gendered as feminine, and a masculinized imperial hegemony.[6]

Certainly Rudolf Cronau was impressed enough with this Pears imperial vignette to *want* to reproduce an illustration. Of course, Germans were not personally involved with the heroic death of Gordon in the same manner as the London public, and so they had little need for a commodified "redemption" of imperialism in the face of military failure. For a German audience, however, the Pears slogan could be illustrative of imperial possibility—a call to overseas boundary-marking of their own. On a simpler plane, however, the image of a soap slogan inscribed on a remote landscape offered an irresistible illustration (in all senses of the word) of the span of modern advertising. The modern brand name—a recent English invention—had the power to appear everywhere.

Yet Cronau revealingly did not reproduce the dramatic Pears advertisement itself, so captivating to Londoners then (and scholars today). Instead, he offered the 1885 woodcut from the "Illustrated London News." There could be many reasons for this; perhaps the "Registered Copyright" in the lower left of the actual Pears 1887 ad dissuaded reproduction. The most likely reason, however, is that Cronau, publishing his book the same year as the spectacularly imperial Pears advertisement, could not secure the original engraving or lithograph stone. Image *reproduction* was becoming cheaper, but image production was still costly. Indeed, the illustration of the rocks that Cronau did use (and reproduced here as Figure 3.1) is reproduced in his book at a much poorer print quality than that originally seen in the *Illustrated London News*; the block itself seems to have become worn, and may have been purchased secondhand. In fact, the original block (from London) might itself have been an alteration of a preexisting engraving plate from a different scene entirely; the three white figures in flowing white robes (each with, perhaps, a halo around his head) and the black figures handling the two camels, seem out of place. As for the slogan, in relief printing it is quite easy to add white by further etching. What German or even British viewer could question that these particular rocks were not actually those very ones in the Sudan?

Yet the absence of a dramatic scene of genuflecting Madhists makes the scene appear a more authentic illustration of Robinson's story. The engraving of the rock pile is more in line with the types of illustrations one might find in a German illustrated middle-class magazine, such as *Over Land and Sea,* in the 1870s and early 1880s. Such engraved illustrations, realistically carved after photographs, were respectable. As we have seen at numerous points already, respectability was an issue for German visual culture in the 1880s. Respectability was also the precondition for the very profession of advertising, like the practice of commodity display and the figuration of spectacular exoticism, to enter into bourgeois German culture. "Empire," as the collective effort of the nation (*pace* Fabri), was eminently respectable, even if some of its more sensationalistic illustrations (in British soap ads) still might have seemed a bit much.

At the time of Cronau's publication in 1887, the German colonial empire was barely two years old. Cronau's presentation of the vignette in the Sudan could connect with two different social milieus in Germany: imperialists and advertisers. Both social milieus were interested in just such illustrations of possibility. Early German colonialists, organized around the German Colonial Society, lobbied for an expansion of German overseas imperial activities; they looked to the British empire as their model. Early German advertising pioneers, on the other hand, were the first in a new profession, and they looked to Britain's modernity as their model. Each of these milieus, advertisers and imperialists, would define itself through print culture over the decade of the 1890s. Yet they remained profoundly separated from each other, not just in terms of their professional institutions, but even socially. Indeed, at times they seem to represent two completely different Germanys, presenting two very different paths to the future—and two different flavors of modernity.[7] Far from cooperating in some larger, overarching colonial project, advertisers and colonialists would emerge as competitors in the 1890s, at least indirectly in the cultural realm, over who would become the masters of the modern exotic.

Advertising in Germany did not begin with the publication of Rudolf Cronau's handbook, of course, just as colonialism did not begin with the pamphleteering of Friedrich Fabri (as we saw in Chapter 1). Many elements that fed into advertising practice had been long in germinating. Classifieds and other paid announcements appeared at the back of newspapers and journals in the eighteenth century and earlier. The press liberalization laws of the 1850s fed the growth of such classifieds enormously, and a few independent brokers of newspaper classified sections (*Annoncen* agencies) began to appear in Germany as early as the late 1860s.[8] But classified advertising remained largely a haphazard and amateurish affair in Germany through the 1870s. Long, dense lists of text generally gave assurances that merchants' wares were "known to be the best *(Anerkannt das Beste*) (Figure 3.3). Such classifieds, moreover, remained spatially segregated at the back of books or periodicals. Even the introduction of the *Litfaßsäule,* the tall wooden columns that held printed notices and promotional bills first appearing in Berlin in 1855, were less a comment on the prevalence of posters than a way to confine handbills and notices to a sort of cylindrical bulletin board.

In the Germany before the mid-1880s the business of classified ads and posting handbills held an air of disrepute. One can see this reflected in the types of products offered in classified sections, which were fre-

Preisherabsetzung.

Durch das in unserer Fabrik eingeführte Princip, nur eine Art von Nähmaschinen zu bauen und auf diese alle Aufmerksamkeit zu verwenden, ist es uns möglich geworden, eine gediegene **deutsche Wheeler- & Wilson-Nähmaschine** für den enorm billigen Preis von 45 **Thlr.** herzustellen. Den Nr. 2 **Familien-Nähmaschinen** auf elegantem Nußbaum- oder Mahagonitisch mit Verschlußkasten für 50 Thlr. werden außer den allbekannten Hülfsapparaten noch 4 Metallspulen, **6 Glasdrücker, verstellbare Säumer und Bandeinfasser, Bandaufnäher**, eine zweite **Stichplatte für dicke Stoffe** und ein **Kleiderschutz** mit Gummiball zugegeben, sodaß diese Maschinen, obenein mit unserer bequemen **Stichstellung nach Zahlen** versehen, die vollständigsten und preiswerthesten sind. Illustrirte Preiscourante gratis, Verpackung frei.

Garantieleistung. 8567

Frister & Roßmann, Berlin, Leipzigerstr. 112, Ecke der Mauerstraße.

SPECIALITAET FÜR HANDNAEHMASCHINEN

Die Nähmaschinenfabrik von

Bassermann & Mondt

in Mannheim, 8471

im großartigsten amerikanischen Maßstabe angelegt, ausschließlich für die Fabrikation von Handnähmaschinen eingerichtet, liefert in jährlich vielen tausenden Exemplaren

Garantie! | Nähmlich bekannt!

Kleine amerik. Handnähmaschinen

System Raymond à 30 Fl. = 17. Thlr. 5 Ngr.

Non plus ultra

Doppelsteppstich-Handnähmaschine

System Wheeler & Wilson 45 Fl. 30 Xr. = 26 Thlr.

Trittschemel 7 „ — „ = 4 „

Tisch mit Tretvorrichtung 15 „ 45 „ = 9 „

Apparate als Säumer, Bandaufnäher, Litzenaufnäher u. s. w.

Auch können alle sonstigen Sorten Nähmaschinen zu den billigsten Preisen durch uns bezogen werden.

NB. Wiederverkäufer erhalten Rabatt und werden solche überall, wo wir noch nicht vertreten sind, gesucht.

Bassermann & Mondt, Mannheim.

Wichtig für

Comptoirbücher-Fabrikanten,

Liniirer 2c.

Unterzeichneter empfiehlt Linirmaschinen, welche die Vorzüge der Tisch- und Drehmaschinen in sich vereinigen. Dieselben sind mit einer Vorrichtung zum zweimaligen Kopfansetzen versehen, zeichnen Linien von verschiedener Länge zu gleicher Zeit, leisten überhaupt an Accuratesse und Schnelligkeit das, was bisjetzt von keiner derartigen Maschine erreicht worden ist; bedürfen außerdem zum Betriebe nur eines Arbeiters. 8530

Frankirte Anfragen beantwortet ausführlich

J. W. Rossi, Geschäftsbücher-Fabrikant,
Flensburg im Herzogthum Schleswig.

Metachromatypie,

Decalcomanie oder Abziehbilder
in Lack-, Porzellan- und Glasfarben.
Fabrik von C. Hesse in Leipzig, Markt,
Alte Wage, 7718

erstes und größtes Geschäft in diesem Artikel, empfiehlt ihr Fabrikat als billigen und schnellen Ersatz der Malerei den Herren Fabrikanten und Wiederverkäufern. Mustersortimente mit Gebrauchsanweisung à 1—5 Thlr.

Auswahlsendungen auf Referenzen bereitwilligst.

Nebelbilder (dissolving views)

jeder Art, nebst Apparate für Schaustellungen, Familien u. s. w., Preisverzeichniß gratis, empfiehlt 6967

Heinr. R. Böhm, Glasmalerei, Hamburg.

Für Photographen. 7521

Unsere neueste Preisliste mit durchweg ermäßigten Preisen ist erschienen und wird gratis franco gegen franco versandt; sämmtliche Artikel bester Qualität.

Berlin, Kronenstr. 65. Brandt & Wilde,
Manufactur photogr. Artikel.

Photographische Apparate.

Der reich illustrirte Katalog **1867** wird auf frankirte Bestellung gratis versandt. 8400

E. Liesegang, Elberfeld.

Albumin-Papier-Fabrik

von

Georg Wachsmuth & Comp. in Dresden.

Unsere Fabrik von Albumin-Arrow-root und Algein-Papieren in weiß und rosa, welche von den renommirtesten Photographen des In- und Auslandes als vorzüglich empfohlen werden, empfehlen wir hiermit aufs neue einer geneigten Beachtung, da es uns jetzt durch vergrößerte Geschäftslocalitäten möglich ist, jeden Auftrag schnellstens und bestens auszuführen. Proben stehen gratis zu Diensten. 8200

Rive's photograph. Rohpapier,

8 und 10 K^{llo}, bei 8583

Hermann Gompertz, Köln a. Rh.

L. G. Kleffel in Goldberg

(Mecklenburg)

empfiehlt den Herren Photographen sein

weltbekanntes Universal - Collodium,

sowie sein Lager 8118

sämmtlicher Artikel für Photographie.

Geprüfte Objectiv - Köpfe jeglicher Dimension von den ersten Meistern zu **Fabrikpreisen.**

Unterricht in der Photographie gegen billiges Honorar.

Pinaud's Venetianischer Cement

zum Kitten von Glas, Porzellan, Marmor, Metall 2c., auch wird derselbe bei **Holz, Kork,** Pappendeckel und Cartonnagen angewendet. Das beste aller bisjetzt existirenden Bindemittel; hinterläßt keine merklichen Spuren von Schmuz oder Bruch und ist daher in Geschäften und Haushaltungen unentbehrlich. Preis pro Flacon 5 und 10 Sgr, Wiederverkäufern wird ein entsprechender Rabatt eingeräumt und belieben sich wegen Bestellungen an

G. L. Daube & Co. in Frankfurt am Main

zu wenden. 8571

Figure 3.3 Classified ad page from the *Illustrirte Zeitung* of 1867. *Source: Illustrirte Zeitung* 48, no. 1246 (1867): 345.

quently for such dubious products as patent medicines and hair tonic. Other classified services included employment notices, businesses for sale, lotteries, discreet homes for unwanted children, doctoral dissertations for sale ("correctly done and annotated"), and rubber sexual paraphernalia thinly veiled as "hygienic" devices.[9] Indeed, even as late as 1907, commentators railed against advertising as a practice fraught with obscenity.[10] Faced with this reputation of classifieds, the advertising writers of the 1890s often found it necessary to defend their trade by admitting to the "excesses" of earlier forms and practices, thereby drawing a line between the disreputable amateurs of old and the honorable professionals of the new modern age.[11]

Advertising's reputation began to improve in the last quarter of the nineteenth century. In part, this came from necessity intermixed with opportunity. Publishers seeking larger print runs, and faced with greater demand for illustrations, required new means to raise revenue to pay for both. The eminently respectable *Gartenlaube,* for instance, began to include a classified supplement as early as the late 1860s in order to pay for its expensive illustrated pages.[12] The more prevalent advertising became, the more reputable it became—which in turn led ever more publishers to include advertising sections in their publications. By the 1890s even professional trade journals, such as the *Elektrotechnisches Rundschau* and even the Social Democratic Party press, began to include classified advertising sections.[13] The simple economics of illustrated publishing thus provided the backdrop to the rise of professional advertising. However, in Germany, the professionalization of advertising emerged as a transnational engagement—a complex cultural negotiation between the exotic and the familiar.

Travel Engravings and the Modern Exotic: The Worlds of Rudolf Cronau

The aura of exotic travel infused the earliest presentations of illustrated advertising, just as it did commodity display and poster representations. The author of one of the earliest and most important trade books for the nascent advertising profession in Germany, *The Book of Advertising (Das Buch der Reklame)* was the well-known travel writer Rudolf Cronau. A longtime essayist for *Gartenlaube,* Cronau is noted for his vivid (if somewhat fictive) depictions of the United States. He is also known, to a lesser degree, for his amateur anthropological ruminations on Native Americans; he published *Travels in the Land of the Sioux* a mere year before *The Book of Advertising.*[14] His depictions of Native Americans and of other exotic peoples to a German audience were visual as well as literary; he was also a renowned illustrator, and his drawings and illustrations appeared in *Gartenlaube* throughout the 1880s. Illustrations also peppered the pages of his own publications on America.[15] Cronau had gone to the United States as a correspondent for *Gartenlaube* in 1881 on the first leg of a world tour, but returned to Germany in 1883 following an illness. A man of many talents, Cronau even involved himself in exotic show spectacle, helping to stage a *Völkerschau,* leading a troupe of Sioux Indians through Central Europe in 1886.[16]

Given the breadth of Cronau's talents and travels, it is unsurprising that the scope of his *Book of Advertising* is far more expansive than the narrow trade manuals that would follow over the next two decades. Cronau's book offers a stimulating survey of *Reklame* in the very broadest sense of the word—as he puts it, "that which through word, writing, or action excites interest in a thing, person, circumstance, or enterprise."[17] Cronau reproduces many examples of what we would see now as actual advertisements, but armed with such a broad definition of the word, he also amiably meanders far afield. Crafted in the erudite manner of the nineteenth-century *Bildungsbürger,* the book is a bricolage of early professional instruction, anthropological conjecture, and a smattering of classical erudition to round out the work. It moves smoothly from the shop talk of advertising to anthropological ruminations on bizarre traditions of primitive peoples. In this sweep of tales and tidbits, Cronau is undoubtedly following in the footsteps of P. T. Barnum, whose book *The Humbugs of the World: An Account of Humbugs, Delusions, Impositions, Quackeries, Deceits and Deceivers Generally, in all Ages* from twenty years before had used essentially the same approach, though in a less erudite style.[18]

Later advertising experts in Germany, writing in the 1910s (and unaware of the Barnum connection), describe Cronau's book as idiosyncratic. In fact, Cronau's book perfectly captures the essence of early advertising—a bit of classical allusion here, a bit of ethnological rumination there, lingering upon the most curious, the most exotic, and the most sensational. As we will see, his book explicitly advocates the use of exotic spectacle to attract attention. The book itself demonstrates this suggestion, by using these curiosities and exotica to pique the interest of readers and induce them to flip to the next page. It is early advertising in theory *and* practice. And all throughout, his legitimacy is maintained, for this is an educational travel narrative spanning the globe—an ethnology of modernity, if you will.

In his first chapter, Cronau waxes eloquently on the everyday street spectacles that travelers encounter in the worldly cities *(Weltstädte)* of New York, London, and Paris—events and displays staged to promote a multitude of wares and services. He tends to focus particularly upon the most outlandish, often featuring exotic people. Such is the case in his portrayal of a New York advertising wagon:

> As we stride through the bustle of Broadway . . . we are enthralled by the ringing and clanging of a "dumb-bell" wagon. Upon it sits a Negro enthroned, in self-conscious pride of his worth. He is bedecked in a costume whose bits seem to be taken from the most disparate nations and eras. Just as fantastic *(phantastisch)* is the nag pulling the wagon, adorned with thousands of little bells; its legs are stuck into wide puffy pants, and its body covered in a clown-suit made of bright patches and rags. On its head sits a ladies' straw hat bedecked with flowers and ribbons, which lends an entirely too hilarious appearance.[19]

Although Cronau's recounting evinces some skepticism concerning this bizarre spectacle, he nonetheless approves more broadly of its basic attention-getting strategies. Indeed, Cronau enhances this description with an engraved illustration of the scene (Figure 3.4).

Other spectacular New York street displays also won Cronau's approval. These included a parade of sixteen live elephants with a "genuine Indian music-band" and camels ridden by Bedouins marching down a major avenue to plug P. T. Barnum's latest show; a nighttime *laterna magica* display of Niagara Falls, where each slide was interspersed with an advertising blurb; and a mockup of a log cabin—"with living Negroes inside"—pulled through the streets to promote a theater production of *Uncle Tom's Cabin.*[20] It is illuminating to note how many of the American street promotions seemed to involve exotic peoples—costumed Negroes, Indians, Bedouins. Cronau's book suggests such exotic spectacles were everyday encounters on the streets of New York. The ingenuity of P. T. Barnum and other New York promoters who staged these spectacles thereby became not only entertaining reading, but a modus operandi to emulate.[21]

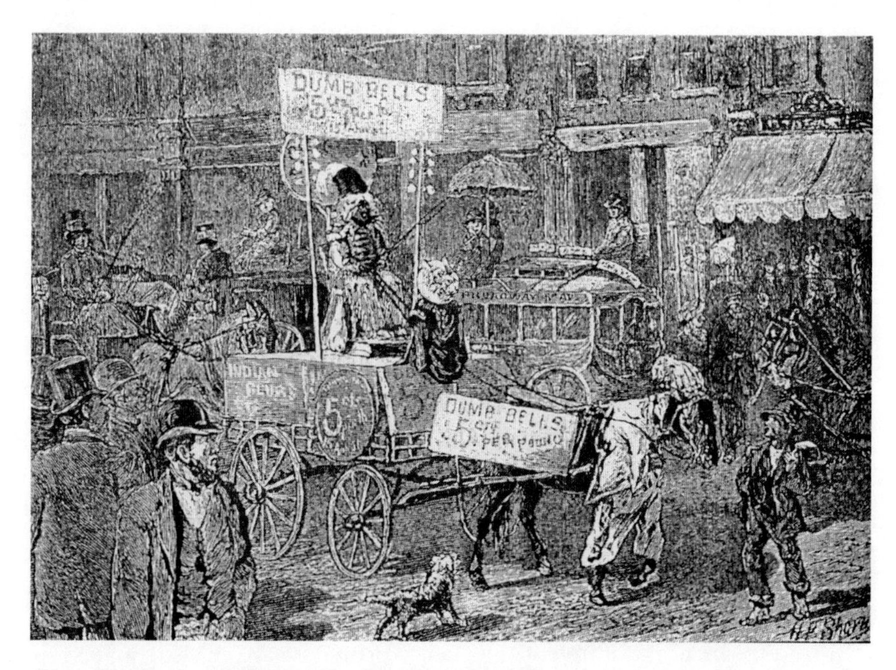

Figure 3.4 Engraved illustration of the Dumb-Bell Wagon, 1887. Reproduced in Rudolf Cronau's *Book of Advertising,* it was plagiarized from *Scribner's Magazine* of 1880. *Sources:* Rudolf Cronau, *Das Buch der Reklame* (Ulm: Wohler'schen, 1887), part I, 44; *Scribner's Magazine* 20, no. 4 (August 1880): 608.

Rudolf Cronau explicitly bases his claim to advertising expertise upon his status as a traveler and firsthand observer of such spectacles. Cronau's travels to London, Paris, and New York in the 1880s establishes this legitimacy of firsthand familiarity: "countless trips in Europe, North Africa, and elsewhere," wrote Cronau in his foreword, "have provided me with the opportunity to gain insight into the lives of the civilized peoples *(Kulturvölker),* and on the basis of these manifold experiences I have composed this work."[22]

Yet Cronau's description of the "dumb-bell wagon" did not, in truth, arise out of his personal experience. Rather, it was plucked (or plagiarized) from an article titled "Curiosities of Advertising" that had appeared in *Scribner's Magazine* in 1880, seven years before the publication of Cronau's book. The comparison of the original English text in *Scribner's* with Cronau's adaptation thereof for his German readers is quite telling. The American article is *far* more critical of this display; the dealer in dumbbells and Indian clubs is derided by *Scribner's* as "evidently somewhat uncertain in ethnology as to the derivation of the name of his principal article . . . [seeming] not to have known whether the muscle-developing implements were an invention of the prairies or of the land of the Taj Mahal, and he has nearly crushed the patient little colored boy, who sits upon the seat with smileless dignity."[23]

In fact, the tone of the *Scribner's* advertising article throughout is more skeptical and more critical than the recapitulation of it in Cronau's book. Though the unnamed American writer for *Scribner's* does grudgingly admit at the end of his essay that pandering to the public's curiosity can be effective, the bulk of his article conveys disdain for such tactics. In effect, then, Cronau took what is essentially an American writer's indictment of advertising *excess,* and remolded it into an archetype of American *success.* Cronau prompts German promoters to emulate the practices of an idealized, unambiguous America—an America of unfettered spectacle and unabashed sensationalism. In a vein of travel writing that stretches back to the days of Tacitus's *Germania,* Cronau's foreign archetypes—idealized to the point of invention—serve primarily as a measuring rod to inspire readers at home.

The modern metropolis, whether that of New York or London, is not the only stop on Cronau's traveling advertising narrative. Cronau's exposition on *Reklame* turns also to the exotic world of primitive peoples. (This ethnographic element distinguishes Cronau's s book from that of his template, P. T. Barnum's 1866 *Humbugs of the World.*) Ethnographic depictions constitute the vast majority of the illustrations sprinkled throughout Cronau's book. Most of these ethnographic illustrations are sensationalist, some of them savagely so. An illustration of "Daut Warriors" returning from the warpath shows these Africans brandishing bloody weapons and blood-soaked clothing ripped off the bodies of their adversaries. An engraving of "dervishes in ecstasy" shows these denizens of the Near East thrusting sharp needles through their own cheeks in a fervor of religious self-mutilation. A sketch of the "warrior rites of the Mandan-Indians" shows them dangling from lodge poles, suspended by hooks in their flesh, fainted from the agony. A profile drawing of "Botokuden from Rio Doce" depicts Africans with large wooden plates inserted into their lips and stretching out their earlobes.[24]

Cronau's excursion into both history and anthropology is fascinating, not the least because it seems to take him so far afield from his topic. In a section on publicity, for instance, the miracles of the early Catholic Church are spoken of in the same breath as the clever tricks that Basuto rainmakers play on their superstitious followers. While not particularly flattering to German Catholics, such parallels are the stock-in-trade of travel writing: startling, even shocking foreignness captures attention, but the "surprising" congruence conveys comprehension—and the sense on the part of the reader that true understanding has been gained. Nonetheless, in Cronau's text, it is the Basuto rainmaker, not the early Catholic priest, that warrants an engraved illustration (Figure 3.5). There is no doubt as to which illustration might better hold a German reader's interest.[25]

The many illustrations of savage warriors, bizarre practices, and horrifying customs therefore cannot help but capture the eye of the reader, who might otherwise lose interest in a topic as mundane as new business practices. On a deeper level, however, these vignettes of exotic "peoples of nature" around the world (and backwards into the mists of time) imply a natural history of advertising. The developmental arc begins with the superstitious prophecies of primitives, up through the sanctifications of medieval rites, to the sly craft of the Oriental hawkers, finally reaching the pinnacle of culture—the modern advertising of America and Britain. Cronau's work, then, not only takes advantage of the attraction of popular ethnography to German readers, but also illustrates the way ethnography can become a powerful explanatory force.[26]

Though Cronau himself was an artist, the ethnographic illustrations throughout his works were rarely (if ever) drawn by him personally. Instead, they are pulled from a wide variety of scientific and popular geography texts of the 1870s and 1880s. The above-mentioned engravings of Basuto rainmakers, cheek-pierced dervishes, and Daut Warriors. for instance, are credited as coming from G. Ebers's *Egypt* (1879), *Le tour du monde* (date unknown), and F. Hellwald's *Naturgeschichte des Menschen* (1882). The dramatic image of the dangling Mandan-Indians, meanwhile, is credited "after a woodcut from Globus" (a German geography journal); but Cronau uses the identical woodcut in a later publication, crediting it to *Le tour du monde.*[27]

In short, Cronau may *claim* personal experience as the basis for his expertise, but the visual elements of his expeditions into anthropological rumination are taken from German and European ethnography publications. Cronau's *Book of Advertising,* therefore, incidentally maps the variety of places that an educated German reader (such as Cronau) encountered

Figure 3.5 Engraved illustration of "A Rainmaker and Witch-Doctor of the Basuto (from Ratzel's *Völkerkunde*)." This image was reused in the 1926 children's book *Tschaka der grosse Zulukönig (Tschaka the Great Zulu King),* by Wilhelm Fintel. *Source:* Rudolf Cronau, *Das Buch der Reklame* (Ulm: Wohler'schen, 1887), part II, 15.

ethnographic imagery: these include such "scientific" works as Bastian's *Geographische und ethnologische Bilder* (1873) and journals like *Globus,* but also family and entertainment journals such as *Daheim,* the *Illustrirte Zeitung,* or *Gartenlaube* (from which images are borrowed). Additionally, Cronau pulls anecdotes from a vast array of travel writing by Holub,

Ein Tramwaywagen der Zukunft.
(Aus den „Fliegenden Blättern".)

Figure 3.6 Illustration of "A Tram-Wagon of the Future," 1887. Reproduced in Rudolf Cronau's *Book of Advertising,* it was originally from the *Fliegende Blätter,* a humor magazine. Note also the dancing black native stick figure, with drum and palm tree, on one of the mock posters advertising cocoa. *Source:* Rudolf Cronau, *Das Buch der Reklame* (Ulm: Wohler'schen, 1887), part I, 37.

Pinkerton, Jacobson, and many others. Given Cronau's inclination for borrowing (as from *Scribner's*), he very likely draws on many more he does not explicitly reference.

The wildly diverse sources of his ethnography are probably the reason for Cronau's fluctuating perspective on exotic others. At times he deploys the staid prose of ethnography, other times he uses more populist, sensationalist language: Native Americans are "peoples of nature" one moment, "redskins" another; Africans are described as "indigenous inhabitants" in one paragraph, as "savages" in the next.[28] He is clearly writing with a variety of open books arranged before him.

When Cronau borrows pictures and transports them to a new context, he repatterns their meaning. A case in point is his illustration of a horse-drawn "tramway car of the future" (Figure 3.6). On this "tramway," every conceivable surface, including the horse and driver, is papered with advertising. This illustration in fact borrowed from the satirical magazine *Fliegende Blätter.* What was initially intended as a satire of the insatiability—perhaps even the insanity—of the new advertising efforts became, in Cronau's recontextualization, a more positive (and positivist) glimpse into its future. Mocking critique was reframed as a vision of progress. Most images, however, were borrowed from more serious books. In his section on "Sorcerers, Shamans, Medicine-Men, and Rain-Makers," Cronau presents a drawing of a Basuto rainmaker as an early "advertiser" who promises (but often fails to deliver) miracle-working (cf. Figure 3.5). This is a very different gloss than that of Friedrich Ratzel's *Völkerkunde* (1884), from which Cronau originally took the image. Forty years later, the same image appeared in a children's book, *Tschaka the Great Zulu King* (1926), but then even the "Basuto" had been lost, and the image was simply "an African Witch-Doctor."[29] In a larger sense, Cronau's advertising book occupies a middle space between the sophistication of ethnography and the simplicity of adventure tales, and highlights ways in which imagery flowed across not only oceans, but also the chasms of social class and eras.

The Book of Advertising was not Cronau's first foray into the world of ethnography. In fact, he had made a career of it. Cronau was personally involved with the *Völkerschau* and wrote pamphlets for a number of them, including Ernst Pinkert's Bedouin Caravan.[30] He spoke about the Sioux, "their land, their customs, and their history" before the Geographical Society of Leipzig.[31] *The Book of Advertising* states that he himself led a *Völkerschau* of Sioux Indians on a tour through Germany, Austria, and Hungary in 1886.[32] More broadly, the *Völkerschauen* form a significant source for his anthropological ruminations. For instance, his discussion of the Aïssaua (an Islamic religious order that supposedly trains its youth to eat poison) relates how the "Truppe Aïssaua" walked barefoot across red-hot iron and razor-sharp swords. The scene he narrates (as if an eyewitness), however, was not in Morocco; it was in Paris, at the World's Fair of 1867.[33] In another section, Cronau mentions in passing the Dahomey and Ashanti penchant for massacre. Coincidentally (or not), both the Dahomey Amazons and the Ashantis were two of the more popular shows of "savages" that were touring Germany the same year he wrote and published his book.[34] The traveling people shows not only fed the visual needs of middle-class entertainment journals, as we saw in the previous chapter, but those of travel writers as well.

Cronau's book thus served as a digest of the exotic and outlandish for those expert advertisers who followed in his footsteps. Cronau's mélange of printed and engraved sources offers a survey of that cosmopolitan, bourgeois leisure in the 1870s and 1880s that related to exotic places and peoples. The scientific treatise, the illustrated family journal, the travel book, and the *Völkerschau* all contributed bits of sensational imagery and provided illustrations for Cronau's global gaze. As a *Bildungsbürger* of the world—an erudite, cosmopolitan bourgeois dabbler—Cronau culled, digested, and simplified these narratives and these images for the expert advertisers of the *neue Mittelstand*—the new professional middle class—that came in the decades after him. The advertisers and graphic artists of 1900 and especially 1910 were more narrowly trained professionals; they may not have heard of Ratzel or Bastian, and likely never traveled "to the land of the Sioux" themselves. But these professionals certainly had a copy of *The Book of Advertising* on their shelves.[35] When wracking their brain for an idea for a chocolate ad or a theme for a poster for laundry soap, Cronau's book beckoned—filled with vivid engravings of African chieftains and self-flagellating dervishes, chock-full of crowded street scenes from exotic Canton, the modern metropolis of New York, and the imperial capital of London. The first German handbook of modern advertising was, at core, a picture book of exotica.

The Mechanics of Mass Culture

Rudolf Cronau's book appeared at a pivotal moment in German technological and commercial history. In the 1890s new technologies came together with new business practices to produce a new visual field: the pictorial advertisement *(Bildreklame).* The pictorial advertisement was more than simply a classified ad with images attached, although it certainly began that way.[36] The pictorial advertisement formed a new world of "commercial visuality," which was simultaneously a business practice that drove an unprecedented expansion of imagery across many different media, and a new and prominent cultural field that changed the very look of Germany.

The rapid expansion of visuality was enabled in part by the new print technologies that were developed in the last third of the nineteenth century. Lithography had entered the German print world substantially in the 1840s, but it was still confined to hand presses until offset printing emerged in the mid-1880s. The introduction of rotation presses after 1872 and of twin rotation presses in 1895 each led to a significant leap in faster and cheaper print production.[37] Developments in secondary technologies, from paper production to rail transportation, facilitated these printing technologies with cheaper raw materials and distribution. The reproduction of quality illustrations (and even photographs) became less expensive in the 1880s using the halftone process, although intaglio processes remained more common in most print media up through 1900.[38] We have seen how chromolithographed posters were used for show and exhibition promotions from the late 1870s and began to promote products in the late 1880s; by the late 1890s chromolithography was cheap enough to be used to advertise just about anything. Chromolithographic printing could also generate a flood of advertising stamps *(Reklamemarken)* and trading cards *(Sammelbilder).* Finally, in the print media itself, advertising inserts increasingly included imagery. Illustrated advertising helped to underwrite the new mass-circulation press, by offering to disseminate commercial messages to a viewing audience of previously unimaginable breadth.

Commercial visuality therefore arose in harness with the new mass media. Illustrated print media was not new in 1887, of course. But new media such as the illustrated tabloids *(Illustrierten)* differed profoundly from the bourgeois magazines of the 1870s and 1880s, not only in cost, but in both aim and scope as well. The most obvious difference was one of scale: the venerable, erudite *Gartenlaube,* for instance, was the most successful of the illustrated bourgeois magazines, with a circulation of 382,000 at its peak in 1875; by 1914 cheap illustrated weeklies such as the *Berliner Illustrirte Zeitung* were churning out a million copies per issue for the Berlin market alone—and this in the thick of intense competition from a half-dozen other mass-circulation papers and illustrated tabloids.[39] In the 1870s illustrated entertainment remained largely the province of the middle classes; by 1900 low-cost, mass-circulation, illustrated tabloids actually reached the whole of the German population.[40] Even the middle-class journals themselves were transformed; the difference in the number and the quality of illustrations in *Over Land and Sea* or *Gartenlaube* between 1875 and 1890 is clear at a glance.

A second essential difference between the bourgeois magazines and the mass-circulation press involved their increasingly commercialized operation. Though classifieds had dotted the appendices of *Gartenlaube* in the 1870s, only the new mass-circulation papers like the *Berliner Lokal-Anzeiger* used advertising as their primary source of revenue, replacing subscription.[41] Larger advertising sections drastically reduced the cost of the paper, which in turn reduced the price, fomenting unprecedented circulation—and the possibility of mass readership. The *Lokal-Anzeiger,* founded in 1883, was the first Berlin paper to follow this formula of a low subscription price coupled with a larger advertising section; five years later it had eclipsed every other newspaper in the city, attaining a daily circulation of 123,500.[42] Other mass papers quickly emerged to follow the *Lokal-Anzeiger's* commercial strategies; between 1894 and 1914 the circulations of this new style of mass media doubled or even tripled.[43] As circulations increased, moreover, revenues gained from individual ads increased as well; businessmen found themselves increasingly willing to countenance larger outlays to promote their goods and services, partly because they knew the scale of the ads' viewers. That the *Lokal-Anzeiger* could claim a daily circulation of 213,500 in 1898 was impressive, but more enlightening was *where* it chose to stake this claim: in a supplement to *Propaganda,* among the earliest advertising trade journals.[44] Advertising agencies could use the figures in such trade journals to make their pitch to businesses for higher fees. The rise of the new mass media was so closely intertwined with advertising, both economically and in the style of communication, that the two phenomena cannot be meaningfully separated.

Businesses needed to be able to purchase such mass dissemination, of course, and those that initially possessed the means to enter into large-scale advertising were the large-scale, capital-saturated manufacturers. The largest businesses also had the motive, seeking to find ways to spur purchasing, in order to cover their outlays for their expensive machinery and organization of labor around mass production. The 1890s saw the emergence of the *Markenartikel,* the mass-produced commodity sold under the aegis of a brand name. The brand was a commercial novelty—a "reputation" established not by word of mouth or through the personal or printed guarantee of the merchant, but more abstractly, through repetition in the emerging mass media. *Markenartikel* included such current brands as Liebig beef bouillon (1865, one of the first), Maggi soup powder (1883), Odol mouthwash (1893), and Persil soap (1907); many of the first *Markenartikel* involved some form of nutrition or hygiene. Prominent among the first brand-name products to appear in Germany in the 1880s were luxury consumables—particularly the so-called *Kolonialwaren,* goods such as chocolate (Sarotti), cocoa (Stollwerck), margarine (Palmin), or tobacco, particularly cigarettes (such as Manoli).[45] In the larger view, the emergence of the brand-name commodity was associated with the effort to connect consumption more closely and directly to meanings that were intentionally produced by advertising. One of the most efficient ways for manufacturers to generate complex meanings was through illustration.

The visuality of advertising played an essential role in the brand-name process in that its images would *show* new meanings—and new cultural configurations—to a viewing audience of unprecedented scope. Like the consumer-oriented mass circulation papers themselves, modern advertising increasingly embraced visuality. The *Bildannonce,* as the large pictorial advertisements were called, offered a perfect complement to the new visuality of the illustrated papers, magazines, and tabloids. A certain number of classifieds over the previous century had been dotted with engravings or cliché blocks; a pointing finger to emphasize the product; a prize medallion to illustrate its excellence; an engraving of the product itself, particularly when it was some sort of mechanical device. The very first illustrated classified appeared in Germany as early as 1854; in the classified pages of the new *Illustrirte Zeitung,* it depicted a fireproof safe surrounded by flames.[46] Yet it was not until the last decade of the nineteenth century that the communicative force of advertisements began to center on the image (Figure 3.7). The new mass-circulation papers, tabloids, and caricature magazines (such as *Simplicissimus*) were the first to embrace the visual ad in the 1890s. The first illustrated advertisement to fill an entire newspaper page appeared in the *Berliner Lokal-Anzeiger* in 1898.[47]

Visual ads began to migrate out of the segregated classified section and into the edited portions of papers and magazines around the same time that visual advertising began to appear en masse on other surfaces. New types of packaging, from cardboard wrapping to cigarette tins, allowed the products themselves to be literally draped in imagery.[48] "Many of them are so beautiful and endearing," Rudolf Cronau wrote of the newly illustrated tin boxes, "that one cheerfully buys the product merely because of its covering."[49] Such illustrated packaging not only attracted attention on the store shelf but also continued to imbue the commodity with imaged meaning back in the home. Chromolithographed posters, meanwhile, were increasingly used to advertise commodities. The early advertising posters of the 1890s tended to drape their commercial message in the ornate decoration of *Jugendstil,* but by the end of the first decade of the twentieth century, advertising posters more frequently evinced the

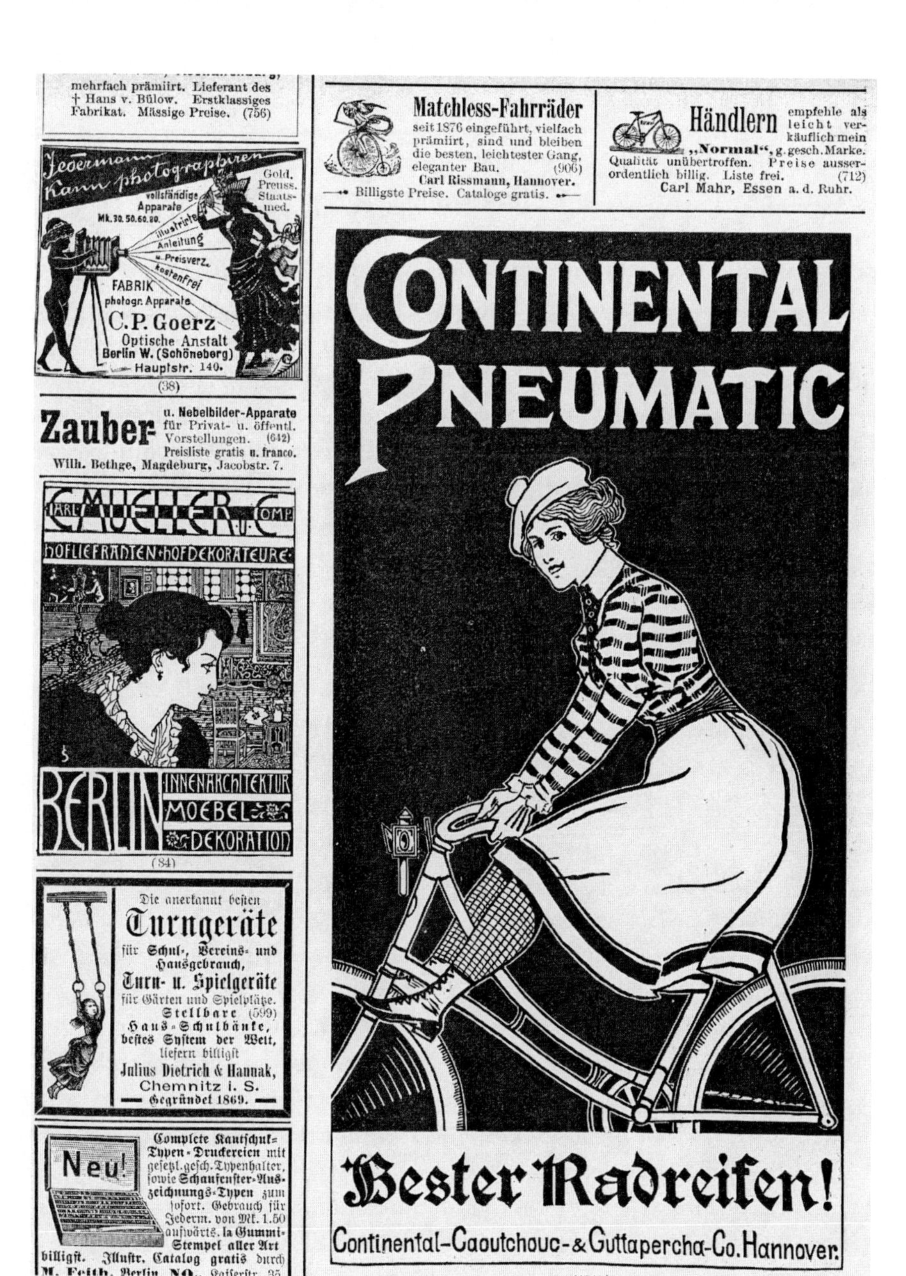

Figure 3.7 Advertising page from the *Illustrirte Zeitung* of 1897. Note how the Continental ad overshadows the adjacent textual classifieds, and how it recenters its message from the product itself (the tires, barely in the frame) to the hips and face of the female figure, each eye-catching white in a black background. *Source: Illustrirte Zeitung* 108, no. 2814 (1897): 701.

stark, textless visuality of the Object Poster *(Sachplakat).*[50] The 1890s witnessed the popularization of chromolithographed trading cards *(Sammelbilder),* given away with the purchase of commodities such as soup powder or chocolate. Cheap color stamps *(Reklamemarken)* were first produced in massive quantities at the Berlin Industrial Exhibition of 1896, and over the next fifteen years they developed into a medium on which advertising images were printed and circulated. Some of these had print runs in the tens of millions.[51] Each of these mass-produced, widely circulating forms of commercial visuality has its own unique antecedents and technological history, but all were in full flower by the end of the 1890s. Collectively they provided a multiplicity of surfaces, plastered, inserted, and circulating, on which meanings and desires could be chromolithographed, engraved, and laminated.[52] By the last decade before the new century, modern commercial visuality had arrived.

The New Masters of the Modern Exotic: Professional Advertisers

We tend to think of "professionalization" as involving the steady accumulation and consolidation of a corpus of specialized knowledge and learned expertise. But the early stages of professionalization, at least with advertising in the late nineteenth century, also required a great deal of both exclusion and self-promotion. First, the lay businessmen who had always promoted their own wares and products needed to be eased out of the emerging field, by highlighting not just the benefits of expertise, but the costs of amateurism as well. Second, the very practice of advertising needed to be "sold" to business owners who would foot the bill for it. Moreover, visual advertising obtrusively transformed the very landscape, and its acceptability therefore needed to be "sold" to those who would see it, namely the German public at large. Advertisers, in their efforts to create, assert, and defend their professional dominion, banked heavily on their claims to special knowledge of the terrain of modernity. Interestingly, in the 1890s much of this modern terrain lay outside the borders of Germany.

The precursors to professional advertisers in Germany were the independent *Annoncen* brokers of the 1860s, who would place classified ads for a businessman—and in the process, often offer advice on wording or layout of the text.[53] The emergence of the visual ad in the 1880s and 1890s demanded more specialization. First, visual composition required artistic training. Moreover, the mass-circulation press commanded far higher advertising premiums for ad space, which made advertising a larger investment, and hence required expertise to ensure the larger investment would not be wasted. By the 1890s, stand-alone advertising agencies that oversaw the whole process of visual advertising, from conception to design, print, and distribution, were becoming increasingly common. By 1900 the largest firms, such as Stollwerck and Bahlsen, had set up advertising departments of their own.[54] The practice of advertising had become the domain of a new class of professionals, a *neue Mittelstand* of graphic artists and admen.[55] Yet no formal professional institution emerged until 1908 (this was the Verein Deutsche Reklamefachleute) and no professional training programs were established until after 1918. In the formative years of the 1890s, then, when advertising began to cohere as a new career, would-be professionals could only exert influence over the direction of the new field informally. Much of this occurred through the world of print.

Between 1891 and 1914, fourteen different advertising journals were published, though many were short-lived.[56] At least sixteen advertising handbooks appeared between 1887 and 1918. Collectively this trade literature offered a wealth of professional commentary, artistic and legal advice, reflection, and injunction. Much of the advice was contradictory, unsurprisingly; this was long before any sort of market research existed, and advertising practice was largely a matter of practical know-how and idiosyncratic "feel." Nonetheless, this trade literature mapped out the contours of professional advertising through text and image, patrolling it through exemplars of "effective" *(wirkungsvoll)* advertisements and critiques of "tasteless" *(geschmacklos)* or "unartistic" renditions.[57] Despite the many different opinions in the literature, some discourses about advertising praxis were persistently reiterated as truisms, finding little contradiction.

Two of these are particularly noteworthy. The first is the general consensus that an advertisement needs to attract attention (to be *auffallend*). This could be through eye-catching motifs, originality, or the appeal to curiosity. The second is that an advertisement must firmly remain within the boundaries of good taste (to be *geschmackvoll*). Both exhortations appear in Robert Exner's early issues of *Die Reklame* in the 1890s, and both would be reiterated decades later in Paul Rubin's 1914 handbook of the same name. These two imperatives, it should be explicitly pointed out, are not congruous. On the most basic level, to stand out involves provoking the public, while to conform to good taste requires *not* provoking the public. Such a philosophical conundrum was not particularly disturbing, however, for it pointed to the need for professionalism: only the advertising expert—advertising literature insisted—could effectively balance such contradictory demands.

The first essay on advertising psychology to appear in Germany, in 1893, insisted that the goal of the modern advertisement was "to hit the senses; to excite sensation; to work sensationally."[58] But how to actually work "sensationally"? Rudolf Cronau's wildly ranging *Book of Advertising* had illustrated this in action by offering spectacular, attention-getting travelogues. But the articles and handbooks of the 1890s eschewed such tangents and meanderings for a tone of focused expertise. A gulf thereby emerged between the suggestions and proscriptions in the ad literature on the one hand, and practice seen on the streets on the other. For instance, we saw in the previous chapter how a spectacular style of promotion emerged on the show posters of Adolph Friedländer and migrated into commodity ads. Yet advertising writers—all too aware of advertising's ill reputation—viewed Friedländer's style with some trepidation. Much of the early professional advertising literature, in fact, enjoined explicitly *against* this "circus-style" of graphic design. In an 1894 article of *Die Reklame* titled "What One Is *Not* Allowed to Do (from American Praxis)," for instance, the long list of maxims includes: "one may not imitate the circus-style; instead, one must be more respectable and discreet!"[59] The "circus style" was linked to P. T. Barnum. And though Barnum was the distant progenitor of German advertising *practice,* he was neither respectable enough nor German enough for its *theory.* This is where the second imperative of the advertising literature entered, namely the necessity of good taste *(geschmackvoll):* just as important as the need to attract attention was the need to avoid offending public sensibilities. And in the 1890s, the identity of "the public" was still often perceived through a bourgeois lens.

Scholars of advertising have often placed this discourse about tasteful advertising within the larger bourgeois worldview of *Bildung* (education or refinement) and thereby treated German advertising before the Weimar years as if it were a projection of the *bürgerlich* worldview onto the larger German public.[60] There can be no doubt that advertising writers validated their profession to the more respectable classes in Germany in part by emphasizing its artistic elements, and stressed that advertising could play an edifying role; indeed, some with a flair for the poetic termed advertising the "art museum of the street."[61] Class predilections and artistic merit each found their way into many individual ads.

Yet these artistic aspirations and exhortations seen in advertising literature should not be taken as descriptive of practice. Even in the 1890s, as we shall later see, the everyday business of advertising had already begun the process of chipping away at middle-class boundaries in the pursuit of a broader appeal. The practice of advertising, as a commercial and ultimately economic endeavor, incorporated basic operations of scale and scope: ads needed to be seen and especially, to be understood, by the broadest possible viewing audience. The injunction to create advertisements "in good taste" was more complicated than merely projecting respectable, bourgeois norms onto a broader public; it incorporated the need to avoid alienating potential customers *across* the social spectrum—not just of the middle-classes—by conforming to prevailing values and prejudices widely shared. The more common the values and prejudices, the better. Given the drive for novelty, however, what was "common" could and did change quite rapidly. To glimpse ahead: advertising would provide an accelerated dynamic of taste, one not dependent upon the literary erudition of the educated middle classes. In this way, "good taste" would prove a great deal more adaptable than one might suspect from reading the ad literature.

Contradictory imperatives to attract attention and avoid alienating the audience factored into the actual historical trajectory of advertising imagery, as we will see in the next chapter. Here I want to emphasize how these themes played a role in professionalization—how they provided tools with which to exclude outsiders and castigate amateurs. If a business owner crafted his own advertisements according to his own inclinations (as he always had in the past), his efforts could be dismissed as too traditional and not sensational enough. Yet if he tried to imitate eye-catching modern ads, his clumsy attempts might very well backfire, the new professionals warned, and offend the sensibilities of the German public.[62] The question then emerged: How could the advertiser convince the business client of his expertise? Since even the most basic public opinion surveys and other forms of market research did not appear in Germany for decades, something else was needed as a yardstick against which the advertiser's efforts could be measured.[63]

The professional advertising writers of the 1890s therefore turned to Britain and the United States for backing. Many Germans saw "America," in particular, as archetypally modern.[64] The recognition of Americans' particular advertising acumen stretched back decades, to Barnum's first German tour of 1858.[65] In the advertising literature of the 1890s, however, British and American modernity became their totem. All advertising writers before the fin de siècle, from the prolific Robert Exner to the scholarly J. L. Sponsel, presented English and American advertising as at the apex of technical capacity, methodological prowess, and unfettered originality.[66] Curiously, though France is often called the birthplace of the artistic poster, France is almost always ignored by the German literature as an advertising role model.[67]

The idealization—or rather, totemization—of Anglo-American advertising in the 1890s served multiple functions. First, it was used as a vehicle to disparage the inadequacy of German amateur advertising efforts. A decade before professional organizations, and two decades before trade schools (and seven decades before any sort of useful market research), the best personal experience was thought to be gained abroad, in nations where advertising was more fully developed. Only professionals who were personally familiar with the latest modern techniques—techniques gleaned by knowledge of overseas trends—possessed the capacity to be effective. Indeed, personal experience overseas was often itself seen as a path to professional success, with German advertisers and designers up through 1900 emphasizing their time working overseas in Britain or the United States as a credential.[68] Familiarity with the Anglo-American model could serve as a professional asset or even certification, essential to an emerging field that as yet had no organized training programs or even widely recognized prerequisites.

The elevation of Britain and America in German advertising writing served another function as well. German professionals were struggling for legitimacy, recognition, and employment in the 1890s, and they often needed to justify their existence to an indifferent business community and a frequently hostile public.[69] Britain and America were widely respected and admired throughout Germany not just for their "modernity" but for their imperial might and commercial ingenuity (respectively). German advertising writers' overseas gaze, therefore, should be seen as akin to their claims of usefulness to the national economy—namely, as a way to demonstrate their economic and social worth in the national arena.[70]

British advertising made such linkages particularly easy. One of the preeminent British advertisers in the 1890s was the Pears soap company, and Pears was, coincidentally or not, also one of the most prodigious generators of advertising that featured imperial and imperialist themes in Britain.[71] Rudolf Cronau had reproduced some of Pears' strategies in his book.[72] And Pears ads continued to feature prominently in the expert literature of the 1890s; the trade journal *Die Reklame,* for instance, discussed the Pears campaign more frequently than that of any other company, foreign or German.[73] When German advertisers read their professional journals, they read about the modernity and the power of Pears. And when they looked at Pears ads in the 1890s, they often saw ads of empire.

Other British soap ads made their way into German advertising literature as well. A British ad for Kirk's White Cloud Floating Soap was reproduced in Robert Exner's *Propaganda.*[74] The scene depicts a white woman, with her shoulder exposed, looking into a hand mirror. Meanwhile, she is attended by two black servants. The text (in English, of course) narrates the tableau: "A bright active woman grasps an addition to her toilet when found to be beneficial to health & comfort. On the soap question, she is firm in accepting Kirk's White Cloud." Most Germans would not catch the political undertones to "On the soap question, she is firm . . ." Yet the would see a scene in which a white woman ignores her black servants, instead gazing at herself in the mirror with all of the self-indulgence of privilege. The black servants above and below her, in turn, mark the white woman's economic and social status. They also contrast visually, highlighting the whiteness of her skin. The white woman's bare arm in the privacy of her toilette, moreover, lends an erotic tinge by means of a bit of voyeurism. A British tableau of race, class, and gender, reproduced in the German journal, thus offers a blend of messages: aestheticized consumption and eroticized domesticity are the core elements of social and racial hierarchy.

The imperial pageantry of Britain was also grist for German expertise. *Die Reklame* reproduced a British ad for Scott's Standard Tyres in 1897; these tires, the text related, would "carry the Hearts of cyclists by storm." The scene to illustrate such a storm was one of high imperial adventure: fierce and determined British colonial troops charge the viewer, urged forward by a heroic, wounded officer, who raises his sword in one hand and the imperial banner in the other.[75] British navalism was also replicated: advertisements with themes of sailors or naval power, such as those used by such British tobacco brands as Ogdens and Capstan Navy Cut, featured prominently in German advertising literature.[76]

Imperialist motifs were not the only themes of British tobacco advertising found compelling by German writers. In 1899 a writer for the trade journal *Propaganda,* discussing the highly competitive British tobacco market, noted how this stiff competition drove the English merchant to invent ever-newer advertising ideas. The German writer commented specifically on the use of humor. Maintaining that "he who has laughter on his side can always be sure of customers," he explained that English tobacco firms "make their fortunes with comical illustrated inserts and posters." The writer continued, "In doing so, they show very good taste. They in no way let the comic element in their announcements degenerate into graphic coarseness. These adverts arouse harmless merriment, without doing damage to good taste."[77]

The repeated insistence that such humorous ads were in good taste seems strange at first but becomes clear when one sees the ad under discussion: a highly racialized caricature of a black man, promoting Ogden's Guinea-Gold tobacco. This Sambo figure, drawn with oversized lips, smoking a cigar, and wearing a floppy hat and a huge smile, declares: "I Feels Puff-ickly Happy!" In 1899 the writers of *Propaganda* clearly needed to reassure their German audience that such an image indeed conformed to public decorum. Though caricaturized depictions of racial difference were common to British and American tobacco advertising in the 1890s, they were just then beginning to appear in Germany.[78]

By 1900 advertising as a profession was largely established in Germany. Perhaps not coincidentally, around that time much of the advertising literature began to turn a more critical eye to the erstwhile modern archetypes, particularly America. Ernst Growald is a perfect example of the new social status of the advertising professional—and new concern about Germanness. Growald was the director of the printing firm Hollerbaum & Schmidt, which by 1900 had grown into one of Berlin's foremost graphic design and advertising companies.[79] He had spotted the talent of the young Lucien Bernhard, the designer who in 1906 crafted a poster for Priester matches that is credited with inaugurating the Object Poster. Growald hired other soon-to-be famous designers, such as Julius Klinger (who designed Eduard Palm's logo) and Hans Rudi Erdt.[80] Growald would go on to become one of the doyens of early advertising. In 1904 he published a small book of advertising maxims, which included such axioms as "thou shalt not imitate the circus poster," "a poster can be hideous, but never tasteless," and "don't come off as an American to the Germans, or it will be all Greek to them."[81] Kevin Repp convincingly argues that Growald's promotion of the Object Poster, featuring little or no text, was a way to assuage Germans' qualms about commercial modernity.[82] In this light, Growald's frequent invocations of the elevated artistry of a uniquely German advertising style should be seen at least partly as a defensive posture. Nonetheless, as a description of practice, Growald's protestations should also be taken with a grain of salt, for as Growald himself wrote, "To judge the posters of a nation, one must not look at the collections in the museums, but those on the street."[83] When Carl Hagenbeck needed a poster to promote his memoir *Of Beasts and Men,* he turned to Growald's firm, Hollerbaum & Schmidt. The firm designed for Hagenbeck a poster that featured a squatting black child, arm in arm with an orangutan. The design elements of the two figures are strikingly similar, inviting a perception of equivalency.[84] The pictorial style clearly anticipated the Object Poster—there is little text, for instance. But the black man/monkey theme came straight out of American visual culture, for it seems to hark back uncomfortably to the poster for Barnum's "What Is It? Or Man-Monkey" racist freak show from 1860.

When the German advertising writers in the 1890s presented British and American advertising as worthy of emulation, it is not surprising that some elements of British and American nation- and race-building projects would be reflected in these lauded examples. This was one of the paths by which imperial and racial imagery came before the eyes of many German advertisers. Yet it was only one path among many. The practice of visual advertising emerged over this same period in a more decentralized fashion than the advertising literature would allow for; advertising came not from the handbooks, but from day-to-day decisions among a plethora of businesses, print shops, packagers, and designers,. The degree to which expert discourse in advertising literature could steer the practice on the street—whether toward artistry or empire—is made questionable by the very different sorts of advertisements seen outside of the pages of the professional magazines. As we will see in the next chapter, the professional literature was not necessarily even in the vanguard of advertising practice, though it claimed to be. What is clear is that the technological capacity, professional skill, and even social status of advertising in the United States and Great Britain were potent totems of modernity to

German advertising writers and advertising practitioners alike, and the colonized lands and racial subordinates in British and American ads appeared as part and parcel of that modernity. From another perspective, however, the imperial ads of Scott's Tyres, or the racial ads of Kirk's soap in the mid-1890s, lent a professional, modern gloss to the enticing ethnographic travelogue offered by Rudolf Cronau a decade before. Cheek-pierced dervishes and Basuto rainmakers had been updated to imperial adventure and white bathing beauties (with black servants), but the images still guaranteed the ad literature would be a page turner.

The Custodians of the Colonies: Professional Colonialists

When Rudolf Cronau set out on his imaginative journey through the worlds of the savage and bizarre peoples of nature, he did not make explicit imaginative stops in the German colonial empire. The German claims to colonies in east, west, and southwest Africa were only two years old at the time of the book's publication, so it is perhaps unsurprising that where references to the German colonies appear in his *Book of Advertising,* they do so almost as afterthoughts. He tacks on a reference here or there to Cameroonians or the Massai of East Africa but is otherwise uninterested in engaging directly with the explicitly *German* colonies.[85] His cultural sensibility seems romantically cosmopolitan rather than parochially nationalist, and his ethnographic gaze flowed more from the transnational, Europe-wide colonial project than from the new Germany's strident push for a "place in the sun."

The German colonies had their own proprietary experts, of course. These included the academics of the colonial sciences, from anthropology to tropical medicine, who increasingly shifted their attentions to Germany's own colonies after 1885, pursuing both governmental resources and political relevance.[86] But in the larger domain of German culture, the German colonies proper fell into the province of a different group—the institutionalized colonial enthusiasts. We saw in Chapter 1 how colonial enthusiasm, originally the beer-hall fantasies of a few middle-class nationalists, became an institutionalized, organized, politicized movement. In 1887—the same year Cronau published his *Book of Advertising*—the German Colonial Society (Deutsche Kolonialgesellschaft) emerged from the union of two rival colonial societies, to become an institutional monopoly on official German colonialism. (This institutional monopoly would last for only a few years; the smaller Pan-German League was formed by frustrated, more radical nationalists in 1891, and it took on colonial affairs as its mandate as well.)[87] The professional secretariat of the German Colonial Society quickly made itself felt. They inserted themselves into Bremen's Trade Pavilion in the exhibition of 1890, for instance, answering the call for alluring exoticism by managing the ethnographic artifacts, art, and other material of the new German colonial project.

Yet the colonialists' own Colonial Exhibition of 1896 in Berlin, as I argued above, laid bare a fundamental disjunction: their exhibition of dry, encyclopedic pedantry paled in comparison to the larger, better-funded, and more spectacular Berlin Industrial Exhibition next door. The primary way they were able to lure in attendees was by pandering to the popularity of the *Völkerschau*—by displaying "real live natives"—even though many members of the Colonial Society were vocal in their discomfort with such populist promotional tactics. Despite their growing political clout in the 1890s, the colonial enthusiasts—with their distrust of popularization, their class-driven political agenda of radical-nationalism (and implicit anti-Socialism), and their cultural conservatism—were increasingly out of touch with the everyday German. Meanwhile, it was the everyday, consuming German whom advertisers were striving to reach.[88]

This does not mean that the official colonialists did not have a large cultural imprint. In the first decade of its life, the membership of the German Colonial Society remained steady, hovering around 17,000 (until an upsurge after 1896). A major draw for the Colonial Society in these early years was bourgeois sociability; the Berlin chapter, for instance, held a weekly *Herrenabend* (Gentlemen's Evening), which featured a lecture or talk, with socializing afterward.[89] The primary significance of these Gentlemen's Evenings was this sociability—to enjoy conversation, brandy, and cigars in the company of like-minded gentlemen.[90] One can see the importance of bourgeois sociability in the Colonial Society's allocation of considerable resources to the construction of a comfortable clubhouse, the *Kolonialheim,* in Berlin, which served after 1897 as colonialism's social and cultural center.[91] The *Kolonialheim* (Colonial Home) was luxuriously decorated, with paintings of colonial landscapes by Rudolf Hellgrewe, who had crafted the murals at Bremen seven years earlier. There were also busts and oil paintings of important personages—the trinity of the kaiser, Bismarck, and colonial enthusiasts' noble patron, Johann Albrecht zu Mecklenburg—blended in with Oriental rugs and tapestries, Massai spears, zebra skins and hyena pelts, antelope horns, and many other artifacts of African natives.[92] In the library, Münchener Bürgerbrau was served on tap, with warm and cold dishes also available to satisfy the appetite. Perhaps unsurprisingly, "German colonial coffee" and New Guinea and Bibundi cigars could all be purchased there. The pleasures of consumption—beer, a cup of coffee, a good cigar—were thereby infused with colonialist meanings both overt and implicit.[93] But the commentary about gatherings in the Colonial Home (or for that matter, in other gatherings, such as public lectures, held in other venues) lingered particularly on the specific aristocrats and notables who were present. The *Colonial News* sometimes read like a nationalist version of a society page—a who's who of the aristocratic right. Since the readership of such commentary comprised the middle- and lower-middle-class members in the chapters—merchants, shopkeepers, or low-ranking bureaucrats—the implied message of colonial enthusiasts' sociability was one of rubbing elbows with a better class of people, including aristocrats, high-ranking officers, and academic mandarins.[94] A few months into 1896, the Berlin chapter boasted of exceeding the 1,000-member mark "because of the creation of the Colonial Home and the growing propaganda efforts."[95] Local chapters in such cities as Kassel began to set up their own Colonial Homes as well.[96] Colonial enthusiasm was not just about politics or colonial knowledge; it was about middle-class pleasures of associating (often vicariously) with elites.

Colonial sociability was larger than just the face-to-face encounters between German Colonial Society members; it occurred virtually, in the world of print. Institutionalized colonial enthusiasm produced a tremendous amount of printed matter. As early as 1891, a mere six years after the establishment of German protectorates, a colonialist librarian wrote that colonial literature had grown into a "deluge."[97] The sheer number of periodicals serving colonial interests alone is astounding: almost two hundred periodicals that relate in some way to German colonialism appeared between 1885 and 1914.[98] This needs to be kept in perspective: the outpouring constituted only a tiny fraction of the printed pages generated by the German mass media over this same period. But considering the rather contained sphere of colonial enthusiasm—bounded first by bourgeois sensibility, and again by its right-wing nationalist politics—the number of printed pages generated for colonial enthusiasts after 1885 is surprising. The publishing empire far eclipsed the actual empire; with fewer than 6,000 European residents in all of the German colonies combined in 1902, it is clear that print culture constituted metropolitan colonialists' primary (and for many, only) "contact" with the African colonies.[99]

The *Colonial News,* the organ of the Colonial Society, was first published in 1884. It became a central generator of colonialist text and imagery, with articles ranging from travel writing to ethnography to treatises on colonial economics. By 1888 the *Colonial News* had a circulation of 18,500. Most of these were the copies sent free to members who paid annual dues of the not-inconsequential sum of six marks, but almost 2,000 copies of the journal were distributed to libraries, offered as promotions, or sold individually. The publication costs of the *Colonial News* in 1888 were quite substantial, at 51,049 marks per annum; in fact, the *Colonial News* remained the largest single expense of the German Colonial Society.[100] There was little hope of it becoming profitable in its own right: its editorial style was stilted and its prose stuffy and convoluted, sometimes tortuously so.[101] In contrast to a magazine like *Over Land and Sea,* its prose was not well-suited to popular readership.[102]

The visual component of the *Colonial News* was also ill suited to compete with the mass-circulation illustrated tabloids. Articles in the *Colonial News* were often accompanied by illustrations; after 1896, additional images began to be included in a separate insert, which incurred significant increases in printing costs.[103] Photographs were the primary visual component, most of which were still reproduced using older photoengraving, not modern halftone. The quality of the photoengravings could vary widely. Some versions of the *Colonial News* were printed as luxury editions on expensive glossy stock, but in the majority, printed on cheaper newsprint, the photographs often did not reproduce well. These photos are likely the work of amateurs; indeed, in 1896 Gustav Meinecke received 1,000 marks from the society's coffers to go on a junket to East Africa, from where he brought back "many worthwhile things" (justifying the expense), including 150 photographs.[104] The primary attraction of these photographs was clearly not the images themselves, for they are boring landscapes, often dimly lit, poorly reproduced, and often not even recognizably "exotic." The appeal of the photoengravings was a factor external to the images themselves, namely, their claim to authenticity: they depicted the colonies "as they really were."

This commitment to photographic authenticity in the *Colonial News* may not have always been an asset. All too often, these photos were of a washed-out desertscape, or a dim clump of tropical trees, or a small, cheap-looking colonial outbuilding. In many of these poorly shot photos of flora or landscape, the subjects are not perceptibly different from those found in Germany or Britain. Is that grainy clump of trees from tropical Africa or from the farm down the road? The only photographs in the *Colonial News* that stand out at all are those of ethnographic subjects. They are usually of higher quality, and pique interest for their humanity in addition to their exoticism. A very few of these ethnographic photos were sensationalized, such as the "Fetish-Girl from Togo" reproduced in 1896, who was photographed only partially clothed.[105] By and large, however, even the ethnographic photos in the *Colonial News* were hardly the sort of illustrations that would grab the eye of the casual peruser. Many illustrated books by colonial publishing houses in the 1890s were not much better than the *Colonial News* at design or visual appeal. Indeed, an attentive viewer sees the same photographs over and over again in different colonialist books and periodicals, making it clear that a fairly small stock of photos were frequently recycled.

The *Colonial News* catered to the circle of *Kolonialfreunden* (Colonial Friends), a group that included members of the Colonial Society, but also those nationally minded persons who purchased colonialist literature. Colonialist publications tended to come out of nationalist publishing houses, such as E. S. Mittler or Dietrich Reimer, but some came from more broad-ranging publishers, even Rudolf Mosse.[106] There was a great deal of back-scratching, mutual praise, and under-the-table subsidies between the Colonial Society and colonial publishers.[107] Expertise in colonial matters, and the dissemination of that expertise to a small niche of the public, thereby became a full-time profession for a small group of nationalists.

One such professional colonialist was Gustav Meinecke, the chief organizer of the 1896 Colonial Exhibition in Berlin, and writer and editor of its luxury-edition guide. Meinecke was the editor of the *Colonial News* until 1899; he also issued a yearly colonial calendar and was involved in an enormous assortment of other publications. His hand can be seen across a tremendous array of essays and articles distributed to the mainstream press: his articles appeared in Scherl's mass-market tabloid *Die Woche,* as well as the more erudite *Illustrirte Zeitung* and *Over Land and Sea;* his ponderous, pedantic, and rather turgid writing style makes his essays stand out noticeably from the flowing, evocative prose more typical of these entertainment magazines. After 1899 Meinecke went on to edit the rival *Colonial Journal (Kolonial Zeitschrift)* and the *Colonial Yearbook (Koloniales Jahrbuch).* Importantly, he was also involved in a number of other commercial enterprises, both in Germany and in the colonies; he was the director of the Kolonialmuseum in Berlin, for instance, and he sat on the board of the East African sugar company, the Pangani-Gesellschaft. The Pangani company even named a steamer after him in 1899. He established his own colonialist publishing house, the Deutscher Kolonialverlag, and published his own book, *The German Colonies in Word and Image,* in 1899 (and an expanded edition in 1901). Boasting "191 illustrations, 17 portraits, and 10 maps," it was among the most heavily illustrated colonialist tomes published before 1905.[108] Most of these illustrations were photoengravings. Photoengravings, it must be noted, were often substantially altered from the original photograph to "clarify" the intended message.[109] One photoengraving, captioned "Gymnastics Instruction in Togo," shows a number of Togolese children in a mission school being "instructed" in morning calisthenics (Figure 3.8). The engraving is signed by Hugo Kaeseberg and Kaspar Erhardt Oertel; since Kaeseberg died in 1893, the plate must have been carved at least six years before it was first published.[110] The image distills the civilizing mission of colonialist ideology: a (white) German instructor, with disciplinary cane, is bringing the childlike Africans into disciplined order. The children's state of undress, meanwhile, suggests that they have still far to come in the civilizing process.

Another professional image maker for the colonial enthusiasts was the aforementioned artist Rudolf Hellgrewe. Hellgrewe was the primary painter for the Trade Hall of Bremen's 1890 exhibition; five years before that, in the very first year of the German colonial empire, he had traveled to East Africa as a study for his work on the Kaiser Diorama. Thereafter he became known as a "colonial-friendly" artist and received a stream of commissions from colonial enthusiasts. He was commissioned to paint the murals in the Colonial Home as well as those in the colonial hall of the Colonial Exhibition—for which he was paid the princely sum of 6,000 marks[111]—and later painted the walls of the Colonial Economic

Figure 3.8 Illustration of "Gymnastics in Togoland" (engraved by Kaeseberg & Oertel, before 1893). *Source:* Gustav Meineke, *Deutschen Kolonien in Wort und Bild* (Leipzig: J. J. Weber, 1901), 16.

Committee's office. His illustrations appeared in many colonialist publications, from the travel narratives of Morgan and Wissmann to the luxury memento book of the 1896 Colonial Exhibition.[112] A decade later his work filled the pages of colonialist serials, such as Süsserott's *Illustrated Colonial Calendar* of 1909. Hellgrewe's work was even sold directly to colonial enthusiasts in the form of wall hangings, postcards, and illustrated children's books (Figure 3.9).[113]

After 1896 the Colonial Society saw a wave of expansion, and the membership had more than doubled in 1900.[114] Membership reached a high-water mark of 43,000 in the tense, politicized nationalism just before the outbreak of the First World War. Nonetheless, the society never attained its goal of breaking into the "wider circles" of the German public; its membership always came entirely from the middle and upper classes. Class prejudices may have hindered the recruitment from the lower classes, although this is difficult to document.[115] Easier to see is the degree to which nationalist, middle-class predilections saturated their social world and broader communicative efforts. As much as the colonial enthusiasts claimed that they wanted to bring the colonial idea to wider circles, it is clear from their self-contained sociability and the cultural rigidity

Figure 3.9 Illustration for a colonialist children's book. "Fifteen little Togo-Negroes / Just as black as the chimney-sweeper / Though they have no shoes or shirt or pants / they thrust their arms with diligence." *Source:* Rudolf Hellgrewe, *Deutsches Kolonial-Bilderbuch* (Dresden: Leutert & Schneidewind, 1899 and 1901), 14.

that marked their broader communicative efforts that this was largely just rhetoric.

Conclusion

The decade before the turn of the twentieth century witnessed an explosion of a new mass-produced, broadly cast visuality into the everyday life of Germans. Advertising drove the expansion of the tabloid press, but it also covered myriad other surfaces, from wall posters to commodity packaging. Unlike the wall prints and illustrated broadsheets from the early nineteenth century, the image itself was not sold; rather, the image was doing the selling. The spread of advertising imagery therefore involved far more than just a new technology, or a new modus operandi in the business world. It involved the fundamental reordering of society's relationship between commerce and customers; in the process, it forged a new cultural field.

The emergence of this new cultural field—and profession practice—went hand in glove with new social strata. This chapter has traced advertising through three different social groupings of the middle class. Rudolf Cronau came from the traditional yet cosmopolitan world of the *Bildungsbürgertum;* as a travel writer, accomplished artist, amateur ethnologist, and erudite jack-of-all-trades, Cronau wrote for illustrated magazines, staged *Völkerschau,* and in passing, wrote the first real advertising handbook. He presented a literary, traveled view of America and of Africans, of England and of Ethiopians—even if (on close examination) these views involved as much armchair plagiarism as actual globe-trotting. Cronau drew on the clamor of American street spectacles and the savage charm of Basuto rainmakers, stimulating the curiosity of the reader and presenting an exotic spectacle of modernity alongside an exotic outlandishness of primitivity.

The second group, the *neue Mittelstand* of professional advertisers, designers, and advertising writers, emerged over the 1890s. Struggling out from under the reputation of patent medicine hucksters, these new tradesmen bolstered their credibility with a transoceanic gaze, extolling Britain and America as modern advertising meccas worthy of imitation. This was one of the many paths by which imperial and racial themes migrated from British and American advertising to Germany. Self-made advertising experts, such as Ernst Growald, first embraced this foreign totem; then, around 1900, with their social and cultural standing assured, they could begin to turn against the rhetoric of Anglo-American modernity to promote German modernity as a unique, indigenous variant. Yet we should not overestimate the degree to which the advertising writers—the self-appointed overseers of their profession—could actually guide the day-to-day practices of a growing swarm of diverse businessmen, designers, merchants, marketers, and other advertisers. The reproduction of imperial slogans by Pears or racial ads like Ogden's were counterbalanced by exhortations to artistic effort and the safeguarding of good taste. Advertising as a visual practice, however, would be significantly less concerned with matters of taste; its discriminations would take a different trajectory.

The third group, the colonial enthusiasts, were less interested in cultural innovation. Their cohesion as a social niche depended to some degree on cultural traditionalism; they catered to like-minded colonial enthusiasts, from reputable aristocrats to nationally minded shopkeepers. Their energies channeled into the realm of politics and ideology. The colonialists produced a great deal of text and imagery of the colonies before 1900, and sold it to their constituents as expertise, with its exotic patina perhaps dulled by layers of ideological orthodoxy and professed authenticity. As consumable literature and imagery, however, it could be repetitive and dry; their grainy, authentic photoengravings had little flash to offer. Their oft-repeated intention to bring "the colonial idea" to wider circles of the German public remained mostly just rhetoric; by the fin de siècle, colonial enthusiast publishing, like other niche markets, was increasingly minor next to the emerging mass media. The colonialists claimed to hold the key to the economic future of Germany, but their methods and their mind-set, as seen in their visual practices, remained rooted firmly in traditional calculations. Nonetheless, the business tactics and print technologies of the world of mass-reproduced imagery were theoretically available to all social strata in Germany. At the turn of the century, it remained to be seen who would emerge as the masters of the modern exotic.

4

PACKAGED EXOTICISM AND COLONIAL RULE

Commercial Visuality at the Fin de Siècle

> He who furnished local tables with the products of far away regions used to exhibit his "colonial wares" in their original casing whenever possible. Undeniably, out of these bright tea canisters painted with Chinese characters, out of these manila sacks, and out of these palm leaf baskets wafted the aroma of distant places, which could so easily captivate an impressionable imagination. Today, instead of the original wrapping of the wares, a new school leads us down the path of a pictorial view *directly into* those distant lands. Here we see a wild Buffalo Bill wrangling a cattle herd, from which he will soon extract exquisite beef bouillon. There, camels wind their way through the deserts of high Asia, heavily laden with crates of tea, on which the import firm "Caravan Teas" is written in massive letters. Over there, the Persian prince who deals in insect powder is a worthy acquaintance, as is the Indian, who carries Arrow-root to us on the backs of his elephants.
>
> —Professor F. Luthmer, in *Die Reklame* (1894)

By the turn of the twentieth century, modern commercial space in Germany was increasingly filled with bright and colorful posters, labels, and packages all clamoring for the customer's attention. The new technologies of illustration now allowed products to be promoted using colorful imagery, and even literally wrapped in it. What had once been an act of personal imagination—divining the "aroma of distant places" from manila sacks or palm leaf baskets—was now materially illustrated in a two-dimensional representation. Commercial visuality could provide the imagination *for* the consumer, to a degree previously undreamed of. Over the decade of the 1890s, a wholesale displacement of imagination had taken place from customer to designer.

In each of the pictorial views that Luthmer mentions above in 1894, an exotic land is epitomized by one of the land's denizens. In the adver-

Figure 4.1 Advertising illustration for cola nut products, 1900, by the Hamburg-Altona Nährmittel GmbH. *Source:* WZB (1900): 1040, reg. no. 46644.

tising and packaging in Germany of the 1890s, commodities originating in the tropics often were advertised with just such a visual theme: an inhabitant of the land offers the raw goods of the exotic land directly to the viewer (and potential purchaser).[1] An image trademarked in 1900 that advertises a product made from cola nuts, for instance, shows a dark-skinned boy holding cola nuts up to the viewer, as if for inspection (Figure 4.1). The background in this engraving is filled with exotic tropical vegetation; the boy seems eager to please, offering his land's natural produce. In some cases, the illustrations for such "representatives" of a foreign land were themselves crafted in that distant land, as with the beautifully chromolithographed cigar tins from Cuba. In tins for Becos cigars, for instance, a classically statuesque woman in white robes smokes a cigar while holding up a row of tobacco leaves, on which the brand name is written; behind her is a verdant, lush landscape around a lagoon.[2] The exotic, idyllic, and tranquil Caribbean is embodied in her very person.

Figure 4.2 Advertising illustration registered by a coffee roasting company, the Gebr. Jurgens (Braunschweig), in 1901. *Source:* WZB (1899): 1086, reg. no. 40943.

Why center such illustrations on a human figure? In advertising, some scholars have argued, the human figure harks back to the days of personal contact between buyer and seller, and is thus a sort of modern reverberation from preindustrial times. An advertising "character type," sympathetic puppet, or homunculus like the Michelin Man takes the place of a spokesman to win the trust of the public.[3] There can be no doubt that human figures personalize an ad's appeal. A packaging illustration by a Braunschweig coffee and tea manufacturer in 1899 offers a useful contrast to the cola nut ad above; it depicts a street scene in the tropics, where an oxcart is being loaded with sacks (Figure 4.2). The palm trees and flat-roofed dwellings mark the scene as a tropical locale, which offers "a view into a distant land" and thereby implies or certifies the coffee's exotic origins. Yet the palm tree that serves as the optical focus of this tropical tableau is not nearly as arresting, I would suggest, as the indigenous inhabitant in Figure 4.1. The parked oxcart seems oddly placid when compared to the movement implied by the young boy's gesture of holding cola nuts aloft. Moreover, neither of these tropical scenes—the boy amid lush vegetation, the laden oxcart on the street—is very adaptable to different types of reproduction. The details of the two scenes are not easily discerned from a distance or in a cheap print, and neither scene is easily scaled up or down to fit into different newspaper spaces or different sizes of packaging. A human figure without all of the surrounding detail is more easily recognized and can be more easily reproportioned to fit available media, as will become apparent with many of the examples in the following chapters.

Human figures are common to advertising everywhere, but the precise manner in which such figures are depicted, and the context in which those depictions circulate, is inextricably interwoven with perceptions of power. These perceptions of power are multidimensional: they include the power relations depicted within the image, the power of the image over the perceptions of the viewer, and the collective power of patterns of imagery over image viewers and image producers alike. All illustrations of human figures are not equal. The image for cola nuts (Figure 4.1), for instance, could certainly fit comfortably into a colonialist ideological framework or worldview, but (unlike some of the imagery discussed below) does not necessarily *generate* that ideology or worldview. While one could summon to mind the connection of cola nuts to colonial economic systems, there is no explicit visual reference to colonial authority anywhere in the illustration. Circulating in the Germany at the fin de siècle, the figure could just as easily be seen, like allegorical clichés or tranquil *Völkerschau* engravings, as a stand-in for exoticism or an embodiment of a distant land. Yet by the turn of the twentieth century, certain lands increasingly came to be particularly inscribed with specific and explicit representations of power. In German commercial visuality after 1900, the "distant lands" most suited to illustrate power using human figures was Africa.

Fabricating an Exotic Aura

From the 1890s, products from exotic lands were increasingly wrapped in illustrations that allowed a viewer to see "directly into" the distant land of origin, whether cigars from Cuba, cigarettes from Egypt, or tea from the Far East. Interestingly, Luthmer emphasized the "original wrappings" of the wares in natural terms, such as palm leaf baskets, manila sacs, and tea canisters. Yet a great deal of the early innovative imagery of overseas products was itself produced overseas, at least initially. Chromolithographed tins were produced in Cuba, Egypt, and China for the emerging global commodities market. A significant number of the cigar tins found in German museums today are in fact of Cuban origin; the romanticized, idyllic Caribbean chromolithographed onto these tins assured European and American purchasers that the cigars indeed came from that locale.[4] Egyptian cigarette manufacturers, first among them Nestor Giancalis, also turned to chromolithographed tins, not only to preserve the tobacco as it traveled overseas, but to wrap it alluringly in romanticized pictures of its supposed land of origin, "the Orient."[5] Exoticism was a visual selling point in the European markets, and the promise of travel to distant lands (the mysterious Near East) by means of ordinary consumption (smoking) proved inordinately appealing. By 1903 Germany was importing more than 240,000 kilograms of cigarettes from Egypt annually.[6]

Illustrated landscapes—packaged exoticism—were too useful to not carry over from imports to domestic production. Goods meant to be seen *as* foreign, even though domestically produced, offered the easy, early crossover. Dyes and dyed goods, for instance, had been imported from the East in previous centuries, and they certainly would have been included in Luthmer's list of goods made exotic by their faraway source and original wrapping. By the 1890s, dyes were synthetically manufactured by German chemical industries. However, the new chemical giants, such as Höchst, and small dye companies, such as Holzkapfel, continued to trade on dye's exotic associations. They trademarked illustrations of elephant caravans in India and of camel caravans in Arabia to advertise their manufactures that were produced domestically. Bayer even trademarked more thrilling scenes; one from 1895 shows turbaned hunters, riding on the backs of elephants, shooting at a pouncing tiger.[7] The Actien-Gesellschaft für Anilin-Fabrikation—known today by its acronym AGFA—was particularly enamored of scenes of India, judging by its numerous trademarks around the turn of the twentieth century.[8] India and Ceylon appeared prominently in German illustrated trademark registrations before 1900 across a wide range of products for several years. The fact that both India and Ceylon lay firmly within the British Empire, and

Figure 4.3 Cigarette packaging by the Demeter Dimitriadis Company, Hamburg. *Source:* WZB (1898): 203, reg. no. 29086.

the fact that the dyes or photographic supplies came from German chemical factories rather than overseas trade, proved not to diminish the value of offering a pictorial look "directly into" a distant land.

The quintessentially modern manufacture to be advertised with fabricated exoticism was the cigarette. German machine-rolled cigarettes were packaged and sold in beautifully chromolithographed tins that featured scenes of pyramids and minarets, desert oases, turbaned camel riders, and palm trees (Figure 4.3). Such packaging, along with its associated print advertising, envisioned Oriental origins for the ware, even though the cigarettes were produced in German cities with American tobacco. Brands such as Salem Aliekum, Sulima, Kios, Ramses, and Nessim all emerged out of the factories in Dresden and Berlin. The cigarette had originally come from Turkey and Egypt, and its exotic flair drew partly from this sensibility of the Orient as the cigarette's original source.[9] Yet commercial visuality played even more of an important role. The first chromolithographed cigarette tins themselves came from Egypt, and early German domestic imitators merely duplicated those tins' orientalizing motifs. In the Germany of the 1880s, Egyptian tins and early German imitations of Egyptian tins were among the very first lavishly illustrated packaging to circulate widely.[10] Germans repackaged and mass-produced an exotic Orient that astute Middle-Eastern producers had previously exported to them.

The rise of cigarette consumption was the first widely recognized "victory" of advertising in Germany.[11] The eye-catching tins themselves, circulating in the 1880s, and the frequent exhortations by professional advertising writers in the 1890s, each offered strong publicity not just for the ongoing success of the cigarette, but for the possibilities inherent in exotic packaging more broadly. The mystical, magical Orient would reign supreme among exotic lands in German commercial visuality for decades. Its mystique was intensified by the escalation of countless other sorts of commercial enterprises, from the small Oriental cupola in 1890 Bremen to the grand Exhibition Kairo of 1896 Berlin, or from the *Völkerchauen* of Tripolitans and Nubians to the "scenes from the Tunisian Harem" in the Panoptikum. In the 1890s, cigarette packaging began to personalize this exotic appeal, shifting their Orientalist fantasy from fantastic cityscapes toward the reclining odalisque. As early as 1894, Professor Luthmer in *Die Reklame* wrote admiringly of the "smoking concubines" who "reveal to us the secrets of the harem."[12] The Orient had been the site of exotic luxury; now the harem girl became the premier embodiment of exotic eroticism. Unsurprisingly, Oriental motifs began to migrate from products that had ostensible Oriental links, such as cigarettes, to those where the linkages were far more tenuous, such as with margarine. Over the first decade of the mass production of commercial imagery, the Orient remained the quintessential land of luxury goods. After 1900, however, a new land of fantasy was increasingly affixed to such products as cigarettes, coffee, tobacco, and dyes—a land that offered something that the tranquil tropics, caravans of India, and resplendent Orient did not.

It might seem surprising that, as late as 1894, Africa and Africans remain palpably absent from Professor Luthmer's panoply of distant lands, even though his figures ranged over the plains of America, the desert highlands of Asia, the kingdoms of India, and a few paragraphs further on (not quoted), the mysterious Orient as well. Despite an official German presence for more than a decade on the African continent at the time of Luthmer's quote in 1894, Africa and its inhabitants had yet to make a strong appearance in the burgeoning world of commercial imagery. In other areas Africa was becoming, as one handbook from the Bremen exhibition called it, "the continent most in fashion," as seen in international political posturing that fed into (and fed from) news reports and editorials on the Berlin Conference, or as seen in the ethnographic collections at trade shows and in the spectacular people shows of the 1890s. [13] Yet by the mid-1890s it had not yet become fashionable in the germinating field of German advertising.

Africa would play a different role than just one more exotic land with exotic wares. After 1900, German commercial images of Africa—or more precisely, of Africans—constructed dense networks of visual power that wove German traditions into modern inventions, and naturalized colonialist ideology by tying it to racial difference. Some of these presentations of power went hand-in-glove with the German colonial project, while others reworked or even subverted the colonialists' ideology. In either case, the institutions of colonial enthusiasm played only a minor role. This chapter charts the emergence of the image of the African native around the turn of the century, tracing the contexts in which it emerged, and the implications of the way in which the figure came to be embedded in positions of visual power. This visual power could draw from and reinforce pictorializations of race (as Chapters 5 and 6 will show) but it was not synonymous with depictions of racial difference.

Around the turn of the twentieth century a new advertising motif began to appear in trademark registrations across a broad range of firms, brands, and product categories—the figure of the African "native," usually clad only in a grass skirt or loincloth (Figure 4.4). The figure would often be depicted either explicitly vis-à-vis another figure in the scene, or implicitly in relationship to the viewer, in a manner framed as "colonial." The African native might be transfixed by a German commodity, for instance, or the figure might be laboring under a burden of supposed colonial goods or wares (Figure 4.5). This motif began to appear in advertising and product packaging in the last years of the 1890s, but 1900 was the watershed in which the figure was used to promote a host of products,

Figure 4.4 Advertisement for tobacco snuff by A. Wünschhüttl, Tirschenreuth, from 1902. "I snort only genuine Tirschenreuth Glasshütten schmalzer." (Schmalzer is a snuff style.) *Source:* WZB (1902): 682, reg. no. 55142.

from coffee and chocolate to shoe polish and accordions. The prominence of this motif has gone entirely unrecognized.

The timing of the appearance of this "colonial" figuration of the African native is significant; it began to manifest fifteen years *after* the advent of official German colonial rule in Africa. It was therefore not a byproduct of the initial groundswell of nationalistic enthusiasm for colonies back in the mid-1880s, nor did it derive from public discussions over colonialist principles after 1905. Neither did it connect to actual articulations of German colonial policy.[14] More importantly, the pervasiveness of the figure in the commercial realm did not correlate with ongoing efforts to extract resources from Germany's African colonies. Even by 1900, the

Figure 4.5 A generic illustration for Universal Coffee, trademarked by the Leipzig firm of Hermann Riechel in 1904. *Source:* WZB (1904): 679, reg. no. 67825.

colonial economy remained insignificant to that of the German metropole. Neither was it the small German colonial companies from Africa—ineptly managed and hemorrhaging capital—that were the first to turn to the most colonialism-steeped commercial images. Instead, it was often the domestic companies, among them the largest mass marketers of the global economy, that turned to this image—companies that imported their cocoa not from East Africa but from Ecuador, and received their coffee not from Cameroon but from Colombia.[15]

So the question becomes: why 1900? In fact, the manifestation of this motif in commercial imagery came at the confluence of a great many forces and influences. In the previous three chapters we have already seen the interplay of broader political, social, and cultural forces in commercial imagery, from the rise of panoramic exhibition displays to the interventions of institutionalized colonialists, from the popularity of spectacles of Africans to the overseas gaze of professionalizing advertisers. Each of these forces, gathering in the 1880s and 1890s, factored into the new penchant for commercialized images of "colonized" Africans around 1900. There were also a number of more proximate factors still to be addressed: these included the reinscription of traditional images, the saliency of colonial warfare, and the implementation of powerful pictorial techniques crafted around visual logic and optical power. Exploring each of these different proximate factors in turn, we can chart the way in which a specific commercial motif was patterned, and thereby see traces of the complex functioning of commercial visuality.

From the Middle Ages, trade guilds used marks to identify their artisans' wares. These were simple marks of origination, however, largely bereft of any broader associative implications. This changed in seventeenth-century Europe, when woodblock printing and other methods of early-modern illustration began to be used to link a commercial good with its distant land of origin. One of the first deployments of such pictures. as we have seen, involved a figure of blackness, the *Tabakmohr* (Tobacco Moor), that was associated with tobacco for well over 300 years in the commercial culture of all western European nations. In English the figure was called a Blackamoor, in Dutch a *Tabak Neger.* American tobacco culture also initially shared this iconography, called "Black Boys" or "Virginians," before ultimately morphing into the more familiar "Cigar Store Indian."[16] Probably the oldest example of this figure is that seen printed on a brown paper wrapper that appears in a painting, a 1644 still life by Hubert van Ravesteijn.[17] All Tobacco Moor figures, whether printed from a woodcut block, sewn onto a sack, or as statuettes in a tobacconist's shop, tapped the allegorical iconography of the New World, the birthplace of tobacco. The figure usually included a bow, and a feather headdress and skirt. Often the figure wore a skirt of tobacco leaves rather than feathers (see the figures at the opening of Chapter 2). The figure relied upon prior familiarity to be meaningful, but the purchasers of tobacco in the eighteenth and early nineteenth centuries usually came from the middle classes and could be expected to have seen allegorical representations of New World noble savages.[18]

Figure 4.6 Three Moors tobacco label, likely from the 1870s. *Source:* Fritz Helmut Ehmcke, *Wahrzeichen, Warenzeichen* (Berlin: Hermann Reckendorf, 1921), 12.

Though the Tobacco Moor may have initially flowed from and symbolized London's or Amsterdam's colonial connections, by the eighteenth century it was inextricably woven into local German commercial culture. German tobacconists in Cologne took venerable Dutch icons and reissued them as their own (Figure 4.6). In the early nineteenth century, block-printed labels with *Tabakmohren* were wrapped around many a cigar, and German tobacconists began to use woodcuts of *Tabakmohren* as a rudimentary form of illustrated advertising in the classifieds by the 1830s.[19] The image had become part of the German culture of tobacco among the urban middle class. Even a century later, a Weimar-era collector of early nineteenth-century cigar paraphernalia wrote keenly of the visions that seemed to almost leap off of the paper labels; "the mythological beasts, the blacks, the palm trees, and the tobacco plants," the collector wrote, brought "the soulful yearning for distant worlds, for incredible adventures, and for enormous riches."[20] Such early tobacco imagery was another small way, alongside the Robinsonades or travel accounts of Patagonia described by Suzanne Zantop, that middle-class Germans participated imaginatively and vicariously in the colonialism of other European nations in the eighteenth and nineteenth centuries.[21] And like colonialism itself, the icon of the *Tabakmohr* was ultimately "Germanized" after the 1880s. Late nineteenth-century German advertising writers insisted that *Tabakmohr* images constituted an age-old *German* tradition. These writers had a larger agenda: they were legitimizing cigarette advertising in Germany, by linking it to a specifically German past. They thereby played down the figure's origins in early Dutch and English culture. Cigarette manufacturing giants such as Joseph Feinhals and Emil Garbaty joined in this reinvention of tradition by sponsoring treatises on tobacco—part essay, part advertisement—that placed these black figures within a long and explicitly German tobacco culture.[22]

When new printing technologies in lithography and chromolithography appeared in the last third of the nineteenth century, they made high-quality prints available at disposable prices. In the world of commerce, however, new technological capacity did not immediately lead to a flood of new motifs. Germans led the world in planographic printing methods and produced many of the earliest forms of chromolithographed commercial imagery, such as postcards or trading cards *(Sammelbilder),* yet they continued to use such traditional allegorical icons as the *Tabakmohr;* indeed, variations on *Tabakmohr*-style figures continued to be regularly registered as trademarks up until just before 1900. Trademarked Tobacco Moor figures continued to be drawn with all of the allegorical signifiers of the traditional motif, but increasingly included the artistic detail afforded by modern print technologies.[23] For all of the penchant for racial typologies in scientific circles after the 1850s, and for all of the meticulous categorizations in academic ethnography in the 1880s, and for all the choreographed savagery of African people shows in the 1890s, many young advertisers and businesses in the 1890s were still proffering more generalized figurations of exoticism, based on long-circulating allegorical representations of the noble savage.

Consuming Colonial Warfare at the Fin de Siècle: Boxers, Battleships, and Boers

Archaic allegorical icons were not the only way to promote tobacco. In 1894 the advertising journal *Die Reklame* suggested a promotional tactic for cigar-store owners. With a one-word title—"Korea!"—an essay described how, in previous wars, cigar retailers would lay out a large map of the theater of war in the display window and affix small flags to pinpoint the locations of the combating armies. These flags would then be frequently repositioned, according to the most recent news arriving via telegram from the front. This up-to-the-minute depiction of the battlefield captivated onlookers, the article claimed, and the implication was that such interest would generate greater cigar sales. The article went on to lament how such maps had not been seen of late. As a remedy it offered up the current war in Korea as one that was, perhaps, "not without merit." Indeed, the article wrote encouragingly, a good map of Korea and the surrounding backwaters would not be that expensive, and a smart businessman "should not let this opportunity slip past."[24]

Despite such an emphatic recommendation, however, the Sino-Japanese War of 1894 over the fate of Korea was not compelling enough for German cigar stores to orient their marketing strategies around. A war between rival Asian powers was distant and of little interest to Germans. The recommendation was prescient in one sense, however. A few years later Germany itself became directly involved in the Far East. In 1897 Germany seized the territory around Kiautschou (Jiaozhou Bay), which included the port city of Tsingtau. Though long-planned by the German navy, the seizure was carried out under the pretext of retaliation for the murder of two German Catholic missionaries. The acquisition of the new colony was greeted with a great deal of official imperialist fanfare. This was the moment that the *Staatsekretär* of foreign affairs, Bernhard von Bülow, chose to deliver his notorious demand that the time was ripe for Germany to receive its own "place in the sun." Nationalist organizations, from the Colonial Society to the Pan-German League, applauded Bülow's official repudiation of the lower-key, more cautious imperialism characteristic of the previous chancellor, Leo von Caprivi.[25]

The seizure of Kiautschou represented the beginning of a more aggressive imperialist German stance in geopolitics. It coincided with one of the first instances where the new commercial forces in German public life engaged directly with official imperialism. Almost before Bülow's bellicose words had stopped ringing in the halls of the Reichstag, Germans in the metropole received a glimpse of what this "place in the sun" looked like through an array of new media. A *Völkerschau* was staged in 1898 by the Circus Schuman under the title "Those of Ours in Kiautschou." Its bellicose promotional poster, by the firm of Adolph Friedländer, shows Chinese being put in their places as colonial subjects: Chinese boys are made to sing for a German corporal's dog, for instance, while nearby a German sailor lasciviously eyes a Chinese girl as he puts his arm around her. In the poster's background, wagons full of Chinese girls arrive—one load pulled by horses, the other by camels—and a Chinese soldier is carried by the nape of his neck—like some mischievous house pet—by a spike-helmeted Prussian. At the center of the poster is an inset of a German warship.[26] Meanwhile, the Passage Panopticum presented a show titled "China in Berlin"; its promotional poster, designed by E. Eden, elicited great acclaim from advertising writers in the years after its appearance.[27]

The chromolithographed postcard—which had emerged in the previous decade—offered an even wider scope for imperial, martial imagery. A slew of particularly bombastic full-color postcards were rushed off the presses; they sold widely and flowed through the German postal system. The Emil Dotzert Verlag of Frankfurt produced a number of five-color postcards depicting cute Chinese children supporting their new German imperial "masters"; the children are drawn wearing Prussian helmets and saluting the German flag. On one a child holds a sign that reads "Deutschland, Deutschland über Alles"; on another a Chinese boy sings, "I am a German, do know you my colors?"[28] Some of these postcards were vicious: one draws a German soldier sitting on the back of a genuflecting Chinese man while using the back of another Chinese man as a writing table.[29] The new imperialism in the Far East evidently stirred up a great deal of bellicose nationalism, and this created an opportunity to see how well imperialist themes did with the German public more widely. A number of clichés (saleable illustrations) and postcards celebrating the "acquisition" were reproduced in the pages of ad journals such as *Propaganda*. Firms related in the ad journal that they were offering postcards "priced for mass consumption."[30] Advertising suggestions also appeared; the 1899 issue of *Propaganda* devoted a page to reproducing a joint advertisement by the Opel and Henkell companies. It depicted Chinese coolies with a crate of Henkell champagne slung between them, a camel laden with Opel tires, with what might (or might not) be a German imperial marine marching alongside. The labels on these crates are the only text in the entire ad, and this was the aspect that particularly impressed the writers of *Propaganda*.[31]

Following the trend, German companies across the board introduced new products and issued new ads to tap into the new German imperial engagement in the Far East. An advertisement for Chinese Kiautschou Liquor promised the product would be "Easily Digestable" and "Stomach-Strengthening"—a not-so-subtle metaphor for Germany's new colonial authority in Asia. Only two months after the German occupation of Tsingtao, Kiaotschou Cakes appeared in Dresden, Prince Henry Kiao-Tchau tea appeared in Frankfurt, and Kia King Cigars—featuring a caricature of an evil-looking Chinese face—appeared in Strassburg.[32] Even the German Kolonialhaus—the two-year-old German colonialist retail chain loosely affiliated with the German Colonial Society—made a somewhat feeble attempt to join the fray, introducing Kiautschou Cigarettes.[33] Indeed, the rush of new product registrations was so great that the 1899 issue of *Propaganda* found it necessary to reiterate the limits on using the word "Kiautschou" under the 1894 trademark law. They pointed out that the Patent Office had rejected applications seeking to register the name "Kiautschou" for an array of products that did not actually originate in this new German protectorate.[34] Other firms, meanwhile, sought to *counter* this flood of Kiautschou-themed imagery by issuing "defensive" advertisements. Otto Sehrndt of Berlin trademarked an advertisement, "The *German People* drinks *German* Tea!"; the illustration shows a Chinese man, sobbing, kept out by a high fence topped with barbed wire.[35]

Some of this advertising and packaging went beyond just jingoistic sloganeering or topical trademarking and sought new ways to directly illustrate the new colonial relationship between Germany and the Far East—a relationship drawn as a sexualized encounter. Tsung-li-Yamen, registered in 1899, was billed as a "German-Chinese Friendship Liquor." Tsung-li-Yamen was the name of the Chinese foreign office, and the "Friendship" label does seem to denote peaceful cultural exchange. The label's image, however, indicates something quite different (Figure 4.7): three German sailors, fresh off of a warship, appraise (and molest?) a Chinese girl as she serves them schnapps. She is depicted as flattered by the attention. Meanwhile, the German imperial flag on the launch flutters

Figure 4.7 Trademark for Tsung-li-Yamen German-Chinese Friendship Liquor from 1899, by Louis Ackermann Jr. of Berlin. *Source:* WZB (1899): 140, reg. no. 35469.

behind her, implicitly marking the land—and her body—as German territory.

The illustration of sexualized power here is quite apparent and hardly needs to be belabored. It draws on a long-established European discourse of colonialism as a gendered interaction, where the colonized land is personified as a desirable, partially reluctant female and the colonizer as a heroic, conquering male. Its proximate visual antecedents were the sexualized postcards made for German soldiers or sailors in the Far East, with captions such as "A Conqueror" or "Seaman's Love," which depicted

German sailors strutting about with one or two Chinese girls hanging on their arms.[36] But introducing this cliché as an advertisement adds an additional layer of complexity. The liquor label is not just a snapshot of a gendered colonial swagger—a nasty but funny postcard to send home to friends—but a scene meant to inspire purchase. The operating assumption behind the Tsung-li-Yamen label flatters the colonizer's ego by depicting the conqueror as masculine and the subjects as feminine eroticized objects. More importantly, however, it also assumes that a German viewer will be so enticed—so *enthused*—in seeing such a gendered encounter performed before his very eyes that he will immediately desire to purchase the liquor.

The commercial frenzy with respect to China lasted for several years. It was reinvigorated by German participation in the war against the Boxer uprising. In 1900 around 900 German marines participated in a multinational military expedition to counter the Boxers' siege of the Legation Quarter in Peking. Meanwhile, a much larger contingent was sent from Germany; the embarkation of the troops at Bremerhaven saw the occasion of Kaiser Wilhelm's infamous "hun" speech, exhorting the departing soldiers to give no quarter and take no prisoners. As a harbinger of things to come, the German pacification of several provinces in China was marked by extreme brutality. Back in Germany, meanwhile, the Boxer campaign was accompanied by an escalating rhetoric of militaristic, imperialistic nationalism—a rhetoric laced with no small amount of racism.

As soldiers were rushed to China to help suppress the uprising, postcard printers rushed to supply Germans with appropriately jingoistic visions. This round of postcard printing offered far more violent fare.[37] Cartoons showed German marines beating Chinese men with rods and yanking on their mustaches; meanwhile, photographs of the Chinese beheading criminals purported to reveal the cruelties of "Chinese Justice."[38] The rubber manufacturing giant Hannoverian Gummi Kamm Co. AG issued an advertising postcard for their Excelsior bicycle tires that showed a mustached German marine—riding a bicycle—while shooting a sword-wielding, evil-faced Chinese through the heart with his pistol.[39] The Passage Panopticum added wax displays of Chinese Tortures to its installations.[40] Carl Röchling's bellicose and instantly famous 1902 painting *The Germans to the Front!* was reproduced as a postcard for mass-market sales.[41] The painting, and its postcard replication, shows German marines striding purposefully into China as injured British naval officers wave them gratefully by. What is rarely recognized is that the painter Röchling was reworking William Heysham Overend's bellicose chromolithograph "Blue Jackets to the Front!" which had been printed in the *Illustrated London News* back in 1885, in celebration of the war against the Madhists in the Sudan.[42] The British imperial venture in the Sudan in the 1880s had a long reach, at least in the visual realm.

The seizure of Kiautschou and the suppression of the Boxer uprising each fed into and accelerated German navalism. Naval enthusiasm, like colonial enthusiasm, was organized around a political institution, the Navy League. Navalism was also potent cultural theater, a "bread and circuses" for the German public.[43] Just as importantly, it was potent *commercial* theater as well. In 1900 the advertising writer Robert Exner likened the role of a fleet to the role of advertising, musing that, just as advertising creates an aura of prestige for the commodity, so too does "a proud armored colossus" sent to a Far Eastern harbor "create an aura of prestige" for the European nation.[44] A subsequent issue of his journal offered suggestions as to how to tap into naval enthusiasm. He proposed that a tobacco merchant might lay out cigars in the outline of warships in his display windows; underneath this cigar fleet he could place signs like "A mighty fleet is assured, therefore, smoke on contentedly with my 5-penny *Sea Dog* Cigars" or "Full Steam Ahead! is now the watchword with us; and so it should be . . . until sold out." The text goes on to explain why such a display would attract attention: "Ships in advertising inserts are quite eye-catching, given the current public debates over the Naval Bill."[45]

Advertising could circulate images of strident navalism to a German public beyond the social boundaries of Navy League members, however. The spice and powdered soup giant Maggi issued advertising postcards of warships, including one in 1898 of German warships on "shooting exercises" off the Chinese coast; and these were collected by Germans of all political persuasions. Two years later, during the commercial craze surrounding the Boxer uprising, navalism was explicitly linked to imperialism in the far East: the multinational Liebig Company, the margarine giant Jurgens and Prinzen, and the ersatz-coffee company Aecht Pfeiffer and Diller all issued cards that, with "Kiautschou" as their rubric, featured steaming warships (instead of scenes from the colony itself).[46] In some advertising trading cards, illustrations of Germany's battle fleet were often

Figure 4.8 Collectible trading card, Liebig bouillon company, from 1900. The Liebig series "Germany Overseas" includes this card of a "Sunday market" in German East Africa. The Africans are drawn in the ethnographic style common to popular magazines, yet a white pith-helmed instructor and a white trader, each positioned below an inset cruiser, visually establishes a colonial-naval connection. *Source:* Liebig card no. 458/4.

juxtaposed against ethnographic illustrations of natives in German colonies, making the association between Germany's fleets and Germany's colonial subjects explicit (Figure 4.8). As a visual strategy, ethnography and navalism clearly played comparable roles.[47] Ultimately, though the Navy League may have been the largest of the radical nationalist organizations, the powdered soup, bouillon, and margarine giants were larger still, and could carry imperially themed navalism into the homes of even the Navy League's working-class adversaries.[48]

A further excursion into the relationship between bellicose navalism and German consumer culture would take us beyond the scope of this book. It is clear, however, that referencing the new colony of Kiautschou in product advertising and packaging demonstrated a useful convergence; a gripping current event, when overlaid with colonial fantasy, presented tremendous commercial opportunity. The seizure of Kiautschou and the suppression of the Boxer uprising fused Far Eastern fantasy with the fetishization of naval technology, at least in the realm of commercial visuality. Warships paraded as manifestations of modernity and icons of national greatness; and transshipping them to Far Eastern harbors perfumed them with the scent of the exotic. This allows us a new perspective on German navalism: did it find popularity in Germany not only for its strident claims to hard-nosed *Weltpolitik,* but also *because* it could blend technophilic fantasy with colonial fantasy? If so, then no small degree of that fantasy was forged in the commercial world. Nonetheless, in the long run the commercialized celebration of Kiautschou proved ephemeral: motifs concerning China did not find sustained resonance in German advertising for more than a few years, outside of a few very specific commodities, such as lacquer or tea.[49]

A colonial engagement slightly closer to home proved to be a catalyst for a more enduring visual engagement. In March 1900 an advertising journal recommended the following window display:

> A Maxim gun, of the type everyone's talked about since the war between England and Transvaal began, should be arranged out of cigars for cigar merchants to place in their shop windows. The gun carriage, consisting of a simple three-legged frame, could be fabricated either from wood or from large cigars. The position of the gun barrel should be represented by a very large cigar, to which the peculiar Maxim-cartridges, made from cigarettes, are connected. Were the arrangement to perhaps be accompanied by the inscription "Captured in the Transvaal War," the whole *Schauobjekt* would be truly delightful.[50]

Why "delightful"? Though the German government cautiously and superficially aligned itself with the Boer camp after the Transvaal crisis in 1895, the German public's engagement was far less restrained. Long-running German sympathy for the Boers can be traced back to the 1880s; none other than Heinrich von Treitschke described the descendants of Dutch settlers in southern Africa as "Teutonic" and called for Germany to protect its ethnic cousins against the British. Trade connections between Germans and Afrikaners extended back even further.[51] Yet neither ethnic affinity nor economic ties can fully explain the upsurge in popular support evidenced in Germany in favor of the Boers at the outbreak of the Anglo-Boer War in November 1899, which shocked outside observers. Bülow's government used this popular commotion to their advantage in the diplomatic arena, taking pains to convey to the British that they were doing all they could to restrain anti-English sentiment in the German daily press; they gained Samoa as a reward for this "restraint" and for Germany's official neutrality during the Boer War itself.[52]

Some historians have seen German popular support for the Boers as an outgrowth of successful propaganda efforts by the more radical nationalist organizations, especially the Pan-German League. Others have argued the reverse—that the Pan-German League's quick-footed self-promotion, seizing the mantle of "protector of the brave little Boers," tapped into existing currents of pro-Boer support, propelling the organization into the limelight and the peak of its pre-1914 financial strength and popular appeal.[53] To both of these formulations needs to be added a new factor, namely the dynamic of the emerging mass media (barely a decade old) with its commercial model that depended upon attention-getting devices. The new mass media commercialized the very attention of the public itself. Current events became an exciting, unifying social experience by purchasing of a tabloid.[54] The Anglo-Boer War offered a perfect convergence, where the mass media could sell news from a gripping conflict set in an exotic locale.

The year 1900 was a particularly propitious time in Germany to mass-market a war. Advances in printing technologies allowed even more opportunities for the circulation and sale of images, and the course of the war was pursued avidly in the illustrated mass press of Germany just as in Great Britain.[55] Since the new halftone printing process allowed for the inexpensive publication of photographs from the field of battle, war photographs appeared in the pages of illustrated mass dailies, such as the *Berliner Illustrirte Zeitung*. The illustrated humor magazine *Lüstige Blätter* put out a special "Boer" issue and commissioned the graphic artist Julius Klinger to create a poster advertising it.[56] Small maps of southern Africa found their way into the daily press, and full-sized maps, complete with troop movements printed on them, sold widely. Popular publishers such as Liebelschen rushed books off the printing presses—revealingly, the authors of these books had also churned out mass-market books on the Boxer uprising.[57] Such books as *Victory or Death: the Heroes of the Boer War* boasted 119 illustrations, mostly photographs, and featured a full-color cover.[58]

Chromolithographed postcards lionized the heroism of the Boers' fight for self-determination.[59] And during the course of the war itself, various impresarios—from the Circus Blumenfeld, to the Circus Lorch, to the Circus Althoff—staged shows reenacting daring Boer raids against the British. The promotional posters for these circus shows—printed by Adolph Friedländer, of course—depict dramatic scenes of battle, with British lines falling under attack by dashing Boer cavalry.[60] In short, the unanimity of support for the Boers *itself* became a commodity—imaged, packaged, circulated, marketed, and sold to a consuming public on a massive scale.

Such activity, it should be pointed out, contrasted markedly with the public indifference that greeted Germany's *own* early colonial wars in western and eastern Africa a decade earlier. The small-scale military engagements that secured German rule in Cameroon (1891–1894), East Africa (1888–1890), and Southwest Africa (1883–1884 and 1896–1898) occasionally manifested in journals such as the *Illustrirte Zeitung* and *Over Land and Sea,* but overall this warfare escaped the notice of both the public and early advertisers. One difference was scale: the Anglo-Boer conflict was far larger and more dramatic than that of Germany's early colonial battles. But another factor was visual: imagery of the early German warfare in Africa was not widely available—indeed, it was almost entirely lacking. Apart from some caricature broadsheets, the first time a broad spectrum of the German public actually saw Hermann von Wissmann's military successes against the Arab uprising in East Africa in 1890 was in the carefully re-created displays of the Berlin Colonial Exhibition, more than six years later. After 1900 the earlier German colonial African wars in the 1880s and early 1890s were feted retrospectively in chromolithographed cards by cocoa firms, such as Hildebrand and Richter.[61] But these wars had no visual footprint at the time, as a current event. The Boer War captured greater public attention than Germany's own earlier battles at least in part because it was more widely *visible.*

With the copious mass-media coverage of the Boer War as an illustrated backdrop, manufacturers leapt into the breach. Trademarks for goods from Boer Victory Cookies to Boer Cheese were registered by bakeries and dairies across Germany, satisfying the public taste for the conflict. The imagery for these new products—or for old products being remarketed as new products—grew to become remarkably consistent, despite their decentralized genesis: the images invariably focused on the figure of the Boer himself, as a lone white man on the frontier, wearing a beard, and with a wide-brimmed hat, cartridge belt, and rifle[62] (Figure 4.9). This visual imagery engaged with discourses about the Boer's sup-

Figure 4.9 Label for Boer Refresher chocolate, trademarked by the Gebrüder Nolting of Herford in 1900. *Source:* WZB (1900): 525, reg. no. 43740.

posed racial role in sub-Saharan African colonialism: as a "Stammbruder" (ethnic or tribal brother), the Boer was expected "to fulfill a great historical mission in the midst of the 'black hordes.'"[63] Commercial connections were often framed in German discourse in the language of ethnic affinity. German businessmen fantasized how, after the war, German products would find a new market in the Boer Republics, not just from widespread appreciation for Germany's military support, but because of the Boer's natural (ethnic) affinity for German products.[64]

The popular and commercial engagement with the Boer War was a catalyst that accelerated a larger transformation in the patterns of German visual mass culture itself, in that it steered the eyes of the German public toward the African continent—and toward Africans. We see the roots of this as early as 1897, when a Transvaal Exhibition was staged in Berlin. The Transvaal Exhibition, on the heels of the Colonial Exhibition, appeared two years before the Anglo-Boer War broke out. The Transvaal exhibition gave Berliners not only a staged glimpse of Boer life, but also an encounter with the racial exoticism of southern Africa, for the centerpiece of the exhibition was a *Völkerschau* of Balobedu. The poster promoting the *Völkerschau* shows a shirtless, muscular Balobedu warrior, shield upraised, wearing a zebra-skin headdress and necklaces. Rounded huts are being constructed by women and children in the background.[65] If the

Figure 4.10 Collectible trading card, Liebig bouillon company, from 1899. "Pictures from the Transvaal—A Village of Natives." *Source:* Liebig card no. 420/6.

Boers were depicted as lone white pioneers of southern Africa, their representational foil was a typified African warrior. In the simple binary of commercial visuality, the African native emerged to fulfill the role of "Indian" to the Boer's "cowboy."[66]

This dichotomy was directly imaged. In 1899 the Liebig Company issued a collectible card series titled "Pictures from the Transvaal." The series of six cards illustrates a narrative of Boer civilization-building: the first shows President Krüger's residence (with modern telegraph poles prominently out front), and subsequent cards show scenes of a stagecoach, a typical Boer farm, and two different scenes of gold mining. Collectively these cards construct a story of the development of the frontier. The final card, however, is "A Village of Natives" (Figure 4.10). It shows natives in brightly colored shawls and wraps, and a small native boy dressed only in a grass skirt, in front of grass-roofed huts—the scene could well have been drawn from a poster for a people show. The last in the series, this card would have been eagerly anticipated by collectors, typically offering a resolution to the series' narrative arc. Visually, at least, the narrative arc of the Transvaal leads to the African native.

Staking a Claim: Drawing Nationalist Politics into Advertising

In 1896 the prolific advertising expert Robert Exner published a guide to modern, effective window displays. He reiterated the potential for map displays in cigar and grocery store windows, but where *Die Reklame* of two years earlier had suggested charting the imperialist war in Korea, Exner now recommended a terrain closer to Germany and German interests: "One lays a large map of Africa in the window and erects, where we have colonies, a grand flagpole—certainly no thin twig—with a German flag that hangs from a proper miniature flagpole rope. Next to the flagpole, bundle African artifacts." He added, "Especially effective when one carries goods from the German colonies."[67]

In case the point was missed, he illustrated it with a rather amateurish drawing for a window display for cigars and other goods, such as pineapples and coffee beans (Figure 4.11). The admonition at the end of Exner's advice is rather curious. He noted that the display would be "especially effective" when one carried goods from the German colonies. But that admonition also implies that the display would still be effective (just not "especially") even without them. This seemingly innocuous comment reflects the confused interplay of substance and fantasy in the culture of official German colonialism. At this point in German colonial history, exports of consumables from the German colonies to the German metropole were sparse. The chances that any given cigar store in 1896 would actually carry tobacco "from the German colonies" was very slight.[68] And while tobacco would be exported from New Guinea with some success, tobacco production in Germany's African colonies would never rise to significance. Yet the mental association between a so-called colonial good *(Kolonialwaren)* such as tobacco with a colonialist claim to African territory represented by a German imperial flag staked into a map was already present—at least, enough for a professional such as Exner to be able to claim that such an advertising display would be effective.

Exner's professional advice in 1896 stood at a midpoint of sorts in the German colonial project. The Scramble for Africa had begun a decade earlier, touched off in part by a new German policy in which the interests of ambitious adventurers in Africa dovetailed with the diplomatic calculations of Bismarck. In the 1880s German "dominion" over the coastal regions of west, south-west, and east Africa was established symbolically, by hoisting the German imperial flag. These small flag-raising ceremonies at

Cigarren, Diverse. Kravatten.

Figure 4.11 Sketch of recommended store window displays for cigars and for miscellaneous goods, featuring a map of German East Africa with German naval flag, along with a display for neckties. *Source:* Robert Exner, *Moderne Schaufenster-Reklame* (Berlin: Verlag der Robert Exner Kommand-Ges., 1896), 80.

Angra Pequena (present-day Lüderitz) and in small villages of the Cameroon and East African coast were irrelevant, except to counter claims by other Europeans, for actual German sovereignty of these coastal areas would have to be negotiated for (as in south-west Africa) or established by warfare (as in Cameroon).[69] The flag-raising ceremonieswere significant, however, in the way that they were narrated and illustrated in the colonialist press and, to a lesser degree, in journals such as *Over Land and Sea;* they symbolically demonstrated the German colonial empire to some of the German public. The illustrations of the flag-raising ceremonies were all cut from the same cloth: a flagpole stands in front of some grass-roofed buildings, while two or three whites in pith helmets raise or salute the naval flag; meanwhile, a cohort of black auxiliary troops stand by at attention, and half-dressed African natives idle curiously around the fringes of the central area.[70] Such tableaux, cycled and recycled through colonialist publications, distilled the originating moment of Germany's official colonial policy; they remained a prominent visual starting point for subsequent colonialist literature. Yet this tableau quickly vanished from the broader media after the buzz over the new German colonies died down. Except for colonial enthusiasts, the vision of a fluttering flag, no matter how heroically hoisted, remained a frozen symbol. As such it was likely a bit dull.

One immediate visual referent for Exner's flag in the ground can be found in connection with Berlin's Colonial Exhibition, which took place in 1896, the same year the window display suggestion appeared in *Propaganda.* Ludwig Sütterlin's gripping hammer poster was the official promotional icon for the Berlin Industrial Exhibition, of course (see Figure 1.3); but the Colonial Exhibition drafted its own icon—an African, most certainly meant to be an Askari from East Africa, with bare feet, dressed in a waist-and-shoulder wrap, with a rifle in one hand and, most prominently, a German flag in the other (see Figure 1.4). Designed by Walter Peck, this poster (like Sütterlin's) found its way into Justus Brinckmann's 1896 poster exhibition in Hamburg's Museum für Kunst und Gewerbe—a seminal moment in the development of German graphic design. Unlike that of Sütterlin, Peck's Colonial Exhibition poster did not win any lasting recognition.

The Askari figure was not, however, Walter Peck's own inspiration. He in fact was closely imitating the cover illustration for Carl Peters's 1891 book *Die deutsche Emin-Pascha Expedition* (Figure 4.12). The book itself was illustrated by Rudolf Hellgrewe—the circle producing colonialist imagery was indeed quite small.[71] The two versions of this African figure are worth comparing to demonstrate the subtle yet distinct differences in the way they are presented. Both are barefoot, in a similar stance, in similar dress, grasping the German flag on a spear. The earlier one on Peters's cover has a stern, almost grim expression on his face, and his weapon is a pistol—more challenging because it is a close-quarters weapon, usually reserved for officers. The pistol seems as if it could be raised at any moment to point toward the viewer. The figure's musculature is emphasized; the forearms imply strength. Five years later, Peck's exhibition poster shows the native soldier holding a rifle instead—a weapon of a foot soldier, not an officer. And the Askari has a much less forbidding expression. A postcard version of the Colonial Exhibition's emblematic flag-carrying Askari even gives the figure a friendly smile.[72] Peck's poster figure is also far thinner than Meisenbach's earlier image—seemingly almost malnourished, with forearm hidden by the flag—clearly less powerful and less threatening. This general

Figure 4.12 Advertisement in colonialist literature for Carl Peters's book *Die deutsche Emin-Pascha Expedition*. The ad promises the book is "richly illustrated." *Source: Des Deutschen Reiches Kolonial-Litteratur* [*sic*] *der letzten Zehn Jahre* (Nuremberg: J. P. Raw, 1891), 44.

theme, of a loyal native holding a flag, would echo throughout colonialist imagery. It would eventually be adopted on tins for cocoa by the German East Africa Company; yet the cocoa-tin illustration not only disarmed the figure, but also drew from a number of other broader trends in commercial visuality explained below (Plate 11). Even photographs were deliberately staged in such a way as to echo the widely disseminated illustrations.[73]

By the First World War, then, there was a well-established foundation in the visual realm upon which to anchor the legend of Lettow-Vorbeck's "loyal Askari," that is, faithful East African soldiers, trained and civilized by German colonizers, whose fidelity to the German war effort justified German imperial rule post hoc.[74] Germans could *see* the loyalty—fluttering behind, in black, white, and red.

Showing something as abstract as land as "belonging" to Germany is no easy task. The notion of national sovereignty is likewise notoriously difficult to actually work into an illustration. The Leibig company, for instance, typically attempted to illustrate Italian or Greek "national identity" by drawing a map or by depicting figures in national costumes, but both of these strategies had their limitations. The complexity of protectorate rule—the colonized "belonged" to Germany, but yet were not "Germans"—was even more difficult to literally draw. Flags were one of the few ways to mark something as abstract as national sovereignty, or claims by one nation to sovereignty over a landscape. Just before 1900, German flags became one of the means by which to mark scenes of tropical exchange (or commerce) as explicitly "German"—and thereby to mark it as colonial.

In the last years of the 1890s a few German advertisements and packaging trademarks began to symbolically show German dominion over African territory as a relationship of Africans to the German flag. An illustrated packaging label for Oldenburger's Angra Pequena German Colony-Bitter (a liquor) offers one case in point (Figure 4.13). Angra Pequena was Germany's first overseas territory; it was claimed by the merchant-adventurer Adolf Lüderitz, and today bears his name. The product label for the liquor depicts an idealized colonial relationship. The German sailor—seen as German by the tricolor standard he bears—arrives on tropical shores and is met by a dark-skinned African woman in a dress, with necklace, bracelets, and a headband. She steps out of the jungle to pour the sailor a drink. The colonial relationship here is figured as a gendered relationship of a subordinate, colonial "wife" serving her patriarch. It is expressly *not* one of sexual access, as seen with the Kiautschou postcards of the same period. Instead, it shows domesticity—colonialism illustrated as a "marriage."[75] This depiction of a serving African woman, in fact, harkens back to earlier allegorical representations of Africa as a woman, where all continents were represented by female figures. This embodiment would not become standard, however; indeed, the representation of African women overall remained much rarer

Figure 4.13 Label for Angra Pequena (German Colonial Bitter) liquor. A number of features in this scene are vaguely reminiscent of the layout of some German orientalist cigarette tins, namely the pyramidlike hill between them, the outstretched hand, and the female figure's serving pose. The inset scene, featuring canoes, a sailboat, and an acropolis-like structure, is difficult to fathom. *Source:* WZB (1892): 884, reg. no. 7639.

in German commercial visuality of the Kaiserreich than, for instance, in French or British advertising.

A very different figuration of the colonial relationship is found in an illustration for Kaufmann's coffee, "Coffee with the German Flag," which shows a German sailor hoisting a German flag above the fallen body of an African (Figure 4.14). The unmistakable bellicosity of the scene is striking. Has the African native been pushed to the ground by the German sailor? Or has he been rendered prostrate by the flag itself—or by his awe of the flag? Either way, the flag is the most central element. The sailor

Figure 4.14 Advertising illustration for "Coffee with the German Flag," trademarked by J. Kaufmann of Hilden in 1900. *Source:* WZB (1900): 146, reg. no. 41728.

himself is of secondary importance in the scene; with his back to the viewer, we can barely make out his features. His function is to point upward—an indicative gesture that is visually echoed by the native's outstretched arm. This tableau, along with the brand name itself, establishes the ascendancy of "Germanness" (and by extension this German brand of coffee). But the broader meaning otherwise remains a bit puzzling. The nationalist overtones implicit in the appellation, "Coffee with the *German* Flag," moreover, are unusual for this early date.[76]

Both of these scenes represent colonial relationships: the first, of gendered tropical marriage; the second, more violent, and with nationalistic overtones. Despite the vastly different inflections, each ad explicitly hitches its company's product to German colonialism by means of emblems. Significantly, the German flags deployed in these illustrations are not the same. The first is the black, white, and red tricolor of the German national flag, associated with the merchant marine.[77] Before 1900 it was the most common flag used in trademark registrations. For the more bellicose "Coffee with the German Flag," the artist drew the imperial naval war flag, white with a black cross and an iron cross in the corner. Less typically seen in commercial imagery before 1900, it became almost de rigueur afterward. The seizure of Kiautschou likely contributed to this iconographic shift, for Kiautschou came under the rule of the German Imperial Navy and hence under the naval (i.e., war) flag. When postcards of German colonialism on the Chinese coast circulated widely through the German metropole, they all accurately showed the naval war flag and thereby visually associated that particular flag with colonial claims.

Other commercial interests also incorporated such symbolism and implicitly demarcated an overseas territory as "German," even when the exotic locale lay within the domain of a rival European colonial power. One early example is an illustration for Eduard Schmidt coffee, trademarked in 1898 (Figure 4.15). Schmidt's ad features a black figure in a turban and sarong holding a German flag, yet the lands from which the labeled goods originate—Ceylon, Java—lay outside German colonial control, in the British sphere.

A different means to illustrate expressly German colonial dominion was to show the German military or administrative presence, as with a label for Schutztruppe Export Bier, named after the "Protection Force" of the German colonies, which appeared in 1898. In the illustration (not pictured), a well-equipped soldier with high boots, pith helmet, and rifle stands in the colonial landscape of palm trees and mountains.[78] Similar images of an upright white male standing alone in the tropics, wearing a pith helmet and other equipment, permeated the advertising pages of the literature printed by the German Colonial Society. Schutztruppe beer may have been intended for export to the colonies (although the term "export" on the label refers to a particular style of beer), or the company, the Flensburger Joint-Stock Brewery, may have had some direct or indirect affiliation with the German Colonial Society, or it might have been

Figure 4.15 Coffee advertisement by Eduard Schmidt of Wickrathsberg, trademarked in 1898. Java and Ceylon lay within the colonial empires of the Dutch and British, respectively. *Source:* WZB (1898): 710, reg. no. 32506.

the only image of a militaristic colonizing presence familiar to the graphic artists working for the firm.[79] Imagery of colonial troopers, however, remained quite rare in German advertising until 1904.

For products that truly originated in the German colonies, the visual certification of German colonial origins was the flag. And flags were de rigueur for German colonial companies that sold goods directly to the German public. The earliest companies selling products such as cocoa from the German colony of Kamerun often deployed quite conservative forms of packaging art—a picture of a cocoa bean, for instance, decorated with a chromatic reference to Germany's flag that tapped into nationalistic sentiment.[80] Without research into each individual firm, there can be no definitive conclusion about why the companies most directly involved in the colonial economy evinced a reluctance to deploy the most power-laden imagery of colonialism seen below.[81] However, the visual traditionalism of colonial companies and colonial-enthusiast enterprises is likely connected to the fact that they aimed their advertising appeals at a far more bounded audience—the patriotic middle class already interested in German colonialism.[82]

Ultimately, Exner's suggestion for a window display in a professional advertising journal in 1896 stands at the brink of a larger transformation, namely the reordering of the consumer imaginary along "colonial" lines. However, it would not be along the lines that Exner so insistently advocated. The fundamental problem with the sorts of colonialist visual appeals seen thus far in this section—namely, staking claims to territories and native bodies by means of imperial flags—is that it requires a predisposition toward those national symbols in the first place. Many German nationalists would respond to the German flag in the anticipated way—namely, they would pay attention to it, and perhaps even be prompted to make a patriotically inspired purchase. Other nationalists might bridle at the crass commercialization of their country's colors. The flag could also fail to inspire many Germans. Would a pipe fitter—someone used to seeing the flag used as the decorative emblem of the nationalist right, and immersed in the culture of his Social-Democratic soccer club that called for international solidarity in a brotherhood of workers—be so moved by the imperial flag that he would purchase the product? Flags could be potent symbols, but many potential purchasers, from Rhineland liberals, to Bavarian Catholics, to Berlin socialists, might not see the national flag in a way that it would drive them to buy a product.

The *Kaiserreich*'s authoritarian political system could afford to overlook the wide diversity of opinion among the larger German public. Advertisers and commercial artists, however, were in the business of searching for appeals that would "work" with the broadest possible public. The future of advertising did not lay with appeals to narrowly nationalistic symbols such as marines, colonial troopers, or the German imperial flag. There were other ways to "colonize" a land—or for that matter, a commercial illustration—with more subtlety and a wider resonance.

The Colonizing Commodity

In the 1890s a pioneer of commercial imagery, the multinational Liebig Company, showed another path, one less overtly politicized. Founded in

1865, the Liebig Company was one of the first true multinationals, with German leadership and technical expertise, British capital, and a Uruguayan production site providing the land, cattle, and labor. "Liebig's Extract of Meat" was one of the very first brand-name products, and the company was one of the first to engage intensively in modern forms of advertising in the early 1870s.[83] (This was a full decade before the more well-known advertising efforts of the Pears soap company.) The company's earliest and most successful form of advertising was the collectible chromolithographed trading card, which it began to print in Paris in 1875.[84] Some of the first wildly successful visual advertising strategies to appear in Germany, then, were produced by a multinational company, for a multinational audience. In German commercial culture, the Liebig Company's creations were often in the vanguard by a decade or more.

Liebig's advertising cards exhibited extraordinary artistry. The level of detail in their early, cheaply produced chromolithography is astounding and is prized by collectors. These cards initially followed older pictorial traditions, such as allegorical representations of continents, or romantic figurations of childhood. In the 1880s they also began to offer vignettes of different lands and peoples from around the world, becoming almost a two-dimensional cardstock version of the commercial exhibitions popular in that decade. After 1890, however, a growing number turned explicitly to the colonial project, offering colorful scenes of "a typical day" in a European colony or illustrating a dramatic tableau of colonialist ideology. One of the most striking is an early series from 1891 titled "The Extract of Beef in Africa." On the first card, "The Loading," a giant jar of Liebig's Extract of Beef is being hoisted by steam crane onto an oceangoing freighter. A would-be explorer (and colonizer), well-equipped with rifle, high boots, and pith helmet, oversees the loading of this and other crucial gear and provisions. In the second frame, "The Unloading," the precious commodity is being removed from the longboat under the watchful eye of the explorer/colonist. In the background the steamer lies anchored in the harbor, and a well-built house testifies to the European influence on the coast. In the third, "The Caravan," native African porters carry the prized cargo on their shoulders through the dense jungle (Plate 12A). Other porters carry crates of other goods on their heads—all under the watchful direction of the mounted European. The caravan arrives at an inland native village—it is here that we learn Liebig's commodity is "the Gift for the King" (not pictured). In the ensuing scene, labeled "Negro

Joy," the natives dance around and/or even worship the great commodity while the king shares a drink with the European (Plate 12B). In the last scene we see the king, now standing in respect, showing his return gifts: ivory, gold, gems, a live antelope (or eland?), gourds of liquids, handicrafts, and other items (Plate 12C). Only in this last scene does the European's full intent become clear: he is a trader, who brings manufactured goods into darkest Africa, and emerges from the jungle laden with its bountiful natural wealth. There is abundant symbolism throughout these colorfully drawn images, but one particular detail is worth pointing out. In the first five scenes, the white European is the most prominent figure; he is either the tallest figure (whether in the foreground, on horseback, or standing over the king) or he is otherwise separated from the others. Only in the final scene does he blend in with the African crowd, yet his white pith helmet still sets him apart.

This series constructs two diametrically opposite worlds—modern Europe and primitive Africa—and maps out an idealized relationship between them, framed as an exchange of modern manufactures for indigenous raw materials. This exchange of manufactures for materials forms one pillar of colonial ideology, but Liebig's scenes are more than a mere reflection of ideology; they offer a striking new visual strategy. The scenes illustrate the "modernity" of a new commodity like Liebig's processed beef bouillon: the product packaging is juxtaposed against a group of dancing, worshipful primitives. The scenes also demonstrate how necessary the product is, for the six cards collectively depict it as the single most important element of the European explorer's preparations. Finally, in several of the scenes, the brand name rises above all else, literally being hoisted aloft onto the shoulders of the awed, subordinate native porters.

In 1900 an essay on Liebig's cards appeared in the professional advertising journal *Die Reklame.* The essay at first focused on the growing value of these *Liebigbilder,* which had become the "victims of collecting-mania *(Sammelwut).*" Around twenty-five years earlier, the essay tells us, the Liebig Company began giving out the picture cards gratis with every purchase; now a complete collection has come to be worth perhaps 30,000 marks. The essay concludes, however, with a reflection on the transnationality of this particular form of advertising: "A fact to be kept in mind," *Die Reklame* wrote, "is that the pictures must be appropriate for the taste of the different nations, because the company has its customers in all parts of the world. A series like 'The Travels of the German Kaiser' would find little appreciation in England or France, while it would find particular applause with us in Germany. Naturally, there are comparatively few series for specific lands. The large majority, then, are of a 'neutral character.' "[85]

What would count as "neutral?" Here we see another factor behind the prominence of colonial themes in Liebig's trading cards. Printed for distribution in England, Italy, Germany, and France (with the same image, but the text in different languages), the illustrations for most of the series needed to be both interesting and "neutral" in the sense that they illustrate something common to each of these very different national cultures, and yet are inoffensive to all. Colonial themes offered one solution; they were common to many European nations and yet unique ("collect each colony!"), and they operated within a larger sense of shared, collective enterprise. Colonial themes became quite prominent in Liebig cards, particularly after the 1880s. Liebig's chromolithographs reached an enormous audience; the print run for each series was from 750,000 to 3 million copies per card.[86] Equally, this set the standard for other, later collectible advertising cards by other firms, such as the chocolate company Stollwerck (1897–1918) or the margarine brand Palmin (1903–1914). The influence of Liebig on German advertising, and on British and French advertising as well, was enormous.

The day-to-day advertising in the streets of the German cities, however, had to function differently from the cloistered world of the trading card collector. In public advertising, as opposed to a collectible series, the "story" had to be compressed into a single, eye-catching scene. This meant distilling the exaltation of the commodity into a single tableau, but one that could attract attention in an instant. As German advertising theorists such as Victor Mataja maintained, an advertising poster must be recognizable at a distance; an ad insert must stand out from the surrounding clutter of the other classifieds; a packaging label must look appealing; a brand logo must carry emblematic weight.[87] Detailed, complicated storylines over multiple scenes are less than ideal for these purposes.

A colonizing narrative encompassed in a single scene can be seen in a German advertisement for accordions by the firm of Carl Essbach in Brunndöbra. It depicts a European, in the comfort and safety of his tent, distributing his merchandise to jubilant African natives (Figure 4.16). The image implies that, from this sanctuary of "civilization," replete with table, chair, and lamp, and a cleared path through the foliage, German

Figure 4.16 Packaging trademarked by an accordion manufacturer in Brunndöbra. Note the European wearing a full suit and hat in the tent, and the black figures wearing the striped shorts. This scene is copied from a Liebig trading card of the previous decade. The text, "Made in Germany" and "Trade Mark Liberty," marks the product for export, most likely to the United States. *Source:* WZB (1899): 448, reg. no. 37232.

commerce is spreading outward and civilizing the land—in the form of accordion sales.[88] The potency of this image does not require a flag planted in the African soil; for the implication is that the commodity itself will do the colonizing. The primary focus—at the center of the composition—is the sheer joy of the native with his new purchase/gift. Some accordions were actually introduced in west and south Africa, particularly by missionaries; nonetheless, the scene in some ways seems a bit odd for product packaging. As it turns out, this 1899 ad is a direct plagiarism of a Liebig trading card from 1891, "Alexander von Humboldt: the Exploration of Brazil." The Liebig card shows the same scene—the same tent, the same white figure, the same foliage and mountains, even the same number of figures—only on the Liebig card, instead of a joyous African native running with an accordion, there is a sophisticated Brazilian in straw hat, shawl, coat, and pants, with books and a walking stick. And on Liebig's card the sitting black figure, in a red sarong, has no object in hand, but merely sits patiently.[89] With Essbach's ad, on the other hand, the sitting black figure, dressed in striped shorts, clutches his own accordion (or accordion box?). As we will see below, the striped shorts are no accident of the engraver's stylus, but an increasingly important marker.

The displacement of Essbach's tableau of commercial delight onto natives lends extra importance to the featured commodity. Unlike Europeans, "natives" are not awash in commodities; an accordion, carried by a native who does not even own proper clothes, takes on the status not merely of prized possession, but of *sole* possession. The accordion then takes on yet another role, an added dimension; it is the material embodiment of Europe itself. At the turn of the twentieth century it was not symbols of sovereignty—flags, uniforms—but the preeminence of the commodity that would define the terms of the "colonial relationship," imaged again and again in commercial culture. The figure of the African native would become the main means to demonstrate that preeminence *ad oculus.*

Picturing Conformity

Depictions of the African native in advertising accelerated markedly in the years immediately following 1900. The earliest incarnations of the figure seemed to play a similar role as that of the venerable Tobacco Moor, discussed at the beginning of this chapter—namely, to serve as the embodiment of a distant land, and in the process, certify the authenticity of the tropical, or allegedly colonial, product. For instance, an advertisement for a sizing agent for textiles by the Cologne firm Jean Cremer & Co. shows a number of the hallmarks of the Tobacco Moor figure (Figure 4.17). It sketches a palm tree and a black figure in a position of repose, with the figure's hand resting on the cargo. But the differences are noteworthy: the basic markers of the black figure have changed. Instead of a headdress, feather skirt, and bow, the African native consistently shows native jewelry of some sort (big, looping earrings), a waist wrap, and bare feet. The cargo is no longer raw tobacco but the brand-name packaged product, Congolin. The brand name itself tells us that this native must be in the Congo. The basic tableau of the Tobacco Moor has been retained (cf. Figure 4.18) but the allegorical figure, of a vague but indeterminate exotic identity for five centuries, has been reconfigured as as an African native.

Figure 4.17 Packaging label for Congolin, a sizing agent for textiles, by Jean Cremer & Co., Köln, 1899. An identical image was re-trademarked by a different company, Mayer & Deroubaix of Köpenick (near Berlin) three years later. *Sources:* WZB (1899): 133, reg. no. 35519, and WZB (1902): 849, reg. no. 55984.

Did the use of the figure of the African native reflect either larger shifting patterns of trade or actual new sources of raw materials for German products? Sometimes, but usually not. In German product registrations, African names were often fashionable rather than descriptive, and this is particularly true in the textile industry. "Congo Red" dye, for instance, was first sold by AGFA in 1885. The dye had nothing to do with the Congo—the name seems to have been chosen because of the newsworthiness of the Berlin West Africa Conference held at the time of the dye's initial appearance. The new dye made a fortune for AGFA, certainly in part because of the exotic-sounding name. Imitators of both the manufacture and the marketing soon followed suit: by 1910 textile dyes were marketed with such names as Congo Corinth, Congo Rubine, Congo

Blue, and Congo Brown, among others. Sudan Black and Somalia Yellow also emerged around this time.[90] Like the analine dyes, the "Congo" here was not a description of origin but exotic marketing. Cremer's brand Congolin (Figure 4.17) merely followed in AGFA's footsteps.

Africa was therefore the continent newly in fashion, not just in the news but in brand names as well. But how to illustrate it? The figure of "the" African should not be seen as a preexisting, recognizable visual category. Representations of Africa could range from the classically composed allegory of eighteenth-century frontispieces (usually a women draped in robes, similar to Europa or Asia but for her darker skin), to the engraved ethnographic subject of the middle-class journals, to the wild, colorful savage on the show posters. The Tobacco Moor also continued to be used on tobacco labels up through the 1870s and beyond, even when the figure had an African ascription. By the 1890s, however, even tobacco advertising began to change the contours of the figure. In trademarks, the standard allegorical accoutrements of the figure (such as the bow) disappeared, and the feathered or tobacco-leaf skirt was increasingly replaced by a cloth waist wrap.[91] In an 1898 ad for Mohr tobacco, for instance, the graphic artist drew the figure in a waist wrap, but then added folds in the fabric to call to mind the traditional feather or leaf skirts (Figure 4.18). No bow or totemic feather headdress was included (cf. Figure 2.3); such timeless allegorical fixtures perhaps looked increasingly confused in the face of the growing circulation of other more ethnographically rigorous depictions of Africans. Instead, other iconic accoutrements emerged, particularly native jewelry, such as an armband or earrings.

On the other hand, compare Mohr tobacco with the previous image, for Congoline sizing agent (Figure 4.17). On the larger level, the two images are uncannily similar; both feature a gesturing black figure, seated on the commodity, in a similar posture, barefoot and in a waistcloth. A tall palm tree stands behind each, and the brand name runs across the sky. Yet the 1899 image for Congoline is unmistakably an African, while the 1898 image for Mohr is a more liminal figure—still close enough to the ill-defined Tobacco Moor as to be ambiguous. In the half-decade between 1895 and 1900 many "transitional" images in fact blended older Tobacco Moor and newer African native conventions.[92] It would be incorrect to see the emergence of the black qua African as a coherent, well-defined figure simply replacing a previously defined predecessor, the black qua Tobacco Moor. It would be more accurate to say that, over a relatively short span

Figure 4.18 Mohr tobacco packaging from 1898, by van Delden & Zoonen of Cologne. Note similar features to a Tobacco Moor figure, such as posture, cargo, palm trees, and sailing ship, but updated in style and technique. *Source:* WZB (1898): 557, reg. no. 30617.

(five to seven years), one image gradually morphed into the other in a step-by-step process that occurred piecemeal, from one trademark to another.

After 1900, however, images of the African native rapidly became standardized. Within the first five years after the fin de siècle the variety of clothing—loincloths, leaf skirts, toga wraps, feathered headdresses—had largely given way to a single, universal marker: striped shorts (cf. Figure 4.4 above and Figure 4.28 below). In color depictions, these shorts were red and white. Their real-world counterpart was likely the cheap muslin often used as a staple fabric in colonized Africa (and other parts of the world as well); but as we will see in Chapter 5, the red-and-white colonial shorts dovetailed with another very different pictorial pattern as well, this one imported from the United States. Overall, the markers deployed to identify and characterize figures as African natives became increasingly similar, even across competing brands and different products, crafted by different advertisers, and trademarked in different regions of Germany.

Standardized markers of "the" African might be assumed to be a simple reflection of colonialist discourses or ideologies. Juxtaposing the striped shorts against the invariably bare feet (see Figure 4.4), for instance, offers a visual shorthand of the civilizing mission: textiles manufactured in Europe were sent to clothe the otherwise-naked natives in Africa, but the feet remained bare—hinting that Africans would never completely escape their primitive nature. This juxtaposition of dress against undress could be argued to be both referencing the progress of the civilizing mission and at the same time marking its ultimate limits.

Depictions of native jewelry might also be read for colonialist symbolism. The use of necklaces, armbands, and pierced earrings might very well have been deployed to feminize the African figure according to late nineteenth-century gendered European norms of accoutrement. Native jewelry might thereby hint at feminized status (and, in a patriarchal society, this meant subordinate status). Ankle bracelets could echo older depictions of African slaves, in ankle chains. A different interpretation is that jewelry symbolizes the latent wealth in the colonized land: mineral wealth is so plentiful in Africa, this reading would imply, that even a barefoot, uncivilized native is adorned by gold jewelry. Another even more subtle interpretation would be that gold earrings or armbands on the very body of the native represent the wealth inherent *in* the native—namely, his "natural skill" or embodied labor that can be put in the service of the colonizers—as a way to symbolize (and visualize) the wealth of native labor potentially available to the German metropolitan economy.[93]

These readings of such symbolic markers as striped shorts, bare feet, and tribal jewelry are not the only possible readings, of course, and one cannot be sure that any of these meanings would be understood by the intended audience—viewers passing by with their attention distracted or viewers coming from a multiplicity of backgrounds and social classes. Symbolism was undeniably used, intentionally and unintentionally, by individual advertisers and designers. But no symbolic interpretation of the new markers of the African can explain these markers' rapid standardization. The meaning for allegorical identifiers (such as a headdress) accumulated over centuries and were used haphazardly; a colonial marker (such as striped shorts) became uniform in a few years. Why?

Quite apart from any single symbolic interpretation, the growing conventionality of these markers themselves fed into yet more standardization. Advertising of the late nineteenth century was not generally original; countless images were not only imitated but stolen outright. In the decade after Sütterlin's famous hammer poster, for instance (see Figure 1.3), the trademark rolls are filled with countless illustrations featuring hands bursting up through the ground clutching some particular item. (e.g., Figure 1.5). References to, imitations of, or plagiarizations of commercial images thought to be successful tended to make the whole corpus of commercial imagery look increasingly similar across the board. Most importantly, as ever-more-standardized images of colonized African figures were increasingly circulated and seen en masse, the uniformity and ubiquity together may well have generated broad-based expectations that this newly common figure—the barefoot black, wearing striped shorts, and jewelry-bedecked—was what an African did and should look like.

After the 1890s, advertisers increasingly saw themselves as needing to tailor their designs to the expectations of the public. The more standardized images of Africans became, the more graphic artists had to adhere to these standardized depictions if they wanted to deploy the figure to generate a message that was broadly and instantaneously decipherable. This had less and less to do with the personal desires or artistic intentions of the designer.[94] We can examine the symbolic elements in any single advertisement for a larger meaning—to discern, for instance, what colonial shorts and bare feet indicate about the pervasiveness of the ideology of the civilizing mission. Viewed collectively, however, commercial imagery is something more: it is a dynamic interplay between repetition and perception (in the visual, rather than cognitive sense). As markers such as shorts and native jewelry became not only standardized but pervasive, they themselves became indispensable in visually identifying the figure itself as *being* an African native in the first place.

The Visual Logic of Colonial Power

One crucial factor behind the standardization of the African native stemmed from that figure's potential to visually demonstrate the power of the commodity through the "logic" of colonial power. There are countless power-laden relationships depicted in commercial visuality that have nothing to do with the colonial realm, of course. Drawings of parents with children show generational power, or illustrate gender roles. Depictions of servants and aristocrats mark out social class. Nonetheless, the visualization of power operating in a colonial framework offers two elements that other forms of illustrated power do not. The first is the cachet of exoticism. The second is the placement—or rather, displacement—of the pictorial power into a realm seen as foreign, and thereby less antagonizing to German viewers.

The notion of visual logic is best demonstrated by example. In an early collectible trading card for the coffee manufacturer Aecht Frank, a white European accepts coffee from a black serving woman while a darker-skinned subordinate stands at attention (Figure 4.19). One crucial pictorial detail here involves dress. The European is figured as a colonizer by his pith helmet and his white tropical suit and is clearly "civilized"—in that, despite the heat of the tropics, he wears a tie, and his black shoes have a polished shine. The serving woman, on the other hand, is dressed as a domestic with apron and plain, functional clothing, while the colonized subordinate is dressed in a uniform but has no shoes. The boy stands at rigid attention, ready to obey every command of the European, while the serving woman stands demurely but also obediently. The colonizer's back is to the male subordinate, but the colonizer leans forward toward the coffee, which is also (not coincidentally) toward the woman. The literary theme of the obedient black servant is hardly new; the advertising card draws from widely circulating colonial discourse, from Robinson Crusoe's Friday to David Livingstone's Susi. The card also draws from a centuries-old theme in high art, of the exotic Other placed in the service of Europeans.[95] But there is a great deal more going on in this picture. All the main elements of colonial ideology are encompassed in this Aecht Frank ad: the cultural superiority of the colonizer (a European without any more specifically defined nationality) is suggested through dress; the educability of the native to obedience is suggested through posture; the subservience of the colonized woman, with the vaguest of hints that other services might be included, is indicated through the angle of the white figure's body and the eager gaze of the black female.

What makes the Aecht Frank advertising scene different from colonial literary discourse or artistic tradition is that the focal point of the illustration is the colonial commodity: coffee. The commodity is pictured

Figure 4.19 Collectible trading card for Aecht ("Real") Frank Coffee, "Known to be the best coffee substitute," from 1895. *Source:* from Erhard Ciolina and Evamaria Ciolina, *Reklamebilder und Sammelalben* (Augsburg: Battenberg, 1995), 21. Copyright: Gietl Verlag.

in a steaming cup, as well as in crates that bear the all-important brand name. The presence of the colonial subordinates attests to its colonial authenticity. The irony, of course, is that Aecht Frank ("Real" Frank) was not a colonial commodity at all, but rather a coffee substitute, brewed from chicory in a factory in Ludwigsburg.[96] The aim of this colonial scene was duplicitous—to legitimize Aecht Frank as a colonial good even though, as a domestically manufactured *ersatz,* it was decidedly not. Such implicit misrepresentations saturate German advertising: the Schultz Brothers' Ivory Soap packaging, for example, featured African native figures carrying ivory on their shoulders to visually verify for the viewer that the commodity was, in fact, authentic "ivory" *(Elfenbein)* soap (Figure 4.20). In fact, the soap had nothing to do with ivory; it was a German manufacturer's appropriation of Procter & Gamble's massively successful brand Ivory Soap, introduced in 1879, which itself had been

Figure 4.20 Packaging for the Gebr. Schutze's Ivory Soap from 1906. The Procter & Gamble Company first marketed its "Ivory Soap" in the 1880s. Note the ivory tusks, certifying this as "real" ivory soap. *Source:* WZB (1906): 1285, reg. no. 89348.

named after a biblical passage. The Schultz Brothers sought to authenticate their (imitation) product by spurious association with ivory—and hence, Africa—by means of images of African natives. Most importantly, if the Schultz Brothers had *written* that their soap was made from real ivory or somehow related to Africa, their claim would have been prima facie absurd and, moreover, subject to Germany's new laws on unlawful competition. But since this claim is made in the visual field, it is immune to logical fallacies or legal charges of false advertising. Most important, the image conveys the spurious information instantly without engaging the more critical level of consciousness demanded by reading text.[97]

In the first decade of the twentieth century, representations of colonial hierarchy often became more explicit in German advertising. Black figures increasingly shoulder heavy burdens—most often the commodity itself but sometimes the firm's logo or a representation of the raw material involved in the product's manufacture, such as a sack of coffee. African workers performing this labor tend to fall into one of two pictorial patterns: either they are pictured at a great distance so as to be completely anonymous, or else as close-up images that meet the gaze of the viewer, offering their wares (see Figure 4.21). This figuration of labor, as it appears in advertising and packaging, emphasizes the subordination of the black within the larger hierarchy of the colonialist system. In the vast majority of these images, furthermore, the black colonial subject carries the burden directly to the viewer. In this way, the advertisement implicates the viewer in the colonial system, as he or she visually becomes the recipient of the colonial goods.

Another advertisement that evokes a colonial hierarchy but in a very different way is an illustration for Reithoffer Pneumatic bicycle tires (Figure 4.22). Reithoffer's advertisement purports to show "elementary instruction in the Congo." An acerbic-looking missionary schoolmaster, with an elongated stovepipe hat, instructs a row of small naked black African children with the lesson that "Reithoffer's Pneumatic Is Simply the Best." This is an unusual ad, both in its design—particularly its dramatic use of blacks and whites—and in its approach, at least for the Germany of the late 1890s. Why should a German company be referencing the Belgian Congo? The easy answer, of course, is rubber. At the turn of the century, the raw material for pneumatic tires came largely from the Congo, and so it might seem natural to advertise a product by drawing a scene from its land of origin. But there is a great deal more going on here. First, there is its topicality: the ad plays upon the brewing notoriety of the Congo. Leopold had made the "humanitarian" face of the civilizing mission the centerpiece of his campaign to establish the Congo Free State under private control in the 1880s. The rubber boom took off the following decade, and missionary accounts of widespread atrocities associated with rubber harvesting were beginning to circulate in the European press as early as 1896. This ad for Reithoffer emerged at a specific *media* moment: after the civilizing mission was beginning to become tainted with

Figure 4.21 Trademark for A. Zuntz Roasted Coffee. The firm of Zuntz supplied "German African Coffee" to the 1896 Colonial Exhibition in Berlin. *Source:* WZB (1901): 594, reg. no. 49696.

scandal but before anti-Congo political activism turned the very name "Belgian Congo" into a byword for brutality. This advertisement surfaced when the Congo was scandalously topical, but not yet so repugnant as to alienate.

Despite the politicized context of the ad, however, the message contained within the scene remains ambiguous. For instance, the instruction of the children could be understood as part of Leopold's "civilizing mission"—a vignette that justifies the extraction of the colonial commodity (rubber) by showing its colonial reciprocity—namely, the humanitarian effort to educate the heathens. In this sort of reading, the viewer is meant to imagine the missionary teaching the row of naked children to read, to wear clothes, and perhaps someday even ride that most modern contraption, a bicycle. Yet the scene could also be read as a comment on the futility of the colonial mission to civilize the heathens: after all, the children are naked savages—what possible use do they have for this information about a bicycle tire, a product they have never seen, and given their state of nature, never will use? Another

Figure 4.22 Advertisement for Reithoffer from 1898, showing "Elementary instruction in the Congo," where "Reithoffer's Tires are definitely the best." This ad was designed by the Hollerbaum & Schmidt agency of Berlin and was reproduced in the advertising journal *Propaganda*. *Source: Propaganda* 1, no. 7 (1898): 379.

interpretation could be one of development: just as the missionary must teach them the basics of literacy, so too must he teach them how to correctly use their native raw material—rubber—so that it can be made into the modern commodity (the Reithoffer tire). Or the image could be a simple, blunt celebration of raw colonial power: the rod of instruction—of correction?—is poised over the child figures' heads; the figures on the left seem to shy away from its power (the figure second from the right, holding his wrist behind him, has perhaps just had his hands firmly smacked).

Finally, certain stylistic details suggest more critical readings: the hunched back of the missionary as he looms over the naked innocents, in particular, strikes me as remarkably sinister. Might it be a subtle, early indictment of the cruelty of whites in the Congo?

This interpretive ambiguity might at first seem to be a flaw in the advertisement's message. It is not. Ambiguity can be extraordinarily useful because images with multiple interpretations on a train-station wall or circulating in a widely read tabloid can capture attention without necessarily alienating potential purchasers of any social class or political opinion.

The operations of visual power in the scene, however, are less open to interpretation. The bicycle was a modern product, and its success in the 1890s, like that of other modern manufactures such as the cigarette, was dependent upon advertising: as there was no preexisting demand for pneumatic-tired bicycles, Germans had to be told to buy them. The anonymous interchangeability of the row of naked black African children is particularly relevant; as the missionary instructs the natives that Reithoffer's Pneumatic is "Simply the Best," the ad also "instructs" the viewer (and potential consumer) of this key information about Reithoffer. But because the viewer is an individualized, clothes-wearing, literate, adult, white German, he cannot *possibly* be considered in the same category as the numerous interchangeable, small, black, naked natives depicted in the scene. The child native needs this instruction in order to become (perhaps) civilized; the adult German is already civilized and has no need of such edification; he is defined to be already familiar with the Reithoffer brand name, even if this was not the case.

The "instruction" of the German viewer allows him to chuckle at the hapless, childlike natives who are ignorant of the supremacy of Reithoffer—even if the viewer also had never heard of Reithoffer up to the moment he or she saw the ad. Thus the image strives to give consumers pleasure by implying their own position of superior knowledge—even when that knowledge is carried within the image itself and given to them at the instant of viewing the ad.

In the early 1900s the African native continued to play an authenticating role—a role that was increasingly enmeshed in the visual logic of the colonial hierarchy that facilitated the power of the advertisement. In a widely circulated ad by the Mannheim margarine giant Schlinck & Co., crafted in 1905, a chubby black child figure cheerfully directs the viewer's attention to the product (Figure 4.23). The slogan tells us, "*This* is the

Figure 4.23 Advertisement for Palmin margarine, a brand of the Schlinck Company of Mannheim in 1905. "*This* is the new Palmin packaging. Beware of imitations!" The commodity itself occupies the central position in the illustration; the black child-figure must raise an arm upward to point at it, while leaning on another iteration. It was designed by Ivo Puhonny as a newspaper insert and lauded in a trade publication. *Source:* Curt Busch, *Von der Reklame des Kaufmanns* (Hamburg: Lüdeking, 1909), 144.

new Palmin packaging. So beware of imitations!" The visual composition works on a number of levels. First, the figure is drawn with the now-standard markers of the African native (which were relatively fixed by 1905); a small waist wrap preserves modesty, but the figure is otherwise unclothed, and the feet are bare. The figure is bedecked with native jewelry, but the lack of clothing and especially the absence of shoes show the primitive nature of the native waiting patiently to be "civilized." (The unshod feet are accentuated optically by the background of the black-and-white checked floor.)[98] This African native, certified as "real" by the newly standardized markers, served to demonstrate the commodity's tropical bona fides. "Beware of imitations!" the figure warns us—and as a native of the land of palm trees, he is capable of certifying the "reality" of the tropical origins of Palmin. To optically underscore the visual logic, the African figure certifies the brand by pointing to it.

Second, the scene shows German viewers the rewards of colonialism, by encapsulating it within the proffered product. Palmin is a wondrous modern commodity, only recently introduced to European society (in the 1870s), but the raw materials for the product (namely, palm oil) come from the tropics. Unlike Liebig's collectible card from 1891 (cf. Plate 12), this is no trade between adults; the immaturity of the African figure immediately places the figure in a subordinate role to the viewer. The childlike African native is helpless; he is undressed and clearly without tools, manufacturing capability, or money. Therefore, he has no means to obtain a modern manufactured commodity like Palmin. He can point and certify, but he cannot make, purchase, or consume. Moreover, there is a flattering visual logic to the scene that works through contrasts; it suggests that the viewer is modern by showing the figure as primitive. It casts the viewer as civilized by showing the figure as a naked savage. And even though the figure verifies the commodity as authentic, the visual logic casts the viewer as knowledgeable by showing the figure as childlike.

Third, the subordinate role played by the figure is crucial. As with the ad for Reithoffer five years before, it effaces the power of the advertisement itself. In the social world in which this illustration is situated, the African figure not only stands *as* an authority (attesting to the veracity of Palmin) but acts *with* authority: the African child's gaze is pointedly at the viewer, and his finger directs us to where *we* should look; the figure is commanding our attention, directing our gaze, and pressing claims upon us. But depicting the African as a child—and equally, as a childlike native—draws the viewer into the comforting paternalism of the colonialist hierarchy, so offense at the imposition cannot be taken. Indeed, since the half-naked African child is clearly the one in need of education, viewers may not even recognize that the information within the ad is, in fact, being pressed upon them, for it comes from a figure that is visibly constituted as an inferior. This particular advertisement was crafted by the renowned graphic artist Ivo Puhonny and reproduced in advertising journals.[99] And no wonder it found acclaim, for it masterfully displaces the intrusion of the advertisement itself. In today's era of advertising saturation, we hardly recognize advertising as an imposition, but in fin de siècle Germany, when advertising was relatively new, it engaged the wrath of all manner of moral crusaders and landscape preservationists. To be able to displace the intrusion of the ad was not an opportunity that German advertisers would easily pass up. Other themes also could displace advertising's power,[100] but the figuration of the child as an African translocated the scene into the distant realm and framed the whole hierarchy as natural, both of which made the ad even more difficult to recognize as an imposition.

To return to the advertisement for Wünschhüttl's snuff that opened this chapter, the African native is depicted as expressing amazement at the wonders contained within the crate (see Figure 4.4). The trope of the native transfixed by the products of European technology is fundamental to the literature of exploration in the second half of the nineteenth century, particularly that of the British.[101] From such travel writing, the motif of the cargo cult became common currency in all Western cultures. In German advertising imagery of 1900, however, the appearance of an African native in this role was quite novel.

The first element of the appeal is the evident awe on the part of the native when faced with the commodity. The scene of the enraptured African is meant to pique initial curiosity—to entice the casual passerby or the distracted reader spotting the advertisement to follow the eyes of the African to the crate. This is reinforced by some of the pictorial techniques employed in the image. The African colonial subject is behind the box of snuff, which itself takes center stage. The figure almost seems to curve around the commodity—and in a very primal way, I might add. The focal point of the image is the native's captivated gaze; clearly this is meant to escape the confines of the picture to similarly captivate the viewer. What is so fascinating is the modern commodity itself—a shorthand, as we have seen, for Western civilization. This image, then, is one that visually constructs a tableau of the cargo cult.[102] The native has stumbled across an artifact of modern civilization and is simultaneously overawed, overjoyed, and unable to entirely understand what he sees. (We will see this last point, incomprehension, illustrated far more clearly in later advertisements circa 1910.)

At the same time, the German viewer can rest assured that he is not being placed on the same level as the African, namely, in a position of awe and incomprehension in the presence of the advertised commodity. This assurance arises out of the visual logic of the scene: the African figure is drawn with the triad of the standardized markers of the colonized African native (striped colonial shorts; native jewelry; bare feet). In the conventionalized world of mass culture, the figure is thereby established as a diametric opposite to the appropriately adorned, clothed, and shod European viewer.

This disassociation of viewer from figure masks the power of the advertisement itself. As with Reithoffer's Pneumatic, the advertisement here "enlightens" the German viewer as to the importance of this particular brand: Wünschhüttl's Tirschentreuther Glashütten snuff is so superior that even a savage prefers it. In this cargo-cult tableau the commodity represents the fruits of modern Western civilization itself—as underscored by the native's fascination. Since the savage is uncivilized, the product must therefore already be familiar to any "civilized" viewer—even if it is not. The disassociation facilitates a two-tiered interpretation; it places the viewer and potential consumer in a position of subordination *to* the advertising image and of superiority to the African *in* the image. The first interpretation (that the snuff is the best) is masked by the second (displacing the effect of the "realization" onto an unmistakable social subordinate). In this way, the advertising image can simultaneously command and flatter the consumer.

Again, it is important to recognize that such a visual logic appeals to a broad audience; it does not depend on the viewer's particular stance on the merits or morality of colonialism. A German viewer could look on this colonized native with amusement or with self-importance, with philanthropy or with pity, with curiosity or even with disgust or fear. But regardless of the individual's ideas about the African native in general, the visual logic still unerringly illustrates the power of the brand. This ad could appeal to both middle-class monarchists and working-class socialists. And the formulation of such cross-class appeals—to bourgeois and to worker, to urban and to rural—was the first step in what would eventually break down those class barriers in favor of a new identity.

The Optics of Colonial Rule

It is useful to note that the size of the snuff box in Wünschhüttl's advertisement, usually pocket-sized, is as large as the African native—a distortion of real-world scale that is easily overlooked (see Figure 4.4). As we saw

Figure 4.24 Packaging trademark for Primeval Forest bananas from 1910 (Robert Wolff, importer, Mannheim). *Source:* WZB (1910): 1417, reg. no. 131392.

with Liebig's mammoth jar in 1891 (cf. Plate 12), scaling up the commodity optically is one way to magnify its symbolic importance. On the most basic level, enlarging the commodity in the image gives the product more of the available space in the visual field, which makes it, quite simply, more visible. After 1900 the burdens borne by black figures tended to become physically larger in proportion to the bearer: a label for Primeval Forest Bananas in 1910 shows two black figures straining under the load (Figure 4.24); in one Tengelmann advertisement for coffee, the cup is larger than the two abstracted natives holding it up, and a later coffee advertisement for Tengelmann shows a line of colonized natives, the coffee sacks on their backs half as large as they are (Figure 4.25).

There are a number of possible explanations for this general trend. One might again look to colonialist ideology and note a correlation between the growing burden of commercial imagery in Africa and the heightened emphasis upon "labor" in the discourse of German colonial-

Figure 4.25 Advertising illustration, without any text, trademarked by the Tengelmann coffee company in 1914. *Source:* WZB (1914): 788, reg. no. 189550.

ists. In the writings of both colonial enthusiasts and politicians in the early years of German colonial activities, the native featured centrally in legitimizing the German colonial project as the subject of ethnography or the object of missionary work and other civilizing efforts. The economic role of the German colonies began to take precedence after 1900, however, and the native was written about increasingly from the standpoint of providing a colonial labor force. Particularly after the Dernburg reforms of 1907, Africans were increasingly described in economic, utilitarian terms.[103] Were these exchanges among the Colonial Office or in the publications of the German Colonial Society picked up by the media and refracted into the broader commercial world? To some degree, for certain. Alternately, other scholars have seen the diminished stature of Africans overall as a defensive measure—to make them seem less threatening, particularly in the face of growing resistance in the colonies after 1900.[104] Violent events in the colonies certainly had their reverberations in the metropole, as we will see in Chapter 6.

The metropolitan aims of advertisers and other commercial interests, however, need to also be taken into account. I would argue that the gradual increase in the size of the burden in such images over time points to another process at work—a visuality-driven dynamic of exaggeration. At the root of the issue lies a conundrum; as depictions of African workers carrying burdens became more and more prevalent, they also became merely common. The lifeblood of advertising, however, is to stand out—as German advertising professionals expounded at every turn. There were limits to how much one could *truly* stand out, however; advertisers could ill afford to contradict or offend the public taste or especially the "common sense" of the audience. The emerging professional norms of advertising demanded that the graphic artist create ads that dramatized, yet conformed and were easily understood. One solution designed to meet these countervailing requirements was to deploy a widely used artistic convention but to further exaggerate it.

Even as the optical size of the colonial subject's burden was exaggerated, so too did advertising exaggerate the visual logic of the native's work. An advertisement from 1904, for instance, trademarked by a grocery supplier depicts a black native picking coffee beans (Figure 4.26). The implication is that the black colonial worker is picking the crop for the German purchaser. In an ad seven years later, however, the work has magnified to a massive scale: the black native uses Colonisol machine oil to smooth the very rotation of the globe itself on a giant machine axle (Figure 4.27). In effect, the colonized native keeps the whole world rotating through his labor—and, naturally, through using the product, Colonisol. Notice, however, that the native, despite his well-defined muscles, is kneeling in a position that almost implies supplication. This is no valorization of labor; rather, the native here is diligent, obedient, and nonthreatening. The figure's work itself is marginalized, furthermore, by placing the figure off center; it is the globe—and the product—that occupies the focal point of the illustration.

Conclusion

The visual colonization of the black figure in German advertising that began in 1900 was largely complete only a half-decade later. Two advertisements that appeared closely thereafter encapsulate two different varieties of this visual colonization, which I have termed visual logic and optics. The label for Hunter-Tobacco, appearing in 1908, stages a scene that is explicitly colonial in its visual logic, namely in its setting and in the relationship between the figures in the tableau (Figure 4.28). Two Europeans in full tropical outfit enjoy the thrill of the hunt in the colonies, with their bush hats, crisp white clothing, and high, sturdy boots to protect and insulate them from the tropical environment. Meanwhile, the almost

Figure 4.26 Illustration trademarked by a grocer, Paul Schneider of Zeitz, in 1904. Note the large earring and almost feminine features and pose. *Source:* WZB (1904): 265, reg. no. 66084.

naked, barefoot black African native bears a large burden on his head—not coincidentally, a sizeable quantity of Jäger brand tobacco. With his back to the threat, the native is either terrified (and ready to run) or oblivious to the danger; either way, he is in dire need of the Europeans' protection. Like the Oriental or tropical tableaus of the mid-1890s, this tobacco ad offers (in the words of Luthmer) a "look directly into distant lands"; unlike the exotic landscapes, this colonial landscape includes a tableau of power based upon the style and position of the figures. This dramatic scene lays out the essential dichotomy of colonial ideology pictorially; the colonizers possess modern equipment (rifles, boots, pith helmets) and modern consuming desires (the pleasures of the safari). The colonized

Figure 4.27 Advertisement trademarked by the Westfälische Stanzwerke GmbH of Aplerbeck for its Colonisol machine oil. Note the unusually defined musculature of the figure. *Source:* WZB (1911): 1549, reg. no. 146279.

African native, on the other hand, is bare except for colonial shorts. The African possesses only anonymous labor. The African's labor is twofold, each role equally essential: first, the figure authenticates the tobacco by linking it pictorially to an exotic land (even though Wilhelm Kisker certainly imported little or no tobacco from Africa). Second, the African lifts the commodity in the optical plane, placing it above all of the human figures. But only the African must suffer "under" or "beneath" the exalted commodity—the Europeans are left free to play, shoot, consume.

The second advertisement, one for coffee from 1909, engages the viewer more directly and personally with a colonialist hierarchy. Much of its "colonial" message works at the level of optics. The black figure—with well-defined musculature—bears the weight of the entire world on his shoulders, even as he supports the cup of Krelhaus coffee (Figure 4.29). Most importantly, he carries this burden to the viewer, who is implicitly

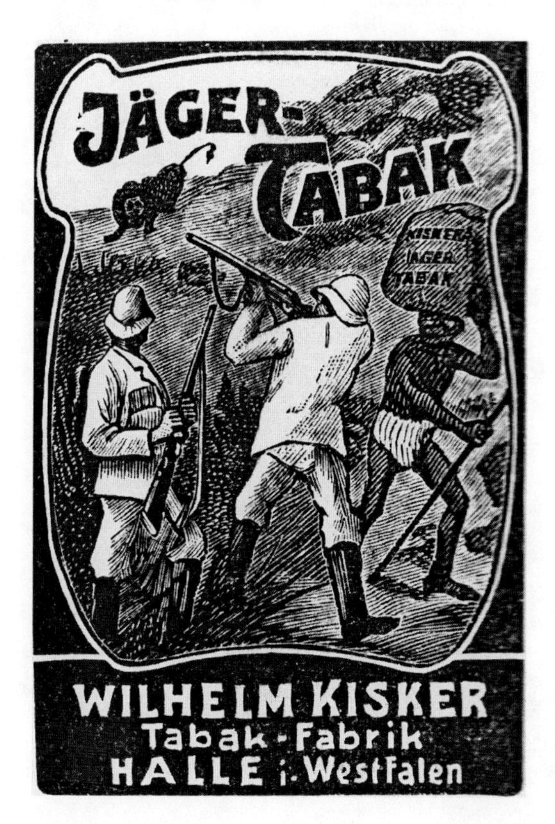

Figure 4.28 Advertising and packaging for Hunter tobacco. Trademarked by Wilhelm Kisker of Halle in 1908. *Source:* WZB (1908): 2048, reg. no. 112462.

the beneficiary of this colonized labor. A closer look at the geometry of the composition, however, is revealing. In fact, it is the Krelhaus coffee cup at the very base of the globe that supports it. The labor of the black subject is therefore only an intermediate element. The black figure is, somewhat perversely, rendered both indispensable and yet unimportant. The figure is indispensable as a generalized representation of labor—a visual clue as to the enormous work that went into crafting such a quality product. Moreover, the figure works as a visual confirmation for the coffee's slogan, in which it claims to be the "most authentic" *(reellste)* coffee in the world. (Coffee comes from "somewhere exotic," and the figure *is* that exotic land, personified.) Finally, the figure's efforts are the means by which the ad personally involves the viewer; the suspended cup is almost extended *to* the viewer, as an offer (from a server) that you are just about to receive.

Figure 4.29 Advertisement for Krellhaus coffee, "the most authentic and reasonably priced coffee in the world," trademarked in 1909. *Source:* WZB (1909): 1874, reg. no. 121631.

At the same instant, the figure is made unimportant. First, because he is graphically sidelined. His head is pushed to the side by the globe and—most importantly—by the brand name, Krellhaus-Coffee. The head of the African is thus out of line with the axis formed between the commodity and the world. Equally, the image reproduces a typology of subordination that by 1909 had become fixed in the consumer imaginary. The African is there to do the work so that you (the viewer) can consume. Finally, regardless of ideology or the vagaries of idiosyncratic interpretation, certain spatial elements are not subject to misinterpretation. The brand name is literally above the human plane. The brand name is also literally in the foreground, implicitly about to be extended to the viewer. Both brand names rest literally upon the dark body of the African. And the body of the Africa offers a dark backdrop—a chromatic contrast—against which to see the whiteness of the commodity and the whiteness of the world.

The difference between an exotified and a colonialist apprehension of distant lands and peoples, then, is in essence a visualization of power. This power was not the product of any single organization or even profession. The contributors to German commercial culture—from advertisers to designers to businessmen to viewers—were diffuse and decentralized. Collectively, however, myriad producers of commercial imagery embraced the new pictorial technologies and new thematic motifs at the conjunction of different contexts, impelled by different forces. The pictorial traditions of the Tobacco Moor were taken up and reinvented, to provide a human figure to stand as a visual argument for origination in an exotic land. From an entirely different direction, opportunities to capitalize on public interest in colonial warfare in China and South Africa steered attention first toward the German colonies in the Far East, then toward the Dark Continent. Institutions, such as the Colonial Society and its circle of colonial enthusiasts, were not guiding such visual shifts; at best, they were on the sidelines, though providing some motifs, such as fluttering imperial flags, for others to use and adapt. Their propaganda and official ideology, however, offered little visual appeal beyond the boundaries of the colonialists' narrower circle defined primarily by its nationalism.

More expansive modes of illustrating colonial rule emerged, embodied in the African native. These other modes became standardized—and the African native became "colonized"—through repetition and mass reproduction, and by advertisers seeking instantaneous comprehension. Colonial scenes became useful, for their visual logic allowed advertisers to make spurious associations, flatter the viewer in subtle ways, and mask the intrusive operations of the advertisement. Equally useful were the emerging optical relationships in the image itself, which could highlight the essential message—first and foremost, the elevation of the modern commodity—in ways that were both unprecedented and unmistakable.

African figures were not the only visual tools that could accomplish these commercial aims, of course. In the same way that the noble primitive was reconfigured in tobacco ads, allegorical traditions of the Madonna were reconfigured in chocolate ads. Just as the Colonial Society generated images, *Heimat* preservation societies generated images of local landmarks and monuments to "Germanness" that were adopted and adapted by advertisers. The visual construction of idealized womanhood, too, offered its own visual logic to veil the intrusive power of the advertising message. And depictions of children also provided opportunities to unmistakably emphasize and elevate the commodity on the optical plane—just as with the African native.[105]

The figure of the colonized African, however, held advantages that these other motifs and themes did not. First, since actual Africans were far away, depictions of them held more sway. Images of Africans, like images of women, were embedded in hierarchies that were claimed to be natural, but unlike domestic gender ideologies, colonialist framings brooked no possibility for firsthand interaction (in the metropole) that might counter or undermine said ideology. As an imaginative device, African figures were thereby all the more useful for their remoteness. Second, Africa as a region was a relative newcomer to the German cultural sphere, which allowed it to be more easily mapped and remapped with new commercial motifs. China was just as "exotic" and plenty distant; but 300 years of imported decorated porcelain (as one example) presented an imposing corpus of Chinese illustration that left less space, visually, for Germans to draw their own fantasies. Finally, as the next two chapters will show, African figures offered greater opportunity to build hierarchies of power directly into the bodies of the figures. The same forces of German mass culture that built a colonial rule into tableaux with African figures would also work on the body of the black; the next chapters will trace the slightly different path by which signifiers of racial difference emerged, circulated, and became hegemonic within the sphere of German visual culture.

Plate 1 Palm cigar poster, trademarked in 1911. *Source:* Staatsgalerie Stuttgart, Graphische Sammlung. © Photo: Staatsgalerie Stuttgart.

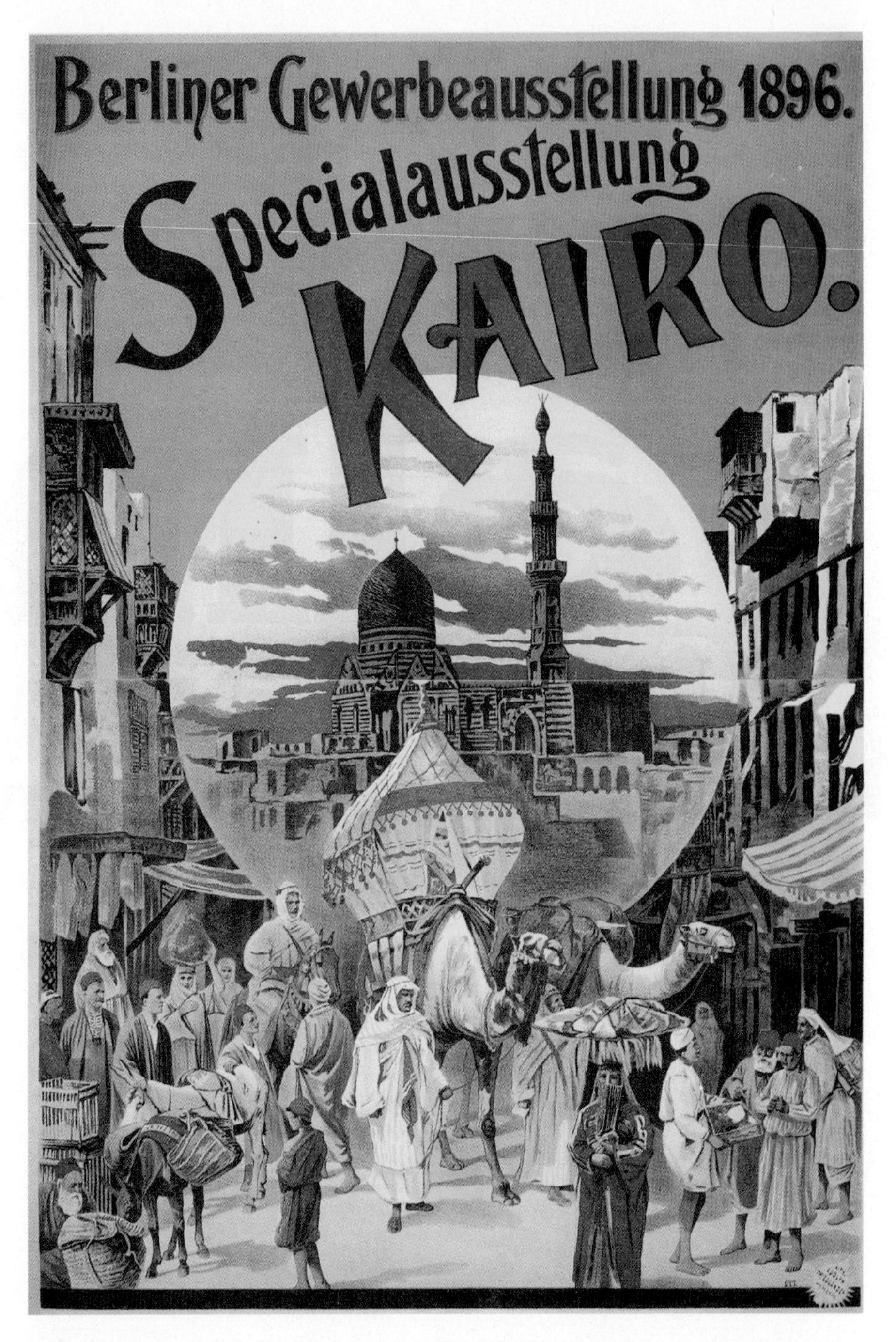

Plate 2 Promotional poster for the 1896 Berlin Industrial Exhibition—Special Exhibition Kairo, printed by the Hamburg firm of Adolph Friedländer. *Source:* With permission from the Museum für Kunst und Gewerbe Hamburg.

Plate 3 Poster for W. Süring's Universum wax museum, from 1892. Printed by Adolph Friedländer, no. 0296. *Source:* Circus Museum Netherlands, Stichting Circusarchief Jaap Best/www.circusmuseum.nl.

Plate 4 Promotional poster for Hagenbeck's International Circus and Menagerie out of Hamburg, 1887. Promotional poster printed by Adolph Friedländer. *Source:* Circus Museum Netherlands, Stichting Circusarchief Jaap Best/www.circusmuseum.nl.

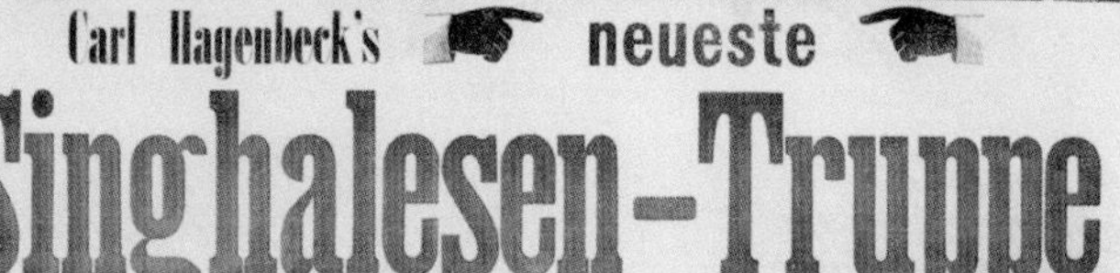

Plate 5 Promotional poster for Umlauff's Weltmuseum for *Völkerschau* from 1883; printed by Adolph Friedländer. "Hagenbeck's *newest*. Singhalese-troupe, men and women (natives from the Isle Ceylon) contains devil's dance, Udaky-dance, stick-dance, pot-dance, and the Singhalese dwarf 'Verama,' 25 years old and 90 centimeters tall." *Source:* With permission from the Museum für Kunst und Gewerbe Hamburg.

Plate 6 Packaging for Ceylon Crème Chocolates by the Stollwerck firm, Cologne, circa 1900. *Source:* Courtesy of Boecher Brand + Package Design Collection.

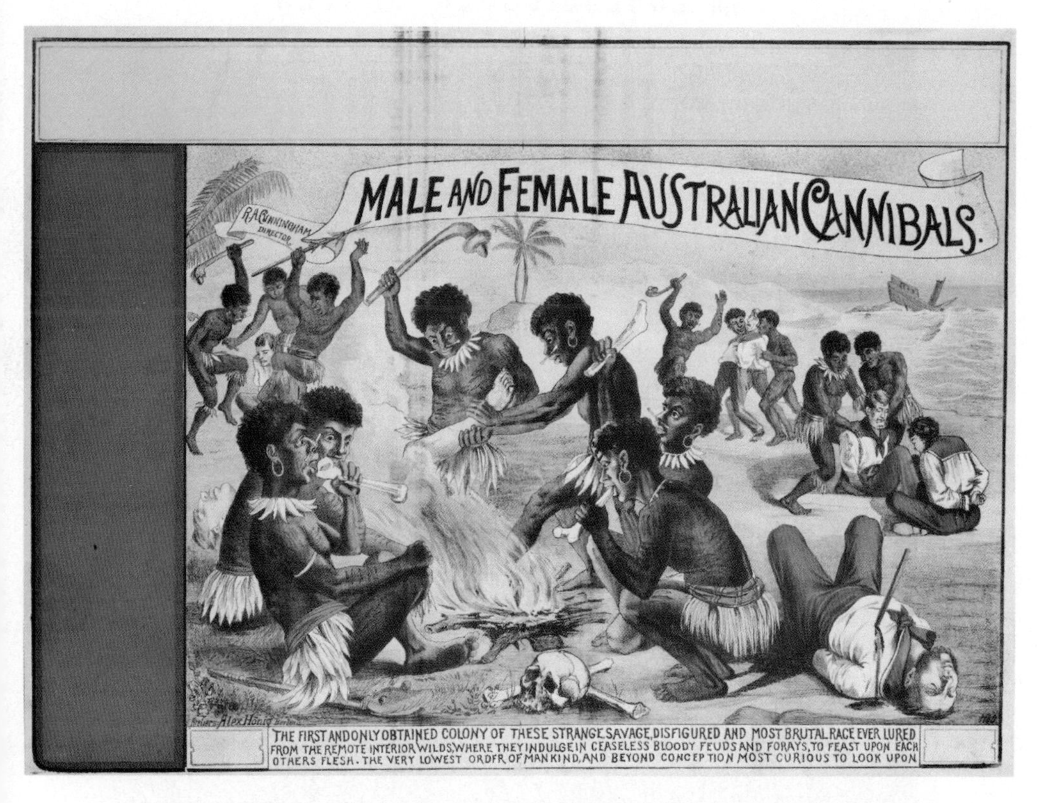

Plate 7 Poster of a *Völkerschau* of "Australian cannibals" from 1885, printed by Nauck & Hartmann (Berlin), atelier Alex Hönig. *Source:* Historisches Museum Frankfurt; Copyright: Historisches Museum Frankfurt/Main. Photograph: Horst Ziegenfusz.

Plate 8 Poster of a *Völkerschau* of the Amazon Corps at the Frankfurt Zoo in 1891, printed by Adolph Friedländer. *Source:* Historisches Museum Frankfurt; Copyright: Historisches Museum Frankfurt/Main. Photograph: Horst Ziegenfusz.

Plate 9 Poster for "The Original Amazons" show appearing in Castan's Panopticum, Berlin, 1893. Printed by Adolph Friedländer. Like Sütterlin's hammer poster, this poster, designed by Christian Bettels, was part of Justus Brinckmann's exhibition of "artistic" posters at the Museum for Arts and Crafts in Hamburg in 1896. The image is a likeness of the performer herself. *Source:* With permission from the Museum für Kunst und Gewerbe Hamburg.

Plate 10 Poster for Albert Urbach's "Wild Women of Dahomey." Variations on this scene, some far more violent, were used to promote this show in Frankfurt in 1899 and in Riga in 1901. Friedländer poster no. 2280. *Source:* Circus Museum Netherlands, Stichting Circusarchief Jaap Best/www.circusmuseum.nl.

Plate 11 Cocoa packaging by the German East Africa Company (before 1914). *Source:* Deutsches Historisches Museum (DHM), ak 94/516.3526.

A

B

C

Plate 12 Collectible trading cards, Liebig bouillon company, 1891. A: Liebig 179/2 1891. B: Liebig 179/3 1891. C: Liebig 179/5 1891.

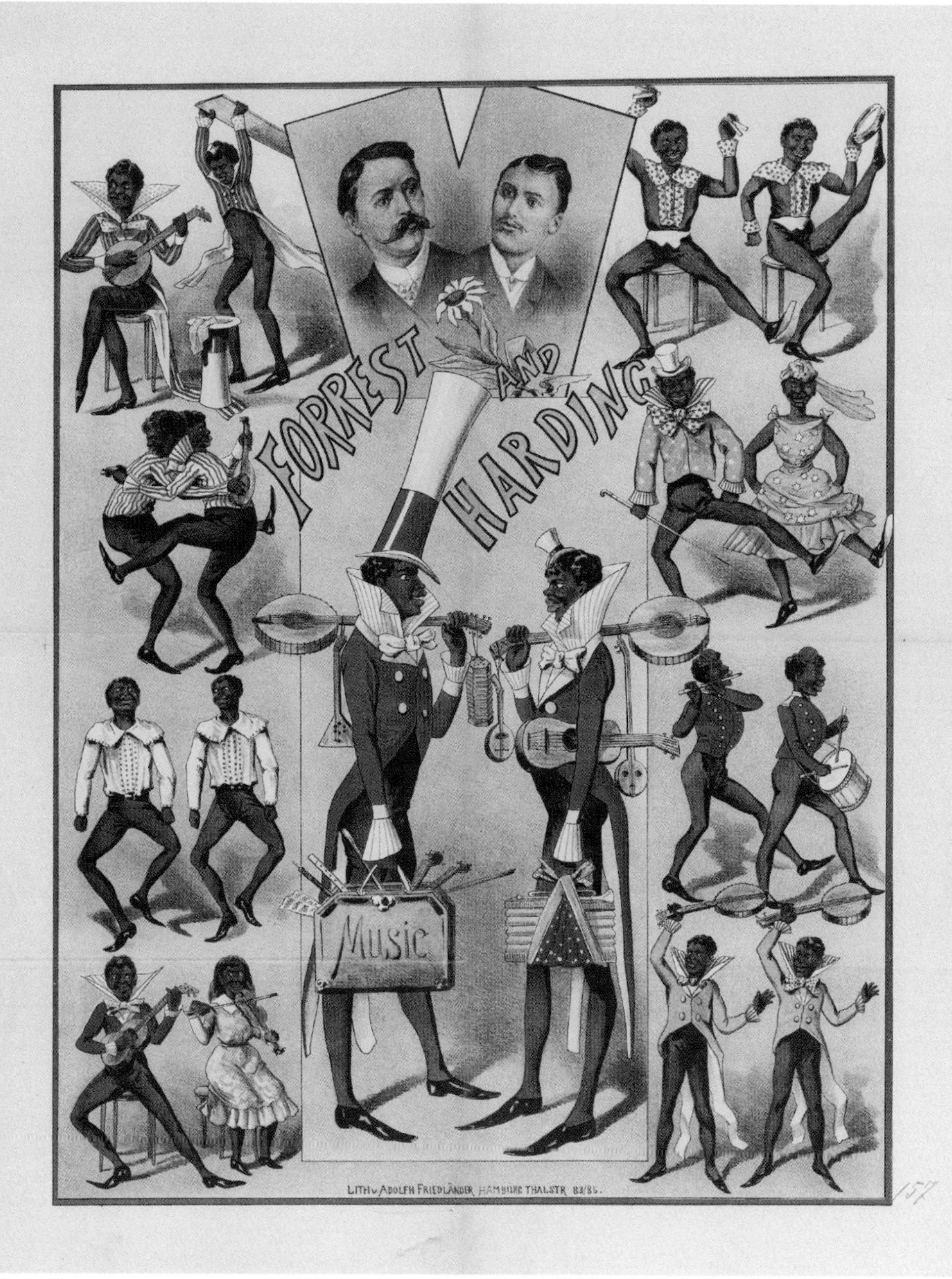

Plate 13 Poster for Forrest & Harding's Minstrel Show (from the United States), touring in Germany in the 1880s. Friedländer poster no. 0157. *Source:* Circus Museum Netherlands, Stichting Circusarchief Jaap Best/www.circusmuseum.nl.

Plate 14 Sheet music for Paul Lincke (Apollo Verlag), 1903. *Source:* author's collection.

Plate 15 Tin for Black Boy shoe polish (date unverified; perhaps circa 1910). *Source:* Deutsches Historisches Museum (DHM) AK 94/516.4704.

Plate 16 Advertising stamp for Palm cigars. *Source: Das Plakat* (1914).

Plate 17 Poster for Palm cigars, circa 1914, from the Berlin agency Hollerbaum & Schmidt. *Source:* Paul Ruben, *Die Reklame* vol. 1 (Berlin, 1914), 56.

Plate 18 Poster for the Odeon Café, 1908, by Ludwig Hohlwein. © 2010 Artists Rights Society (ARS), New York/VG Bild-Kunst, Bonn. Image: Hans Moor, *Reklame-Lexicon* (Leipzig: Phönix-Verlag, 1908), 158, and Kunstbibliothek, Staatliche Museen zu Berlin, Preußische Kulturbesitz.

Plate 19 Advertising poster for Palmin margarine, circa 1913, by Ludwig Hohlwein for Schlink Company, Mannheim. © 2010 Artists Rights Society (ARS), New York/VG Bild-Kunst, Bonn. Image: Staatsgalerie Stuttgart, Graphische Sammlung. © Photo: Staatsgalerie Stuttgart.

Plate 20 Palmona margarine advertising stamp, circa 1913, designed by Ludwig Hohlwein. H. Schlink & Co., Mannheim. *Source:* Museum Europäischer Kulturen Berlin no. 260/2012. Copyright: Staatliche Museen zu Berlin—Museum Europäischer Kulturen, Stiftung Preußischer Kulturbesitz.

Plate 21 Advertising stamp for Cobu margarine, issued after 1909 by F. A. Isserstedt, Leberfeld. Note the repeating of the image on the packaging, implying a recurring tableau *ad infinitum*. *Source:* Museum Europäischer Kulturen Berlin 33 Q 2031, p. 2. Copyright: Staatliche Museen zu Berlin—Museum Europäischer Kulturen, Stiftung Preußischer Kulturbesitz.

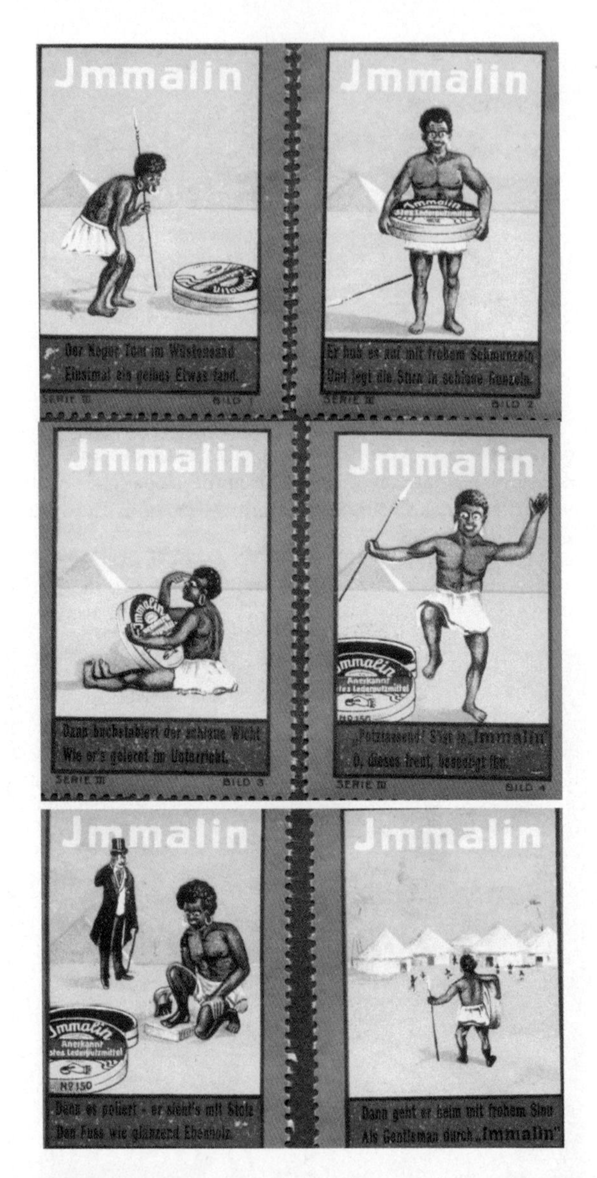

Plate 22 Advertising stamp series for Immalin shoe polish issued by the Chem. Fabrik Eisendrath GmbH, Mettmann, trademarked in 1913; see WZB (1913): 2831, reg. no. 182571. "Nigger Tom in the desert sands, once found something yellow / He lifted it up with a happy smile and knit his brow in a sly furrow / The clever scoundrel spelled it out just like he'd been taught / 'Bless my soul! It's Immalin' Oh the joy that filled his soul / For it polishes (he saw with pride) his feet, to gleam like ebony / Then home he went in happy spirits, made a gentleman by Immalin." *Source:* Museum Europäischer Kulturen Berlin 33 Q 1454F. Copyright: Staatliche Museen zu Berlin—Museum Europäischer Kulturen, Stiftung Preußischer Kulturbesitz.

Plate 23 Poster for Sarotti's Banana-Cocoa, circa 1911, crafted by Julius Gipkens. *Sources: Mitteilungen des Vereins Deutscher Reklamefachleute* 42 (1913): 1; *Monographien Deutscher Reklamekünstler Heft* 6 (1914).

Plate 24 Advertising stamp for soap by A. L. Mohr. *Source:* Günter Schweiger's virtuelles Reklamemarkenmuseum; see also Günter Schweiger and Gerlinde Spicko, *Die Reklamemarke—Das Werbemittel der Gründerzeit* (Vienna: Bibliophile Edition, 2008).

Plate 25 Advertising stamp for Trab-Trab shoe polish, circa 1910. The figures are performing a cake-walk dance, tracing back to American sheet music covers. *Source:* Museum Europäischer Kulturen Berlin. Copyright: Staatliche Museen zu Berlin—Museum Europäischer Kulturen, Stiftung Preußischer Kulturbesitz.

Plate 26 Advertising stamp for Bullrich Magensalz (sodium bicarbonate). In his unfinished work on the Arcades Project, the Weimar writer and critic Walter Benjamin wrote of a moment when, as a child, he saw an advertising poster that struck him "with such violence, that it broke though the ground of consciousness." That poster was an ad for Bullrich Salt, picturing a laden freight-wagon, pulled by horses, making its way slowly across the desert—even as salt trickled from one of the sacks, to form the words "Bullrich Salt" in the trail behind. "Was not the pre-established harmony of Leibniz mere child's play," Benjamin wonders, "compared to this tightly orchestrated predestination in the desert?" This advertising stamp here is another image in the same series, and its predestination is the unending labor of the African. *Source:* author's collection.

Plate 27 Advertisement for Goldene Haus cigarettes, 1916. *Source:* Deutsches Historisches Museum (DHM), Sammlung Plakate.

5

FEATURING RACE

Patterns of Racialization before 1900

In 1903 a rather startling image was trademarked in the Trademark Registration Rolls of the Imperial Patent Office by a small chemical firm not too far from Württemburg whose manufactured goods included shoe polish and ink (Figure 5.1). The sign "Mohren-" (meaning Moor's or Moorish) leaves blank space for the actual commodity (ink, soap, shoe polish) to be named later, but this trademark was most likely intended for ink, for the composition as a whole conveys a certain sense of blotted fluidity, evocative of that liquid's properties. The stylistic conventions used with the black figure holding the sign are astounding for a German advertisement of the time: they reflect an early commercial deployment of the most extreme conventions of racialization. Notice the massively oversized lips, with tiny white-dotted teeth that graphically accent the twin white gashes of the lips. The ears are also greatly exaggerated; given the composition's minimalism, it is impossible to tell whether the ears are long and deformed, or if they are meant to represent earrings or some other form of native jewelry. The nose is akin to the snout of a pig, and the bumpy head is meant to allude to kinky hair. The feet are huge, bare, and deformed; peeking out from under the blank whiteness of the sign, the feet instantly attract the viewer's eye. Only after the face and the feet are both

Figure 5.1 Trademark for Mohren ink from 1903, by the chemical manufacturer Grau & Locher in Schwäbisch Gmünd. This design is unusual for 1903, both for its focus on physical features of racial differentiation and for the minimalism of its pictorial style. *Source:* WZB (1903): 1239, reg. no. 62916.

seen will the viewer then realize how diminutive the figure is. For how could the feet be that close to the head unless the figure was either torturously contorted (hidden by the sign) or the body were abnormally stunted?

In the public sphere of Leipzig in 1903, this image would have been jarring. And not just for its racism; the image's pictorial style is almost as unusual. The stark contrast of black and white (without shading or grays) and the focus on nothing else but a single central figure differentiate it stylistically from late nineteenth-century ads almost as much as its overt racism.[1] In fact, the racism of the image is not so separable from its pictorial style. Its visual syntax comes at the intersection of message and mode. And as unusual as both its message and mode were in 1903, a mere seven years later it would be ordinary, as we will see in the next chapter. This ad for Mohren ink was a forerunner; it emerged a few years before a surge in advertisements and illustrated packaging that placed just this sort of simplified graphic emphasis upon features of racial difference. Particularly after 1905, racial difference came to be depicted in increasingly stark and simple terms throughout German commercial visuality.

This image's status as forerunner depends also upon the context of its circulation, namely as an advertisement that was mass-reproduced. As we will see throughout this chapter (and have glimpsed at several points in this book), the stylistic racialization of black figures appears at different times—sometimes much earlier—in different contexts, in different types of media directed at very specific audiences. The historical trajectory of racial differentiation is not a linear one, nor is it attributable to a simple causative force. Most importantly, this historical trajectory of racial imagery remains, surprisingly, quite distinct from the history of intellectual theorizations of "race" and their subsequent popularizations.[2] Elements of racialized depiction first became evident in certain types of advertisements in the 1890s (and earlier for specific cases), but it was only after 1904–1905 that racializing elements and styles, previously seen only sporadically with certain products by some companies, spread to become a broader, almost codified strategy of depiction throughout German consumer visuality.

Scholars have noted a broad correspondence between the European colonial project and images of racially differentiated and subordinate blacks in European culture. A closer look at these images—at the paths they took, their permutations, and the forces driving their dissemination—can tell us a great deal more about the complex relationship of colonialism—and the development of colonialism as a cultural practice—to the emergence of modernity itself. Surprisingly, the racialization of advertising imagery in Germany did not emerge in lockstep with official or scientific colonialism. Neither the growth of German colonial sciences, such as anthropology, after the 1870s nor the beginning of direct German colonial rule in 1884 had much impact on commercial articulations within the German metropole. The construction of a racial—and ultimately racist—imaginary of colonialism in Germany can be traced instead to preoccupations with a land far removed from the German colonial orbit. They flowed not from the established ideologies of race science or colonialism but rather from the new connections of commerce.

Entertaining Americanization: Featuring the Minstrel Show in the 1880s

In the 1893 issue of *Die Reklame,* the Metz firm J. Bouchy & Sons printed a cluster of clichés (stock illustrations to be put to any purpose) for resale to other advertisers or businesses. Among this group of clichés, one stood out for its use of the grotesque, in the art-historical sense of the word (Figure 5.2). Bouchy & Sons' 1893 image incorporated some of the markers

Figure 5.2 A purchasable stock illustration, or cliché, from 1893, offered by J. Bouchy & Sohn of Metz. *Source: Die Reklame* 3, no. 8 (1893): 175.

of race seen in the Mohren ink advertisement from ten years later that opened this chapter; it included a pictorial emphasis on the figure's lips and on the white (and somewhat bulging) eyes; a few crooked and broken teeth, askew in a gaping mouth; a bizarre styling of hair; and a disproportionate body that featured a massive, oversize foot, on which was displayed a mock-up advertising slogan for shoes. The illustration, as many today would recognize, is a minstrel, a figure drawn from American popular culture of the mid-nineteenth century. It is identified largely through its accoutrements, from striped pants to mismatched vest and coat, from oversize spats to a tattered hat, and especially the banjo. Yet no matter how recognizable to scholars today, it was a decidedly odd illustration for a German advertiser to try to sell to German businessmen more than a

Figure 5.3 Advertisement for office supplies, trademarked in 1906 by E. W. Leo, Nachfolger (Leipzig). *Source:* WZB (1906): 1272, reg. no. 88725.

century ago. How could such a jarring American image be seen—and sold—as a necessary business expenditure in Germany? And if it were purchased and used in an advertisement, would a welder from Bochum or a clerk from Potsdam even understand what the figure was, let alone what it was meant to connote?

More than a decade later, in 1906, the cliché had found a buyer: a Leipzig producer of office supplies trademarked a more or less identical figure (Figure 5.3). The alterations relate to the recent developments in printing technology and advertising technique, but that is a topic for the next chapter. This new trademark was used not to sell shoes, but for office supplies—likely ink. The associational link to ink is equally puzzling. Why would a minstrel figure, a staple of *American* popular entertainment, be seen by commercial artists as relevant to hawk shoes in the German marketplace in 1893—and then in the Germany of 1906, be seen as so valuable in selling ink that it needed the protection of a commercial copyright? The answer to this question is not simple, and it takes us back to the discussion of American modernity.

American racism had long fascinated Europeans, and this was particularly evident in the field of entertainment. In the United States the minstrel show emerged in the 1820s to become the quintessence of American entertainment for the next one hundred years. It could also be performed by Americans as their national culture; in 1854, in the ceremonial exchange before the signing of an American-Japanese trade treaty aboard the *Commodore Matthew C. Perry,* for instance, Japan presented demonstrations of sumo wrestling and ceremonial dancing, while the American sailors responded by offering a minstrel show of "colored Gemmen of the North" and "niggas of the South."[3] As an American export, minstrelsy also proved magnetic to European audiences throughout the nineteenth century. The catchphrase "jumping Jim Crow," for example, had entered into the European vocabulary as early as 1834, when Thomas Rice's one-man minstrel show first left the United States to tour London and the Continent. Following in his footsteps, American minstrel shows criss-crossed Britain and the Continent over the next seventy-five years. They reached their zenith of popularity in Europe in the 1880s.[4]

While London and Paris remained primary destinations, German cities also proved profitable venues on the show circuit. Charles Hicks had led the very first troupe of black minstrels to Germany in 1870.[5] The subtle discriminations inherent in these performances, however, could sometimes be lost on German viewers. When Haverly's Mastodon Minstrels toured Germany in the early 1880s, they were threatened with arrest by the police. This was not for the charge of affronting public decency—the most common charge in the *Kaiserreich* levied against any type of entertainment that was seen to be outside of German bourgeois or parochial norms. Instead, the charge was "a fraudulent attempt to deceive the German public." The audience was apparently outraged that the show was not performed by *real* Negroes—but rather by whites in blackface.[6] Such a seemingly minor incident is revealing, for it raises questions about the nature of the appeal of the minstrel shows in European culture. Were they understood as parody (or multiple layers of parody)? Or were they merely seen as yet another performance of exoticist ethnography—as a *Völkerschau* of the Deep South?

In the broader view, minstrelsy found purchase in Europe because it entertained on more than one level. Just as with white American audiences, minstrelsy's celebration of racial hierarchy and unrestrained ribaldry flattered and titillated white European audiences. At the same time, the very "foreignness" of the form allowed European audiences an additional layer of pleasure—namely, to feel a sense of self-satisfied superiority vis-à-vis that ill-bred "America," which produced and genuinely delighted in such crude amusement in the first place.[7] Just as minstrelsy in the United States could resonate with both proslavery and abolitionist attitudes, in Europe it could resonate with both pro- and anti-American sentiments.[8] Minstrelsy's "Americanness" may have been overstated, however; in 1822, more than a decade before Thomas Rice's trip to London, the English comedian and actor Charles Matthews delighted British and Continental audiences with his one-man show "A Trip to America," which featured him singing in blackface.[9] Some scholars of minstrelsy have argued that the form itself can be traced back to European folk rituals of blacking up in mummers' plays and shivarees.[10] The European roots of minstrelsy extended to its imagery: for centuries, woodcuts of "wild native" dancing and carousing had illustrated travel writing, as Christopher Steiner has shown, and the carefree slapstick jig of minstrelsy fits comfortably into this primitivist mold.[11] Regardless of the precise reasons for their appeal in Europe, American minstrel shows toured Europe from the mid-nineteenth century onward and, in the process, familiarized European and German audiences with the racial stereotypes that were common in the slaveholding and postslavery segregated United States.

The imagery of American minstrelsy in the mid-nineteenth century had a transnational reach of its own—indeed, it often crossed borders ahead of the shows themselves. This was partly due to the expense of engraving; well-crafted images were frequently borrowed or pirated and recirculated. For example, a British lithograph from 1844, "Master James Crow" by Thomas Fairland, was reproduced in Germany as a *Bilderbogen* (wall hanging) for German audiences by the Danzig printer Friedrich Samuel Gerhard.[12] Such lithographs were likely intended to function in the manner of a film poster today—namely, as a souvenir of an appreciated show. But while minstrel shows were all the rage in the London of the 1840s, none had made its way as far east as Danzig at this early date. How many of these east-Elbian Germans who saw Gerhard's lithograph recognized it as caricature rather than ethnography? Indeed, the promotional practices surrounding minstrel shows contributed to such confusion. John H. Haverly, nearly arrested in Hamburg, had multiple minstrel troupes. In addition to his mammoth Mastodon Minstrel company, he also ran the Genuine Negro Minstrel & Jubilee Company, which toured Britain in 1881. The Genuine Negro Minstrel show was "genuine" in the sense that it consisted of African Americans performing in blackface. But from the European perspective, if minstrelsy was whites performing as blacks, would blacks actually be "genuine" minstrels?[13] The promotional posters for the two troupes—white minstrels and black minstrels—gave no visual clue that there was any difference between the shows other than the names; the representational styles and subject matter are virtually identical. In this light, the Hamburgers' assumption that Haverly's minstrels were real African Americans—perhaps even an ethnography of the Deep South—seems less German provincialism and more planographic syllogism.

At the end of the nineteenth century the new scale of image reproduction lent the visuality of American minstrelsy a wider scope. In the age of mechanical reproduction, the geographic and social reach of minstrel imagery became far greater than that of the shows themselves. Minstrel show posters were among the very first posters printed by the firm Adolph Friedländer; such traveling shows sometimes brought the lithographic stone with them for a local printer to run off copies, but other times the printer crafted the posters according to a model. Friedländer's firm ran off posters for the American minstrel acts of Brooks and Duncan (1873), Forrest and Harding, Edwards and Harris (1882), and Astor and Belmont (1884).[14] In the 1880s and 1890s minstrel acts were also often part of larger circus acts, and their posters correspondingly included blackface tomfoolery.[15] One of these circus posters might even have provided the model for Bouchy & Sons' 1893 cliché (see Figure 5.2); the poster, for Jack Barett's American minstrel show touring through Germany in 1891, includes (as one of many small background minstrel figures) a seated banjo player quite similar to that offered by Bouchy & Sons.[16]

A chromolithographed poster, perhaps from 1885, depicts the touring American minstrels Forrest and Harding (Plate 13). They are drawn in a quasi-realistic fashion at top—perhaps to emphasize their show is not a *Völkerschau*—while other scenes purport to show them in their blackface, as they clown, sing, dance, and play banjo (and two scenes in drag, no less). These illustrations are expertly crafted. Note particularly how the use of shadows lends a sense of movement, which, together with the extreme exaggeration of the blackface physiognomies, adeptly captures the carnivalesque elements of minstrelsy. It is important to recognize that the graphic racialization of the black figures' features on the poster is not merely extreme but *misleading;* no amount of makeup could alter the physiognomy of the actors so completely. The legs could not possibly be that thin; and the physiognomic transformation would require a rubber face mask, not the standard bit of burnt cork. In this promotional poster, the dramatic distortion of the black figures juxtaposed against the more true-to-life depiction of the white figures is one way to visually illustrate their comedic transformation. In a visual language akin to circus posters, the scene exaggerates the transformation to the point of impossibility.

In the 1880s, as we saw in Chapters 1 and 2, the German public still placed a strong emphasis on authenticity to justify exhibitions and even ethnographic shows. The extremism of the Forrest and Harding poster is at odds with this ethos, and correspondingly, with most other German posters of the 1880s. Indeed, when we scan to the bottom and see that this poster was printed by the firm of Adolph Friedländer, the puzzlement only grows. Friedländer's posters for the circus, *Varieté,* and *Völkerschau* performances were certainly sensationalist, as we have seen, but in the 1880s they were rarely built around such racial demarcations. Apparently, however, these American styles of pictorial representation were acceptable in the German public sphere for *American* entertainment acts.

In 1900 a Hannoverian rubber giant used a highly racialized black figure to advertise its Excelsior brand bicycle tires (Figure 5.4). The company's Excelsior brand was heavily advertised; a typical poster for its tires featured a thin, modernly dressed white woman riding a bicycle. Here, however, the company deployed a minstrel figure, complete with top hat, tails, high-water pants, and spats; smoking a cigar, the black figure rides a unicycle precariously over a road of broken bottles, thorns, and sharp spikes. This scene is clearly drawn from a comedic minstrel show; riding a unicycle over broken glass is an act of clowning, and the massive white lips are drawn in such a way as to show that it is makeup. The massive ears and spindly legs, however, are not; they are meant to be real bodily attributes. But even as late as 1900, in Germany such an image could meet with criticism. One advertising editor (most likely Robert Exner) dismissed the Hannoverian Rubber Company's ad as inappropriate: "the Negro-motif is quite popular in America," he bristled, "but on a *German* poster, and particularly from such an eminent German firm, we would rather *not* have seen it."[17] Revealingly, the editor did not seem to recognize the Excelsior illustration as a reference to an *entertainment* scene; it was just a generic popular American "Negro-motif" that, as of 1900 at least, was still not entirely respectable in Germany. The admonishments of advertising

Figure 5.4 Advertisement for Excelsior pneumatic bicycle tires from 1900. "Dependable. Long-lasting. Flexible. Elegant. Fast. Light." Note the broken glass being ridden over. *Source: Propaganda* 3, no. 10 (1900): 342.

writers need to be weighed against the actual visual record, however; and by 1900, many other German firms were turning to such imagery to sell their wares.

Minstrelsy was merely the first in a wave of American shows and fads focused on blackness to cross the Atlantic. Close on the heels of minstrelsy—and feeding from the minstrel show's popularity—was the European mania for *Uncle Tom's Cabin* in the 1860s and 1870s.[18] A third wave swept over Germany in 1903, when the cakewalk craze hit Berlin. The cakewalk was a high-kick dance performance that originated in slaves' shows in the antebellum United States; these shows initially mocked the strutting habits of white owners but were eventually performed by Northern whites in blackface as a mockery of black efforts to rise above their station. After the cakewalk came to Europe, the German composer Paul Lincke's popular tune "Coon's Birthday" *(Neger's Geburtstag)* became an international hit. The success of the song in turn inspired a great many imitators, including "Meine kleine Braune" in 1904, "Das kleine Niggergirl" in 1908, and "Molly, mein kleiner Nigger" in 1910.[19] And such musical fads spilled over into the commercial world. The phrase "nigger girl" from the 1908 song, for example, was trademarked for use by a German biscuit and chocolate manufacturer in Rybnik six years later, on the eve of the war.[20]

The bright illustration on the cover of Paul Lincke's 1903 music depicted a strutting male and female, with masklike black faces and extraordinarily bright red lips (Plate 14). This emphasis on the lips drew straight from the iconography of minstrelsy, but it was less immediately recognizable as theatrical makeup. Even more than the promotional posters of minstrelsy, those for Lincke's music might have easily been seen as depicting real African Americans.

Regardless, there is no doubt that the cakewalk craze—and *especially* its attendant visuality—exerted a significant influence on German commercial visuality otherwise far removed from the world of entertainment or dance.[21] A German baked-goods manufacturer, for instance, sought to take advantage of the cakewalk fad to sell its Kummer's ready-made cake mix; an advertising poster, trademarked in 1904 by Krewel & Co., depicts a black dandy in top hat, tails, and spats, carrying a cake while being escorted by a white woman in a cakewalk (Figure 5.5).[22] The scene in fact is borrowed directly from the covers of American cakewalk sheet music—or, more correctly, French and German covers of American cakewalk music.[23] There is one crucial difference, however: the German advertisement depicts a white female figure cavorting with a black figure. Interracial pairings are seldom seen in American sheet-music covers. Moreover, the woman's clothing in the Kummer's cake mix ad is not the dandified fashion of the cakewalk genre—that is, short hems and frills—but rather the flowing finery of a German woman drawn in full *Jugendstil* mode. The Kummer's ad shows a contemporary, modern German woman dancing with a cake-bearing black American dandy—a real shocker. The pictorial details played upon the type of cake mix itself: it is chocolate

Figure 5.5 Advertising poster for Kummer's Ready-Made Cake Mix, by Krewel & Co. GmbH, Cöln, from 1904. The cakewalk craze hit Germany in 1903. *Source:* WZB (1904): 2306, reg. no. 74090. (A poster of this is in the Historisches Museum Frankfurt am Main.)

cake with white frosting. The black figure on the advertising poster is racialized a bit, with some exaggeration of the lips, and would likely be far greater in a color depiction, where the lips would be bright red.

The cakewalk genre had many other pictorial ripples through German commercial imagery apart from racialization of facial features, of course. An advertising poster for a Munich bar in 1908, for instance, shows postures and lines of movement that clearly hark back to cakewalk imagery, even if the figures in this dance are white.[24] One might even go so far as to suggest that the common imagery of the Weimar cabaret—with its white bodies at extreme angles—derived from, or at least was influenced by, this commercial visuality of the cakewalk. It might even be possible to trace many iconic representations in the Weimar Republic—from 1920s café advertisements to paintings by Otto Dix—directly back to images of American blackness circulating on the show circuit and in advertising at the fin de siècle. But it is clear that minstrelsy and the cakewalk were two primary avenues by which graphic racialization entered mainstream German visual culture, and this racialization became more extreme as the minstrel and cakewalk themes continued to be popular in German commercial imagery well into the next decades. If the angled, oddly posed Charleston dancers represented the bright, modern future of Weimar Germany, the negro minstrel remained the dark Other of the *Kaiserreich*.

The Trade in Race: Transatlantic Packaging

The march of the minstrels across German stages and German billboards was one of the first avenues by which American racial imagery came into Germany, but there were others as well. From the mid-1890s onward, American visions of race—which were at the same time self-reflective visions of America—crossed the Atlantic in myriad ways, for even in the new era of mechanical reproduction, images continued to be not only bought, but borrowed, plagiarized, and in many cases, stolen outright. Among the most recognized visions of America at the time were those that illustrated the Wild West, and these are still prominent in German visual culture today. In the German commercial culture of the 1890s, however, those that mapped the Deep South were even more prevalent. The attraction of the wild frontier is easily understood; but the allure of the bucolic, racially stratified South is more puzzling. Why did American racial themes spread beyond the narrow field of entertainment to eventually resonate with advertisers, designers, and the German public, particularly in the production of meanings meant to affix to everyday commodities?

Racial imagery saturated the advertising of the United States. Racial motifs appear in American postcards, trading cards, and collectibles back to the first commercial use of chromolithography. But racial and racist imagery took center stage beginning in the 1880s. The obvious icon here is the figure of Aunt Jemima, which dates to 1889. Unlike today's benevolent African American matron, however, the original images of Aunt Jemima were highly racialized. Figures such as Aunt Jemima and Rastus (the Cream of Wheat chef since 1893) are merely the survivors of tens of thousands of others long since disappeared and forgotten.[25] These black figures, willingly and warmly serving commodities to a white audience or serving as objects of clownishness or ridicule, are so prominent in the advertising of the 1880s that scholars have seen the imagery itself as pivotal in the development of American mass culture. Racial and racist advertising served as a sort of reconciliation of North and South after the Civil War, cementing postslavery racial barriers in the South, but offering an illusion of an idealized racial harmony in the North. At the same time, racial advertising reinforced class and gender roles for white Americans. Racialized advertising may even have legitimized and facilitated the consumerist ideal itself.[26] While images of inviolable racial hierarchy were as old as slavery in some media, the emerging commercial practices of the 1880s in the United States caused a surge in such imagery. And this surge in racial imagery was highly visible to the new German specialists.

As we saw in Chapter 3, early German advertising writers embraced American modernity as a rhetorical device to solidify their own precarious social status. (Whether American advertising was actually more "advanced" than that of Germany in the 1890s is another story.)[27] When German advertising writers held up America as a model of advertising methodology, they pointed to strategies and tactics that were claimed to "work," and many of these seemed to be (or were held to be) racial and racist ones. German advertisers, however, often had to go to great pains to fathom *why* they supposedly were effective. In 1894 one German advertising writer, Professor F. Luthmer, rhapsodized over the artistry evident in an American poster for shoe polish that featured a black man: "the moor's blue-black *physiognomy itself* shines with incredible highlights," he wrote, "which demonstrates *to our very eyes* the *actual effects* of a new American shoe polish."[28] At the risk of belaboring the obvious, it is worth mentioning that to apply shoe polish to human skin of any shade creates a dull, smudgy mess, not a lustrous, patent-leather shine. But Luthmer felt the need to provide some explanation for the juxtaposition of black shoe polish with a black figure. The more obvious connection probably escaped him, because it lay an ocean (and a culture) away: black shoe-shine boys were a fact of everyday life in every American city. A black figure on an American package of shoe polish served as visual certification of the polish quality, as testified to by an expert. In Germany, however, there were no black bootblacks, and so a convoluted argument about tincturo-luminosity was put forward.

Figure 5.6 Advertisement for boot wax from 1899 by Rasche & Co., Minden. *Source:* WZB (1899): 522, reg. no. 38174.

By the mid-1890s, German shoe polish manufacturers were using American black figures in their own advertisements.[29] In an ad by a Minden company for boot polish-wax, for instance, the black figure is not far removed from a realistic portrayal (Figure 5.6). Notice, however, the pictorial emphasis on the lips, which are not only exceptionally large but also drawn in white so as to be more prominent on the black figure's face. And note especially the "shine" of light on the black figure's cheek and forehead—a "shine" that perhaps, as Luthmer reported, "demonstrates to the eye" the lustrous shine provided by the Rasche Fettglanz brand itself.

Given the prevalence of the shoe-shine boy in American advertising motifs for shoe polish in the 1890s, it is no surprise that the graphic artists Bouchy & Sons steered their 1893 minstrel cliché for a German business toward the expectation that it would sell shoes (see Figure 5.2). Shoe polish was one of the first manufactures in which American racial stereotypes, with all of their corresponding conventions of pictorial racialization, became visible in German promotional imagery. And it is through this circumlocutory route that a black-tinted product, such as shoe polish, became indelibly associated with blackness as a racial category and as a graphic style. By the First World War, shoes, shoe polish, and other shoe accessories in Germany had become thoroughly infused with the "shoeshine boy" motif (despite the figure's absence from everyday German street life) (Plate 15). Like the tin for Black Boy shoe polish, these images invariably adopted racializing conventions, most often a deliberate emphasis upon the figure's lips.

American racial themes found entry into German commercial imagery in conjunction with other specific products as well. New products of the late nineteenth century—the cigarette, the bicycle (and its rubber tires), the safety razor, reservoir fountain pens, toothpaste in tubes, and a range of others—had no preexisting clientele; they therefore seemed particularly suited for the most modern promotional strategies. As a result, advertisers concentrated their efforts on selling their services to firms making these types of products.[30] Many of these inventions and entrepreneurial innovations, from the safety razor to the toothpaste tube, also originated in the United States. For German advertisers, modern strategies meant strategies notionally linked to an America defined as modern by virtue of its entrepreneurial innovation.

Preeminent among such new manufactures was the bicycle. As we saw earlier, the Excelsior ad of 1900, which featured a black minstrel unicycle rider, was criticized by the professional advertising journal *Propaganda* for its use of the "Negro-motif popular in America" (Figure 5.5). Yet such criticism did not prevent other German tire firms from following suit. The firm Reithoffer, for instance, deployed the motif of a black American minstrel (or rather, dandy) as well. Its poster features four identical well-dressed black "dandy" figures in top hats and coats, with starched collars, boutonnières, and gloves, looking over a fence. Each tips his hats toward the viewer while holding a sign that spells the firm's name. And each figure is drawn to emphasize bright red lips and a gleaming white smile.[31] This scene of black faces peering over a fence proved quite popular, and it was much imitated in subsequent German advertising.

Toothpaste offers another example of a modern manufacture. It had first appeared in the 1850s, but in a celebrated story of American ingenuity, toothpaste was first packaged in an easy-access tube in 1892, and sales then skyrocketed. Toothpaste is a quintessentially modern product. It fundamentally altered traditional habits and ingrained behavior, and required the powerful cultural pressure of advertising to do so. Imitating American companies' successes, the powerful German chemical industry quickly turned to toothpaste production themselves, and when faced with the dilemma of how to market a habit-changing personal hygiene product, they often turned to the "modern" methods of American companies,

Figure 5.7 Advertisement for toothpaste from 1899 by W. Seeger of Berlin. *Source:* WZB (1899): 262, reg. no. 35997.

namely, utilizing images of American blacks. The toothpaste ad of the Berlin firm of Seeger from 1899, for instance, depicts a black minstrel-type figure in a mismatched vest and jacket, with his shirt cuffs sticking out of the too-short sleeves (Figure 5.7).[32] This figure displays overemphasized lips (as if he were wearing black lipstick), large ears, a lumpy face, and a stretched neck, which optically correlates with the short sleeves and exposed cuffs.

The Seeger ad offers a hint at the *reception* of advertising by designers and among the public. As a decontextualized commercial image, the ad makes little sense: why would a German purchaser be inspired to purchase toothpaste by a smiling black American? Its very functionality depended upon the growing *range* of visibility of a specific racial image. Black figures beginning to circulate through German commercial culture over the previous decades—on minstrel show posters and *Völkerschau* posters in the 1880s, on shoe polish ads in the 1890s—had been drawn with large, bright white teeth. Only in the context of the growing visibility of racial images of Africans in the 1890s would a German viewer recognize the specific joke here: blacks have such bright, shiny teeth *because* they use toothpaste—specifically, Seeger's toothpaste.

Incorporating this joke plays another role, moreover, which is to resolve a difficult design issue. In four- or five-color printing, how does an artist make white teeth really stand out on a white figure? The solution is to use a black figure. In fact, advertising themes that do not immediately make sense, such as black figures selling toothpaste in a nation where there are few blacks, provide some of the best evidence we have that advertising images were seen and that they made an impact. Over the ensuing decade, many other German toothpaste manufacturers followed suit, deploying black American figures in their advertising, including the two Berlin firms, the Florian Chemical Works (with their packaging featuring two black boys with pearly white teeth hugging) and R. Barnick GmBH's with its famous brand Komasept, featuring a black figure in a red jacket, with red lips, grinning widely into a hand mirror.[33]

When American racialized types were first deployed outside this very specific zone of modern products, audiences and advertisers alike could be uncomprehending. In 1895, for instance, a German advertising writer critiqued an American ad that featured a large black woman, with racialized features, holding what looked like a rolling pin. The German author complained that the American ad was totally misleading; he declared that one expected the ad to be "for noodles or baked goods."[34] The American ad, however, actually promoted ink rollers. The German writer's confusion of the sketch of an ink roller for one of a rolling pin (used in Germany to make such staples as *Badische Schupfnudeln*) was not the central problem. The crucial misunderstanding came out of the fact that, as of 1895, there was no automatic associational link between African Americans and ink. There was—at this point—no widespread understanding among advertisers that it made sense to sell a black commodity like ink using black people.

A decade later this had changed. By 1904 the notional link between ink and black skin had become strong enough that an office supply company in Hannover saw fit to trademark an ad for ink rollers based around a black figure. The figure, in a dated top hat and coat, demonstrates the

Figure 5.8 Advertisement for ink rollers from 1904 by Westenhoff & Co., Hannover. *Source:* WZB (1904): 83, reg. no. 65237.

action of the device, rolling out countless copies of the brand name, Optimus (Figure 5.8). It has been argued that advertisers played upon natural color associations of black products, such as shoe polish, coffee, chocolate, and ink, to black skin pigmentation. In fact, there was nothing "natural" about this association at all—it was constructed historically through repetitions just such as these. What had been nonsensical a mere decade before had become widely comprehensible by 1904. The notional blackness of a product entered Germany in the wake of other stronger associational links, like that of "American" to "modern." The linkage of black figures to ink, shoe polish, tires, and other black-appearing commodities was forged visually—through mass reproduction and mass dissemination of borrowed commercial imagery.

Regardless of how they were initially forged, linkages between blackness and ink proved to be quite durable. When the Hannoverian pen and ink company Günter Wagner introduced its Pelikan ink, for instance, the packaging sported a pelican, which was the crest of the Wagner family, but the image showed two caricatured black child figures fending off the pelican with an oversize fountain pen.[35] Clearly the association between ink and blackness had solidified. Borrowed from the American cultural context, motifs of blackness, from minstrels to dandies, from shoe-shine boys to pickaninnies, from Uncle Toms to bellhops, all appeared in German advertising with a steadily increasing frequency from the mid-1890s onward.[36] And bound up with this steady inclusion of American blacks were the pictorial techniques of racialization that American commercial artists had used for decades to define and mark such figures.

"Made in Germany": Self-Fashioning through the Export Market

Advertising motifs could sometimes be carried directly through the new streams of transatlantic trade, as product packaging. American products, packaged for domestic consumption, were also shipped overseas, with their packaging logos as well. The N. K. Fairbanks Company, famous for its Gold Dust brand of soap that featured racialized depictions of two black children in a washtub, exported a range of products to Germany. And to protect the label from German knock-offs, the company registered the Gold Dust Twins with the Imperial German Patent Office (through a German middleman) in 1901.[37] Meanwhile, the Johnson & Johnson Company, the pharmaceutical giant from New Jersey, registered their trademark of a racialized black figure strumming a banjo sitting on a bale of cotton.[38]

German businessmen, intent on exporting their products to the United States, familiarized themselves with American racial motifs as a necessary business practice. For instance, the Nuremberg pencil manufacturer J. S. Staedtler (founded in 1835) trademarked its famous Minerva brand pencils in 1895 for the German market. In 1896, however, Staedtler also trademarked a different brand: The Negro. With its English-language logo, and featuring the smiling, friendly face of a black boy with chubby cheeks, white teeth, large lips and forehead, and tiny nose, it was designed for the export market to the United States. Clearly Staedtler's executives, advertisers, and designers had attuned themselves to American motifs. Their competitor, Faber Gmbh, had trademarked the brand name Congo for its pens the previous year.[39]

Figure 5.9 Packaging for accordions from 1904 by G. A. Dörfel of Brunndöbra. *Source:* WZB (1904): 60, reg. no. 65398.

With such manufactures as musical instruments and toys, German industry secured a commanding position in the second half of the nineteenth century. And German manufacturers in these areas crafted cover illustrations and packaging that they thought Americans would find appealing. The trademarked packaging for a concertina (an accordionlike musical instrument) by the Dörfel company in Brunndöbra, Saxony, in 1904 is a case in point[40] (Figure 5.9). With English text and a scene meant to evoke the Mississippi, this packaging was evidently crafted for export to the American market. In the United States, such "black romances" had been common for decades even with products marketed to white consumers. The scene is affectionate and even romanticized; yet the racialization of the figures' lips nonetheless is a major element of the characterization. Many of the details are discordant. The earrings on the male figure are evocative of images of Africans, and palm trees have similarly been somehow transplanted to the shores of the Mississippi. Images like this one

Figure 5.10 Packaging for Sambo shoe polish from 1900 by Jaeger & Kiesslich, Berlin. This packaging was intended for export as well as for the German market, as the multilingual text attests. Note the figure's earring. *Source:* WZB (1900): 478, reg. no. 44027.

sought to imitate American motifs for an American purchaser. But they registered the trademark in Germany. From this, it was a short step to redeploy such imagery in the German market. And indeed harmonicas, accordions, and other musical instruments were frequently prominent vectors of racialized imagery within Germany.[41]

American visions of race were eventually blended into a mishmash of tropes by German advertisers trying to make their appeals sensible to multiple audiences both in the United States and in Germany. Take the packaging for Sambo Blacking, trademarked by the Berlin shoe polish company Jaeger & Kiesslich in 1900 (Figure 5.10). The name "Sambo," of course, was meant to resonate with an American purchaser. The primary panel of the packaging is in English—it is "the best Waterproof Polish in the World . . ."—and the emphasis on the word "blacking" (instead of *wichse*) suggests that it was primarily intended for American store shelves. Yet one full panel holds German text, suggesting that Sambo Blacking (now Sambo-*Wichse*) circulated in the German market as well. The illustration on the packaging does not use an American racial type, however. It employs the conventions of the African native: the figure is undressed, he wears tribal jewelry, and his curly hair is close-cropped rather than the wooly disarray of the American minstrel type. Around 1900 this illustration was far closer to German figurations of Africans than to American figurations of blacks. The packaging may have been destined for America, with its associational linkage of shoe polish to blackness of American origin, but the pictorial style reflected German colonial culture.

Africanizing American Depictions

Curiously, racial images of American blacks were also transported to the framework of the German colonial project for commercial use. The German cocoa giant Theodor Reichardt, for instance, trademarked an image for Cameroon Cocoa in 1898 (Figure 5.11). Cocoa from that German West African colony counted as one of the very few successes of the German colonial economy, and nationalist and colonialist circles therefore ardently promoted it as an important step to autarky, even though total cocoa imports from all the German colonies (including Cameroon) accounted for only 2 percent of German domestic consumption. It is not surprising, then, that the Reichardt GmbH would market a brand of German colonial cocoa to cater to this vocal constituency. Reichardt's choice of illustrations, however, does not derive from the growing reservoir of colonialist and ethnographic imagery seen in earlier chapters. For one thing, the children's clothing is wrong; the raincoat and rain hat on the leftmost figure pictorially suggests that Africans are as in need of protection from the elements as Europeans—these are not depictions of "peoples of nature" *(Naturvölker)*. Second, the racialization of the figures is likewise premature for a cocoa ad from 1898: the pictorial emphasis on the lips and nose stands out in particular.

As it turns out, the image is a blatant theft of an American illustrated advertisement by the Peters Shoe Company in St. Louis, for Diamond Brand Shoes (Figure 5.12). This Diamond Shoes ad, in turn, might be a commercial reworking of Winslow Homer's 1876 painting *The Watermelon Boys*. In the Diamond Shoes ad, the cherry-red lips of the black children are as typical for American advertising of the 1890s as the old,

Figure 5.11 Trademarked illustration and slogan for Cameroon cocoa by the Kakao-Company Theodor Reichardt GmbH of Halle in 1898. *Source:* WZB (1898): 807, reg. no. 32986.

Figure 5.12 Poster for Diamond Brand (Peters Shoe Company), date unknown. *Source:* Image from Douglas Congdon-Martin, *Images in Black: 150 Years of Black Collectables* (West Chester, PA: Schiffer, 1990), 60. Courtesy of Schiffer Publ. Ltd., Atglen, PA and Holt's Country Store, Grandview, MO.

rumpled clothing they wear. A comparison of the American and German versions is worthwhile; note particularly the manner in which the German version in black and white pares down the level of detail to maximize impact. The expressiveness of the faces in the American shoe ad is lost—the mischievous gleam in the boy's eye and the rather glum look of the middle girl are missing from the German version. Instead, it is the racial identifiers (prominent lips) that are retained and intensified. Reichardt's ad reflects a precise moment in German commercial imagery; in 1898, American images of race had been circulated through German commercial visuality for a decade or more on the wrappings of specific products or on show posters; yet a coherent, German vision of Africa had not yet fully emerged. German advertisers therefore mapped familiar American illustrations over onto Africa.

The Americanization of German commercial visuality and the concomitant embrace of American racial types and styles did not take place without reaction. Indeed, a rhetorical backlash against the American style of advertising began as early as 1900 from German advertising writers, and this criticism became increasingly vociferous after 1905. As we will see at the end of this book, by 1912 even self-proclaimed admirers of the United States, such as Hans Sachs, the renowned poster collector, called themselves "cured from [their] enthusiasm for America." He continued, "We all consider America to be the land of the screaming advertisement, the loud imposition, the tasteless presumption." Sachs went on to frame his criticisms of America in racial terms, misreading the work of the anthropologist Franz Boas in the process.[42] Advertising writers' attacks on America in the first decade of the twentieth century coincided with a gathering anti-Americanism in Germany more broadly.[43] Like all fashions, "America" was a fad—and certain to become tiresome—and a tempting target for all manner of social critics.

"German" Humor: Caricature and Its Commercial Counterparts

> In America, advertising is allowed to run around brazen and naked. In Germany, though, it must be draped with a good cloak. One can best weave this cloak out of art and humor.
>
> —Ernst Growald, "Amerikanische und Deutsche Reklame" (1914)

American racial types and stylistic conventions had an enormous impact on German visual culture, but other forces at the roots of the racialization of German visual culture were more homegrown. One influence that was local in its very essence, or at least appeared so, was humor. Ernst Growald, in a retrospective on German and American advertising published just before the First World War, posited a national dichotomy of commercial culture: American advertising was brazen and often naked—in other words, allowed to be as indecent as business may require. In Germany, however, advertising was adorned with art or with humor—in other words, with attributes often claimed as central to German cultural identity.

Humor is a culture-specific form of communication that creates and reinforces social bonds; it not only reflects hegemony but also constructs and enforces hegemony. For German advertisers, however, sociological definitions of humor were beside the point. Instead, humor was a practical tool—something to arouse interest, attract attention, and make connections between illustration and viewer. Humor was interesting inasmuch as it was effective. Humor attracted not only the interest of the passing public, but the attention of the business and professional world as well. Humorous ads revolving around visual puns or jokes permeated the examples reproduced in German advertising journals like *Die Reklame*. After all, editors of ad journals were concerned with increasing their own readership; what better way to do this than by reproducing ads that would make the journal itself a pleasure to peruse? The appearance of the humorous ad in the 1890s should therefore be considered in two contexts: first, to capture attention for the advertised product, but also to attract the attention of ad-journal editors in order to garner professional recognition.

For humor to be effective, of course, the viewer (or editor) had to "get" the joke. Since humor could vary significantly by locality and social class, the humor that advertisers most often deployed tended to be popular, in the strict sense of the word. Advertisers turned to the most widespread folktales and childhood tales—taken to be the most broadly familiar sort of humor—to tweak or play upon them. In choosing proverbs or folktales taken to be popular "across Germany" and then physically broadcasting those themes across Germany, advertisers fulfilled their own prophecies. Advertisers' riffs on "common" tales or "national" styles, disseminated to a truly national broader public, helped to standardize elements that had once been bounded by locale, region, or social class—just as the Brothers Grimm had done when they published their collections of

"German" fairy tales eighty years earlier.[44] In this way, advertising should be counted among the modern forces that transformed particularistic, local, and variegated folktales into coherent myths that could be played as the core components of a German national identity.[45]

An example of this process at work, and one that is particularly relevant to the imagery of race in Germany, can be found in the adage of the *Mohrenwäsche.* The German idiom *"einen Mohren weiss waschen wollen"* ("trying to wash a Moor white") is a centuries-old shorthand for attempting something fundamentally impossible. At first glance, the idiom seems to have a lengthy German pedigree; the entry for "einen Mohren waschen" in the 1922 edition of Grimm's Dictionary, for instance, cites usages by august personages such as Goethe and Kant.[46] In the nineteenth century the origin of the notion was often taken to be a biblical passage.[47] In point of fact, the homily of the futility of "washing an Ethiopian" stretches further back to Greco-Roman antiquity, first recorded in Lucian, and likely came into European Renaissance culture by way of Erasmus.[48] In German the proverb is often condensed to a single word—*Mohrenwäsche*—but the notion is not particular to Germany at all but rather a legacy of the Europe-wide humanist tradition of the sixteenth century. Similar expressions are found in English, French, Dutch, and other European languages.

The history of the visual trope of washing the Ethiopian is no less pan-European. Jean Michel Massing has sketched the trajectory of this pictorial theme from its roots in early Christian iconography and Renaissance illustration, up through sixteenth-century emblem books and engravings. The theme appeared in paintings by Rembrandt and migrated to eighteenth-century portraiture (with white women washing their black pages) and late eighteenth-century English satirical prints. It also appeared on late nineteenth-century French *Imagerie d'Epinal* (engraved prints made for a popular audience, akin to *Bilderbogen*) before finally materializing in British advertising of the 1890s. The endurance of this pictorial theme is remarkable, and certainly has a great deal to do with chains of artistic influence and cross cultural borrowings over generations. It was, in this way, not unlike the long history of the Tobacco Moor.

Yet the theme of the *Mohrenwäsche* offers a functionalism as well, for it allows artists to make intangible characteristics visible by playing upon chromatic associations. In the symbolic order of Western art, black was to dirt (or corruption, particularly bodily corruption) as white was to cleanliness (or purity, particularly spiritual purity), and this chromatic symbolism was frequently embodied in human figures.[49] Given this symbolic convention, how better to depict an abstract notion such as purity—the cleanliness of the soul—than to personify it in a figure of pristine whiteness, diligently endeavoring to scrub away the indelible stain of blackness? Not only could such color contrasts be visually striking, but the ability to figure an abstraction in visual mode was simply too useful to resist. In the late nineteenth century, the graphic artists were desperate for just such a useful embodiments of abstraction than their "high"-art predecessors of previous centuries. The theme of washing the Moor began to appear in the soap advertisements of every Western European nation after the 1880s; it appeared particularly early in Great Britain and the United States (both leaders in brand-name soap manufacture) but was used in France, the Netherlands, and even Switzerland.[50]

In 1897 *Die Reklame* devoted an entire page and three expensive intaglio illustrations to show a mechanical window display device that featured this "supremely original" theme (as the advertising journal termed it). In the mechanical display, a lead figurine of a "Moor-boy" *(Mohrenknabe)* flits in through the open window and plunges into a waiting washtub. Then the figurine of the German housewife begins to "energetically" scrub the boy (now referred to as a "Negro-child," *Negersprößling)* with soap. Finally, the Moor emerges from the tub, and the housewife stares at him in astonishment, for he stands in front of her in his "irreproachable whiteness" (as the editors termed it). Then the whole mechanical cycle begins anew, showing a successful washing of the Moor ad infinitum with the indefatigable repetition afforded by mechanization. The editors emphasized that the movement of the mechanical display occurs quite slowly, "forcing the public to wait until the whole scene has been observed." The whole device, the article concluded helpfully, was made from the finest of lithographed lead and available from a firm in Buchholz for only 25 marks: "it is recommended to any store where soap is sold."[51] Did this mechanical advertisement receive the editor's approbation because of its ingenious machinery, evocative of mechanical figures of so many German clock towers? Or from its arresting theme of the *Mohrenwäsche?* Or because the device's makers employed some connection to get into *Die Reklame*'s pages? Impossible to say. Yet the allure of the *Mohrenwäsche* theme for a cleansing commodity is obvious. It highlights the potency of the commodity by *showing* the product attaining the impossible. The modern commodity is such that tasks that were traditionally impossible are now easily accomplished. But it also calls upon an adage familiar to most everyone, and thereby seeks to establish a common visual language by playing upon a common *folk* language. Interestingly, this early deployment of the *Mohrenwäsche* was sold as a stand-alone advertising machine—and hence emerged without any connection to a specific brand name.

Curiously, German advertisers generally took up the *Mohrenwäsche* theme later than other Western nations. One of the first German firms to deploy it was Ribot. Founded as the Royal Bavarian Court Soap Factory in Schwabach in 1849 by Philipp Benjamin Ribot, the firm expanded dramatically under his son Fritz's leadership, exporting soap worldwide. As one of its expansion strategies, the firm began distributing postcard-size *Sammelbilder* with soap purchases in 1890, and many of these collectible cards illustrated the *Mohrenwäsche,* with black, cherubic children being scrubbed white.[52] Nonetheless, though British, French, and American advertising prominently featured the theme in ads by such brands as Pears, Sodex, and Gold Dust in the 1880s and early 1890s, the theme took off in Germany only after 1905.

There are many possible reasons why Germany adopted the theme of blacks and soap later than did the United States, Britain, and France, despite the transatlantic borrowing of advertising themes. One possible factor lies with Germany's relatively slower adoption of racial styles in product advertising more broadly, given the demands of the visual logic of the theme as a soap advertisement. For the premise of the *Mohrenwäsche* is about impossibility; it illustrates that which cannot be done, in order to represent an abstract concept—namely, that of futility. As an artistic theme, it "works" through an optical juxtaposition of unalterable difference—you cannot turn black into white. When advertisers played with that tradition of futility to illustrate the power of the modern commodity to accomplish that heretofore impossible task, the message of the theme itself morphed. Instead of illustrating the abstract concept of futility, the theme in a soap ad portrays a different abstract concept—that of *capability.* Yet such a shift of message immediately raises other vexing questions. The first is motive: Why would one want to wash a Moor white? (When the task is impossible, the question of motive is less pressing.) The second is more subtle, yet more troubling: If the new brand-name soap

Figure 5.13 Advertisement for soap from 1905 by Aug. Luhn & Co. GmbH of Barmen, using an early halftone technique. *Source:* WZB (1905): 1051, reg. no. 79677.

can—right before your very eyes!—turn black into white, the power of the commodity can undermine the inequality of difference—the inequality of difference upon which the theme visually depends. If the Moor *can* be washed white by the power of soap, then difference between whites and blacks can be erased with a good scrubbing. The problem here is that this erasure of difference (promised in the immediate future—the implied "after" picture of the ad) destabilizes the power dynamic between the white and black figure, which could entail undesired consequences or meanings.

This dilemma can be seen in a 1905 German advertisement for Abrador brand soap. Interestingly, the illustration is not an intaglio but uses the new halftone process. Even more interesting is the frozen tableau: the white man, with soiled hands, lunges for the soap—soap that is so powerful it has washed the blackness off the hands of the African native (Figure 5.13). The overall composition is poorly executed; for instance, the African's head is practically invisible, lost in the German's dark shirt. Yet it deploys an engaging metaphor reinforced by pictorial elements. The tableau equates dirt with blackness. This metaphorical linkage is underscored by eye-catching contrast of a white figure with black hands juxtaposed against a black figure with white hands. The upturned black mustache echoes the white, toothy smile. The larger implications of this scene might be disturbing: can the African indeed "wash himself white" with Abrador? And if so, would the status between the two figures then be equalized? The scene seems to speak to this, for the black figure holds the soap—controlling access, if you will—while the white figure's eyes bulge with fear. (The eye-widening fear also makes a visual correspondence between the supposedly naturally bulging eyes of the black figure.) From a larger view, then, the advertisement as a whole sets up uncomfortable resonances. Will the white figure succumb to the blackness crawling up his arms? Will the grinning black figure—dangling his soap tauntingly before the desperate white—decide *not* to "share" it? Could the next scene actually show the two figures have reversed places—the white turned black, corrupted, the black become white, purified? The comfortable visual tradition of the *Möhrenwasche* theme from the Renaissance—a white, patiently scrubbing away at a docile Moor—is shattered.

German soap advertisers turned to a variety of tricks to attempt to escape the disorientation that the visual logic of the theme could engender. The Melsbach firm's ad for laundry soap, likely for its Sahara brand, humorously inverts the normal telling of the tale (Figure 5.14). Instead of a white launderer attempting to wash a Moor white, the whitewashing in this ad is inadvertent: the black mother, drawn in the fashion of an American mammy figure, is aghast that her son has jumped into the washtub, as the powerful laundry soap whitens her black child. Because of the "accidental" nature of the scene, vexing questions of motive do not arise. No one wanted to wash the black child white—it happened by mistake. The power of the Melsbach firm's product just happened to be demonstrated, by mistake. The ad thereby sets up a very different humorous reaction: the black mother is not pleased at the new whiteness of her child, but just as horrified at her child's transformation as any white mother would be were the reverse to have occurred.

As British, French, and American advertisers had hit upon a decade earlier, there was an easier resolution to this thorny dilemma of confusing visual logic: namely, to present racial differentiation as something that remains regardless of black skin tone.[53] Graphic racial differentiation could evade questions about intention or disturbed hierarchy by moving

Figure 5.14 Advertisement for laundry soap from 1905 by W & H Meslbach, Crefeld. *Source:* WZB (1905): 1047, reg. no. 79421.

the core concept back to one of futility: racial differentiation through physiognomy and other bodily markers visually confirms the impossibility of any *true* metamorphosis, even if skin color were to be changed by the commodity. In a 1910 advertisement from the S. Mohr soap company (see Plate 24, discussed in Chapter 6), it is clear that no amount of whitening can transform the race of the black native, because other markers—enormous lips, immaturity, nakedness, distorted skull or leg shapes—reassure the viewer that race goes deeper than skin tone. The designer can then play with the idea that blackness washes off because the subversive potential of the advertisement has been neatly eliminated. The moral of the story returns to one of futility, even while the power of the soap is demonstrated *ad oculus*.

It is impossible to ascertain how deeply the tale of the *Mohrenwäsche* was embedded in the fabric of German popular culture before the era of mass culture, and before the decade in which it was widely deployed to sell soap. One thing we can be certain of, however, is that advertising's visual presentation of washing the Moor directed its appeal at a new, nationwide audience. The *Mohrenwäsche* was not a story particular to Bavarians or to the bourgeoisie; it was a visual tale for a new social category—every German who purchased soap. As we will see in the next chapter, by 1910 the association between blackness and soap had become so entrenched in German consumer visuality that advertisers continued to play with the notion long after more direct references to washing the Moor had faded into the realm of passé. The traditional, popular audience, familiar with the fable of the *Mohrenwäsche,* had been replaced by a new German viewer—a purchaser who saw for himself that soap was a requisite product for whiteness.

Victor Mataja, the first German theorist of advertising, mused in his 1910 work *Die Reklame* that grotesque imagery or humorous twists are forms of "sensational advertising" that seize the attention of the public and thereby attain sensational efficacy.[54] Mataja's alignment of "grotesque" with "humorous" is no coincidence. What exactly did he mean by the word "grotesque"? The art-historical sense of the term is perhaps most apt: the grotesque refers to a carnivalesque configuration of the bizarre, the ridiculous, the excessive, and the unreal, in a way meant to induce both empathy and disgust. The popular printed form of the grotesque in the nineteenth century was caricature.

Caricature has been defined as the "grotesque or ludicrous representation of persons or things by exaggeration of their most characteristic or striking feature."[55] Caricature is as old as drawing itself, although the form, execution, and meaning of caricature has changed markedly over the centuries. Nineteenth-century caricature traces its intellectual roots back to the work of the physiognomists, who looked for a direct correspondence between inner nature and outer appearance.[56] As a form of visual communication, however, caricature was inherently populist; its entire rationale was for its visual codes to be easily and widely understood.[57] Caricature became one of the earliest mass-oriented visual forms in Germany, for it offered easily decipherable meanings, which appealed to an audience of the widest possible range, from the distracted commuter to the barely literate, from the consummate appreciator of biting political satire to the enthused child.[58]

Caricature may have taken off in France in the 1840s with the work of such lithographic artists as Honoré Daumier, but by the 1870s Germany had moved to the forefront.[59] As early as midcentury, magazines such as *Fliegende Blätter* (appearing in 1844) and *Kladderadatsch* (1848) emerged, purveying broadsheets of satirical prose accompanied by humorous caricatured illustrations to large audiences. The circulation of *Kladderadatsch* was in the vicinity of 20,000 in 1852, which was a huge number by the standards of the day.[60] By the turn of the twentieth century, satirical magazines such as *Simplicissimus* (1896) and *Jugend* (1896) grew to circulations five times that, and they were dominated by caricature illustrations. Satirical magazines of caricature could be found in every nation (see *Punch* or *Le Charivari*) but only in Germany was caricature elevated to the level of national culture. Indeed, *Jugend* became so influential as to become the eponym for the German inflection of Art Nouveau.

The work of Wilhelm Busch (1832–1908) had a great deal to do with the early success of caricature in Germany. Busch was an accomplished essayist, poet, and artist (who studied at Düsseldorf); after 1859 he published for the satirical journals *Fliegende Blätter* and *Münchner Bilderbogen* and, after 1867, in the more staid forerunners of the mass media, such as the illustrated family journal *Over Land and Sea*.[61] But it was Busch's so-called picture tales from the 1870s that spread his renown throughout Germany and then Europe, and ultimately cemented his status as the father of the modern comic strip. In the process, he established caricature as a legitimate form of expression in its own right; Busch always insisted that his work was more for adults than for children. Among his illustrated stories, Busch's most famous are of the naughty children Max and Moritz. Yet while Max and Moritz were crafted in 1865, it was not until a full twenty years later that Busch gained a truly mass audience. Busch's original cartoons (for Caspar Braun's *Fliegende Blätter*) were hampered by their poor reproduction; the engravers were not skilled enough to carve the woodblock against the grain. Only in the late 1870s could Busch's drawings be transferred photomechanically onto the wooden block, where skilled engravers could render it more closely to his originals.[62] The first mass-produced *Wilhelm-Busch-Album* appeared only in 1885, and it sold hundreds of thousands of copies. Editions of Busch compendium reprints continue to appear with unceasing regularity down to the present day.

One of Busch's extraordinarily popular tales offers an insightful glimpse into the consonance and dissonance of caricature with the workings of visual racialization. This is "Fipps der Affe" (1879), a story of a clever and malicious monkey who terrorizes local African natives until he is captured and brought to Bremen. In the Hansa city, he alternately tries to fit in with the German burghers and wreaks havoc upon them. Ultimately, they kill him. One reading of "Fipps the Monkey" (as the tale would come to be known in English) is anticolonial: Fipps thrived in Africa, and it is only after being dragged out of his habitat, for the entertainment of Germans, that chaos erupts. Since much of that chaos comes from the monkey's attempts to imitate the German lifestyle, it is poignant when he is killed by the enraged burghers for reverting to his true nature. It contains an implicit indictment of colonialism's "civilizing mission," appearing the very same year as Friedrich Fabri's influential *Does Germany Need Colonies?* which called upon Germans to embrace colonization as a cultural mission and national destiny.

The illustrations of the African native from the earliest part of the story are of particular interest here (Figure 5.15). In Busch's 1879 drawing we can see the emphasis on physical features of racial differentiation that would permeate German advertising thirty-five years later. The black African figure, clothed only in a loincloth in other scenes, is drawn with oversized lips. (In Busch's original oil paint/sketch, the lips are further emphasized by being colored red.) Busch's native African wears a giant nose ring; indeed, the nose ring is the instrument of the native's undoing at Fipps's cruelly ingenious hands. And in Busch's story line the African possesses a charming simplicity and bumbling naïveté that corresponds with colonialist discourses about childlike natives.[63] Indeed, colonialists sometimes appropriated Busch for their own purposes; when H. F. von Behr published his memoir *Scenes of War from the Arab Uprising in German East Africa* in 1891, he quoted Wilhelm Busch when describing the Africans' resistance to wearing clothing.[64]

There is more to the story, however. As befits a talented artist who was also a talented writer, the textual elements of his story line are crafted as a counterpoint to the pictorial elements. Indeed, despite the caricatured features, Busch's prose seems at pains to point out the parallels, rather than the distinctions, between Africans and Europeans—whether in their self-satisfied sense of their own worth or in their love of adornment. One could claim, therefore, that while the images establish difference through the exaggeration of caricature, the text forges connections through empathic connections. This tension between difference and similarity, caricature and empathy, is provocative and is the crux of Busch's artistry, placing it in the realm of the best satire. It sketches the simplistic codes of mid-nineteenth-century colonialist notions (including those of the

Es wohnte da ein schwarzer Mann,

Der Affen fing und briet sie dann.

Besonders hat er junge gern,
Viel lieber als die ältern Herrn.
„Ein alter Herr ist immer zäh!“
So spricht er oft und macht „Bebä!“

Um seine Zwecke zu erfüllen,
Wählt er drei leere Kürbishüllen.

Für auf den Kopf die große eine,
Für an die Hände noch zwei kleine.

Figure 5.15 Excerpt from Wilhelm Busch, *Fipps, der Affe,* from 1879. *Source:* Wilhelm Busch, *Fipps, der Affe* (Munich: Fr. Bassermann, 1879), 4.

physiognomists) in a way that simultaneously takes a playful jab at them.[65] "Fipps the Monkey" is both a mischievous and touching tale, with lessons that undermine the facile cultural narcissism of "civilizing mission" ideology.

The imitators and plagiarizers who capitalized on Busch's popularity, however, were less concerned with humanist subtlety, narrative tension, or satirically pointed excess. It was Busch's commercial success, rather than his creative genius, that attracted attention. Busch's work was shamelessly copied and reproduced in Germany and throughout Europe; it even crossed the Atlantic to the United States. Indeed, a whole array of cheap magazines built their circulations around plagiarizing Busch's illustrations. The New York penny magazine *Puck,* for instance, published "Fipps the Monkey" in 1881 as its own creation; the illustrations were copied verbatim but the text was reworked to appeal to American audiences, and its sophistication was scaled back to appeal to the "juvenile masses." Recastings of the text around the imagery also occurred in England and France.[66]

In Germany a similar process of simplification can be seen in the 1880s. Busch's picture stories were first reproduced and widely sold as illustrated broadsheets for wall decoration. They offered a dramatic change from the usual, more sober religious or militarist themes. Firms such as Gustav Kuhn printed satirical broadsheets on a range of topical issues, including some in the late 1880s on the new German colonies.[67] The success of these caricature broadsheets led to a boom in the market for illustrated children's books in the 1880s, and scholars have noted how the treatment of Africans in such mass-produced books became harsher as Africans became adversaries in tales of exploration and colonial adventure or objects of childish mischief.[68] In 1885, for instance, F. H. Benary published the enduring story of the "Ten Little Niggers" *(Zehn kleine Negerlein)* where small black children from Cameroon one by one meet a grim fate. As it turns out, Benary blatantly pirated the children's poem from a wildly successful 1868 American minstrel show song. (That same minstrel show song, in turn, also inspired the "Ten Little Indians" nursery rhyme later popular in the United States.) In 1885 Germany the colonial empire was brand new, and Benary seized the opportunity to graft the popularity of American minstrelsy onto German colonialism. He had the artist Christian Wilhelm Allers draw up exaggerated caricatures of the ten little black African children meeting their gruesome fates and published it under the title that translates as *Out of Cameroon: A Picture-Book for Children, Little and Big.*[69] Caricature thus was one bridge between transgressive minstrelsy and colonialist child's play. More broadly, caricature thus came to be marketed to multiple audiences, from sophisticated readers of the educated middle classes to marginally literate groups, such as children. The flexibility of caricature was such that it could appeal broadly; as the audiences broadened, however, the sophistication often receded, as we see with Benary's cruelly humorous constructions.

By 1905 the illustrated satirical magazines, such as *Simplicissimus, Der Wahre Jakob,* and *Jugend,* boasted of circulations of up to 100,000.[70] Such popularity stemmed partially from caricatured satire as a readily grasped cultural form. Yet also had to do with new business practices, for these magazines were at the vanguard of the mass media in drawing most of their revenue from advertising, which lowered the cover price to within reach of a broader reading public. The new dominance of the satirical magazines, therefore, stemmed from a multifaceted modus operandi: provocative critique, popular appeal, and modern business model. Humor magazines such as *Simplicissimus* in turn served to stimulate the practice of advertising itself, for the magazines offered forums for novel strategies and provocative experiments unfit for more restrained publications, such as the family journals.[71] In the 1890s a great many graphic artists cut their teeth as caricaturists for these satirical magazines before going on to make their careers in advertising. Julius Klinger, whose glowering ad for Palm cigars opened the introduction of this book, was one of these; he worked for Munich's *Meggendorfer Blätter* in 1896 and also contributed to *Jugend.* After moving to Berlin in 1897, he drew for such magazines as *Das kleine Witzblatt* and the *Lustige Blätter;* only then did he join Hollerbaum & Schmidt, the premier poster-design firm in Germany.[72] Thomas Theodor Heine was another caricaturist-turned-advertiser. He was the artistic force behind *Simplicissimus,* but he also crafted advertisements for such firms as Otto Ring and Brakls.[73] These artists moved freely between political satire and advertising, and they brought their stylistic tools of caricature with them. Many advertisements after 1900 drew their caricatures of Africans from satirical broadsheets and children's books alike.[74]

One of the hallmarks of caricature as a mode of mass communication is the exaggeration of a single feature—the feature best suited to capture the "essence" of the person or the type. The exaggeration of specific features, however, can often hold subtle ramifications. A trademark from 1902 by a company that produced gardening tools offers a good case in point (Figure 5.16). The advertiser is led to adopt a humorous motif based on the name of the firm: Mohrenweiser, literally "Moor-white." The advertiser explores the apparent oxymoron of the name by means of visual dichotomy: we thus get a Janus-faced depiction in which the white element is represented by a German shopkeeper, parodied by an enormous

Figure 5.16 Trademark from 1902 by the Chrn. Mohrenweiser firm of Altenweddingen. The company sells gardening tools and seed. The name of the firm—"Moor-White"—is the inspiration for the use of a black/white figure in the graphic. *Source:* WZB (1902): 249, reg. no. 53287.

mustache, juxtaposed against a Moor—a black in livery, with collar and epaulettes, and parodied by oversize lips. The humor so graphically illustrated, however, involves more than just a pun on the name of the firm; it also plays upon the physiognomists' sense that a single feature can represent fundamental essences—in this illustration, the German *is* to his mustache, as the African *is* to his lips. Since a mustache is a manifestation of culture, grown and shaped according to the dictates of fashion, but facial features are an immutable fact of nature, this advertisement for garden tools also offers a graphic vision of the culture/nature divide common to German colonial discourse.

Mass marketers did not miss the opportunity to capitalize on the popularity of caricature. The earliest advertising writers, such as Rudolf Cronau in 1887, praised the use of humor: "It's been proven that the public more quickly forgives an advertisement that bears the stamp of humorous overstatement than one of an upright earnestness of dissembling transparent lies."[75] Cronau then reproduced a starch advertisement for Hoffmann & Schmidt, featuring a preening African family, strutting through the palm trees in gleaming white starched cufflinks and ruffles, with

Figure 5.17 Advertisement for Syndetikon glue from 1895. "Otto Ring's Syndetikon adheres, glues, cements everything!" "Available everywhere." *Source: Die Reklame* 5, no. 19 (1895): 335.

canes—and bare feet. The clothing and postures of the Africans came from the minstrel show; the graphic style came straight out of the broadsheets.[76] Later, *Die Reklame* specifically praised the use of caricature for poster advertising, likening it to medieval heraldry for its "instant legibility."[77]

In fact, many early German advertisements drew their inspiration from the Wilhelm-Busch style of caricature, even if they lacked any hint of Busch's empathic subtlety. In an ad for Syndetikon glue, where a lion has its tail affixed to a palm tree by a mischievous black native (Figure 5.17), the native is barely visible but the overall shape of the body is substantially distorted; the oversized head, lack of neck, curving arms, and stance lend the figure a monkeylike appearance. This African native seems to be a cognate of Fipps; the humanlike monkey in a children's tale has been replaced by an apelike African in an advertisement. The Syndetikon ad was reproduced in the section "How One Advertises in Germany" in the 1895 issue of *Die Reklame.* The accompanying commentary assured readers that the ad was "humorous" and "fittingly aimed at the incredibly popular

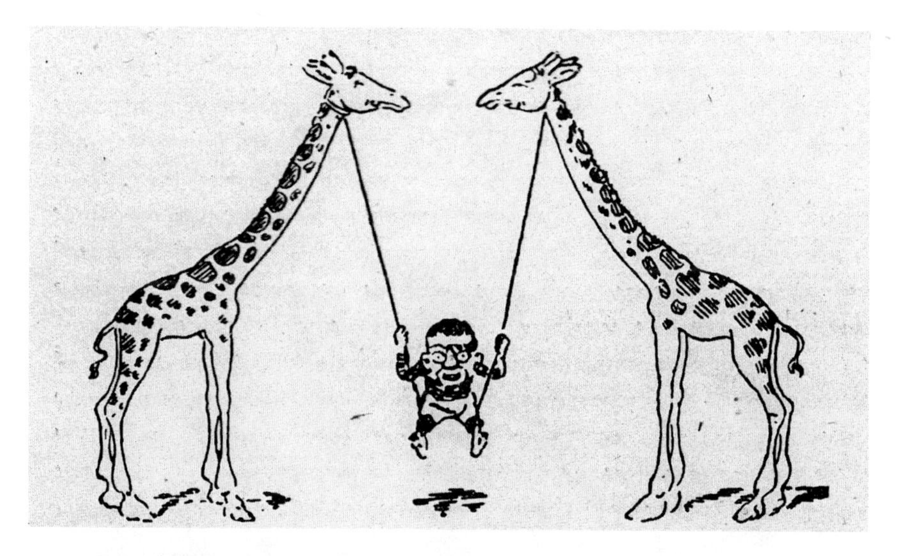

Figure 5.18 Trademark by import/export firm of Siemssen & Co. (Hamburg) in 1900. *Source:* WZB (1900): 1005, reg. no. 45910.

field of the most modern African culture. . . . The lion, whose tail has been firmly glued to the tree to the great amusement of a few Kaffer, will certainly delight and make a lasting impression."[78] The firm of Otto Ring had been far more traditional in its advertisements just a few years earlier; an advertising poster for the Syndetikon from around 1890, for instance, featured ornate script in a traditional style and included a vignette of a bourgeois father using the glue to repair various objects brought to him by his doting wife and children. In another famous Otto Ring poster from 1899, designed by Fernand Schultz-Wettel and often considered a masterpiece of *Jugendstil,* a beautiful female seraph glues broken hearts back together with the powerful paste. Next to these sentimental ads of bourgeois domesticity and aestheticized gendered romance, the "humorous" and "fitting" illustration of an African's prank seems more than a little mean-spirited. But perhaps that was exactly the point.

In a trademark from 1900 by an import/export firm in Hamburg, in which a caricatured black boy swings between the necks of two giraffes (Figure 5.18), the humor of the improbable scene is graphically underscored through two devices of caricature: the first is the closed-eyed grimaces of the giraffes (which perhaps evokes the facial expressions of harried but

Figure 5.19 Trademark for Mammoth Mark iron fastenings, Robert Zinn & Co., Barmen-Rittershausen. *Source:* WZB (1900): 941, reg. no. 46083.

happy parents); the second is the over-the-top racialization of the black figure, pop-eyed and with huge lips and gaping mouth.

Another early example, far more unkind, is an advertisement for Mammoth brand steel fasteners from 1900 that emphasizes the massive strength of the product by depicting a hapless elephant trying to pull the fastener from its moorings—and ripping off its own trunk instead (Figure 5.19)! The effect tends toward the cruel or the gruesome, yet the "fun" in the composition is preserved by graphic caricature techniques. The first such element is the wide astonishment evident in the eyes of the elephant, and the second is the improbable contortion of the elephant's body; together they convey an exaggerated sense of surprise that partially mitigates the shock of seeing blood spurting from the ruptured trunk. Finally, the tiny, equally caricatured African, with clawlike hands and extremely exaggerated features, spasms in evident sympathetic horror, further accentuating the humor of the tableau. This ad featured prominently in a compendium of *Trademark Humor,* a book of the "best" humorous advertisements and logos compiled and published in 1916 by a government clerk from the Imperial Patent Office.[79]

In each of these examples—Janus-faced puns, super-glued tiger tails, bug-eyed swingers, or sundering elephant trunks—the grotesque style and oftentimes gruesome overstatement of the great caricaturists are faithfully adopted. Yet they are also adapted. The graphic techniques are imitated without the corresponding sympathy or in some cases profound insight afforded by the suffering that is narrated by the cartoonists' or satirists' text. Instead of satirizing, these images sell.

As caricature moved from the realm of nascent mass communication in the 1870s into the realm of nascent mass consumption around 1900, the meanings conveyed by the style itself were fundamentally transformed. When the graphic stylistic techniques of caricature were reproduced en masse in German consumer visuality, the "codes" to interpret them may also have been transferred, but the larger context of the communication behind the codes changed. Caricature was no longer sold and consumed for its own sake—as an entertaining yet provocative carnival of absurd exaggeration. Instead, the commercialized caricature that emerged in advertising at the fin de siècle used those codes to confirm and correlate viewers' judgments and prejudices, all in the effort to sell more products. Its critical edge was lost. This shift from critique to confirmation may be subtle, but the distinction lies at the heart of the difference between exaggerated communicative code and stereotype.

Conclusion

German visual culture of the nineteenth century offered a mélange of early styles of racial otherness mapped onto the form of black figures. The three wellsprings of racial imagery discussed in this chapter—the entertainment of minstrelsy, the transatlantic traffic in American commodity-racism, and the popularization and Germanization of caricature—were the most central to later developments in German commercial visuality. Each dovetailed with a different facet of emerging commodity culture: entertainment, circulation, popularization.

American minstrelsy offered a form of entertainment that enticingly blended romanticized foreignness with transgressive comedic ribaldry. German advertisers of the 1890s, in the same way they had drawn from the sensationalism of *Völkerschau* imagery, drew from the images of minstrelsy, attempting to tap into its entertainment value. From Reithoffer's tires to Kummer's cake mix, German firms large and small mimicked the pantomime visual style from minstrel-show posters, transferring it onto product packaging. Whether the visual trope of minstrelsy, and the ads that later played upon this trope, was recognized as the exaggeration of theater is an open question. To an even greater degree than with the *Völkerschauen,* the vast majority of the Germans never saw such a show; they encountered only its visuality by means of planographic reproduction. Friedländer's minstrel posters, side by side with their *Völkerschau* posters, may well have appeared as nothing more than an ethnographic show of American blacks. More importantly, the spread of the racial techniques of American minstrelsy into *every* other visual field of German commercial culture—visual fields that had nothing to do with America or entertainment whatsoever—is highly illustrative of the power of mass reproduction. It is not that many Germans did not "get" the joke of minstrelsy. It is more that, by 1910, there were simply no other images of blacks available in Germany against which one might compare, and thereby see that minstrelsy even *was* a joke.

Minstrelsy was not the only American vision of blackness that found purchase in Germany. The tendrils of transatlantic commerce circulated many others, in a piecemeal process that began in earnest in the mid-1890s. Over the last decade of the nineteenth century, American black types like the minstrel, the shoe-shine boy, the Uncle Tom, the dandy, and the pickaninny were adopted to lend an air of Americanness to new products appearing for the first time on the German market, such as toothpaste or bicycle tires. Such imagery was as important for its certification of Americanness as for its presentation of blackness, because American meant modern, and modern meant desirable, to designer and purchaser alike. Embedded in these American racial types, however, were American stylistic conventions of racial difference. Thus, in the German advertising of the 1890s, the physical features of black figures were first exaggerated in association with the most modern products, whether fountain pens or bicycle tires.

The expansion of racial motifs into other product categories, such as toothpaste, speaks to the reception of such racial imagery. Certain advertisements, such as that for Seeger's toothpaste, simply make no sense without the larger visual context of other images of blacks and Africans circulating in public; to be understandable, other images *had* to have been seen.

This does not mean that such images were static. German advertisers and graphic artists ultimately reworked these adopted American types and styles. American visions of racial hierarchy would remain popular in German advertising up through the Weimar Republic, and would even provide an attractive theme on which the new German masters of graphic design, such as Ludwig Hohlwein, could whet their artistic teeth. Yet as we will see in the next chapter, German designers also translated such types into illustrations that spoke more directly to them—and to their role as colonizers of Africa. In the process, German advertisers forged some of the most visually striking imagery of colonial power to emerge out of Europe.

A third font of racialization, one more explicitly German, or at least perceived to be such, was humor in the pictorial form of caricature. The pictorial exaggerations of German caricature initially came from the inkwells of artist-writers and satirists in the 1850s through the 1880s. In the new mass market of the 1890s, caricature's visual character expanded the appeal of satire beyond urban sophisticates to a truly mass audience. It was, in the process, adopted by advertisers. In advertising, caricature could be seen as a "German" counterweight to the perceptions of and unease with Americanization. When advertisers adopted these stylistic tools of caricature, however, they profoundly transformed the nature of the communication. The satirist's caricature captures a trait (or alleged trait) by comic visual exaggeration and deploys it to mock otherwise untouchable subjects. The marketer's caricature, however, engages audiences by reification rather than provocation. It is aimed not to satirize, but to sell. In this way, commercialized caricature was shorn of its critical edge.

These examples demonstrate three roots of racialization as a pictorial style in Germany. There are others, too, of course. It would take a political event, however—an event of extreme violence—to provide an impetus for the adoption of racialization across all imagery in the consumer imaginary. That event was war. The uprisings of colonial subjects, first in German South-West Africa in 1904, and then in German East Africa in 1905, were suppressed with extreme brutality—a brutality that, in the case of South-West Africa, was genocidal. The violence of these colonial wars was refracted and reflected in German consumer culture as well, with unsettling consequences for long-term German national identity. Shortly after the bloody suppression of the Maji Maji uprising of 1905, the

East-African News insisted that the indigenous Africans "are and will remain forever at a lower cultural level. And whoever among them rises up, wanting to achieve the level of Europeans, will become instead only a caricature."[80] As a description of German *perceptions* of Africans, the newspaper was speaking the literal truth.

6

RACIAL IMPERIUM

> The portrayal must be so graphic that the meaning forces itself upon the spectator, to lastingly imprint itself.
>
> —Ernst Growald, advertiser, 1904

By the fin de siècle, imagery that explicitly demarcated racial difference had begun to circulate through Germany. As we saw in the previous chapter, much of the racial imagery circulating in the commercial realm was imported from "modern" America, whether on posters for minstrel shows or on tins for American products, such as shoe polish. A very different font of racial imagery, meanwhile, was more homegrown. The "German" humor of caricature and pictorial exaggeration in satirical magazines and children's picture books also moved into commercial imagery, perhaps as a specifically German counterpoint (or even antidote) to perceived Americanization. The early business pioneers of the 1890s, such as Ribot and Odol, turned to newly rediscovered humorous folk anecdotes and fables as they searched for arresting ways to display the power of their cleansing commodities. By and large, however, the pictorial dissemination of racial difference in commercial imagery before 1900 remained particular to certain types of product packaging (such as that for American-style shoe polish) or very specific media contexts (such as caricature magazines or satirical broadsheets).

In 1910 the Düsseldorf firm Heinemann & Co. trademarked an image for laundry soap (Figure 6.1). This particular version was bereft of

Figure 6.1 Advertisement for Heinemann's laundry soap from 1910. *Source:* WZB (1910): 1626, reg. no. 133159.

text—as we will see below, a later version would add a slogan—but text was not needed, because by the early twentieth century, commercial imagery was increasingly crafted to be understandable on a purely visual plane. The central "joke" here, of course, revolves around the scanty beaded loincloths of the two cute African children. Their skimpy vestments are a travesty of real clothing. These Africans, with but a few strings of beads over their otherwise naked bodies, clearly have no real *need* for laundry soap. (This advertisement would be particularly striking on a typical ad page, where it would be juxtaposed against department store ads, for instance, with illustrations of women modeling the latest fashions in hats, gloves, or overcoats.) Their nakedness is covered by a conveniently placed fence—a fence oddly out of place in their supposed African environment. With their wide eyes looking at you, the viewer, the figures seem to be making direct communicative contact. Using eye contact as a means to capture attention was just on the verge of becoming a new and pervasive advertising technique.[1] And in this communicative exchange, one of the children points to the clothing behind them with eagerness and pride. It is as if these childish figures are keen to show off their own laundry, to prove to you that they, too, can be civilized. The second level of the "joke" here, then, is that they clearly cannot. This whole ritual of bodily cleanliness—a ritual that only over the last decades had become increasingly central to European identity through advertising—is ultimately one that they can only mimic, at best. No amount of laundry soap will raise their social status to the level of Western civilization, and no amount of earnest pride will make them truly equals.

How do we *see* this in the ad? Through differentiation, using markers of race; the graphic artist emphasizes their lips by whitening them—a technique common to minstrel imagery, as we saw in the last chapter—oversizes their ears and their eye sockets, enlarges their heads (notice that the tips of their ears are almost as far apart as their shoulders), and highlights their faces with a "shine" to emphasize their black skin. Their figuration as children, furthermore, not only makes the figures arrestingly cute, but also underlines the fact that they are too immature to recognize their savage state, or understand their social and racial inferiority.

Finally, this illustration also works from a third, more subtle level of humor. In linking black figures to soap (even laundry soap), it draws on the centuries-old adage of the *Mohrenwäsche*—that Aesopian fable about the futility of washing the Moor white, which, as we have seen, was refracted through European painting and engraving for centuries before being popularized through mass-circulated soap advertising in the 1890s. When face to face with the Heinemann firm's startling image of otherness, the familiarity of the tale of the *Mohrenwäsche* might provide a German viewer with a comforting cultural referent that seemingly traces back to the distant German past.[2]

But how German was this Heinemann ad? As we have already seen, British companies had advertised soap using visions of civilization, of colonialism, and of race for almost two decades, going back to the late 1880s.[3] And indeed, it turns out that Heinemann's ad is a direct theft from British commercial culture: the image is stolen from a 1906 ad for the British market for Sunlight soap (Figure 6.2). "We wash *all* our clothes with Sunligt Soap," the two native children boast to their British audience (with the brand name endearingly misspelled). In fact, Sunlight was a direct competitor of Heinemann's. It was one of several brands marketed by the international soap-manufacturing powerhouse, the Lever company, which was

Figure 6.2 Advertisement for Sunlight soap (Great Britain). Note the misspelling. *Source: The Graphic* (3 March 1906).

one of the first multinational corporations and did a great deal of business in Germany. (In Gemany, Lever's Sunlight brand was cleverly renamed "Sunlicht," with a small, stylized uptick on the bottom of the capital *C* to Germanize the name while still capitalizing on the cachet of the British brand.)

Though the Lever company was multinational, it did not simply shift its colonialist, race-laden advertising from Britain over to the markets of other nations. In fact, Lever quite deliberately directed its advertising to

Figure 6.3 Advertising poster for Sunlicht soap (Germany), 1905, by H. Eichrodt, reproduced as a paradigm in an advertising trade journal. *Source:* Curt Busch, *Von der Reklame des Kaufmanns* ((Hamburg: Lüdeking, 1909).

what was seen as appropriate to each specific national market. For Sunlight ads in the American market, for instance, Lever ratcheted up the racism; it used a black mammy figure with enormous red lips to drawl out the slogan "I'se middlin' proud!" as she gazes over her white laundry.[4] For the German market at the fin de siècle, however, Lever dialed it down (Figure 6.3). The company utilized more traditional staples of early German commercial

Figure 6.4 Advertisement for laundry soap, 1910, by C. A. Heinemann & Co., Düsseldorf. *Source:* WZB (1910): 2218, reg. no. 135996.

visuality, from angelic white children to stern-looking white maternal figures.

The visual tale of Heinemann's soap does not end with this trans-channel theft. Only a few months later in 1910, the Heinemann firm trademarked a second image (Figure 6.4), which was clearly a reworking of the one initially pirated from Lever. The first was likely a trademark placeholder, to beat Lever to the punch—or more precisely, to the patent clerk. In the new scene, drawn by Heinemann's graphic artists explicitly for the German market, *four* black childlike figures are doing their laundry (such as it is) with Heinemann's laundry soap. This later version incorporated a slogan, with a subtle change from the

Lever firm's original. "We wash *all* of our clothes . . ." became "*Even we* wash 'all' of our clothes . . . !" The change in word emphasis is important. The British text draws attention to the difference in clothing, The German slogan draws attention to the difference of the Africans themselves.

In this reworking by Heinemann, the "humor" of the joke is hammered home by a significantly greater distortion of the black figures' physiognomy. This distortion is particularly stark for the faces of the two added figures on either side—a distortion so extreme that they are not even necessarily recognizable as human. Their massively oversized ears are half as large as their heads. The lips of the facing figures are exaggerated even more than the original pair. Their eye sockets are darker and even more cavernous, to better emphasize their wide, round eyes, and the leftmost added figure's profile is distorted so completely as to resemble a mask. The eyes of the two original figures, meanwhile, are redrawn to pop out crazily—an alteration that ruins the direct-eye-contact effect. All of the figures are drawn with further distorted bodies; the figures have been moved up to sit atop the fence (though with legs modestly crossed) so that the artists can show how their bellies are swollen, their legs are spindly, and their feet are bare.

The larger visual arc of this laundry-soap imagery is quite revealing. In 1900 the commercially savvy Lever Brothers deployed a conventional, gendered vision of whiteness to advertise in Germany. A decade later Heinemann stole Lever's imagery of racialized blackness that had been designed for the British market, transported it to Germany, and then further exaggerated the racial elements. Clearly something significant took place in Germany in the first decade of the twentieth century. This chapter will explore that transformation by looking at three elements, each coming from different directions, but all tightly interlaced. The first involves a new dynamic in the commercialization of politics, when this commercialization is faced with the new magnitude of visual advertising. The second stems from the "optics" of the commodity fetish where "power" came to be visually conveyed in unmistakable ways. The third involves the means by which a visual hegemony emerged—a pervasive way of depicting, and therefore of seeing. Together these elements transformed the way Germans literally saw Africans.

Selling Genocide

A dramatic surge in the prevalence of racialized advertising in Germany can be seen over the first decade of the twentieth century. Behind it looms the first act of genocide in the history of the new German nation. In 1904 the Herero, one of the largest socioethnic groups in South-West Africa, took up arms against the growing impositions of German colonial rule, and the German high command assembled a large army to crush the rebellion. In the German metropole the Herero War galvanized public opinion; this was, after all, the first major war since the founding of the Reich in 1870. Some scholars have pointed to a broad-based escalation of racist rhetoric and racism in German culture as a result of the Herero War.[5] Others have argued that older discourses of race and colonialism structured the terms around which the conflict was discussed and debated.[6] Both are true. In newspapers and in the halls of the Reichstag, wartime nationalist rhetoric lamented the slaughter of German innocents and excoriated the Herero as barbarous savages. At the same time, even the opponents of the war, the Social Democrats, drew upon the use of racial stereotypes, particularly that of the helpless, childlike native, to make their antiwar arguments.

The visual representation of the uprising, however, was more complicated. On the one hand, some visions of the uprising (as opposed to textual and rhetorical invocations of race in newspapers and parliamentary debates) were not merely illustrative devices but broadcast and sold as commodities in and of themselves. On the other hand, advertisers—by then one of the most significant purveyors of imagery—had very different concerns and constraints: they needed to pique interest, to stimulate sensation, to *show*—but at the same time, to make positive associations, to endear, to charm. These competing imperatives of commercial imagery are important to keep in mind, for as we will see below, the tension between them is crucial to understanding the connection between the politics of genocide and the escalation of racial differentiation—a relationship that is in many ways counterintuitive.

In January 1904, after the rapid and unrelenting expansion of German settlers at the expense of the indigenous population, the Herero rose in revolt against the Germans under the leadership of Samuel Maharero.[7] In the first stages of the war more than 100 German male settlers were killed; German women and children, non-Germans (Boers and English), and missionaries were all deliberately spared.[8] In the following months, a German expeditionary force was amassed, ultimately reaching 19,000 soldiers. The execution of the war eventually came under the command of General Lothar von Trotha, who had built his military career leading ruthless campaigns of reprisal in East Africa and China. In August the German expeditionary force decisively defeated the Herero at Waterberg, but the planned elimination of the Herero failed when many Herero broke through the encirclement and fled into the Omaheke desert. Trotha's forces pursued and secured the watering holes, from which they engaged in sorties against the dispersed and demoralized Herero survivors. Two months later Trotha issued his infamous declaration: "inside German territory every Herero tribesman, armed or unarmed, with or without cattle, will be shot. No women and children will be allowed into the territory; they will be driven back to their people or fired upon." Even though Berlin officially rescinded this policy of extermination several months later, Trotha continued to pursue it until he was physically recalled the following year. By war's end only perhaps 20,000 of an original population of anywhere from 40,000 to 80,000 Herero had survived.[9] Most of the survivors were confined in forced-labor camps for another decade, where as many as half died of starvation and disease. With up to 65,000 Herero killed, it was, by most senses of the word, a genocide.[10]

Back in Germany, criticism and even dismay erupted over the handling of the war. In the Reichstag, critics of the war and of its conduct used debates over the colonial budget to increasingly attack government policy. Even a number of colonial enthusiasts voiced their dismay, publicly fretting over the need to preserve the indigenous labor force that was so pivotal to the colonial economy in South-West Africa. For many others in Germany, however, colonial warfare was increasingly framed as race war. Count Alfred von Schlieffen of the German General Staff defended Trotha's policy: "After what has happened, the co-existence of whites and blacks will be very difficult, unless the blacks are kept in a state of forced labor, indeed in a kind of slavery. Racial war, once it has broken out, can only be ended by the destruction of one of the parties."[11] Trotha, Schlieffen, the General Staff, and countless others clearly viewed the war not as a police action against a military opponent but as a comprehensive strategy against a threat to social and racial order.[12] In German South-West Africa, the implementation of this racial war was restrained only by the demands of German settlers to preserve "their" native labor forces.

This was not the last of Germany's colonial wars. Just after the Herero revolt was crushed, the Nama in South-West Africa under Hendrik Witbooi rose in revolt—at least in part because of the German brutality they witnessed in the Herero campaign. The Nama (called Hottentots in Germany) were eventually suppressed after three years of guerrilla warfare; they suffered a similar fate to that of the Herero—shootings, starvation, and incarceration in forced-labor camps.[13] And in 1905 the Maji Maji revolt broke out in German East Africa. It was ultimately crushed with similar ruthlessness, including the summary execution of prisoners and a scorched-earth campaign that brought dire famine to an entire region. The death toll has been estimated as high as 250,000 or even 300,000 African lives.[14] "Total war" against any indigenous rebellion had become the norm.

The war played out in German domestic politics in all-too-predictable ways. The Reichstag elections of late 1906 were an opportunity to put the government's colonial policies up to national referendum. The Center party and the Social Democrats (SPD), along with the Progressives (Freisinnige Vereinigung), seized on the wars in South-West and East Africa as a way to attack an aloof and distant imperial government.[15] Reichstag opposition, however, generally centered on the economic mismanagement in German colonial rule rather than the inhumanity of the genocidal policies. Chancellor Bernhard von Bülow manipulated this opposition into a political confrontation and then dissolved the Reichstag. For its part, the imperial government cooperated with colonialist and radical nationalist pressure groups to stir up nationalistic support; a newly energized bloc of the nationalist right strove to equate support for the war with German patriotism, and any critique of it with treason.

An important aspect to this electioneering was the manner in which the prowar contingent campaigned. They tapped into nationalism and wartime jingoism, but they also underscored that the threat facing the German nation was a racial one. Helpless German settlers, according to this political propaganda, needed to be protected from murderous, racially inferior savages. One campaign flyer included a bloody illustration of the Herero and Nama uprisings by the colonial artist Rudolf Hellgrewe. Such electoral propaganda overall crafted "vivid stories—the bloodier the better"; for its part, the German Colonial Society pinned its tactics firmly on its audience, claiming that "the melodramatic requirements of the masses" demanded it.[16] In what became known thereafter as the Hottentot elections of early 1907, deputies hostile to colonialism, and particularly the SPD, lost seats. Chancellor Bülow was thereafter able to count on the support of a nationalist, procolonial bloc, at least for a few years.[17] Meanwhile, the imperial government claimed a mandate supporting colonialist policy but nonetheless introduced a reorganization of the colonial administration. These reforms signaled the intensification of German colonial rule, marked by a greater economic, military, administrative, and psychological investment in the colonies.

A political propaganda of "race war" therefore structured the political debates and maneuverings of late 1906. This politicized propaganda, however, had been preceded by private commercial engagement that began earlier, in 1904. As with the seizure of Kiautschou and the Anglo-Boer War, the war in South-West Africa afforded unmatched commercial opportunities. In the months following the initial Herero attacks, the mass media threw themselves into the fray, reporting on the atrocities of the Herero and berating the government for inaction. As the war unfolded, the tabloids lionized the brave lieutenants of the colonial forces and boasted of exclusive access to up-to-date information and photographs from the battlefield. Entertainment personalities rallied around the cause: Carl Hagenbeck sent 2,000 camels to South-West Africa as his personal—and well-publicized—contribution to the war effort.[18] A 1907 trademark by a Hamburg import/export firm appears to illustrate Hagenbeck's promotional coup by showing German colonial troops riding in line formation . . . on camelback.[19] The satirical humor magazines were drawn into the conflict; in 1904 *Simplicissimus* produced a "Kolonial-Spezial-Nummer" devoted entirely to colonialism. Though its critique of colonialism was both pointed and bitter, its caricature of Africans as savage cannibals was equally sharp.[20] Indeed, all of the satirical magazines, from the venerable *Kladderadatsch* to the socialist *Der Wahre Jacob,* portrayed Africans in a highly caricatured fashion.[21] Even as these popular magazines cast a critical eye on the war itself, they spread visions of savage, caricatured Africans to a broad audience, whose attention was now firmly fixed on Africa.

The growing media interest in—if not mania for—the war in South-West Africa offered businesses a new field of opportunity. Almost immediately in 1904, a pay-for-admission panorama of the Herero uprising appeared in Berlin.[22] A great many illustrated wall prints were churned out by such firms as Gustav Kühn and were soon decorating homes with

Figure 6.5 Wall print, "Uprising of the Herero," from 1905, by the printing firm of Gustav Kühn. This image also circulated as a collectible trading card. *Source:* Stefan Brakensiek, Regina Krull, and Irina Rockel, eds., *Neuruppiner Bilderbogen: Ein Massenmedium des 19. Jahrhunderts* (Bielefeld: Verlag für Regionalgeschichte, 1993), 149.

heroic scenes of courageous German colonial troopers battling fierce and relentless African hordes (Figure 6.5).[23] A more or less identical version was printed and circulated as a chromolithographed trading card by the Tribus and Sundheim coffee company.[24] In the immediate aftermath of the war, a surge of soldiers' and settlers' memoirs appeared, as participants sought to capitalize on their supposed eyewitness accounts.[25] Many of these soldiers and former colonists (including many women) published their own war memoirs and were then drawn into the publishing circuit of the colonial enthusiasts. The most famous of these accounts was a work of fiction; this was Gustav Frenssen's *Peter Moors fahrt nach Südwest: Ein Feldzugsbericht* (1906), which sold well over a million copies before 1945. The cover illustrations of most of these books showed either a threatening, looming Herero savage, or a triumphant German colonial soldier smiting a cowering brute.[26]

Some of the most widely disseminated imagery was that circulated on collectible trading cards of companies such as Aecht Frank (coffee [e.g., Figure 2.11]), Erkel (soap), Theodor Hildebrand (cocoa), and Walser & Schwarz. The first image of such card series often showed a scene of savage Herero murdering and pillaging, sometimes with cowering German women nearby to suggest the threat of rape.[27] (Later cards in the series would show captured Herero prisoners.) Collections of published photographs also appeared; these offered images of the defeated foe—a veritable photographic procession of desperate-looking chained or imprisoned Herero.[28] Thus images of the Herero War circulated widely through the German metropole, both as commercial opportunism and as visual commodities in their own right. Collectively, this suffusion offered visions of Africans in one of two motifs: as rebellious savages, drawn to look as murderous as possible, or as vanquished foes in ethnographic-style photographs of the enchained.

To what degree did this commercialized imagery from the war make its way into advertising more specifically? Indeed, advertising almost immediately began to reference the war in South-West Africa directly. In the midst of the war enthusiasm of 1904, the colonial soldier of the *Schutztruppe* with the iconic Southwester hat and rifle appeared across a range of products. Some were by small firms, such as Carl Warmann & Co., which had issued a China Fighter cigarette after the Boxer Rebellion, and now turned toward Africa with its German Knights cigarette, featuring charging colonial cavalry. Others were large-scale manufacturers, such as the Dresden cigarette manufacturer Jasmatzi and the Mainz champagne giant Kupferberg, which each deployed themes of the colonial soldier. Some advertising effaced the harsh realities of war—and the brutality of German soldiers' actions—by depicting Germany's adversaries metaphorically: on the label for August Deter's German-Southwest cigarettes, a colonial trooper aimed his rifle at a menacing lion. The lion—a stand-in for the Herero?—is perched atop stacked cigarette boxes.[29] Colonial troopers became the new hot "brand," both metaphorically and literally.

Advertising images of the Herero, however, were more problematic. According to the dicta of advertising writers, imagery must be sensational enough to attract but not so horrific as to repel. A trademark of a Herero

Figure 6.6 Trademark featuring a "Herero" warrior from 1905, by Carl Henckell, a Hamburg import/export company. It was trademarked for an enormous range of products that ran on for several pages and was likely drawn from Friedrich Meister's 1904 *Muhérero riKárera*, a book for young readers. *Source:* WZB (1905): 1417, reg. no. 80815.

warrior by the import/export company Carl Henckell seems surprisingly placid, particularly given the charged atmosphere of war (Figure 6.6). The pose is increasingly atypical after the fin de siècle, for it echoes many of the older conventions of ethnographic drawings that emphasized the nobility of the subject. For 1905 the image seems oddly ambivalent in the way it eschews the sensationalism currently saturating the new tabloids. It may have been intended as authentic; it looks almost identical to the Herero on the cover of Friedrich Meister's 1904 *Muhérero riKárera (Beware, Herero),* which itself looks to be borrowed from a previous ethnographic work. (Meister himself had churned out books on the Boer War and on the Germans in China.)[30] In the context of war, the Herero figure might also be intended as a pictorial version of an old trope of colonialist literature—that the savages were noble yet doomed to extinction by Darwinian inexorability.[31] Other companies trademarked brand names that merely referenced colonial wars—names such as Hottentotten (for cigarettes) or Nama (for groceries).[32] These brands may have been nothing more than a commercial echo of words made fashionable by the stimulating events of the war, or they may have carried more freighted implications relating to the appropriation of the names of defeated foes. Regardless, images like that of Carl Henckell's Herero, above, were rare and became more scarce as the decade wore on. Such noble depictions of Africans became increasingly out of place amid the visuality of brutal savagery in other media.

On the other end of the spectrum, some ads celebrated the German victory over the Herero with downright savage glee. For instance, a trademarked bottle label from a small liquor manufacturer in Stettin features a racist caricature of a Herero, dancing for the amusement of a German sailor as he prepares to swig the advertised product (Figure 6.7). The figure is graphically racialized for such an early date (1904)—the lips of the black native are exaggerated, the nose and ears massive. Interestingly, this rendition differs from those seen thus far: the facial features are not so much caricatured as they are deformed, in an apparent attempt to illustrate racial degeneracy. The eyebrows slant the eyes in an evil-faced caricature more common to images from the Boxer uprising. The crosshatching on the arms and legs perhaps represents filth or hair; both would animalize the figure. The fact that it is a German sailor forcing the Herero to "dance" again traces back to the imagery of the seizure of Kiautschou and the Boxer war. The composition of this ad is amateurish and probably represents a hasty effort by a small business to capitalize on postvictory jingoism. Certainly, the figure's most dehumanizing components, particularly the attempt to illustrate dirtiness, are extremely unusual for product labels. Even with the most exaggerated racial stereotypes, as we will see below, consumer imagery presented images that were as crisp and clean in their delineations as they were in their discriminations. Consumer imaginary was meant to entice, not disgust.

Another apparent offshoot of the heightened bellicosity surrounding the Herero War was that images that never would have passed governmental censorship before 1904 were allowed to appear during and after it. Images of questionable taste or morality but that played into patriotic

Figure 6.7 Trademarked label for Herero liquor from 1904 by R. Paulini & Co., Stettin. The watching German is a sailor, rather than a soldier of the Colonial Defense Forces *(Schutztruppe)*. *Source:* WZB (1904): 1606, reg. no. 71685.

nationalism enjoyed a greater degree of latitude from the authorities. In the most startling example I have found, a Dresden cigar firm trademarked a photograph of a supine and totally nude black woman in a pose of blatant eroticism (Figure 6.8). Nude or seminude photographs of African or South Pacific women often appeared in ethnographic books and journals, of course, but even textual classifieds offering such books could meet strong opposition.[33] Publicly circulated imagery was held to a far stricter standard.[34] Copyrighted trademarks, moreover, went through a lengthy bureaucratic process with the Patent Office. This image of a "Herero Girl" is the first full nude photograph—ever—to appear in the German Imperial Trademark Registration Rolls. The cigars were a house brand from a cigar store in Dresden and were named after a coastal town in German South-West Africa, which suggests that the store might have had some connection to the German Colonial Society. The gender of the registrant, Frau Taeß, may also have helped to slip this image past the

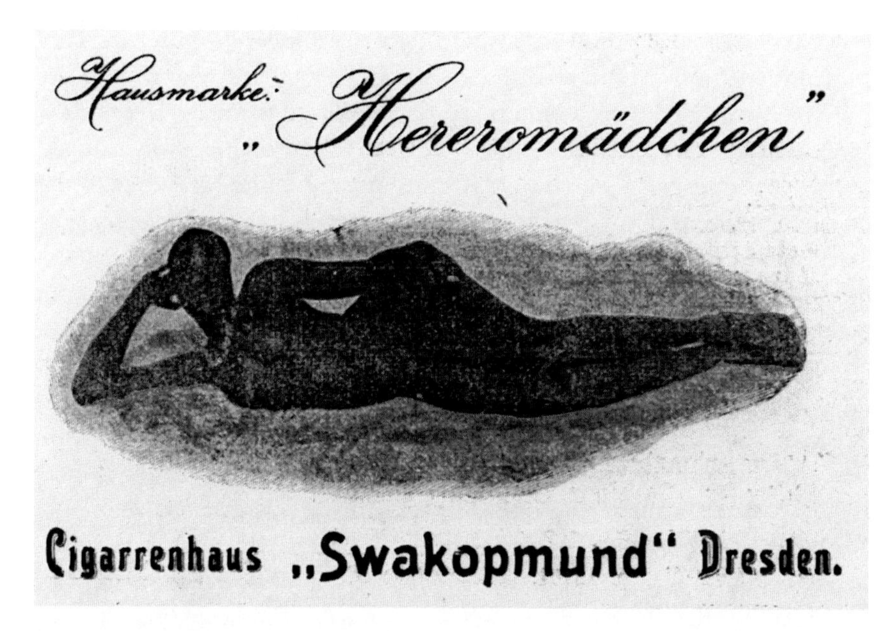

Figure 6.8 Photoengraved trademark for "Herero-Girl" cigars, 1908, from the Swakopmund cigar house in Dresden, registered by Frau Gertrud Taeß. The original in the Trademark Registration rolls is somewhat more clear than the poor reproduction here; the figure is nude with the image seemingly carved from a photograph. The image makes no gesture toward preserving the "modesty" of the figure; images such as this did not often slip past the censors before the First World War, let alone get trademarked by a state agency. *Source:* WZB (1908): 2055, reg. no. 112947.

censors. But the image remains startling; in the context of war, reprisal, repression, and genocide—the survivors of Trotha's genocidal policy were at this point suffering forced labor, starvation, and disease in concentration camps in Swakopmund—the proffered nudity and sexual access of the "Herero Girl" cannot help but be evocative of symbolic rape. Yet it was an outlier; no similar images were trademarked.

The more typical engagement of advertising in Germany with the foes of the German colonial forces, at least among the firms and businesses that invested large sums in advertising, played in more ambiguous spaces. On the one hand, such firms sought to exploit on the peaks of popular interest; this meant they sought to deploy images to reference the thrilling headlines of colonial warfare in South-West Africa, to capitalize upon them. On the other hand, they needed to skirt direct endorsement of a procolonial or even prowar position, since prospective purchasers included the legions of the working class, a great many of whom were Social Democrats and thereby in official opposition to the colonial policy of the German state. Colonial policy, as the Hottentot Elections showed, could be as divisive as integrative. Commercially astute businessmen had no wish to alienate any prospective purchasers. In a broader sense, mass marketers in recent years increasingly sought to address Germans as theoretically classless consumers, using themes devoid of politics. This left a conundrum: how to avoid divisive political issues—even as the thrill of political events offered unparalleled opportunity? One approach for treating politically charged topics was through the avenue of humor.

Some of the larger companies' advertisements referenced the South-West African war euphemistically, by portraying the threat of the Herero as, for instance, a menacing lion. Other companies, however, dealt with the threat of the Herero more directly. An ad for Müller's ink remover, registered by an office-supply firm in Stettin, is a subtle yet shocking case in point (Figure 6.9). The advertisement exhorts: "Eradicate your writing mistakes and blots with Müller's ink remover." It seeks to draw from two different fonts of humor, both discussed in the last chapter: the first is the growing linkage of black products (such as ink) to black figures; the second is soap advertisements' version of the *Mohrenwäsche,* where a black figure finds his skin color mistakenly washed off by the power of modern cleaners. In this ad for Müller's ink remover, then, the inclusion of the black African figure provides a visual link to both of these twin themes to evoke familiar humor. The figure's entanglement in these larger, humorous visual lineages is therefore disarming, *de*politicizing the image to some extent.

Yet the symbolic and metaphorical implications of this advertisement are quite sinister. Given the heightened racial rhetoric saturating the mass media in 1904, the choice of words—*vertilgen,* meaning to destroy, eradicate, exterminate—to "correct" the "mistake" of too much blackness can hardly be accidental. The visual elements are even more ominous. The ink is literally dissolving the blackness of the African. In a startling and powerful visual gesture, the figure has inadvertently transferred some of the ink remover to his neck—a mistake that has left, quite literally, a white hand gripping the African's throat. Another striking element of the ad is the figure's graphic racialization: the deliberately elongated skull, receding hairline (to better emphasize the oblong skull), wide eyes, and

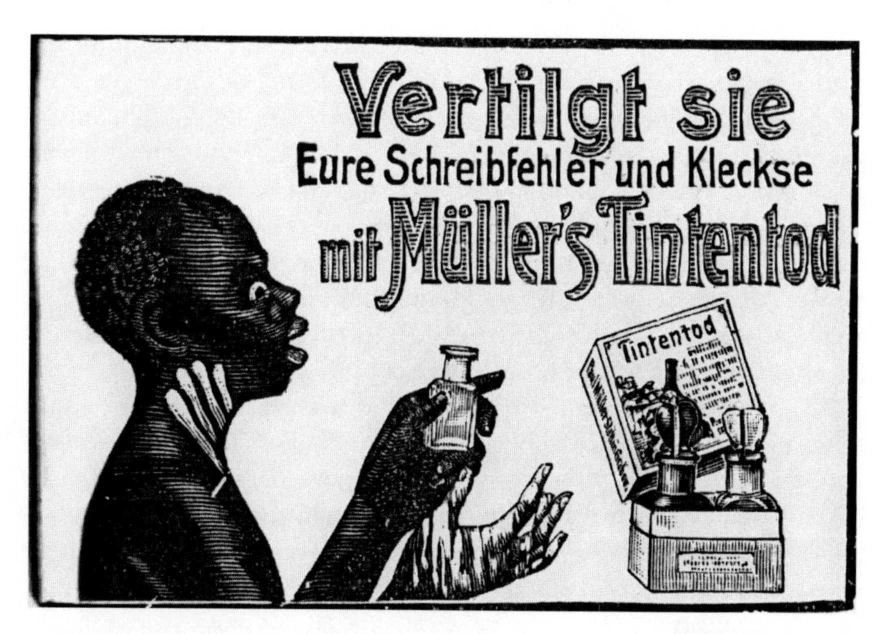

Figure 6.9 Advertisement for Müller's ink remover from 1904 by Paul Müller of Stettin-Grabow. *Source:* WZB (1904): 2071, reg. no. 73662.

exaggerated lips would be quite dramatic for a commercial image of an African in 1904. But the "humor" of the figure—the way the facial expression is drawn, the caricature of physiognomic features (harkening back to the humor magazines), and the comic tableau itself (he's erasing himself!)—all serve to make palatable the basic, brutal visual logic of eradication.

Reducing the African, 1904–1908

The war in South-West Africa was one key factor in a larger shift in nascent German consumer imagery. That shift has three strands. The first is an acceleration of the tendency to deploy images of African natives in advertising. We have seen how, around the fin de siècle, African figures became increasingly common, when the thrill of geopolitics came together with the new needs of commercial imagery as a visual form. After 1904, however, the deployment of African figures escalated further. Even more than the Boxer or Boer wars, the Herero War became a modern media event, which galvanized the interest of both advertisers and the public and amplified the interest of both in African figures. The incongruity of the political and commercial worlds is important to expressly point out: at a time of spiraling rhetoric about race war, of growing skepticism about colonialism's "loftier" aims (such as the civilizing mission) in the face of supposed racial inferiority, and of the explosion of alarming, sensationalized scenes of Africans committing murder and rape, Africans were increasingly seen everywhere—deployed by advertisers in the expectation that such imagery would attract purchasers.[35]

The new prevalence of African imagery was accompanied by a shift in the pictorial styles used to illustrate African figures. The racialization of the African in Müller's 1904 ad above (see Figure 6.9) was unusual for the time. Racialization, as we saw in the last chapter, had circulated through the Germany of the 1890s, but usually in certain media, such as caricature magazines, and in advertising with explicit connections to such topics as American minstrelsy. At the fin de siècle, many if not most African figures in trademark registrations were portrayed in distinctly nonracial ways. (They were pictured as romanticized noble savages, for instance, or as ethnographic curiosities.) Yet by the first decade of the twentieth century, these racializing conventions migrated onto *all* African figures. By 1908 racializing styles were ubiquitous, and by 1911 there were virtually no images of blacks registered that did *not* apply exactly this type of racialization of facial and bodily features. Africans were everywhere depicted with the styles that German artists, in imitation of the American style, once reserved for cakewalking dandies or pickaninnies.

In the aftermath of the Herero War, we can trace both the prevalence of the African figure and its racialization across a range of products. For instance, a Gondarin shoe polish ad, trademarked by a small Wuppertal firm in 1904, shows three identical African heads, each with the earrings marking the figure as a native (Figure 6.10). Gondar was the old imperial capital of Ethiopia, and the name therefore offered a tenuous link between this brand of shoe polish and the pictorial use of three Africans to illustrate it. As we saw in the previous chapter, however, a firm link between the black of shoe polish and the black of black figures had already been established in Germany back in the 1890s, importing the American motif of the black shoe-shine boy. The Gondarin shoe polish ad of 1904, then, transports the connection between black faces and black products

Figure 6.10 Trademark for Gondarin shoe polish from 1904 by Herman Meyerdrees of Elberfeld. Gondarin is an old name for Ethiopia. *Source:* WZB (1904): 220, reg. no. 66402.

from an entertaining America to a mythologized Africa (of "Gondar"). Shoe polish ads shifted from a locale of modern exoticism to one of primitive exoticism, yet the pictorial practice of racial differentiation was retained.

American-style racialization was more than merely transported: it was honed and, in the process, transformed. Though American minstrel visuality had always emphasized large lips, German graphic designers by mid-decade were drafting entire commercial compositions around this archetypal "racial" feature. In the Gondarin ad, for instance, the lips of the three black faces dominate the figures' faces, and (not unlike the minstrel figures of the 1880s) they are drawn as totally white to maximize the contrast against the figures' black skin. When one looks closely at the geometry of the composition as a whole, however, the centrality of the lips emerges even more clearly. First, each set of lips is the primary focal point for each face. This is accomplished by leaving the lower third of each face dark, except the stark white of the lips, and then engraving the figures' foreheads and cheeks to shine with reflected light. This device has the optical effect of drawing even more attention to the white lips, by making them into almost a glaring beacon. On the horizontal axis, meanwhile, each set of lips is bracketed between equidistant, looping earrings. Moreover, the lips of the three faces together comprise a white horizontal line that bisects the top half of the illustration—a line that parallels the white brand name Gondarin in the lower half. In the composition as a whole, therefore, the lips are as much an eye-catching line as the brand name itself; they are not just part of the composition's aesthetics but integrated into its optical geometry.

As we saw in Chapter 4, African figures were increasingly used as testifiers of authenticity. In Ivo Puhonny's Palmin ad for the Mannheim margarine giant Schlinck & Co. (see Figure 4.23), the commodity, palm-oil margarine, occupies the pivotal point in a triangular relationship that includes the figure and (implicitly) the viewer. The commodity is not just a product of colonialism—made from raw materials extracted from the colonized tropics—but also a manufacture of European technology, and thereby a distillation of modern civilization. The African figure is therefore a middleman—an authority that verifies the product's authenticity to the viewer, and at the same time an inferior against which the (German) viewer can measure and recognize his own superiority. The viewer is therefore the pupil—enlightened by the information about Palmin in the ad—but also is presented as the instructor—namely, the colonizer who will potentially educate the barefoot, childlike native. In each of these subtle interplays of visual power the figuration of the African as a child helps to mask the power of the advertisement itself and to mask the implicit authority of the native figure; it does this by flattering the viewer. Such dynamic operations of visual power—flattering the viewer by presenting a minor as visual spokesman—could and did work with *white* children in advertisements as well. Indeed, ads in the 1880s deployed children as an endearing veil to soften the command (to the viewer) contained within the advertisement itself. But, as popular as they were, the power dynamics of white children (vis-à-vis German adults) had only the masking element of age difference; they lacked the further disguise element of racial difference.

The date of Puhonny's illustration makes it worth revisiting from a different perspective. In 1905 a veil was needed to mask another and markedly different operation of visual power. Consider the violence of the imagery that was then permeating the public sphere during the Herero War and its aftermath. Collectible trading cards and covers of colonial memoirs circulated images of savage warriors about to burn farmhouses and rape virtuous German women (see Figure 2.11). Thrilling imagery, for certain, but to place such a scene of African savagery in an advertisement for a product like Palmin to demonstrate its authenticity would be highly problematic, to say the least. In fact, given the imagery of violent struggle omnipresent in the German public sphere around 1905, depicting any adult African might well evoke unwelcome or unpleasant associations. True, the goal was to seize attention, but an image that made the viewer feel threatened would be undesirable. Yet as we saw in Chapter 4, the African figure was incredibly useful—perhaps too useful to abandon. And the additional topicality of thrilling warfare in South-West Africa lent it even greater reverberation. The answer advertisers hit upon was to diminish the figure. In the Palmin advertisement, note how passive the African figure is. In the larger context of violence and genocide, the small size and passivity of the African figure disarm the figure's capacity for violence while retaining some of its topical, savage allure.

We can see this diminution at work across an array of commercial images after 1904, where the violent imagery of the Herero War in the German metropole was refracted in commercial imagery in subtle and often playful ways. After 1904, trademarks for German products that depicted black native figures, for instance, were far more frequently depicted carrying spears. Spears appear in the 1904 ad for WiTco conserves (Figure 6.11); Thurmann's chocolate from 1906; Bergmann's soap of 1905 (see Figures 6.12 and 6.13); and even Henckell's ethnographic Herero warrior of 1905 (see Figure 6.6). The spear as a symbolic referent to the potential danger posed by the African native was far less common in illustrations crafted before 1904, and it would again decline after 1910. For a few years after 1905, however, drawing a spear as an accoutrement became the norm. Such an inclusion may not have been intentional, in the common understanding of the word. Given the heightened awareness of violence during and after the uprising, this accessory may have just felt right to graphic artists and advertisers. But it served two distinct purposes. The first was to subtly reference the possibility of danger—to show that the African native offering you chocolate or soap with such docility was in fact kindred of those brutal, murdering savages imaged in the pages of the *Berliner Illustrirte Zeitung*. But once this thrilling danger was evoked, it then needed to be managed, if not dissipated—or else unpleasant associations might then be linked to the product. The weapon itself therefore was usually drawn as short and harmless-looking. It is worth pointing out that while the Herero were well armed with modern rifles in the South-West African war, many depictions of the war in German mass culture

Figure 6.11 Advertisement for WiTco canned tortoise meat from 1904 by the firm of Gustav Hennssen, Hamburg. *Source:* WZB (1904): 1000, reg. no. 69214.

drew them attacking with spears or even clubs. Such mischaracterization succinctly illustrated the savagery of Germany's foes, but it also traced a direct visual line back to Adolph Friedländer's figurations for the African (and Amazon) shows from the 1890s.

Short, cute spears can still be dangerous—but not if they are wielded by short, cute natives. The post-1904 penchant for depicting Africans as children therefore makes a great deal of sense in the context of the visual logic of Herero War imagery. Were children perhaps *too* cute, though? Images of children, psychologists tell us, elicit paternal or maternal feelings at a very basic level, and these empathic or even caring feelings might interfere with the portrayals of power that we have seen were increasingly important to consumer-oriented imagery. Regardless of whether a graphic artist would balk at drawing an African child under-

Figure 6.12 Trademark for chocolate, 1906, by the Berliner Couvertüren Special Fabrik Otto Thurmann, Berlin. *Source:* WZB (1906): 2070, reg. no. 92475.

going backbreaking labor for the viewer, such an image might just feel odd. German advertisers, then, hit upon an ingenious pictorial compromise. In an advertisement by the Hamburg firm of Gustav Hennssen from 1904 for WiTco canned tortoise, the figure is neither adult nor child but rather a man-child (Figure 6.11). This optical effect is achieved in part by drawing the head disproportionately large for the body and by drawing wide, round eyes; both are characteristics that evoke the features of children. Here, however, these childlike features are paired incongruously with the well-defined musculature characteristic of a young man or adult—the bicep of this figure is particularly well developed. Given these contradictory visual clues, the figure cannot be other than of indeterminate age.

The head-to-body disproportion is even more clearly seen in a chocolate trademark from 1906 (Figure 6.12). With the stance and accoutrements of a warrior, this native type should by all accounts fall into the category of adult. Yet the diminution of the figure, primarily through the disproportion of the head to the body, suggests instead physical immaturity.

Figure 6.13 Advertisement for Bergmann's Hobby Horse Lily Soap from before 1909. This advertisement later appeared in colonialist journals, such as *Süsserott's Illustrated Colonial Calendar*, but was crafted for the mass market. *Source: Illustrirte Zeitung* (1909): 636.

This pictorial strategy of diminution was most common with colonized images of blacks, such as the types of the colonized native discussed in Chapter 4. It also frequently appeared in other manifestations of black figures, such as that of the liveried servant. One of the essential reasons for this reducing of African figures, I argue, is to *preserve* them—to be able to keep deploying these indispensable figures in a context of escalating violence and race war (Figure 6.13).

Consumer images in Germany quickly began to incorporate all of these racially differentiating features as a coherent set. In a 1905 trademark from another Hamburg firm, Steffens, a black figure dressed in a cook's outfit carries the product package (Figure 6.14). The figure here incorporates all of the major features of racialization, with tactical tricks deployed to emphasize each. First and foremost is the by now familiar emphasis upon the lips; here they not only are stark white to contrast vividly against the figure's black face, but the exaggeration is carried to an

Figure 6.14 Advertisement from 1905 by the import/export firm of Alfred B. Steffens, Hamburg. *Source:* WZB (1905): 1280, reg. no. 80430.

extreme degree. Along similar lines, the kinky hair is cleverly highlighted by drawing it in front of the bright white backdrop of the chef's hat, rough and chaotic against the smooth and even line formed by the hat's base. The eyes are wide and staring (and a little maniacal, if looked at too closely). Even the flatness of the nose is brought up from total invisibility against a black face, by clever deployment of highlights and shadows. Finally, the entire figure is diminished—neither adult nor child, but a curious man-child. His miniature size is driven home by the inclusion of an enormous spoon tucked under his arm—or perhaps "her" arm: the racial features are so graphically dominant that it is difficult to find clues that attest to the gender of the figure.

Despite the cook's attire, other markers are included that identify the figure as a native. The figure has bare feet—a point cleverly emphasized by drawing cuffs on the pants, articulating the detail of the toes, and placing the feet at the very border and foreground of the composition. Furthermore, the oversized ear might be lost against the background if not for the tribal earring glinting and thereby accenting it. Thus, in this advertisement and the many that followed, the signifiers for the colonial native (bare feet, native jewelry) became so tightly interlaced with markers of race that they became *compositionally* interdependent. Colonial power—the visual logic of physical servitude—became increasingly intertwined with racial power—the visuality of bodily difference. In consumer-oriented imagery, this came about at least partly for simple reasons of making the actual picture as clear as possible.

The Optics of Race

In the long tradition of painting and engraving in Western art more broadly, black figures were not infrequently depicted as small or child-like or were pushed to the margins of the composition. Paintings of European aristocratic or bourgeois subjects in the eighteenth century, for instance, were often juxtaposed against youthful or boyish Moor servant figures.[36] Scholars generally have seen the small stature of black figures in high art and popular art in one of two contexts: either as reflective of social inequity, representing the real marginality of blacks in slaveholding and colonial societies, or as detached symbols, where a black figure might, for instance, symbolically sexualize a scene and be drawn as small to preclude competition.[37] While interpretations involving the reflective or the symbolic are each quite valid ways to analyze visual representations, a different logic drives this diminution of blacks in German commercial visuality after the fin de siècle—a logic less interpretive than optical. Since the formulation of Marx's notion of "commodity fetishism," scholars have reflected on the elevation of the commodity as a pivotal feature of modern cultural life.[38] I argue that advertising took commodity fetishism (the elevation of the brand-name product) not just as an economic strategy or even as a cultural practice, but as a scopic imperative. As commercial imagery emerged as both a new business tactic and as a new cultural practice in its own right, it sought to establish this ascendancy visually. One of the most effective ways to elevate a brand-name product visually was through comparison, and increasingly after 1900, advertising scenes graphically established the primacy of the product relative to something else.

A close look at an advertisement from the coffee manufacturer and grocery giant Emil Tengelmann can shed more light on this point. The company began in 1867 as Wilhelm Schmitz-Scholl, a coffee and cocoa importer in Mühheim; its first grocery store affiliate opened as Tengelmann (named after Schmitz's procurer) in Düsseldorf in 1893 and expanded dramatically, with 560 Tengelmann stores by the beginning of the First World War. Today, the Tengelmann group is one of the world's largest retail chains.[39] Both the Schmitz-Scholl coffee and Tengelmann grocery branches began deploying many racialized images of Africans after 1907. Emil Tengemann in Bochum trademarked the text slogan "Tengelmann's Negerbrot" as early as 1898.[40] The Schmitz-Scholl firm's ad for Frau Professor Luise Holle's Finest Household Margarine was trademarked in 1913 (Figure 6.15). With a racialized black figure in a chef's outfit carrying the product, it is at least somewhat derivative of the Steffens firm's earlier ad from 1905 (cf. Figure 6.14). The Tengelmann ad for Professor Luise Holle margarine takes place in two panes; read from left to right, the first panel gives the visual story and the second its resolution—"fabricated from only the best raw materials, and in every category of usage, on par with BUTTER"—presenting a steaming roast bird as testimony of this truth. The visual story of the first pane, however, is quite sophisticated. The first point to emphasize is the relative size of the black figure: he is just over half the size of the German *Hausfrau* because of his position in the background, farther away from the viewer. This placement yields the optical effect of dramatically magnifying the housewife within the space of the illustration; she dominates the pane. This tactic is reminiscent of the way noblewomen are depicted with their chamber-moors in eighteenth-century painting. Yet there is a significant addition. The product itself is huge relative to the black figure; indeed, the square of margarine is practically as large as the black figure's head! Optically, then, the small black figure serves twice as a spatial measure; he magnifies the dominant Frau Professor, and he magnifies the product. Revealingly, the dimensions of the white woman vis-à-vis the commodity are true to life.

A second point to mention in this packaging illustration is the clashing artistic styles. The white figure, like the abstract design around the slogan in the following pane, seems to draw artistically from Art Nouveau or *Jugendstil;* the woman's gaze, lifted up and away from the viewer, perhaps even evokes some of the distracted etherealness of an Alfons Mucha print.[41] And, as often is found in *Jugendstil,* there could be subtle eroticism here too—look how close the lips of the two figures are to each other, separated only by the margarine. Yet the style of the black figure is

Figure 6.15 Packaging for Frau Professor Luise Holle's margarine from 1913; this was a brand of Hamburg's Tengelmann firm. *Source:* WZB (1913): 2887, reg. no. 183010.

far different. The massive lips, odd nose (lightened to appear snoutlike), staring eyes, and clumsy hash marks for the black skin come from a very different stylistic template. Note also the high pant cuffs, a marker of the minstrel figure. These clashing styles further exaggerate the pictorialization of racial difference.

This use of different artistic styles—more representational for German figures, more abstract for Africans—became a common tactic in the years before the war. A reverse polarity—a more representational African juxtaposed against a more abstracted white—was never, ever used. One might even argue that this particular form of representational whiteness was codified in contrast to—in opposition to—the codification of blackness. In attempting to appeal to as large a community of potential consumers as possible, advertisers sought to find a common visual language to cross class divides and breach political fissures. In Tengelmann's Professor Luise Holle's ad, for instance (see Figure 6.15), the woman is clearly drawn to represent the upper middle class: her attire, her well-outfitted kitchen, her servant, even her delicate cheek mole all indicate her high social status. The product being advertised, however, is margarine—a less expensive substitute for butter, consumed largely by the working classes. Would a working-class mother see such indicators of status and feel envious or alienated? In increasingly politically divided times—1913 was the year that the largely working-class Social Democratic Party secured an absolute majority in the Reichstag yet still faced an intransigent bourgeois bloc—how would a perspective customer of any class perceive, and respond to, the subtle class codings? One cannot tell (then or now), but the inclusion of a radically differentiated figure in the illustration overshadows—by means of visual contrast—any potential perception of difference between the illustrated white figure and the possible working-class or bourgeois viewer. The racial contrast of this ad implicitly lumps white viewers together by juxtaposing whiteness against blackness in the *optical* field—through stark color contrasts. It is literally more difficult to see different shades of a color (such as white) when set against its chromatic opposite. Advertisers were searching for a generic "consumer" long before there ever was such a category, and in the first decade of the twentieth century, they could figuratively "whitewash" their own presentation of Germanness by highlighting its chromatic *and* essential opposite.

By using imagery to differentiate and optically diminish groups that lay outside of the sphere of potential consumers, racial differentiation resolved two problems. It established the ascendancy of the featured product (Figure 6.16). And it implied a commonality among all members of the potential audience. It may seem trite to restate the maxim that successful mass culture divides the world into "insiders" and "others," but it is important to recognize that this occurs not just in the construction of the meaning of the image but also through *optical* means, such as scaling. To use semiotic terms, commodity scaling operated at not just the level of the sign, but at the level of the signifier itself.[42] Colonized black figures are made physically insignificant in comparison to the commodity, to a representative of European race, or to a manifestation of Western technology. Examples of this tendency abound: the tiny size of the Palmin child (see Figure 4.23) exaggerates the size of the margarine's box and demonstrates the centrality of the commodified luxury to civilization. The tiny size of the Little Coco (see Figure C.1) in comparison to the German children exaggerates the importance of the German child, and the enormous spoon in the crook of the native chef's arm (see Figure 6.14) exaggerates even the everyday implements of Western technology. Taken collectively, such ads optically magnify the commodity, European culture, and Western technology, and link the three meaningfully in a triumvirate of European colonialist identity. Though each individual

Figure 6.16 Advertisement for Immalin metal polish, 1911, by the Chem. Fabrik Eisendrath GmbH, Mettmann. *Source:* WZB (1911): 351, reg. no. 139965.

consumer image may have been constructed tactically to serve a discrete and focused purpose, such ads taken collectively reveal that racial identity not only played a role in visually certifying the broader virtues of consumer capitalism as a whole, but that race could be constructed as an ancillary operation of consumer capitalism's most basic needs. The racialized Other was a means to illustrate the generic consumer, and simultaneously, also a way to efface the subordination of this generic consumer to the commodity—a subordination that operated as much in the visual world as in the tactile world.

Racial Hegemony, 1908–1912

> Seen again day after day, hour after hour, the forms, colors, and fonts of the poster imprint themselves quite deeply.
>
> —Ludwig Lindner, "Warenanpreisung und Läden" (1914)

The rapidity with which strategies of racial depiction became ubiquitous after 1905 is astounding. The exaggeration of the lips, the enlarging of ears and bare feet, and the diminution of the body appeared with growing frequency and growing uniformity: this increasingly coherent set of racializing conventions was often used in its entirety. In 1905, illustrations of colonized blacks might only slightly exaggerate the lips. In trademarks from 1908 through 1912, the racialization is uniform: the racialized lips are not only massively oversized but tend toward the grotesque; the ears of each figure are deformed; visual emphasis is laid upon the flatness of or distortion of the nose; the hair is uniformly depicted as kinky. In each figure the distortion of bodily proportions lends an air of immaturity to the figure, even those clearly meant to be adult natives. By the time of the Hottentot elections of 1907, with the heightened rhetoric of race war and demand for racial exclusion (and even extermination), racialized images of blacks were increasingly ubiquitous. In the years after the elections, particularly between 1908 and 1912, the numbers of new trademarked illustrations that featured racialized black figures peaked. By the First World War, the conventions of racialization were so widely established in consumer culture that it is nearly impossible to find images of blacks that do *not* deploy them (Figure 6.17). I have found only a handful of black figures in the Trademark Registration Rolls that eschew racializing techniques after 1910.[43] Over the course of little more than half a decade, the racialization of the black figure had become hegemonic. The question then arises: how does such a hegemony emerge?

One component of visual hegemony was the new cult of the great designer. From its shady origins in the 1880s, advertising had grown into a fully established profession by 1910. With this new legitimacy came the rise of a new kind of graphic designer—the German master. We have already seen how as early as the late 1880s and especially the 1890s, advertising publications had demarcated and policed the profession, decades before institutions such as professional organizations or training programs

Figure 6.17 Trademark for a pharmaceutical and medical supply company in 1910 by Nietzschmann & Hildebrandt of Leipzig. *Source:* WZB (1910): 1933, reg. no. 135348.

existed. Professional publications originally held up British and American methods, motifs, and styles to buttress their claims, but by the first decade of the twentieth century, overseas legitimacy was no longer required. After 1900, foreign designs were no longer privileged; instead, journals foregrounded the work of the new German masters of illustration.

One of the earliest recognized masters was the graphic artist Julius Klinger, whose famous trademark for Palm cigars that opened this book was still in use as recently as the 1980s. Klinger, an Austrian, moved to Munich in 1896, first drawing for the satirical magazine *Meggendorfer Blätter* and then working as a commercial artist. He moved to Berlin the following year and was soon working for Ernst Growald's firm, Hollerbaum & Schmidt, which by that time had become the premier poster-design firm in Germany.[44] Klinger's logo for Palm cigars was designed as early as 1906, but curiously not trademarked until 1911.[45] It ranked among the most well-known advertising icons of the *Kaiserreich,* appearing on a great variety of surfaces, from storefront signs, to the side panels of delivery trucks, to advertising stamps (Plate 16). This image also circulated through the professional advertising literature; it was referenced widely in advertising trade journals and handbooks, and was lauded as a triumph of color and form.[46] It quickly found its way into exhibitions of the best poster art, and the *Bulletin of the Association of Advertising Experts* even used it as an example of how a well-crafted ad could become "so popular so quickly" that it could turn into the firm's de facto trademark, even if it had not originally been intended as such.[47]

Art historians have echoed Klinger's contemporaries in praising the ad's composition.[48] But the degree to which the ascribed popularity of the image flowed naturally from the success or merits of its design alone is questionable. Some of the mechanisms of popularization will be discussed below; here I want to underscore the point that Klinger's approach was hardly original. As the images throughout this and the previous chapter have shown, the signifiers used by Klinger—bright red lips, oversize ears, rounded skull, wide, white eyes, infantilized and diminutive body—were drawn from an increasingly common repository of artistic conventions. I would suggest that the recognition and professional success he gained for this design stemmed in part from timing: in 1906—on the heels of the Herero War—Klinger deployed the crystallizing canon of racial conventions boldly at exactly the right moment—after such conventions were familiar enough to conform to public perceptions of appropriateness but before they were so ubiquitous as to be seen as merely commonplace.

It is instructive to see how later reproductions of Klinger's work stripped away his artistic touches, reducing idiosyncrasy to conventionality. The reproduction of the Palm ad in Paul Ruben's 1914 advertising handbook, for instance, removed the glowering, sinister eyes from the figure, replacing them with wide, rounded eyes more in line with a solidifying stereotype (Plate 17). In part, of course, this simplification also derives from the shift from five-color to four-color printing. Yet such simplifications of design to suit print technology were, in fact, exactly the point—and one of the mechanisms manufacturing hegemony. Advertising imagery—even the work of a renowned master—needed to be cheaply reproduced, and this meant distilled to its bare essentials. Interestingly, though Klinger's poster for the Palm firm remained his most renowned work, he rarely drew black figures. One of the few other instances is the abstract representation of the heavyweight boxing champion Jack Johnson in a 1910 poster for Bruno lightbulbs. ("Johnson" in that famous design is an inky splash of black, with bright red lips, white eyes, and white gloves.)[49] The mainstay of Klinger's designs, even for such products as Excelsior rubber shoe heels, were of caricatured white figures or abstracted stick figures. His most popular design, therefore, was not at all typical of his oeuvre, and it just happened to also be his most racialized design.

The graphic artist who would come to be recognized as the undisputed master of the German modern was Ludwig Hohlwein. Renowned in Germany even before the First World War, Hohlwein's fame ultimately spread far beyond the borders of Germany; by the 1920s he was one of the most prominent graphic designers in the world. Even in his early career during the *Kaiserreich,* Hohlwein's works were loudly applauded by the advertising establishment as masterpieces of clarity and artistry, and his posters often found their way into museum exhibitions. Much of Hohlwein's work tended to reference or play upon racial hierarchy. Indeed, one of his favorite themes involved portraying blacks in service to whites.[50] Often these scenes of racial power drew from the American influences seen in the previous chapter, but he also crafted a number of images that powerfully evoked the colonial realm, particularly later in his career.

One of Hohlwein's earliest posters to win acclaim was a 1906 design for the Palast Café, which featured a diminutive black serving boy in uniform (Figure 6.18). The figure is racialized, with emphasis upon the lips, an extremely rounded skull, and a diminished stature. In a touch that would become a Hohlwein signature, the eyes are hidden in shadow. This poster was reproduced as a black-and-white image in a number of advertising trade publications, including Hans Moor's *Reklame-Lexicon* in 1908. In Moor's handbook, moreover, Hohlwein's Palast Café poster was paired with another racial ad—a soap poster by J. B. Maier of a black dandy (in white suit with pink top hat, tie, and cane), which also found lasting renown; artistic mastery seems to have increasingly involved race.[51] Hohlwein would certainly play with racializing convention; in a 1910 ad for Marco Polo Tea, for instance, he drew a somewhat racialized black servant figure, but wearing Chinese attire, complete with a long topknot.[52] The composition is often reproduced in art-historical literature as an example of innovative use of color contrasts, yet its odd intermingling of racial types often goes unmentioned.

Hohlwein's later posters for Eppan champagne (1909) and for an exhibition at the Odeon (1908) each recycle his Palast Café servant-theme (Plate 18). For Eppan, Hohlwein colors the figure's lips bright red—so much so that it almost appears to be bright red lipstick.[53] For the Café Odeon illustration, the diminished black serving figure is drawn with a native earring and with a massively elongated skull that makes the figure look almost simian. Hohlwein then juxtaposes this small, sober, racialized black figure with a smiling, white male consumer, in stylish vest and

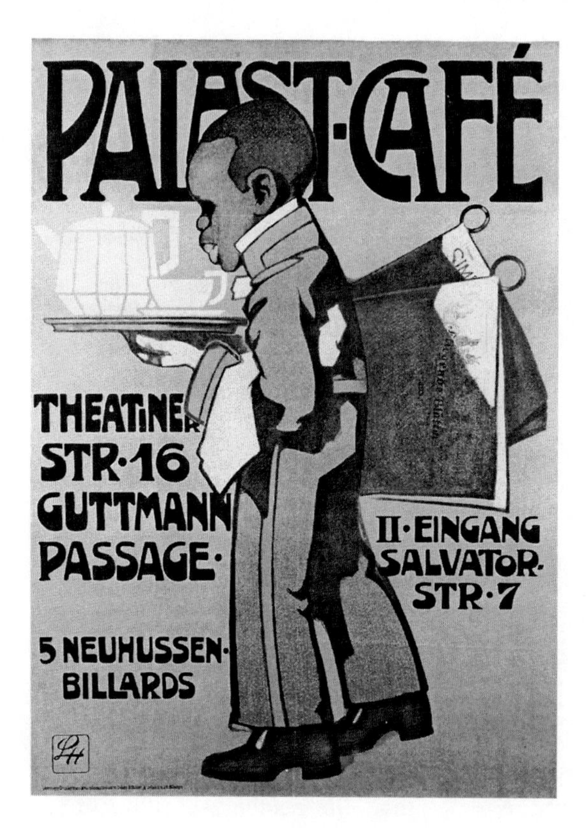

Figure 6.18 Poster for the Palast Café from 1906, by Ludwig Hohlwein. © 2010 Artists Rights Society (ARS), New York/VG Bild-Kunst, Bonn. Image: Hans Moor, *Reklame-Lexicon* (Leipzig: Phönix-Verlag, 1908), 158.

spats, sleeves rolled up rakishly. The line of the black servant's livery parallels the pool cue nestled in the crook of the coffee consumer's arm. Hohlwein would revisit this theme of blacks offering goods or service to whites continuously throughout his career, well into the Weimar era. It was often imitated by other designers, sometimes exactly.[54]

In fact, the black figures of Hohlwein's design should be thought of always in relation to his white figures. Oftentimes this is explicitly expressed in a composition, as with the poster for the Café Odeon (see Plate 18). At other times the chromatic and racial contrast came from the way in which they were shown: posters of white figures were often checkered with posters of black figures across walls or on poster columns. A photograph of a wall from 1910, for instance, shows Hohlwein's Café Odeon poster plastered repeatedly, in alternating quadrants, with two of his other posters, one featuring three little white girls, the other of three male white bobsledders.[55] Clearly, in presenting these posters to a viewing public, poster hangers thought the blackness of the black figures an excellent juxtaposition to the whiteness of the white figures. It seems plausible that they were crafted with that in mind. It is perhaps not so surprising that Hohlwein also became skilled depicting another vision of race—the square-jawed, powerful blond white male figure that would become the prototypical Aryan of National Socialist graphic design.

In all of his designs, Hohlwein's mastery of color and form is unparalleled, and the geometry of his compositions is gripping. However—to take issue with some of the art-historical critique of his work—Hohlwein's use of black serving figures and his deployment of techniques of racialization were in no way original. Rather, as the last two chapters have shown, Hohlwein's work merely stands at the apex of a rising tide of coherent racial types and standardized graphic conventions. Hohlwein's poster for Palmin margarine, crafted just before the war for the Mannheim margarine manufacturing giant H. Schlinck, shows an exceptional talent for five-color composition (Plate 19). The gold earrings perfectly frame the bright red lips. The twin red nostrils balance the two hashed blue eyebrows above, which in turn bracket (and underscore) the two wide white eyes. The pointed roundness of the turban seems to hold up the blue circular backdrop, which in turn serves as a spotlight on the figure, and, at the same time, as a halo over the packaging. The golden spoon, resting in the figure's lap, lies midpoint between the smile and the brand name; a spoon is the literal (or rather visual) connector between the product and happiness. The figure literally rests upon the packaging. The shine on the red shoes draws the eye, but the playful cock of the foot on the left side points again to the brand name. This is a stunning composition. But the obvious talent that artists such as Ludwig Hohlwein (or for that matter, Julius Klinger) brought to their work should not obscure the ways in which they followed trends in advertising as much as they influenced them. All of the primary pictorial elements in Holhwein's Palmin poster, for instance are evident in compositions a half decade earlier, from the earring-framed smile (Figures 6.12 and 6.14), to the circular "halo" over the commodity (Figure 4.29), to the shiny spats of the American minstrel-dandy (Figures 5.4 and 5.5), to the magnifying of the commodity packaging (Figure 6.13), to the pointing hand or foot (Figures 4.23 and 6.16).

Thus, the advanced techniques of individual advertising artists need to be seen less in terms of innovative artistic genius and more in the context of the gradually accumulating conventions of a consumer society as they were normalized through imagery. As Ernst Growald wrote in 1914, it was the success of advertisements like that for Klinger's Palm cigars (Plate 1) that showed "*how* the new brand-name trademarks *must* be crafted, so that they *can* become popular."[56] In other words, no matter how much they saw themselves as artists with an individual style, graphic designers and advertisers alike were beholden by the nature of their work to cater to what was collectively seen as the bottom line: popular comprehension, popular appeal, powerful message. Advertisers conceived of their work as beholden to the tastes of the broader public; as *Propaganda* explained it back at the turn of the twentieth century, "The young artist must either make extensive concessions to ruling tastes, or he must forgo the sale of his work."[57]

The Stereotype en Masse

The work of the new German masters of graphic design was circulated through new forms that reached ever wider segments of the population. One new medium was the *Reklamemarke*—a small, multicolor stamp originally used to seal packages at grocers. Following in the footsteps of the success of the *Liebigbilder,* these stamps first appeared in the 1890s but achieved their widest distribution two decades later; they were printed and distributed free by the brand-name firm as a new method of advertising. Julius Klinger's design for Palm cigars and Ludwig Hohlwein's designs for Marco Polo tea and Palmona margarine (see Plate 20) were reproduced by the millions as *Reklamemarken.*[58] The images on advertising stamps, however, were pared down to their most basic elements to reduce reproduction costs—namely, by reducing the number of colors. Designs were streamlined to maximize the interpretability of the image by deploying easily recognized, easily understood referents—for the quality of reproduction could be quite poor. To be understood, the *Reklamemarke* relied utterly on codes that had formed and circulated for a decade in commercial visuality. Would the stamp for Palmona margarine (Plate 20) have been even remotely comprehensible without one's having previously seen prior images (Figure 6.14, Plate 19)?

An illustrated trademark for Cobu margarine from 1909 allows a glimpse into the process of distilling meaning down to its most basic elements

Figure 6.19 Advertisement for Cobu margarine, 1909 ("Cobu: the finest vegetable-butter margarine. No animal fat"), by the Bergische-Märkische Margarine-Werke of Elberfeld. *Source:* WZB (1909): 1309, reg. no. 119196.

(Figure 6.19). In the original, a racialized African figure shoos away a sobbing pig. Cobu margarine was a vegetable product, meant to replace cooking fat. For the smaller and later version appearing on an advertising stamp, several adjustments are made to the black figure (Plate 21). First, the most essential racializing feature—the bright red lips—have been further emphasized. Similarly, the body has been diminished, reducing the black from a man to an immature figure of indeterminate age. The distortion of the size of the feet and the arm is retained; but the head has been reproportioned—or rather, malproportioned—to both make the skull seem rounder and evoke a sense of kinky hair. In short, the *Reklamemarke* version is recrafted to look *more* similar to every other racialized, diminished version of the image currently in circulation. Interestingly, the pig in the *Reklamemarke* version is also more clearly distilled down to the essence of pigness by including a few extra lines to emphasize the floppy ears, a porcine snout, and porcine heft. Finally, in the mass-produced stamp version, the product package itself has been further enlarged. This not only makes it more visible, but also increases its scale relative to the African figure at the optical level.

Like the *Sammelbilder* of the Leibig company and others, advertising stamps were often serialized—that is, they were printed in sets of four, six, or ten different stamps, under the presupposition that all would be collected. Public interest in the *Reklamemarke* surged to epidemic proportions by 1912. In the larger view, the tactic of serialization involves a peculiarly modern form of consumption; the expectation was that the incompleteness of the individual stamp—segregated from the rest of the series—would spur consumers to eagerly anticipate and pursue the next installment. These stamps often offered story lines or snapshots of the world and of human history, showcasing differences in peoples, places, and things, and ordering them in sets or narratives to greater heighten the desire to collect.[59] In this form of advertising, the commercial image is consumed wholly as a good in and of itself.

An example of this serialized consumption as it intertwined with the German colonial project can be found in a number of *Reklamemarke* series issued by the Mettmann firm of Eisendrath for the Immalin brand of shoe polish, around 1913 (Plate 22). The signifiers of race and colonial domination in these stamp stories should by this point be familiar: the oversizing of the commodity, the racialization of the native, the earrings and nose ring, the spear; and in the scene with a European, the native is crouched down—polishing his bare feet—and so optically on a lower plane. The integration of the humorous poem with the caricatured illustrations, meanwhile, traces directly back to the children's caricatures of Wilhelm Busch. Unlike the work of Busch, however, the text does not exist in a satirical tension with the exaggeration in the illustrations; instead, both are in the service of lauding the commodity to the consumer by denigrating the African. The effort here is not to play with or invert assumptions, but rather to enlist and enforce them.

As the features of blacks became more standardized in the crucible of mass culture between 1908 and 1912, they became more exaggerated, and as these exaggerations in turn took on a greater centrality to the composition, nonessential details of the figure were frequently dropped. Eventually black figures began to be so racialized, caricatured, and exaggerated

Figure 6.20 Advertisement for Cocosa cocoa-butter margarine, 1910, by the Höllandische Margarine-Werke Jurgens & Prinzen of Goch. This is the most highly racialized variant of "Little Coco," the firm's brand-figure. *Source:* WZB (1901): 301, reg. no. 125812.

that they no longer resembled human beings (see Figure 6.17). In fact, they became abstract reference points to racial otherness. Their iconicity (in the technical sense of the word) became less important than their stereotypic markers. We see this in the ads of the firm of Wilhelm Schmitz-Scholl (Tengelmann), for instance, which began to use more abstracted black natives in 1908 to image its coffee. The figures are almost mere abstract black props, with giant white lips that cover one quarter of their heads. The margarine giant Jurgens & Prinzen (Holländische Margarine-Werke) crafted a racialized, minimalized abstracted native after 1909; this Cocosa Moor promoted their margarine and cocoa butter brands, appearing widely in ads and on product packaging (Figure 6.20). All of the renditions of the Cocosa figure are reduced to the essential racializing features—an abstraction that contrasts strikingly with the more detailed, traditional depictions of white Germans.[60] One most directly tied to the colonial project is that by the chocolate manufacturer Sarotti in 1911 for its Banana-Cocoa (Plate 23), by Julius Gipkins, the same designer who would draft the famous Sarotti Moor several years later.

One lens through which to see the new visuality of abstraction lay with the new science of mass psychology, and the corresponding value it placed upon visual impact. The psychology of advertising emerged in Germany as a subject for scientific investigation around 1910, not from the advertising profession itself but rather from the burgeoning field of mass psychology.[61] The first German-language article on the subject appeared in a philosophical journal in 1906, and it argued among other things that advertising used visual stimulation to transport complete perspectives and judgments *(Ansichten und Urteilen)* into the human mind.[62] Meanwhile, the work of Gustave Le Bon, first translated into German in 1908, stressed the irrationality, impulsiveness, and hotheadedness of the masses, who were said to respond to stimuli like "women, savages, and children."[63] In 1913 an essay by M. Picard appearing in a trade journal drew on Le Bon's work to claim that specific advertising methods could push reason to the background and work upon everyone equally: "the means by which to melt the most heterogeneous individual down into a collective mass is the penetrating repetition of the advertisement, in combination with the liveliness, visuality *(Bildhaftigkeit),* and authoritative certainty of the composition."[64] A 1912 book on industrial psychology included a chapter on advertising that stressed that to be effective, the ad must imprint itself into the mind; it must be easily understandable; but above all, it must make as vivid an impression as possible by means of large size, lively colors, and skillful use of empty spaces.[65] Thus the psychology of advertising began to define and scientize the impact of visuality on the individual and on "the masses." It thereby lent scientific validity to the shift (already well under way) to simpler compositions with clearer, more codified, and more repetitive representations.

By the end of the first decade of the twentieth century, the markers of race had become so commonplace in commercial art that they were able to be deployed independently—as a mere reference that could stand in for the larger implications of racial difference and colonial mastery, wholly defining the figure within that visual and discursive constellation. What drove advertisers and graphic artists in this tendency toward abstracted racial markers? The primary trend in art-historical circles has been to credit the vision of the individual artist. In this vein, art historians have echoed the laurels that advertising writers bestowed on such graphic artists as Julius Klinger, treating his minimalist abstraction for Palm, for instance, as a moment of innovation rather than as merely another iteration of a commercial strategy following a clear trend.[66] Indeed, the minimalism of the "German Modern" and the simplicity of the *Sachplakat* (Object Poster) or *Neue Sachlichkeit* (New Objectivity) in poster art are described most often within a genealogy of German artistic genius, starting with Lucien Bernhard's inspiration and ending with Ludwig Hohlwein's perfection.[67] But the 1903 image that opened up the previous chapter (see Figure 5.1) suggests that abstraction, as a stylistic approach, predated these innovative artists.

The movement in commercial graphics toward abstraction—at least, toward abstraction of fixed stereotypes of racial difference—was inspired by the demands of mass culture, particularly the continuing pull toward exaggeration. Racial markers were beginning to become ubiquitous, which made them understandable to the broadest possible popular audience, even on such reduced forms as advertising stamps. But this also made them more ordinary. As we saw in Chapter 4—where the burdens carried by colonial subjects became larger over time—the contradictory compulsion in advertising to conform to the norms of the audience on the one hand, while nonetheless attracting attention on the other, can lead to the exaggeration of those graphic conventions that are recognized as the norm. This argument applies equally well to racial markers, such as the size of black figures' lips. In the world of mass-circulated imagery, the more ubiquitous the racialization of a certain physical feature became, the more this marker became prerequisite to identify the figure *as* an African. But as the exaggerated racializing convention itself became the new norm, it paradoxically lost its capacity to startle or to capture attention. Ultimately, further exaggeration of the feature within the bounds of a realistic depiction was no longer tenable. Abstraction of the convention itself offered a solution: the artists could reference the hegemonic stereotype that had become standard in the consumer imaginary by making a gesture toward it. Abstraction, in this view, can be seen as a reflection of pictorial hegemony.

We can see the outlines of this at work by returning to Ludwig Hohlwein's poster for H. Schlinck's Palmin (see Plate 19). It is, in fact, a revision of the Palmin ad crafted by Ivo Puhonny in 1905 (see Figure 4.23), and a side-by-side comparison shows how much has changed in eight short years. In each illustration the black figure in this image serves to authenticate the product. Yet Hohlwein's 1913 version is several levels of abstraction away from that childlike native. The composition overall looks "flatter"—as much a referent as a representation. The red lips are the focal point of the composition; their predominance momentarily distracts the eye from the fact that the nose slits are done in red rather than white, which lends a subtle sense of the animal to the figure and further distances the figure from a "human" model. Hohlwein's abstract figuration allows for the easy blending of four different pictorial traditions: the earrings identify the figure as an African, the giant spoon and apron harken back to the black cook-servant of American cooking ads, and the shiny shoes tap into the dandy of American minstrelsy. Finally, for good measure, the chef's hat is actually a Moorish turban, which ties the figure into a fourth pictorial tradition, the venerable incarnations of blackness associated with the Orient. In short, *all* major motifs of black figures in Germany have been neatly fused into one single overarching composite symbol of blackness—a symbol of blackness defined by abstract racial features. Images like this 1913 ad for Palmin cannot begin to be understood without fully appreciating the trajectory of all the different black images that preceded them—and the way that blackness has now been fused into an almost universal stereotype—a stereotype that sits in juxtaposition with the modern commodity.

Conclusion

In all of their incarnations, images of blacks remained only one facet of a complex consumer imaginary of the *Kaiserreich*. While it could be argued that these images were among the most vivid and power-laden, they were by no means the most prevalent. Images of a single thin white woman, for instance, proffered soap more frequently than racially differentiated blacks; images of cherubic white German children decorated more cocoa tins than laboring African colonial subjects. Yet the fact that by the First World War virtually *every* image of blacks deployed fell into the patterns of racialization described in this chapter speaks a great deal about the normative and uniformity-producing potential of mass culture. These increasingly fixed images of Africans were crucial in creating and sustaining these images of whiteness—and of German racial and consumer identity.

A number of disparate forces came together to produce this racialized consumer imaginary. The surge of belligerent nationalism in the popular press after the 1904 uprising in German South-West Africa was a crystallizing moment in its genesis. In the immediate aftermath, a few hastily drafted ads illustrated virulently racist jingoism. The professional designers of the larger firms looking to capitalize on the event, however, deployed imagery both ambiguous and humorous, looking for their images to find broader appeal, appeal that would cross political and class divides. Moreover, though the process of racialization as a pictorial convention had already begun well before 1904, the uprising of the Herero, and the racial war (and genocide) that followed, accelerated and intensified this trend. But the details of this intensification are crucial. The stylistic conventions of racialization and infantilization were not so much to convince the German public—in propagandistic fashion—that Africans in the German colonies were actually harmless or loyal and obedient subjects. Instead, the intensification of racial imagery arose out of a different commercial dynamic. The motif of the African in German advertising had, by 1904, already become too useful to abandon: it was a convenient method to pique curiosity through exoticism; to seize attention through sensationalistic exaggeration; to demonstrate the supremacy of the commodity by juxtaposing it against the unclothed and uncivilized; and to flatter the white viewer by implicating him in a visual constellations of power. Advertisers, in short, increasingly racialized and diminished Africans after the violence of war *in order* to continue to exploit them.

Racialization emerged tactically, from myriad commercial interests, but cohered into a larger visual strategy seeking to reach the broadest range of potential customers. Images of racial difference created an omnipresent racial Other, against which political or social divisions among potential customers would recede. At the same time, racialized colonial imagery could establish the ascendancy of the commodity in the optical plane—a plane all the more powerful in that it remained one step removed from the realm of cognition and interpretation (see Plate 24). In the decentralized but increasingly hegemonic world of mass-produced visuality, allegorical figures gelled into types, types serialized into stereotypes, and stereotypes hammered into racial icons. The emergence of a hegemonic vision of racial uniformity in Germany—of black difference and white supremacy—lay as much in the origins of mass consumer society as in the colonial project itself. The imaginary of colonial power lay close to the heart of modern consumer society.

CONCLUSION

> The advertisement wants mass consumption. To this end, it reshapes the purchasing individual into a mass.
>
> —*Siedels Reklame,* 1913

In the three decades from the mid-1880s until just before the outbreak of the First World War in 1914, Germany was refashioned, in part by means of an overseas gaze. In these thirty years Germany developed into an imperial power, and over these same thirty years it built the foundation for a modern consumer-oriented society. The first of these transformations involved geopolitics; the second, industrial economics. Yet each also involved fundamental shifts in identity and in imagination. Moreover, the imaginative portions of these transformations were steeped in the visual world; Germans saw what they would become before they became it. The possibilities of empire were viewed before they were pursued. The British empire, for its part, was not just a political entity but a powerful spectacle in its own right; imperial exhibitions, Zulu shows, and civilizing soap vignettes demonstrated not just the prestige of empire and not just its political economy, but its potential profitability in the domestic realm as well. The fusion of commodity culture and imperial prestige in Britain looked to be seamless, at least from across the Channel. In Germany the culture-empire nexus was not seamless; there were profound divides between radical nationalists and curious cosmopolitans, between erudite *Bildungsbürger* and modern new professionals, between politically driven activists and professionally driven graphic artists. A common commodity culture of Germany could be built, in part, on a series of powerful images—images that invited viewers—everyday Germans—into the position of colonial master, receiving the goods of the world. The actual fact of the German colonial economy's insolvency was beside the point; after 1900 every German knew what being a colonial ruler—a *world* power—meant, merely by scanning the advertisements in the paper or seeing *Weltpolitik* neatly packaged on the store shelves. Few recognized the very practice of visual advertising that built this vision of German colonial identity was itself an import, first introduced and legitimized by the overseas gaze of pioneers looking at imperial Britain.

The United States was an even more prominent source of inspiration for German commercial interests—a veritable wellspring of modern methods of marketing. The American style of promotion, as characterized by P. T. Barnum, found its way into the sight of Germans as lithographs of the outlandish—in living color. The most prominent American diversion, however, was the minstrel show: its boisterous and witty discriminations proved alluring to German audiences, and its imagery irresistible to German advertisers. This modern, savage America worked its way into the travelogues of the earliest German advertising literature, and if later advertising writers critiqued the "American style" as excessive and overly loud, advertising practitioners were far more embracing.

Germans' cultural practice of advertising drew from these transatlantic modernities but also from a third overseas land—Africa. To British and American imports, Germans added a new gloss from their own transoceanic "engagement"—namely, their own colonial project. Ethnographic edification and geographic elucidation offered a patina of legitimacy, used by exhibition organizers to raise up the "commodity fetish," and used by the Panopticons to mask their lineage from the houses of Barnum and Tussaud. Colonial enthusiasts, meanwhile, sought to direct public attention overseas by means of a well-organized publicity machine, but kept strict focus on scientific authenticity and national authority. Pioneering lithographers were more freewheeling, crafting vivid views of dancing primitives and lunging warriors to captivate the public eye. Individually these groups had no connection with each other, and often worked at cross purposes. Collectively their vision(s) had an enormous impact. In the 1890s Africa was coming into vogue. By the fin de siècle Africa had entered into the emergent, colorful miasma of advertising and packaging as a stimulating terrain for power.

Among all the lands offering exotic allure, from China to the South Pacific to South America, the template for "Africa"—its dark continent a tabula rasa—offered a territory most suited to forging desirable (if spurious) connections. Advertisers could graft the aura of the tropics onto chicory coffee produced in Germany. The colonial tableau could visually exalt a product or commodity in a way that just looked more believable, because its constructions were displaced to a distant, and very different, land. Moreover, the "colonization" of Africa, as a political fact, but equally as a visual pattern, helped to efface the uncomfortable pedantry of visual commands given to German viewers. It did this by displacing such commands onto an obvious inferior: a colonized subordinate. To visually underscore the obviousness of this "inferiority," advertisers developed visual tactics of nakedness (to illustrate lack), diminutive stature, and subordinate posture. When the thus-constituted native was enraptured by the commodity in a pictorial frame of colonized Africa, the tableau could be presented as innately natural, inoffensively humorous, or both.

The figure of the African native had thus become, by 1900, a staple of German visual advertising. It was by no means the most prevalent but it was one of the most visually arresting, and visually powerful. And joining it to another pictorial convention, a separate visual trajectory, would make it more so. German designers and advertisers began to take their imported racial themes, drawn off of minstrel show posters and pulled off of American packaging, and translocate these themes to Africa. Rather contradictorily, this "Africanization" of racial patterns served to Germanize them. The racialization of African figures dovetailed with Germany's own tradition of satirical exaggeration in popular caricature and with pressing geopolitical events.

The 1904 Herero uprising, Germany's first large-scale military operation as a unified nation, offered both possibilities and pitfalls. German military strategy quickly turned ruthless and its policy genocidal; many in the military and among the public saw this as a race war not bound by the norms of civilization. The theme of race war also suited the commercial interests of the new mass-circulation press. For advertising, however, race war brought a set of attendant problems: how could businessmen and designers continue to deploy the useful and ubiquitous figure of the African without activating an undesirable association with violence or with a racial

Figure C.1 Advertisement for Cocosa margarine, 1909, featuring "the Little Coco." Notice how the different children are set into sharp relief by the abstracted black figure; the depiction of the children—itself idealized—comes across as more realistic through stark contrast. Trademarked by the Holländische Margarine-Werke Jurgens & Prinzen GmbH, Goch. *Source:* WZB (1909): 1870, reg. no. 121870.

enemy? The pictorial strategy of racialization became a way to salvage the figure, for it optically defined Africans as both childishly harmless and humorously different. Amplified by the self-reinforcing dynamic of mass culture, such strategies of racial depiction for black figures had become hegemonic by 1910. "Africans" by this time were formed into a coherent stereotype, and this stereotype provided a convenient visual foil. This hegemonic imagery helped—along the line of Siedels's observation that opened this chapter—to form Germans into a mass (Figure C.1). From there it was but a short step into the new category of mass consumer.

This brief visual history of colonial rule and visual history of racial differentiation after 1885 diverges from histories based on textual sources in a number of crucial ways. First, most political and social histories emphasize the widening divisions in Germany in the late nineteenth century, particularly the growing sociopolitical divisions between workers/social democrats and the bourgeoisie/nationalist right. These divisions are seen as only growing sharper leading up to the First World War. Without contradicting that sociopolitical history, commercial visuality shows an opposite development not toward division, but toward integration—integration around hardening visions of race. (Though unfortunately not addressed in this book, a first impression from scanning trademark registrations, posters, and advertising stamps is that other visions also became hegemonic—visions of female domesticity, of idealized childhood, and of militarized masculinity—and these visions were also increasingly "generic," in the sense of offering a new pictorial identity divorced from explicit demarcations of social class.) This hegemony of racial differentiation, moreover, was structured entirely around blackness as the foil for the white German. Anti-Semitism, so venomous in discourse and ideology across the German right and in society more broadly even before 1914, was simply not present in commercial imagery; in advertising's world of expedient color contrasts, race was constructed against Africans, not against Jews.[1]

The visual history of commerce in this book also differs from histories that describe a relative stasis, even stifling conservatism, along the main axes of bourgeois culture—a stasis that drove a small artistic avant-garde into rejecting that culture.[2] The imagery of advertising, to the contrary, shows a very rapid disruption of traditional bourgeois patterns and habits taking place over just a few decades. We see that disruption in the effacement of established authorities (scientific, ideological, political) in favor of raw visual power. And we see it in the abandonment of the respectability of edification in favor of shock value. The new capacity of mass image-reproduction circulated these disruptions to a public that was, if not the entire nation, certainly larger than anything previously seen. Little wonder that the most provocative movement in the early twentieth century, the Dada, named themselves after an advertising slogan—an advertising slogan, moreover, of a company that frequently deployed colonial and racial imagery.[3] The roots of sensationalistic, distracted, profoundly visual modern German consumer society stretches back not to the tumult of Weimar, but earlier—to the Empire. Visuality in Imperial Germany—what Germans saw—was increasingly driven by a visual syntax of advertising that clamored for attention on the one hand, and yet strove to conform to expectations on the other. The dynamic of visual advertising pushed for that which was radical, but yet still felt like common sense (even if that "common sense" emerged through the mass reproduction of its imaginations). The notion of race meshed perfectly with that dynamic. The vision of race became one important element in the construction of advertising's empire.

The Certainties of War

The road to the First World War was paved with diplomatic bungling and economic rivalry, with extreme nationalism and unchecked militarism, and with leaders' efforts to distract their citizenry from demands for political reform. Historians increasingly include the heightened competition in the colonial realm among these contributing elements.[4] In German domestic politics, the naval arms race that proved so destabilizing was fueled by a loudly proclaimed *Weltpolitik,* summarized in Bülow's famous words that proclaimed Germany's *desire* for a "place in the sun." Many historical accounts still treat the notion of this "desire" unproblematically, as if it were a natural or logical outgrowth of Germany's new military and economic strength. But desire, as theorists such as Anne Stoler have argued, is never innate; it is created and propagated.[5] And if the new practice of advertising excelled at anything, it was the creation of desire.

In 1911 Germany sent a gunboat to press its claims to Morocco—claims with a vision of colonial rule not far behind them. Large sections of the German press and public expressed elation. The resulting crisis—the second in the decade to arise out of competing French and German claims to Morocco—led Europe to the brink of war. When the German leadership was forced to back down from their diplomatically untenable claims, this elation turned rapidly into disillusionment, and even proregime elements on the right savaged the German government in their criticism. Similar colonialist moves three decades before, around the first Samoan bill, had met with public apathy, and it should seem puzzling to us why an imperialist gesture in faraway North Africa found such wide resonance in Germany in 1911. Much of this had to do with the political and social mobilization of the extreme right, of course.[6] But the broader public's vision of Morocco—what it was, and what its "ownership" would offer Germans—also fed on or flowed from a consumer imaginary filled with both orientalist and colonialist imagery.

Colonialism was not just international politics; it was a domestic agenda—and grist for advertising to capitalize upon. An advertisement for Pebeco toothpaste from 1911, for instance, offers the following reassurance: "The Congo Accord means that we give up Morocco . . . but not that we give up Pebeco!" (Figure C.2). The Beiersdorf Company in Hamburg, which also manufactured Nivea skin cream, crafted this ad to capture the attention of the public by drawing upon the intensity of interest in the second Morocco crisis.[7] The advertisement is geared to a mass

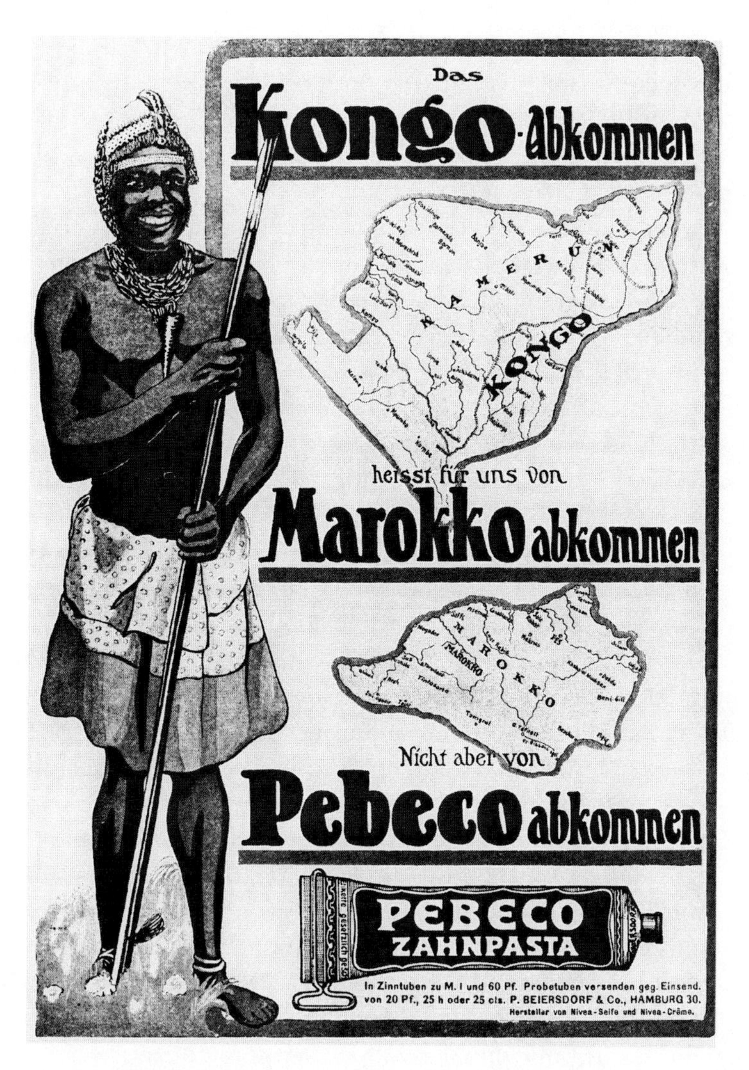

Figure C.2 Advertisement for Pebeco toothpaste from 1911: "The Congo Accord means that we give up Morocco . . . but not that we give up Pebeco!" Pebeco toothpaste was a brand of Beiersdorf & Co. in Hamburg, which also manufactures Nivea skin lotion. *Source: Jugend* no. 52 (1911).

audience and skirts any political divisions: it neither castigates the German government for weakness, nor does it chide German imperialists for their belligerence. Instead, it offers a new solution—the commodity as compensation. The image of the smiling, spear-carrying African in the Pebeco ad offers the visual glue that pulls politically and socially diverse

German viewers together. This African native is depicted in the mode of a colonial subordinate—with partial clothing, bare feet, native jewelry—a mode that by 1911 would have been recognizable to every German. The figure of the African native stands obediently and patiently, providing the attention-arresting element of the composition.

But what does the Morocco-Congo Accord actually have to do with German toothpaste? As we have seen at multiple points, illustrations that do not make sense can offer evidence of the reception of commercial imagery. In this case, the white smile of the African figure is the ostensible reason for the ad's colonial theme, because Africans are "known" to have particularly healthy, white teeth. This "information," however, was conveyed in Germany by two decades of toothpaste advertisements. Brands such as Kalodont, Anumu, Odol, Seefeld's Pulvaton, and Schmittner's "Tooth-balm with the Negro Head" all used images of African figures with gleaming white smiles in the first decade of the twentieth century. These German brands, in turn, were "colonial" reconfigurations of an earlier imagery of the black American minstrel; the white-toothed minstrels had been deployed by German brands such as Komasept, Florian, Sebald, and Seeger. The minstrel-toothpaste imagery had originally come over on American toothpaste tubes (an American invention) and also on American shoe polish tins that featured gleaming white teeth to better juxtapose against shoe-polish-black skin. Beiersdorf's Pebeco ad—starting in the midst of the Moroccan crisis—utterly relies upon this twenty years of German commercial imagery to be meaningful, in order for the Morocco-toothpaste connection not to be bewildering. At the apse of a visual trajectory of racial toothpaste ads, Pebeco's ad about Morocco, interestingly enough, taps into not only the exited international rivalry surrounding French colonial expansion in North Africa, but the excited national apprehension surrounding American cultural expansion across the Atlantic.

The very next year, in 1912, a diatribe against *Dollerika* was published by Hans Sachs. As a young man in the late 1890s, Sachs had been fascinated by posters and became a private collector. He was a founder of the Association of Friends of the Poster in 1905 and became a champion of advertising as art; he was also the editor of *Das Plakat,* the leading journal of German poster design. In the 1912 newsletter of the new Organization of German Advertisers, Sachs began, "I count myself among those who has been cured from his enthusiasm for America." He continued, "We all consider America to be the land of the screaming advertisement, the loud imposition, the tasteless presumption."[8] Sachs went on to frame his criticisms of America—or more accurately, his broader criticisms of modernity articulated *as* America—in a revealing way: America was artistically degenerate, he claimed. And this was because America was *racially* degenerate. As "evidence" of this racial degeneracy, Sachs misrepresented (or misunderstood) the work of the anthropologist Franz Boas, claiming that children born in America were a new race unto themselves:

> Even children who are born just shortly after the arrival of their parents in America develop in a way that is fundamentally different from their own siblings who had been born earlier in Europe. This occurs particularly with the shape of the skull, and the facial features. These features rapidly develop into a type that we all know so well and find so characteristic of the "American." . . . The very notion of "art," with this race, is quite remote.[9]

Sachs was no ultranationalist or Pan-German. He was first and foremost a poster aficionado and aesthete. (And he would ultimately find refuge in the United States in 1938, fleeing Nazi persecution for his Jewish heritage and working as a dentist in New York well into the 1960s.)[10] Nonetheless, Sachs's spirited attack on American style was framed first in racial terms. Advertising writers' attacks on America over the first decade of the twentieth century coincided with a gathering anti-Americanism in Germany more broadly.[11] The broader criticism of America became more and more bound up with racial rhetoric—specifically, rhetoric of American mongrelization. Much of this was due to the popularization of race science, and its growing legitimacy especially among the nationalist right.[12] But the racialized imagery of America circulating in German culture may have been one factor feeding into this rhetoric (see Plate 25). The circulation of black minstrels and tray-carrying servants, of black shoe-shine boys and pickanninies, in commercial visuality presented a two-dimensional black minority in the German public sphere, and it might not be too outlandish to suggest this contributed to the growing notion that America, and to some degree modernity itself, was racially an Other. In the long run, imagery of American blackness may very well have spawned as much racial anxiety as racial validation.

Hans Sachs's diatribe about American excess and the incapacity of the "American race" to appreciate or create art was followed, on the very

Figure C.3 Advertisement for AGFA photographic equipment, reproduced in a professional ad journal as an "exemplary combination of illustration and textual insert." *Source: Mitteilungen des Vereins Deutscher Reklamfachleute* 33 (1912): 10.

next page, by an ad the editor (likely Sachs himself) termed "exemplary." It was an advertisement for AGFA photography gear featuring a white German man, in high boots and pith helmet, with a camera, eagerly looking forward; stooped behind him is an ignored, semidressed African subordinate, rummaging through an AGFA package to find his safarigoing "boss" a new roll of film (Figure C.3). The slogan reads, "dependable and longlasting in the tropics." The German "race" was not only suited to create art; it was suited to colonial rule—at least in the world of imagery.

In the lead-up to the First World War, domestic political divisions, not the least between Social Democrats and the nationalist right, were increasingly sharp, and many Germans of all persuasions craved some sort of unifying ideal or mission. An ad like that of Pebeco or AGFA (see Figures C.2 and C.3) in fact reveals the contours of an integrative imaginative identity, even though it was not consciously recognized as such. Colonialist visions in consumer-oriented imagery could accommodate all political stances, from the Social Democrats of the left to the Pan-Germans of the extreme right, and the racialization of these visions made them look like an unquestionable reflection of the natural order of things. The advantages of a position as beneficiary of colonial labor—and implicitly, as a *Weltmacht*—was paraded daily in front of Germans' very eyes (see Plate 26). The problem with an integrative identity based around colonialist imagination is that, just as it fed *from* imperial rivalry, so too could it feed *into* it. The degree to which convictions of cultural supremacy and racial entitlement, evident in the visual cultures of *all* the belligerent powers, contributed to the outbreak of what Fritz Fischer called the "War of Illusions" must remain a matter of conjecture.[13] But the fact that German superiority (like British superiority or French superiority) was imaged over and over again in the commercial realm—in a new visual syntax of certainty—might very well have contributed to the detachment from realism with which the German public (like those of all the European powers) went to war. Jeffrey Verhey has exposed the myth of German unanimity in support of war; press reports aside, actual German attitudes were more complicated than unrestrained joy.[14] But visual advertising had only one syntax—that of certainty—and only one register: that of enthusiasm. The degree to which the new of advertising might have fueled the drive to war is difficult to answer, but it is an important question to ask.

One effect of advertising on the war is clear. After August 1914 the new war was suddenly, and rather artificially, drawn in racial colors. Official German wartime propaganda generally eschewed the techniques of bestialization or demonization deployed by the English, French, and (eventually) Americans; there was no official German counterpart to the way that Anglo-American propaganda bestialized "the Hun," largely to avoid offending the sensibilities of the German public.[15] Depictions of *non*-white French and British troops were fair game, however. Soldiers from the colonies often became the target of German caricature or propaganda that stressed not only their inferiority, but also their nonhumanity.[16] German satirical magazines in particular obsessed over caricatured depictions of African troops in French and British uniforms. This permissibility of extremist caricature—just so long as it was directed against non-whites—could have interesting implications, when liberally applied (Figure C.4). Magazines like the venerable *Kladderadatsch* or the more provocative *Simplicissimus,* and even the artistically inclined *Jugend,* spent

Figure C.4 Caricature of John Bull from *Kladderadatsch* 68, no. 25 (1915): cover.

a great deal of ink showing how the Allies' deployment of "savages" belied their claims to be civilized nations. All of the techniques carefully developed over the previous decade were used. The seriousness with which these racialized caricatures were taken, and could even intertwine with less jocular racist perceptions, is revealed when, for instance, authorities took racial photographs and measurements of the non-white French and English troops in German and Austrian prisoner-of-war camps.[17] Among other goals, they were seeking empirical validation of racial stereotypes.

The war may have ended in 1918 (at least in the minds of the Allies), but the bestialization of Allied colonial troops did not. In 1920 French soldiers occupied the demilitarized Rhineland; some of these troops came from the French colonies, most from North Africa. In a well-orchestrated campaign that began immediately after the occupation, various groups on the German right, with government support, began a public propaganda campaign to protest the French use of these "black" troops. The campaign against this so-called Black Horror on the Rhine was aimed at two audiences; it was designed on the one hand to unite a politically divided Germany against the occupation, and on the other, to arouse the indignation of an Anglo-American audience.[18] The propaganda itself notoriously deployed a highly sexualized imagery of vicious, subhuman Africans raping young German maidens. Importantly, the black figures in the visual propaganda were all highly racialized, often to the point of making the figure almost nonhuman (Figure C.5). In some cases these figures featured in lurid sexual scenes.[19]

The propaganda campaign rarely bestialized white French occupying troops with the same visceral savagery. The graphic, sexualized imagery of the Black Horror campaign drew its saliency from the circulation of racial imagery in the consumer realm from before the war. The visuality of 1920s propaganda differed markedly from that of the consumer imaginary in the 1910s, of course: commercial scenes of racial difference in the late *Kaiserreich* were constructed to flatter the German viewer. While propagandistic scenes of racial difference in early Weimar were constructed to threaten the German viewer. Yet in some ways the propaganda scenes retain the essential configurations of advertising, namely overstatement, simplified delineation, and repetition of patterns of depiction. The propaganda campaign against the Black Horror inverted some of the basic optics of the power relationship, however: instead of diminishing the racialized figures, for instance, figures were enlarged. Instead of depicting them with large, round eyes (evocative of naïve immaturity), they were depicted with eyes hidden under helmets or heavy brows, to heighten the sense of threat.

Figure C.5 Caricature of the "Black Horror" (French colonial occupation troops) in 1923. *Source: Kladderadatsch* 76, no. 25 (1923).

The End of Colonial Rule?

If racial imagery was enlisted into the German cause in 1914, which lasted well into the 1920s, colonial imagery did not fare quite so well, at least not so overtly. When hostilities broke out the war itself became the primary concern of the commercial mass media, and firms that normally deployed colonial, Oriental, and otherwise exotic motifs tended to drop them, quickly shifting to themes more visibly nationalistic and militaristic. Cigarette tins with colorful Oriental landscapes were literally papered over with stickers of German and Austro-Hungarian flags; this certified not only their Germanness but also the tobacco manufacturer's seriousness and commitment to the national war effort.[20] New brands such as National Pride or Field Gray quickly emerged across every product category. Themes of marching soldiers, of nationalism, and of military technology became dominant commercial motifs almost overnight.[21]

In 1916, however, as war weariness set in, exotic themes once again began to resurface in trademark registrations. The orientalized Moor had come into fashion in commercial imagery around 1912; Julius Staege's coffee brand, featuring a black face with bright red lips wearing a red fez, was trademarked in 1914.[22] All of these orientalized Moor-figures turn to Middle Eastern motifs (and fantasies) by means of costume, namely the "harem" pants, the turban, and the pointed slipper. But the racialized features—large red lips, round white eyes, infantilization—had been honed and perfected on figures of African colonial subjects for a decade before the war. (Indeed, the Staege firm itself had deployed images of *African* colonial subjects in its advertising as early as 1903.) Though military themes briefly dominated in 1914 and 1915, by 1916 these orientalized black figures began to reappear (see Plate 27). Indeed, the Sarotti Moor, which would become one of the most famous commercial icons in German history, was designed by Julius Gipkins in 1918, the last year of the war (see Figure I.4).[23] Gipkins was likely imitating the designs of Staege and Goldenes Haus (and many others besides). Perhaps the new wave of orientalized Moors represented a return to exoticism that could serve as a distraction from the unrelentingly grim news from the front. Trademark registrations overall, however, became increasingly scarce after 1916 due to shortages of paper, of manpower, and of the commodities themselves. (They remained scarce until around 1920 or so.) Rationing and widespread shortages of even the most basic necessities had shrunk the commercial world itself to a pitiful skeleton.

The First World War cost Germany more than 2 million dead. It also spelled the end of the German colonial empire. The colonies were cut off from Germany and lost one by one to Allied military campaigns. Only in

German East Africa did German forces manage to hold out to some degree, waging a successful guerrilla campaign against a numerically superior Allied army right up to the Armistice of 1918. This resistance made its commander, Paul Emil von Lettow-Vorbeck, a hero during the war and generated the myth of the "loyal Askari"—an oft-repeated refrain that colonized Africans had been so devoted to their stern yet beloved German masters that they were willing to die for them.[24] The trope of the loyal Askari validated German colonialism *post facto;* its standard illustration was of an East African holding a German flag—a clear derivation from the emblem of the German Colonial Exhibition of 1896, itself copied from the cover of Carl Peters's 1891 book. In the visual field, the German colonial project had come full circle.

Yet the loss of the colonies was a staggering blow to the relevance of institutionalized colonialism. During the war and after, the ranks of colonial enthusiasts dwindled.[25] German colonial enthusiasts attempted to regroup upon the cessation of hostilities in 1918: a number of small organizations emerged to complement and compete with the German Colonial Society, and these various organizations joined in shrill denunciation of the hated Versailles Treaty (that had permanently ratified the loss of Germany's colonies).[26] The efforts of the old colonialists, however, became largely irrelevant in the shifting political landscape after the 1920s, and it would migrate into a burgeoning colonial nostalgia industry.[27] Hans Grimm's colonialist and anti-Semitic novel *Volk ohne Raum*, appearing in 1926, sold more than 300,000 copies over the following decade; collectible trading cards of the colonies surged, and a feature films about Germany's colonial past were produced.[28] Nonetheless, the mass mobilization of the right in the Weimar years would occur not over colonial revanchism but around the twin poles of militarism and anti-Semitism.

A Look Forward: The Cannibals of Weimar

What about race? What role did the certainties of race, forged in the consumer realm, play in the postwar and postcolonial republic? Though an investigation of the patterns of colonial and racial imagery in Weimar advertising ranges far beyond the scope of this book, it is clear that the imagery of colonial mastery and racialized stereotypes of blackness each continued to circulate through the broadest reaches of the Weimar con-

Figure C.6 Advertisement for abrasive soap powder from 1923 by Wilhelm Nocker of Köln-Mülheim. "White Like Snow." *Source:* WZB (1923): 657, reg. no. 299084.

sumer imaginary (Figure C.6). In consumer-oriented imagery, a glance through the trademark registrations from the 1920s suggests that a common depiction of blackness in the Weimar years reworked the African native into a more "humorous" image: that of the cartoon cannibal. The figure of the cartoon cannibal followed many of the conventions of the racialized native of Imperial Germany, but some the earnestness of racial difference gave way to exaggeration to the point of absurdity. Human bones as hairpins, or faces contorted into farcical or comical expressions, often appeared with products related to modern technology, for instance, seeking to set up a racialized dichotomy of the modern product juxtaposed against the *funny* savage. Significantly, many of these scenes forgo the tableau of colonial power to highlighted the impudent cleverness of the native.[29] Such cartooning of race in Weimar Germany seems to wink at its own patent *in*authenticity. Some of it seems to poke fun at the conventions of racial marking that became so pervasive a decade earlier.

The 1920s also saw a dramatic increase in the numbers of African Americans and even Africans in the German metropole. Former colonial subjects could travel more freely to Germany after 1918; and African American entertainers became popular in jazz clubs and cabarets. Most famously, Josephine Baker's revue played to packed audiences in Berlin and other German cities in the 1920s; her notorious dance wearing nothing but a skirt of bananas was performed in 1928 in Berlin's Theater des Westens. Baker used the stereotype of African savagery to her advantage, as a lure for German urbanites looking for a taste of something wild.[30] She and other black performers also played off of—and played with—stereotypes that had been staples of German consumer fantasy. To give just one example, Baker's famous dance with the banana skirt was performed in front of a curtain decorated with an enormous caricature of her several stories high. This cartoonish image exaggerated her facial features, such as the size of her eyes and mouth, to an absurd degree; it distorted her body to exaggerate her sexuality; and it shortened her banana skirt to the point of immodesty. This backdrop was painted by Benno von Arent (who later became a Nazi and protégé of Hitler). But when Baker performed in front of this curtain, she comically attempted to contort her body into its pose. Her own staging and orchestration of her show exposed the caricature itself, with all of its racial and sexual exaggerations, for what it was: a grotesque distortion. And in her pantomime, she invited her audience of insiders to join her in an enjoyable send-up of it.[31] Thus, in the longer view, the mass-reproduced stereotypes forged in the imperial era on the eve of the First World War were not unrelentingly unidirectional in their presentation of power. The hegemony of racialized depictions before the war could become a theater for irony afterward. "The Negroes Are Conquering Europe," wrote the poet Ivan Goll about the new dances, with approval; "Do the Negroes need us? Or are we not sooner in need of them?"[32]

There were reactions against such playful reinventions. One writer for the Nazi paper *Völkische Beobachter* wrote scornfully of those "belles of the ball" who "enter the paradise of cannibal dances looking totally barbaric."[33] Reactionaries in Weimar overall showed a great deal of discomfort with the black presence in Berlin. When Wilhelm Frick, the first National Socialist to hold a ministerial-level post in Germany, was appointed the Minister of the Interior and of Education in the state government of Thuringia in 1930, one of his first actions was to put into effect an "Ordinance Against Negro Culture." This law was to not only prohibit "foreign" influences, such as jazz or the "negro dances," but curtail all immoral and degenerate forms of modernism in the arts.[34] This was one of the opening salvos of Nazi cultural policy; it found full expression in the 1937 "degenerate art" exhibition and the 1938 exhibition of "degenerate music" by the National Socialist regime. The exhibition poster for the latter is infamously racist; it depicts an extremely caricatured black American saxophonist with lips so enormous as to make the figure completely inhuman. The figure wears a top hat and white gloves like the American minstrel, an earring like the African native, and a star of David pinned to the black figure's tuxedo.[35] As a whole, the poster offers a ludicrous caricature, but in the context of the National Socialist police state, that which was ludicrous always became deadly serious.

Over the past few years scholars have traced lines of continuity between the colonial project of Imperial Germany and the racial state of the National Socialists.[36] Moreover, other scholars have pointed out that National Socialist propagandists deployed the strategies first used by advertisers, including an attention to target groups, appeals to emotion, reductionism, and hammering repetition.[37] Often overlooked are the themes of advertisements themselves—particularly racial themes. The National Socialists took lessons from the Black Horror campaign, melded them with pictorial techniques from the *Kaiserreich*, and deployed blackness as the visual epitome of corruption. In National Socialist propaganda, racist depictions of blacks provided a secondary racial Other, used most frequently to highlight the degeneracy of American culture and of the Weimar-era American imports, particularly jazz.

The primary racial foil for National Socialism, of course, was not the figure of the black but the figure of the Jew: extreme anti-Semitic racialized caricature, often inserted into scenes that were highly sexualized, formed one of the centerpieces of National Socialist propaganda, whether in posters or in the pages of the *Völkische Beobachter*. Anti-Semitism has a very long history in Germany society and culture, but the 1920s seems to be the first time that such racialized and sexualized anti-Semitic imagery was deemed acceptable in the broader reaches of the public realm (and not just because of the liberalization of censorship laws). Anti-Semitism never emerged in the German consumer imagery as a vision that sold commodities; yet the highly racialized imagery of black figures in the German consumer imaginary before 1914 could not but have helped to acquaint, to normalize, and to some degree legitimize the exaggeration of *any* exaggerated presentation of "race" to the German public.[38]

Certainly, specific designers who had built their careers around imaging blacks in the service of whites, most famously Ludwig Hohlwein, became masters at depicting the figure of the whites in the face of all so-called Others, whether slavs, blacks, or Jews. The chiseled Aryan that came to occupy a privileged position in National Socialist imagery was perfected by Hohlwein, who, as we have seen, had built his reputation—and his repertoire of racial constructions—in the 1910s. Before the war his figures of blackness worked as visual foils for building his figures of whiteness. In the Weimar era he would hone this technique further; black figures still sometimes provided a visual foil for his white figures, as his work for Zeiss optics and his famous poster for Kaloderma shaving cream, both built around themes of colonial power, suggest.[39] More often, however, his figures of whiteness—his archetypal Aryan, eyes in shadow—stood alone. The dark contrast to the Aryan lay outside and below the frame of view, perhaps now so familiar as to no longer even be necessary.

For Germany, the commercial visuality of race wound its way to the public through colonialist fantasy—filtered first through Britain and America, then reconfigured by Germans as a view of Africa. Consumer-oriented visuality then streamlined and simplified racialized colonial rule—a visual colonial project—into a mass-reproduced consumer culture with an unprecedented reach. The mass-marketed colonial project constituted a significant component of Germany's own path to modernity: it illustrated a new, modern German, one very different from the German targeted by political organizations on the right or on the left. This generic German consumer—imagined in no small part by advertising—was implicated into visual constellations of colonial power not through political rhetoric but through the more pervasive yet decentralized techniques of the day-to-day practices of business. The generic German consumer, moreover, had been defined by race. When actors in German shopping malls, even in the twenty-first century, dress up in blackface to promote Sarotti chocolates—and children flock around, thrilled—this is more than just an embarrassing anachronism of blackface.[40] It is a performance of a consumer identity marked by race and global power—an identity first glimpsed in the commercial visuality of Imperial Germany.

NOTES

INDEX

NOTES

Abbreviations

BA Bundesarchiv Berlin-Lichterfelde

CMNL Circus Museum Netherlands

DHM Deutsches Historisches Museum

DKZ *Deutsche Kolonialzeitung (German Colonial News)*

MEK Museum Europäischer Kulturen

SAB Staatsarchiv Bremen

SAH Staatsarchiv Hamburg

WZB *Warenzeichenblatt des kaiserliches Patentamt* (Trademark Registration Rolls)

Introduction

1. The Swiss Oettinger/Davidoff group bought Eduard Palm in 1998. *Handelsblatt* 102 (29 May 1998): 19.

2. Jeremy Aynsley, *Graphic Design in Germany, 1890–1945* (Berkeley: University of California Press, 2000). See also Kevin Repp, "Marketing, Modernity, and 'the German People's Soul,'" in *Selling Modernity: Advertising in Twentieth-Century Germany,* ed. Pamela E. Swett, S. Jonathan Wiesen, and Jonathan R. Zatlin (Durham, NC: Duke University Press, 2007); and Steven Heller and Louise Fili, *German Modern: Graphic Design from Wilhelm to Weimar* (San Francisco: Chronicle, 1998).

3. See Stephen Eskilson, *Graphic Design: A New History* (New Haven, CT: Yale University Press, 2007).

4. Jan P. Nederveen Pieterse, *White on Black: Images of Africa and Blacks in Western Popular Culture* (New Haven, CT: Yale University Press, 1992).

5. In Germany, tobacco falls under the category of *Kolonialwaren* (colonial goods), a rubric that lends itself to colonially themed ads: see Stefanie Wolter, *Die Vermarktung des Fremden* (Frankfurt a. M.: Campus, 2005); and Gerhard Pfeisinger and Stefan Schennach, eds., *Kolonialwaren: Die Schaffung der ungleichen Welt* (Göttingen: Lamuv, 1989). An insightful argument linking British advertising to colonial economics is Anandi Ramamurthy, *Imperial Persuaders* (Manchester, UK: Manchester University Press, 2003).

6. On race science and racial "others," see classics such as Elazar Barkan, *The Retreat of Scientific Racism* (New York: Cambridge University Press, 1992); George Mosse, *Toward the Final Solution: A History of European Racism* (New York: Howard Fertig, 1978); and Sander Gilman, *Inscribing the Other* (Lincoln: University of Nebraska Press, 1991). On exoticism, see Hermann Pollig, ed., *Exotische Welten: Europäische Phantasien* (Stuttgart: Edition Cantz, 1987).

7. See Alexander Honold and Klaus R. Scherpe, *Mit Deutschland um die Welt: Eine Kulturgeschichte des Fremden in der Kolonialzeit* (Stuttgart: J. B. Metzler, 2004), 94–105. See also Wolter, *Vermarktung des Fremden,* 45–81, esp. 76.

8. Lamberty, *Reklame;* Clemens Wischermann and Eliot Shore, *Advertising and the European City: Historical Perspectives* (Aldershot, UK: Ashgate, 2000).

9. Benedict Anderson, *Imagined Communities* (New York: Verso, 1983).

10. These will be discussed in later chapters. See also Peter Martin, *Schwarze Teufel, edle Mohren: Afrikaner in Bewußtsein und Geschichte der Deutschen* (Hamburg: Junius, 1993).

11. Eckstein was a Jewish-owned firm that achieved success with its "Da Capo" brand, with more than 2,000 employees by 1914. The firm was ultimately absorbed by the Reemstma company in the 1930s.

12. It was registered with the Imperial German Patent Office for use in Germany; WZB (1905): 675, reg. no. 77688.

13. The seemingly venerable parable was pressed into service by soap advertisers as early as the 1880s; see the discussion in Chapter 5, as well as Jean Michel Massing, "From Greek Proverb to Soap Advert: Washing the Ethiopian," *Journal of the Warburg and Courtauld Institutes* 58 (1995). With such a dense array of references embodied in a playful tableau, the homoerotic overtones of the image would likely be overlooked. Champagne advertisements that would leap out at us today as homoerotic, for instance, were never commented upon as such in fin de siècle sources.

14. The N. K. Fairbanks Company of Chicago first produced an illustration of two black American children scrubbing each other in a tub as a trade card in the 1880s. For the image, see Douglas Congdon-Martin, *Images in Black: 150 Years of Black Collectibles* (West Chester, PA: Schiffer, 1990), 68. The Fairbanks Company registered the logo in Germany: see WZB (1901): 950, reg. no. 51022. On British soap advertising, see Chapter 5 and also Ramamurthy, *Imperial Persuaders,* 24–62.

15. As but one example: when the chemical manufacturer Grau & Locher issued its Othello shoe polish after 1910, it depicted a racialized black figure more akin to Sarotti than to the Othello cigarettes of 1900.

16. See Walter Benjamin, "The Work of Art in the Age of Mechanical Reproduction," in *Illuminations*, ed. Hannah Arendt (London: Pimlico, 1999).

17. See Janet Ward, *Weimar Surfaces: Urban Visual Culture in 1920s Germany* (Berkeley: University of California Press, 2001).

18. I have generally tried to avoid the term "colonial project" in this book, though it is a useful one, since the term can convey either a unity of purpose or a sense of equivalency among free-floating discourses. Both overlook the conflicts and (especially) cross-currents and cross-purposes of the diverse interests seeking to forge and (more importantly) use their own visions. The term can also obscure self-defined institutional boundaries. Overall, "colonial" is used in this book fairly precisely, involving either a politicized and/or institutional focus on "the (German) colonies" on the one hand, or a visual pattern designed to focus on or highlight some presumed relationship in "the colonies" on the other.

19. Susanne Zantop, *Colonial Fantasies: Conquest, Family, and Nation in Precolonial Germany, 1770–1870* (Durham, NC: Duke University Press, 1997). See also Todd Kontje, *German Orientalisms* (Ann Arbor: University of Michigan Press, 2004); Nina Berman, *Orientalismus, Kolonialismus, und Moderne: Zum Bild des Orients in der deutsch-sprachigen Kultur* (Stuttgart: M & P, 1996); Russel Berman, *Enlightenment or Empire: Colonial Discourse in German Culture* (Lincoln: University of Nebraska Press, 1998); and Kirsten Belgum, *Popularizing the Nation: Audience, Representation, and the Production of Identity in Die Gartenlaube, 1853–1900* (Lincoln: University of Nebraska Press, 1998).

20. Birthe Kundrus, ed., *Phantasiereiche: Der deutsche Kolonialismus in kulturgeschichtlicher Perspektive* (New York: Campus, 2003); Alexander Honold and Oliver Simons, eds., *Kolonialismus als Kultur: Literatur, Medien, Wissenschaft in der deutschen Gründerzeit des Fremden* (Tübingen: A. Francke, 2002); Joachim Warmbold, *Germania in Africa: Germany's Colonial Literature* (New York: Lang, 1989); John Noyes, *Colonial Space: Spatiality in the Discourse of German South West Africa, 1884–1915* (Philadelphia: Harwood Academic Publishers, 1992); Marcia Klotz, "Memoirs from a German Colony: What Do White Women Want?" in *Eroticism & Containment: Notes from the Flood Plain*, ed. Carol Siegel and Ann Kibbey, *Genders 20* (New York: New York University Press, 1994); Sara Friedrichsmeyer, Sara Lennox, and Susanne Zantop, eds., *The Imperialist Imagination: German Colonialism and Its Legacy* (Ann Arbor: University of Michigan Press, 1999).

21. George Steinmetz, *The Devil's Handwriting: Precoloniality and the German Colonial State in Qingdao, Samoa, and Southwest Africa* (Chicago: University of Chicago Press, 2007); Jürgen Zimmerer, *Deutsche Herrschaft über Afrikaner: Staatlicher*

Machtanspruch und Wirklichkeit im Kolonialen Namibia (Munster: LIT, 2004); Birthe Kundrus, *Moderne Imperialisten: Das Kaiserreich im Spiegel seiner Kolonien* (Köln: Böhlau, 2003).

22. Lora Wildenthal, "Race, Gender, and Citizenship in the German Colonial Empire," in *Tensions of Empire: Colonial Cultures in a Bourgeois World,* ed. Frederick Cooper and Ann Laura Stoler (Berkeley: University of California Press, 1997); Cornelia Essner, "Zwischen Vernunft und Gefühl: Die Reichstagdebatten von 1912 um koloniale 'Rassenmischehe' und 'Sexualität,'" *Zeitschrift für Geschichtswissenschaft* 6 (1997); Michael Schubert, *Der schwarze Fremde: Das Bild des Schwarzafrikaners in der parlamentarischen und publizistischen Kolonialdiscussion in Deutschland von den 1870er bis in die 1930er Jahre* (Stuttgart: Franz Steiner, 2003).

23. Lora Wildenthal, *German Women for Empire, 1884–1945* (Durham, NC: Duke University Press, 2001); Sandra Mass, *Weisse Helden schwarze Krieger: Zur Geschichte kolonialer Männlichkeit in Deutschland 1918–64* (Cologne: Böhlau, 2006).

24. Pascal Grosse, *Kolonialismus, Eugenik und bürgerliche Gesellschaft in Deutschland 1850–1918* (Frankfurt a. M.: Campus, 2000); Wolfgang U. Eckart, *Medizin und Kolonialimperialismus: Deutschland 1884–1945* (München: Paderborn, 1997); Andrew Zimmerman, *Anthropology and Antihumanism in Imperial Germany* (Chicago: University of Chicago Press, 2001); Matti Bunzl and Glenn Penny, *Worldly Provincialism: German Anthropology in the Age of Empire* (Ann Arbor: University of Michigan Press, 2003); Jens Ruppenthal, *Kolonialismus als "Wissenschaft und Technik": Das Hamburgische Kolonialinstitut 1908 bis 1919* (Stuttgart: Franz Steiner, 2007); Dirk van Laak, *Imperiale Infrastruktur: Deutsche Planungen für eine Erschließung Afrikas 1880–1960* (Schöningh: Paderborn, 2004).

25. For an overview, see Nederveen Pieterse, *White on Black,* chapter 13. For Great Britain, see Ramamurthy, *Imperial Persuaders;* Thomas Richards, *The Commodity Culture of Victorian England: Advertising and Spectacle 1851–1914* (London: Verso, 1990), esp. 119–167; and Anne McClintock, *Imperial Leather: Race, Gender, and Sexuality in the Colonial Contest* (New York: Routledge, 1995). For France, scholarly work has focused on the 1920s: see Dana Hale, *Races on Display: French Representations of Colonized Peoples, 1886–1940* (Bloomington: Indiana University Press, 2008); Brett Berliner, *Ambivalent Desire: The Exotic Black Other in Jazz-Age France* (Amherst: University of Massachusetts Press, 2002); Petrine Archer-Straw, *Negrophilia: Avant-Garde Paris and Black Culture in the 1920s* (New York: Thames & Hudson, 2000). For Italy, see Karen Pinkus, *Bodily Regimes: Italian Advertising under Fascism* (Minneapolis: University of Minnesota Press, 1995), esp. 22–81. For Germany, the scholarly literature on the image of blacks in German culture is referenced extensively in Chapters 5 and 6 of this book.

26. Wolter, *Vermarktung des Fremden;* Thomas Held, "Kolonialismus und Werbung," in *Andenken an den Kolonialismus,* ed. Volker Harms (Tübingen: Attempto, 1984). Most recently, see the intriguing and marvelously illustrated work by Joachim Zeller, *Bilderschule der Herrenmenschen: Koloniale Reklamesammelbilder* (Berlin: Ch. Links, 2008).

27. A key work on colonial visual culture appeared too recently to incorporate here; see Volker Langbehn, ed., *German Colonialism, Visual Culture, and Modern Memory* (New York: Routledge, 2010). See Assenka Oksiloff, *Picturing the Primitive: Visual Culture, Ethnography, and Early German Cinema* (New York: Palgrave, 2001); Wolfgang Struck, "Die Geburt des Abenteuers aus dem Geist des Kolonialismus," in Kundrus, *Phantasiereiche;* Wolfgang Kabatek, *Imagerie des Anderen im Weimarer Kino* (Bielefeld: Transcript, 2003); Wolfgang Fuhrmann, "Locating Early Film Audiences: Voluntary Associations and Colonial Film," *Historical Journal of Film, Radio and Television* 22, no. 3 (2002). Most work on German colonial photography has been on the photos themselves, not mass-produced photoengravings. See Wolfram Hartmann, ed., *Hues between Black and White* (Windhoek: Out of Africa Publishers, 2004); George Steinmetz and Julia Hell, "The Visual Archive of Colonialism: Germany and Namibia," *Public Culture* 18, no. 1 (2006); Eleanor M. Hight and Gary D. Sampson, eds., *Colonialist Photography: Imag(in)ing Race and Place* (New York: Routledge, 2002); Jürg Schneider, Ute Röschenthaler, and Bernhard Gardi, eds., *Fotofieber: Bilder aus West- und Zentralafrika—Die Reisen von Carl Passavant 1883–1885* (Basel: Christoph Merian, 2005); Jutta Engelhard and Peter Mesenhöller, *Bilder aus dem Paradies: Koloniale Fotographie Samoa 1875–1925,* vol. 19 (Köln: Jonas, 1995); Michael Wiener, *Ikonographie des Wilden: Menschen-Bilder in Ethnographie und Photographie zwischen 1850 und 1918* (Munich: Trickster, 1990); Markus Schindlbeck, ed., *Die ethnographische Linse: Photographien aus dem Museum für Völkerkunde Berlin* (Berlin: Museum für Völkerkunde Berlin, 1989). Two works that deal with colonial culture and have extensive visual components are Alexander Honold and Klaus R. Scherpe, *Mit Deutschland um die Welt: Eine Kulturgeschichte des Fremden in der Kolonialzeit* (Stuttgart: J. B. Metzler, 2004); and Ulrich van der Heyden and Joachim Zeller, eds., *Kolonialmetropole Berlin: Eine Spurensuche* (Berlin: Quintessenz, 2002).

28. Peter Borscheid and Clemens Wischermann, eds., *Bilderwelt des Alltags: Werbung in der Konsumgesellschaft des 19. und 20. Jahrhunderts* (Stuttgart: Franz Steiner, 1995).

29. Dirk Reinhardt, *Von der Reklame zum Marketing: Geschichte der Wirtschaftswerbung in Deutschland* (Berlin: Akademie, 1993); see also Christiane Lamberty, *Reklame in Deutschland 1890–1914: Wahrnehmung, Professionalisierung und Kritik der Wirtschaftswerbung* (Berlin: Duncker & Humblot, 2000).

30. See Kevin Repp's essay in Swett, Wiesen, and Zatlin, *Selling Modernity,* 27–51.

31. See Brinckmann's introduction to his 1896 exhibition catalog; *Plakatausstellung: Hamburg, 1896* (Hamburg: Lütcke & Wulff, 1896).

32. Hellmut Rademacher and René Grohnert, *Kunst! Kommerz! Visionen! Deutsche Plakate 1888–1933* (Berlin: Deutsches Historisches Museum, 1992).

33. J. L. Sponsel, *Das Moderne Plakat* (Dresden: Gerhard Kühtmann, 1897); the *Monographien Deutscher Reklamekünstler* was published by the Deutsches Museum für Kunst in Handel und Gewerbe, a sort of virtual museum, existing only in traveling displays and publication. Aynsley, *Graphic Design,* 41–42. The "museum" was initiated by Karl Ernst Osthaus in 1901. *Das Plakat,* first published in 1913, gained an international circulation.

34. See especially Jürgen Schwarz, *Bildannoncen aus der Jahrhundertwende: Studien zur Künstlerischen Reklamegestaltung in Deutschland Zwischen 1896 und 1914* (Frankfurt a. M.: Kunstgeschichtliches Institut der Johann Wolfgang Goethe-Universität, 1990); Jörg Meißner, ed., *Strategien der Werbekunst von 1850–1933* (Berlin: Deutsches Historisches Museum, 2004); and Reinhardt, *Reklame zum Marketing.*

35. Max Horkheimer and Theodor W. Adorno, *Dialectic of Enlightenment: Philosophical Fragments,* ed. Gunzelin Schmid Noerr (Stanford, CA: Stanford University Press, 2002), 94–136. See also, for instance, Herbert Marcuse, *One-Dimensional Man: Studies in the Ideology of Advanced Industrial Society* (London: Routledge, 1964); Stuart Ewen and Elizabeth Ewen, *Channels of Desire: Mass Images and the Shaping of American Consciousness,* 2nd ed. (Minneapolis: University of Minnesota Press, 1992). On a more theoretical plane, the work of Jean Baudrillard moves outward from this starting point, but delves into semiotics and post-structural relationships between symbols.

36. See, for instance, the highly influential Judith Williamson, *Decoding Advertisements* (London: Boyars, 1978); or more broadly, Roland Barthes, *Mythologies* (London: Vintage, 1993). I have generally tried to avoid using the dense and highly specialized language of semiological analysis in this book. This will unfortunately lead to more cumbersome explication, and (in some cases) a dissonance of terminology; but it has the advantage of readability and, of greater importance to a historian, offers a mode of analysis that might well have been comprehensible to someone from that time (perhaps lending additional historial insight).

37. See Lisa Cartwright and Marita Sturken, *Practices of Looking: an Introduction to Visual Culture* (Oxford: Oxford University Press, 2001); Nicolas Mirzoeff, ed., *The Visual Culture Reader* (New York: Routledge, 1998). As W. J. T. Mitchell has said, there are now too many anthologies in visual culture and visual studies to count; W. J. T. Mitchell, *What Do Pictures Want? The Lives and Loves of Images* (Chicago: University of Chicago Press, 2005), 1n1. I have found a useful overview of the debates in visual culture to be Margarita Dikovitskaya, *Visual*

Culture: The Study of the Visual after the Cultural Turn (Cambridge, MA: MIT Press, 2005).

38. Such diverse theoretical frames as Stuart Hall's on the processes of encoding and decoding, or Roland Barthes's on the denotation and connotation of signs, retain at their core some vestige of the notion of a single image seen by an individual observer. These frames essentially extend the conception of an individually created and individually received image into a theory of social operation by repeating the process innumerably or ad infinitum. See Stuart Hall, "Encoding/Decoding," in *Culture, Media, Language: Working Papers in Cultural Studies, 1972–79* (London: Hutchinson, 1980); Roland Barthes, "Rhetoric of the Image," in *Image, Music, Text,* ed. Stephen Heath (New York: Hill and Wang, 1977).

39. The investigation of "visuality" itself distinguishes the emerging academic field of visual culture from traditional modes of art history. It is "a history of images rather than a history of art": Norman Bryson, Michael Ann Holly, and Keith Moxey, *Visual Culture: Images and Interpretations* (Hanover, NH: Wesleyan University Press, 1994), 2. Yet while some argue that the defining feature of the study of visual culture should be the insistence on the social construction of the visual experience (see Peter Erickson and Clark Hulse, eds., *Early Modern Visual Culture: Representation, Race, and Empire in Renaissance England* [Philadelphia: University of Pennsylvania Press, 2000], 1–14), the approach as a whole can become lost in interpretational entropy. One example of a scholar of popular culture who highlights the multiplicity of popular interpretations is John Fiske, *Understanding Popular Culture* (Boston: Unwin Hyman, 1989).

40. The *Gesetz zum Schutz der Waarenbezeichnungen* of 12 May 1894 (replacing the *Reichsgesetzes über Markenschutz* of 30 November 1874) established a central control over the registration, use, and restriction of trademarks. As businesses began to lay out substantial sums of money for advertising campaigns, and professionals built careers around their design of images, the stakes of producing slogans and images became increasingly high, resulting in a growing demand for some form of copyright protection. Hence the registration of "Warenzeichen" was a regular topic in professional advertising journals such as *Die Reklame* from 1894 onward. See also Paul Ruben, "Die Bedeutung der Warenzeichen für die Reklame," in Paul Ruben, *Die Reklame* (Berlin, 1914), 1–17.

41. "Psychologie der Reklame," in Ruben, *Die Reklame,* 18–22.

42. Businesses small and large registered several thousand illustrated advertisements and trademarks in the *Warenzeichenblatt* every year; with the ongoing proliferation of visual mass media, this number doubled by 1910 to very roughly 4,000 per year. These registrations, furthermore, provide a means by which to date the origin of the images, which is almost impossible using advertising journals or the mass media alone. Only a small fraction of advertisements were registered in this manner, of course. Likewise, registration provides no indication

of where a trademarked image was used. The effort and cost of commissioning and registering an illustrated trademark probably guaranteed that it would be put into use. See "Die Vorprüfung der Warenzeichen auf ihre Eintragungsfähigkeit," in Ruben, *Die Reklame,* 183ff.

43. These include more than 5,000 posters published in Klaus Popitz et al., eds., *Das frühe Plakat in Europa und den USA: Band 3: Deutschland* (Berlin: Gebr. Mann, 1980). Still highly useful is Viktoria Schmidt-Linsenhoff, Kurt Wettengl, and Almut Junker, eds., *Plakate 1880–1914* (Frankfurt a. M.: Historisches Museum Frankfurt am Main, 1986). The 3,500 posters of the Jaap Best collection, part of the Circus Museum in the Netherlands (CMNL), offer a remarkable online resource (circusmuseum.nl). Collections of advertising trade cards abound; more than 10,000 images of the Liebig Company's trade cards are digitized in Bernhard Jussen, *Liebig's Sammelbilder* (DVD-ROM) (Berlin: Yorck Project, 2002). Also useful is the compendium of posters in Deutsches Historisches Museum, *Reklame: Produktwerbung im Plakat 1890 bis 1918* (DVD-ROM) (Berlin: Directmedia, 2005), as well as dozens of printed museum catalogs listed in footnotes throughout this book.

44. Henriette Väth-Hinz, *Odol: Reklame-Kunst um 1900* (Gießen: Anabas, 1985); Rita Gudermann and Bernhard Wulff, *Der Sarotti-Mohr: Die bewegte Geschichte einer Werbefigur* (Berlin, 2004).

45. This leads me to a caveat: I use trademark registrations to discuss patterns of commercial imagery, though some of these patterns appear earlier in different media. Thus an advertising image such as that of Eduard Palm, almost unheard of in the world of advertising before 1900 to judge by registrations, has precedents in certain types of postcards in the late 1880s, and in illustrations from children's books in the 1860s, and even all the way back in heraldic devices for the city of Coburg—which later became the trademark for Tucher beer.

46. On this note (but concerning photography) see James Ryan, *Picturing Empire: Photography and the Visualization of the British Empire* (London: Reaktion, 1997), 16–20.

47. Sander L. Gilman, *On Blackness without Blacks: Essays on the Image of the Black in Germany* (Boston: G. K. Hall, 1982).

48. Tina Campt, *Other Germans: Black Germans and the Politics of Race, Gender, and Memory in the Third Reich* (Ann Arbor: University of Michigan Press, 2004); Fatima El-Tayeb, "'If You Can't Pronounce My Name, You Can Just Call Me Pride': Afro-German Activism, Gender, and Hip-Hop," *Gender & History* 15, no. 3 (2003); Patricia Mazon and Reinhild Steingröver, *Not So Plain as Black and White: Afro-German Culture and History, 1890–1920* (Rochester, NY: University of Rochester Press, 2005); May Opitz, Katharina Oguntoye, and Dagmar Schultz, *Showing Our Colors: Afro-German Women Speak Out* (Amherst: University of Massachusetts Press, 1992).

49. Friedrichsmeyer, Lennox, and Zantop, *Imperialist Imagination.* On the danger of reinscribing the erasure of black agency in the analysis of racial advertisements, see Anne Donadey, "'Y'a Bon Banania': Ethics and Cultural Criticism in the Colonial Context," *French Cultural Studies* 11 (2000): 9–29. Imagery is indeed especially effective at effacing the history of the oppressed, the marginalized, and the overlooked. The danger of *not* investigating the history of racial imagery, however—of not gaining a firm historical understanding of where it comes from and what forces create and disseminate it—is equally acute.

50. See Henry John Drewal, "Mami Wata and Santa Marta: Imag(in)ing Selves and Others in Africa and the Americas," in *Images and Empires: Visuality in Colonial and Post-Colonial Africa,* ed. Paul S. Landau and Deborah Kaspin (Berkeley: University of California Press, 2002).

51. See the first chapter of Keven Repp, *Reformers, Critics, and the Paths of German Modernity: Anti-Politics and the Search for Alternatives, 1890–1914* (Cambridge, MA: Harvard University Press, 2000). Far from atavistic or neo-feudal, Germany is increasingly seen as being at the vanguard of a specific inflection of modernity. See Modris Eksteins, *Rites of Spring: the Great War and the Birth of the Modern Age* (Boston: Houghton Mifflin, 1989); Frank Trommler, "The Creation of a Culture of *Sachlichkeit,*" in *Society, Culture, and the State in Germany, 1870–1930,* ed. Geoff Eley (Ann Arbor: University of Michigan Press, 1996). Only recently has German modernism been traced back to the imperial era: see Kundrus, *Moderne Imperialisten;* Sebastian Conrad and Jurgen Osterhammel, eds., *Das Kaiserreich Transnational: Deutschland in der Welt 1871–1914* (Göttingen: Vandenhoeck & Ruprecht, 2004).

52. Jennifer Jenkins, *Provincial Modernity: Local Culture and Liberal Politics in Fin-de Siècle Hamburg* (Ithaca, NY: Cornell University Press, 2003); Celia Applegate, *A Nation of Provincials: the German Idea of Heimat* (Berkeley: University of California Press, 1990); Thomas Lekan, *Imagining the Nation in Nature: Landscape Preservation and German Identity, 1885–1945* (Cambridge, MA: Harvard University Press, 2004); and Thomas Rohkrämer, *Eine andere Moderne? Zivilisationskritik, Natur und Technik in Deutschland 1880–1933* (Paderborn: Schöningh, 1999).

53. Nancy Reagin, *Sweeping the German Nation: Domesticity and National Identity in Germany, 1870–1945* (New York: Cambridge University Press, 2007); Ann Taylor Allen, *Feminism and Motherhood in Germany, 1800–1914* (New Brunswick, NJ: Rutgers University Press, 1991). See also Kathleen Canning, *Languages of Labor and Gender: Female Factory Work in Germany, 1850–1914* (Ithaca, NY: Cornell University Press, 1996); and Wildenthal, *German Women for Empire.* See also Uta Poiger's essay in *The Modern Girl around the World: Consumption, Modernity, and Globalization* (Durham, NC: Duke University Press, 2008).

54. Bernhard Rieger, *Technology and the Culture of Modernity in Britain and Germany, 1890–1945* (New York: Cambridge University Press, 2005); Repp, *Paths of German Modernity.*

1. Exotic Panoramas and Local Color

1. Walter Benjamin, *Gesammelte Schriften,* vol. 5, ed. Rolf Teidemann (Frankfurt a. M.: Suhrkamp, 1982), 267. Translation mine.

2. See Susan Buck-Morss, "Dream World of Mass Culture: Walter Benjamin's Theory of Modernity and the Dialectics of Seeing," in *Modernity and the Hegemony of Vision,* ed. David Michael Leven (Berkeley: University of California Press, 1993), 310.

3. This is a gross simplification of Marx's materialism and his thoughts on commodity fetishism, of course. See Timothy Burke, *Lifebuoy Men, Lux Women: Commodification, Consumption, and Cleanliness in Modern Zimbabwe* (Durham, NC: Duke University Press, 1996); W. J. T. Mitchell, *Iconology: Image, Text, Ideology* (Chicago: University of Chicago Press, 1986), 193–194; Jean Baudrillard, *For a Critique of the Political Economy of the Sign* (St. Louis: Telos Press, 1981), among many others.

4. *Oxford English Dictionary,* 2nd ed. (1989). The utility of the word "fetish" to discriminate between "good" and "bad" objects and sort out the iconoclastic/iconodulist tension is discussed in W. J. T. Mitchell, *What Do Pictures Want? The Lives and Loves of Images* (Chicago: University of Chicago Press, 2005). On the commodity fetish and advertising specifically, see Sut Jhally, *The Codes of Advertising: Fetishism and the Political Economy of Meaning in the Consumer Society* (New York: St. Martin's Press, 1987).

5. Most provocatively, see Anne McClintock, *Imperial Leather: Race, Gender, and Sexuality in the Colonial Contest* (New York: Routledge, 1995). McClintock offers a methodologically intriguing sketch of colonial tropes, including fetishism, that run in and through very different sorts of texts.

6. On Benjamin's biologically based mimetic theory, see Michael Taussig, *Mimesis and Alterity: A Particular History of the Senses* (New York: Routledge, 1993).

7. See Tony Bennett, "The Exhibitionary Complex," in *Culture/Power/History: A Reader in Contemporary Social Theory,* ed. Nicholas B. Dirks, Geoff Eley, and Sherry B. Ortner (Princeton, NJ: Princeton University Press, 1994), 123–154.

8. Walter Benjamin, *The Arcades Project,* trans. Howard Eiland and Kevin McLaughlin (Cambridge, MA: Belknap Press of Harvard University Press, 1999), 7. Italics mine.

9. Berlin's regional trade fair in 1844 may have been an inspiration to London's endeavor in 1851, however. And Berlin did stage small industry-and-trade

exhibitions in 1869 and 1879. The Bavarian King Max II sponsored an industrial exhibition in Munich in 1854 featuring a glass-and-steel structure modeled after the Crystal Palace; in 1882 this building was the site of the first exhibition to be electrified. German cities such as Hamburg also staged specialized international exhibitions, such as the Agricultural Exhibition of 1862. See Hella Kaeselitz, ed., *Die verhinderte Weltausstellung: Beiträge zur Berliner Gewerbeausstellung 1896* (Berlin: Berliner Debatte, 1996).

10. On *Bildung,* see Matthew Jefferies, *Imperial Culture in Germany, 1871–1918* (New York: Palgrave, 2003), 30–31; Jonathan Sperber, "Bürger, Bürgertum, Bürgerlichkeit, Bürgerliche Gesellschaft: Studies of the German (Upper) Middle Class and Its Sociocultural World (Review Essay)," *Journal of Modern History* 69 (1997): 276; and David Blackbourn and Richard Evans, eds., *The German Bourgeoisie* (New York: Routledge, 1991).

11. Thomas Richards, *The Commodity Culture of Victorian England: Advertising and Spectacle, 1851–1914* (London: Verso, 1990), 37; see also Bennett, "Exhibitionary Complex," 134–139.

12. See, for instance, Glenn H. Penny, *Objects of Culture: Ethnology and Ethnographic Museums in Imperial Germany* (Chapel Hill: University of North Carolina Press, 2002).

13. *Illustrirte Zeitung* no. 2094 (Leipzig, 1883): 137–138. See also Kirsten Belgum, *Popularizing the Nation: Audience, Representation, and the Production of Identity in Die Gartenlaube, 1853–1900* (Lincoln: University of Nebraska Press, 1998), 104–108.

14. See K. Lüders, *Das Project einer Weltausstellung zu Berlin im Jahre 1885* (Berlin, 188?); A. Haarmann, *Vor dem Rubicon: Ein letztes Wort der Beherzigung zur Ausstellungsfrage* (Berlin, 1892). Haarmann called for German exhibitions particularly because the world exhibitions in other countries, like that of Paris in 1889, invariably and unfairly favored the manufactures of the country that masterminded the exhibition.

15. *Über Land und Meer* 64, no. 51 (1890): 1027. I have translated "Gewerbe-Ausstellung" throughout this book as "commercial exhibition" (rather than the more literal "trade exhibition") to better capture its nature, and also to differentiate it from its "Handels-Ausstellung" subsections (translated below as either Trade Exhibit, or Hall of Trade).

16. *Illustrirte Zeitung* no. 2457 (Leipzig, 2 August 1890): 122–124.

17. See, for instance, Martin Wörner, *Vergnügung und Belehrung: Volkskultur auf den Weltausstellungen 1851–1900* (Münster: Waxmann, 1999).

18. There are several very brief sketches: see Andreas Lüderwaldt, "Die Handels- und Kolonialausstellung von 1890," in *Bremen: Handelsstadt am Fluß,* ed. Hartmut Roder (Bremen: H. M. Hauschild, 1995); Andreas Lüderwaldt, "'. . . den Warenproben Lokalfarbe zu verleihen . . .' 1890–1990: 100 Jahre

'Handels- und Kolonialausstellung' in Bremen," *Tendenzen 92. Jahrbuch des Übersee-Museums I* (1992): 55–72. Oliver Korn, *Hanseatische Gewerbeausstellungen im 19. Jahrhundert* (Opladen: Leske & Budrich, 1999), 138–154, surveys the Bremen exhibition but does not mention its colonial components.

19. Alison Griffiths, *Wondrous Difference: Cinema, Anthropology, and Turn-of-the-Century Visual Culture* (New York: Columbia University Press, 2002), 60. See especially Paul Greenhalgh, *Ephemeral Vistas: The Expositions Universelles, Great Exhibitions and World's Fairs, 1851–1939* (Manchester, UK: Manchester University Press, 1988), 59, 66, 87–88. The "colonization" of European exhibitions arose out of diverse impulses, from the interests of the state to those of academic disciplines, such as anthropology or medicine. Most important, the theme of "empire" was thought to be popular, and therefore lucrative. The literature on exhibitions is immense: a starting point on the issue of "popularity" of colonial themes in them is, for Britain, John M. MacKenzie, *Propaganda and Empire: The Manipulation of British Public Opinion, 1880–1960* (Manchester, UK: Manchester University Press, 1984); and for France, William H. Schneider, *An Empire for the Masses: The French Popular Image of Africa, 1870–1900* (Westport, CT: Greenwood Press, 1982), and Dana Hale, *Races on Display: French Representations of Colonized Peoples, 1886–1940* (Bloomington: Indiana University Press, 2008).

20. See Belgum, *Popularizing the Nation;* Matthew Fitzpatrick, "Narrating Empire: Die Gartenlaube and Germany's Nineteenth-Century Liberal Expansionism," *German Studies Review* 30, no. 1 (2007).

21. *Über Land und Meer* 64, no. 51 (1890): 1027.

22. The entry fee was 1 mark for adults and 50 pfennig for children. The most widely sold ticket was the expensive season pass, at 20 marks, affordable only for the middle class.

23. "The cupola of the Park House," one writer waxed eloquently about the rounded, orientalist domes on the exhibition halls, "seen against the backdrop of the stars and glow-lamps, leads one to believe that he is in the fairy tale world of '1001 Nights.'" *Über Land und Meer* 64, no. 51 (1890): 1027. A Chinese pagoda, built on a platform standing in the middle of the *Hollersee,* became the icon of the exhibition after it appeared as a full-page engraved illustration in the premier bourgeois family journal, *Die Gartenlaube* (1890): 733.

24. See *Illustrirte Zeitung* no. 2405 (3 August 1889): 122.

25. *Officieller Führer durch die Nordwestdeutsche Gewerbe- und Industrie-Ausstellung und die Stadt Bremen* (Bremen: Rudolf Mosse, 1890), 56. The poster promoting Castan's *Irrgarten* shows an orientalist façade; see Viktoria Schmidt-Linsenhoff, Kurt Wettengl, and Almut Junker, eds., *Plakate 1880–1914* (Frankfurt a. M.: Historisches Museum Frankfurt am Main, 1986), 279, no. 409. The

Castan Brothers were branching out from their Panopticum (wax museum) in nearby Cologne and their original location in Berlin.

26. Hamburg's 1889 exhibition nonetheless received perhaps up to 2 million visitors (mostly locals) and even closed with a profit, however. Korn, *Gewerbeausstellungen,* 135–136.

27. The commentator also complained that, although the exhibition was to promote the city to the surrounding provinces, four-fifths of the visitors were from Hamburg. *Reform* no. 137 (9 June 1889), SAH 614 3/6 sig. 4.

28. *Echo* no. 127 (1 June 1889), SAH 614 3/6 sig. 4.

29. Cf. *Die Nordwestdeutsche Gewerbe-, Industrie-, Handels-, Marine-, Hochseefischerei- und Kunst-Ausstellung: Bremen 1890* (Emmerich: J. L. Romen'schen, 1890), 166. In contrast to the Bremen exhibition literature that paints the earlier effort at Hamburg as a "failure," Oliver Korn places the Hamburg exhibition in a more successful light; Korn, *Gewerbeausstellungen,* 131.

30. *Officieller Katalog der Handels-Ausstellung* (Bremen: Max Nössler's Buchdruckerei, 1890), 2.

31. *Illustrirte Zeitung* no. 2463 (12 September 1890): 280.

32. *Officieller Führer,* 70. This "Official Guide," costing only 50 pfennig, evinces a more populist and "touristic" style of prose.

33. *Illustrirte Zeitung* no. 2457 (2 August 1890): 124.

34. *Officieller Führer,* 70.

35. *Ausstellungs-Zeitung: Nordwestdeutsche Gewerbe- und Industrie-Aussstellung Bremen* no. 1 (2 June 1890): 6. This appears to be a serialized catalog, printed as a newspaper.

36. *Die Nordwestdeutsche Gewerbe- . . . Ausstellung,* 174.

37. See Regine Hrosch, *"Welttheile und Winde": Arthur Fitgers Gemälde im Haus Seefahrt zu Bremen: Eine Studie zur Kunst der Gründerzeit* (Bremen: Edition Temmen, 1996). Fitger was also an accomplished poet.

38. On the poster, the skyline of the exhibition is lost in the ornate decorative border design. See J. L. Sponsel, *Das Moderne Plakat* (Dresden: Gerhard Kühtmann, 1897), 249; see also Klaus Popitz et al., eds., *Das frühe Plakat in Europa und den USA: Band 3: Deutschland* (Berlin: Gebr. Mann, 1980), no. 911.

39. *Officieller Katalog der Handels-Ausstellung,* 1; also in the luxury edition, *Die Nordwestdeutsche Gewerbe- . . . Ausstellung,* 166. Werner Sombart is credited as the "Schriftführer" of the Trade Exhibition in the latter.

40. *Officieller Katalog der Handels-Ausstellung,* 1.

41. Indeed, Eduard Schnitzer/Emin Pasha even became a de facto colonial official for Britain in the Sudan, succeeding Gordon as governor of Equatoria.

42. On German missionaries before official colonialism, see Ulrich van der Heyden and Holger Stoecker, eds., *Mission und Macht im Wandel politischer Orientierungen* (Stuttgart: Steiner, 2005); Klaus J. Bade, ed., *Imperialismus und*

Kolonialmission: Kaiserliches Deutschland und koloniales Imperium (Wiesbaden: Steiner, 1982); and Horst Gründer, "Christian Missionary Activities in Africa in the Age of Imperialism and the Berlin Conference of 1884–1885," in *Bismarck, Europe, and Africa: The Berlin Africa Conference, 1884–1885 and the Onset of Partition*, ed. Stig Forster, Wolfgang J. Mommsen, and Ronald Robinson (Oxford: Oxford University Press, 1988).

43. See Woodruff D. Smith, *Politics and the Sciences of Culture in Germany, 1840–1920* (New York: Oxford University Press, 1991); Bradley Naranch, "Beyond the Fatherland: Colonial Visions, Overseas Expansion, and German Nationalism, 1848–1885" (PhD diss., Johns Hopkins University, 2006), 219–260; Lewis Pyenson, *Cultural Imperialism and the Exact Sciences: German Expansion Overseas, 1900–1930* (New York: Peter Lang, 1985); Belgum, *Popularizing the Nation,* 153–156.

44. Naranch, "Beyond the Fatherland," 204–215; Dirk Bavendamm, ed., *Wagnis Westafrika: 150 Jahre C. Woermann* (Hamburg: Hanseatischer Merkur, 1987); Heiko Möhle, ed., *Branntwein, Bibel und Bananen: Der Deutsche Kolonialismus in Afrika—Eine Spürensuche* (Hamburg: Libertäre Assoziation, 1999); and Renate Hücking and Ekkehard Launer, *Aus Menschen Neger machen: Wie sich das Handelshaus Woermann an Afrika entwickelt hat* (Hamburg: Galgenberg, 1986).

45. Fitzpatrick, "Narrating Empire"; Belgum, *Popularizing the Nation.*

46. Following his expeditions, Alfred Brehm became a regular author for *Die Gartenlaube.* In 1886 and 1887 Finsch published a series of essays in *Die Gartenlaube* about his expeditions to New Guinea; he had also written about his Siberian expedition in *Die Gartenlaube* 26 (1878): 184–187.

47. On this issue, see especially Naranch, "Beyond the Fatherland."

48. Klaus Bade, *Friedrich Fabri und der Imperialismus in der Bismarckzeit* (Freiburg: Atlantis, 1975).

49. E. C. M. Breuning and M. E. Chamberlain, eds., *Bedarf Deutschland der Kolonien?/Does Germany Need Colonies?* (Lewiston, NY: Edwin Mellen Press, 1998), 28.

50. Previously, a small number of linguistic and geography clubs (such as the *Deutsch-Afrikanische Gesellschaft*) had served as meeting grounds for those interested in African affairs. The emphasis on "commerce" added to the raison d'être of geography groups in the 1880s expanded not only their purview but their memberships as well. The Centralverein für Handelsgeographie und Förderung deutscher Interessen im Auslande was founded in Berlin in 1878 by a group of national economists, geographers, and editors under the leadership of Robert Jannasch. Ernst Hasse's Verein für Handelsgeographie und Kolonialpolitik was a loosely affiliated group founded in Leipzig. The Westdeutscher Verein für Kolonisation und Export (WVKE), founded in Düsseldorf by Friedrich

Fabri after 1879, included a higher concentration of businessmen and (small) industrialists. Bade, *Friedrich Fabri,* 237–245. For the WVKE, see also Ulrich S. Soenius, *Koloniale Begeisterung im Rheinland wahrend des Kaiserreichs* (Köln: Rheinisch-Westfalisches Wirtschaftsarchiv zu Koln, 1992), 21–26; and Hans Ulrich Wehler, *Bismarck und der Imperialismus* (Köln: Kiepenheuer & Witsch, 1969), 158–168.

51. Erich Präger, *Die Deutsche Kolonialgesellschaft 1882–1907* (Berlin: Dietrich Reimer/Ernst Vohsen, 1908), 25; this book is the DKG's own "official" history. See also Wehler, *Bismarck und der Imperialismus,* 165.

52. In addition to Hans Ulrich Wehler's classic explanation of social imperialism, see also Forster, Mommsen, and Robinson, *Bismarck, Europe, and Africa;* Axel T. G. Riehl, *Der "Tanz um den Äquator": Bismarck's antienglische Kolonialpolitik und die Erwartung des Thronwechsels in Deutschland 1883 bis 1885* (Berlin: Duncker & Humblot, 1993); and Woodruff D. Smith, *The German Colonial Empire* (Chapel Hill: University of North Carolina Press, 1978), 27–34.

53. For Woermann, see Hücking and Launer, *Aus Menschen;* Arne Perras, *Carl Peters and German Imperialism, 1856–1918: A Political Biography* (Oxford: Oxford University Press, 2004), 42; and Fritz Stern, *Gold and Iron: Bismarck, Bleichröder, and the Building of the German Empire* (New York: Knopf, 1977).

54. Peters intended his Society for German Colonization less as a print-media pressure group (like the German Colonial Society) than as an organization by which to funnel private capital directly to support colonialist ventures and adventures in Africa. It maintained an uneasy and antagonistic relationship with the larger, wealthier, and more decorous Colonial Association. This early history is recounted in Richard Pierard, "The German Colonial Society, 1882–1914" (PhD diss., University of Iowa, 1964); Soenius, *Kolonial Begeisterung;* and Bade, *Friedrich Fabri.*

55. Adolf Woermann did manage to push the Hamburg chamber of commerce to a demand for colonies. Helmut Washausen, *Hamburg und die Kolonialpolitik des Deutschen Reiches, 1880 bis 1890* (Hamburg: H. Christians, 1968).

56. See Klaus Bade, "Imperial Germany and West Africa: Colonial Movement, Business Interests, and Bismarck's 'Colonial Policies,'" in Forster, Mommsen, and Robinson, *Bismarck, Europe, and Africa,* esp. 129–133.

57. The German Colonial Society was a fusion of the German Colonial Association and the Society for German Colonization; the charter is reprinted in *Fünfzig Jahre Deutsche Kolonial Gesellschaft 1882–1932* (Berlin, 1932).

58. Bismarck used his political muscle to force successful Hamburg trading firms operating in Zanzibar, such as O'Swald and Hansing, to defer to Carl Peters's inept colonial concession, the German East Africa Company. Arne Perras, "Colonial Agitation and the Bismarckian State: The Case of Carl Peters," in *Wilhelminism and Its Legacies,* ed. Geoff Eley and James Retallack (New York: Berghahn Books, 2004), 162–163.

59. These companies included J. K. Vietor and Th. Gruner. Bremen trading companies operating in West Africa included Vietor Söhne (1883–); Henry Deitrich & Co.; Compagnie Commerciale Africaine Hans Weber (1904–); and the most successful, F. Oloff & Co. Hartmut Müller, "Bremen und Westafrika. Wirschafts- und Handelsbeziehungen im Zeitalter des Früh- und Hochkolonialismus 1841–1914," *Jahrbuch der Wittheit zu Bremen* 17 (1973): 75–148.

60. Chief among these was the New Guinea Company, which displayed an assortment of tropical wood and a piece of furniture made from it. *Ausstellungs-Zeitung, Bremen* no. 14 (2 September 1890): 6. A South Pacific colonial concern, the New Guinea Company appears to have been attached to the African Hall by virtue of its "German colonial" character; the section was referred to by several publications as "the African and Colonial exhibition."

61. *Ausstellungs-Zeitung, Bremen* no. 14 (2 September 1890): 3. See also *Officieller Katalog der Handels-Ausstellung,* 138–142; *Officieller Führer,* 73; and *Ausstellungs-Zeitung, Bremen* no. 13 (26 August 1890): 1.

62. *Officieller Katalog der Handels-Ausstellung,* 128.

63. *Daheim* 26 (1890), 682. Italics mine.

64. *Illustrirte Zeitung* no. 2463 (12 September 1890): 280.

65. Hellgrewe was trained in the Berlin Art Academy from 1879 to 1883. In 1885 he traveled to East Africa as a study for his work on the Kaiser Diorama, an installation at the Jubilee Exhibition of the Berlin Academy of the Arts. Dolf Sternberger and Joachim Neugroschel, "Panorama of the 19th Century," *October* 4 (Autumn 1977): 15; *Führer durch das Pergamon- und Olympia-Panorama sowie durch das Kaiser-Diorama der centralafrikanischen Erforschungs-Expeditionen,* ed. Ernst Fabricius (Berlin: Berliner Verlags-Comtoir, 1886). He turned to colonial art after that trip; he illustrated Carl Peters's 1891 book on the Emin Pasha expedition, for instance. See also Joachim Zeller, "Berliner Maler und Bildhauer im Dienste der Kolonialidee," in *Kolonialmetropole Berlin,* ed. Ulrich van der Heyden and Joachim Zeller (Berlin: Quintessenz, 2002), 165–167. Hellgrewe later became the artistic director of the German Colonial Exhibition of 1896 and a member of the board of the German Colonial Museum in Berlin after 1896.

66. *Ausstellungs-Zeitung, Bremen* no. 1 (2 June 1890): 6. One of Hellgrewe's color paintings of Kilimanjaro can be found on the plate following p. 122 in Ottomar Beta, *Das Buch von unsern Kolonien* (Leipzig: Ferdinand Hirt, 1908).

67. *Deutsches Kolonialblatt* no. 7 (1890): 113.

68. For later painters, see especially Sabina Wilke, "Romantic Images of Africa: Paradigms of German Colonial Paintings," *German Studies Review* 29, no. 2 (2006): 285–297.

69. *Officieller Katalog der Handels-Ausstellung,* 138. Italics mine.

70. *Officieller Führer,* 73.

71. *Officieller Katalog der Handels-Ausstellung,* 2.

72. See the Heinrich Ad. Meyer firm's many *Elfenbein-Bericht* over the 1890s in BA RKA 1001/6814. These reports reveal that this trading firm increasing deployed colonialist language, apparently in the hope of securing support from the German Colonial Office. They also chart ever-declining "stocks" of ivory, due to the mass killing of elephants.

73. Walther Hoffmann, *Das Wachstum der deutschen Wirtschaft seit der Mitte des 19. Jahrhunderts* (Berlin: Springer, 1965), 526. Germany's total trade with its colonies overall never rose above one-half of 1 percent of its total import/export trade; this statistic includes such things as monetary transfers and import duties on Chinese goods shipped through the German-controlled Chinese city of Kiautschou. Francesca Schinzinger, *Die Kolonien und das Deutsche Reich: Die wirtschaftliche Bedeutung der deutschen Besitzungen in Ubersee* (Stuttgart: F. Steiner, 1984), 125; L. H. Gann and Peter Duignan, *The Rulers of German Africa, 1884–1914* (Stanford, CA: Stanford University Press, 1977), 257. Statistics about German colonial trade are notoriously unreliable; see Helmuth Stoecker, *German Imperialism in Africa,* trans. Bernd Zollner (London: C. Hurst, 1986), 153. One of the very few "successes" of German colonial extraction was cocoa, most of it from Cameroon. Even at peak production in 1912, however, the cocoa imported from the German colonies covered at most 2.2 percent of domestic consumption. Ghana alone produced almost ten times the cocoa of Cameroon that same year.

74. *Officieller Katalog der Handels-Ausstellung,* 9.

75. DKZ 7:17 (1890): 205. Italics mine. This central tobacco display featured the United States and Sumatra.

76. See especially Birthe Kundrus, *Moderne Imperialisten: Das Kaiserreich im Spiegel seiner Kolonien* (Köln: Böhlau, 2003).

77. *Deutsches Kolonialblatt* no. 7 (1890): 114.

78. *Officieller Katalog der Handels-Ausstellung,* 128.

79. *Kulturvölker* and *Naturvölker,* respectively. Ethnographic artifacts represented German colonial might in the crudest sense as well, since they were often acquired through violence, whether as booty or tribute. Andrew Zimmerman, *Anthropology and Antihumanism in Imperial Germany* (Chicago: University of Chicago Press, 2001), 151 and 157. More broadly, see also Elazar Barkan and Ronald Bush, eds., *Prehistories of the Future* (Stanford, CA: Stanford University Press, 1995); and Timothy Mitchell, "The Stage of Modernity," in *Questions of Modernity* (Minneapolis: University of Minnesota Press, 2000).

80. *Officieller Katalog der Handels-Ausstellung,* 135, 136.

81. See *Officieller Katalog der Handels-Ausstellung,* 143–144. See also Otto Finsch, *Gesichtsmasken von Völkertypen der Südsee und dem malayischen Archipel nach Leben abgegossen den den Jahren 1879–1882* (Bremen: Homeyer & Meyer, 1887). The Royal Museum of Ethnology in Berlin had declined to purchase these

masks from Finsch in 1886; see Sierra Bruckner, "The Tingle-Tangle of Modernity: Popular Anthropology and the Cultural Politics of Identity in Imperial Germany" (PhD diss., University of Iowa, 1999), 82; and Zimmerman, *Anthropology and Antihumanism,* 166. A number of these masks have survived to the present day, as seen in the 1998 exhibition *Der neue Mensch* at the Hygiene Museum in Dresden.

82. See DKZ 7:12 (1890): 149–150. One article in the *German Colonial News* on the Trade Exhibition went so far as to say that Bremen's interest in Germany's east African colonies was "unfortunately generally patriotic rather than economic." DKZ 7:20 (1890): 237.

83. *Deutsche Geographische Blätter* 13 (1890): 206.

84. Cf. *Ausstellungs-Zeitung, Bremen* (10 June 1890): 6.

85. *Illustrirte Zeitung* no. 2464 (20 September 1890): 308. Italics mine.

86. *Illustrierter amtlicher Führer durch die Berliner Gewerbe-Ausstellung 1896* (Berlin: Verlag der Expedition des Amtlichen Führers, 1896), 5; Fritz Kühnemann, Heinrich Fränkel, and Albert Willner, eds., *Berlin und seine Arbeit: Amtlicher Bericht der Berliner Gewerbe-Ausstellung 1896, zugleich eine Darstellung des gegenwärtigen Standes unsere gewerblichen Entwickelung* (Berlin: Dietrich Reimer/Ernst Vohsen, 1898), 27 and 89. I follow earlier scholarly literature by translating Berlin's "Gewerbe-Ausstellung" as "industrial exhibition," primarily to avoid confusion with that of Bremen.

87. The costs of the Berlin exhibition were initially estimated at 4.5 million marks; seed money was raised by a consortium of Berlin businessmen, which admission fees and booth space rental were expected to repay. At least 3 million marks were spent by the City of Berlin on transportation infrastructure. Ralf Stremmel, *Modell und Moloch: Berlin in Wahrnehmung deutscher Politiker vom Ende des 19. Jahrhunderts bis zum Zweiten Weltkrieg* (Bonn: Bouvier, 1992), 45. The figure 6 million is in Dorothy Rowe, "Georg Simmel and the Berlin Trade Exhibition of 1896," *Urban History* 22, no. 2 (1995): 222. See also Katja Zelljadt, "Presenting and Consuming the Past: Old Berlin at the Industrial Exhibition Of 1896," *Journal of Urban History* 31, no. 3 (2005): 308; and Kaeselitz, *Die verhinderte Weltausstellung.*

88. *Die Zeit,* 25 July 1896, reproduced in David Frisby, ed., *Georg Simmel in Wien* (Vienna: WUV, 2000), 67.

89. *Illustrirte Zeitung* (1896): 671.

90. "Am Karpfenteich," *Illustrirte Zeitung* no. 2771 (8 August 1896): 158. A full-color illustration of the pavilion appears in Gerhard Genest, *Sechzig Jahre Sarotti* (Berlin: Ecksteins, 1928), 52 and 58.

91. "Alpine Panorama," *Illustrirte Zeitung* no. 2795 (1896): 600.

92. Eric Ames, *Carl Hagenbeck's Empire of Entertainments* (Seattle: University of Washington Press, 2009), 154–157; Nigel Rothfels, *Savages and Beasts: The*

Birth of the Modern Zoo (Baltimore: Johns Hopkins University Press, 2002), 173–174.

93. The poster is in Popitz et al., *Das frühe Plakat,* no. 3904.

94. "Die Wasserbahn im Vergnugungspark," *Illustrirte Zeitung* (1896): 411.

95. Popitz et al., *Das frühe Plakat,* no. 4911.

96. *Deutsche Warte,* 4 September 1896, cited in Bruckner, "Tingle-Tangle," 221.

97. *Illustrirte Zeitung* 106, no. 2760 (23 May 1896): 641–642. This magazine related that the director of the exhibition, Willy Möller, was from an old Hamburg trading family, bringing "that energy of entrepreneurship that possesses all of the men of the Hansa and drives them to worldwide trade." See also Bruckner, "Tingle-Tangle," 143 and 269–274.

98. Kühnemann, Fränkel, and Willner, *Berlin und seine Arbeit,* 78. On the Colonial Exhibition's planning, see Kenneth Holston, "'A Measure of the Nation': Politics, Colonial Enthusiasm and Education in Germany, 1896–1933" (PhD diss., University of Pennsylvania, 1996), chapter 1; Robert Debusmann and János Riesz, eds., *Kolonialausstellungen—Begegnungen mit Afrika?* (Frankfurt a. M.: Verlag für Interkulturelle Kommunikation, 1995); Bruckner, "Tingle-Tangle," 158–185; and Kaeselitz, *Die verhinderte Weltausstellung,* 115–124.

99. Lübeck's Deutsch-Nordische Handels- und Industrie-Ausstellung of 1895 included a Colonial Exhibition built around the theme of a station in German East Africa, and a *Völkerschau* of "Dinka-Neger." The organizers of the exhibition had tried but failed to involve Hagenbeck's company. Korn, *Gewerbeausstellungen,* 169–170. Many of the displays from the Bremen exhibition of 1890, such as paintings by Rudolf Hellgrewe, or Otto Finsch's wax racial masks, were simply trotted out five years later and reused for the Lübeck exhibition, as is evident from the descriptions of the latter. See DKZ (1895): 260–261.

100. On the production and consumption of colonial knowledge as the main occupation of German colonial enthusiasts, see John Phillip Short, "Everyman's Colonial Library: Imperialism and Working-Class Readers In Leipzig, 1890–1914," *German History* 21, no. 4 (2003), and David Ciarlo, "Consuming Race, Envisioning Empire: Colonialism and German Mass Culture, 1887–1914" (PhD diss., University of Wisconsin, Madison, 2003), chapter 5. On colonial science, see Pyenson, *Cultural Imperialism and the Exact Sciences;* Woodruff D. Smith, "Anthropology and German Colonialism," in *Germans in the Tropics,* ed. Arthur J. Knoll and Lewis H. Gann (Westport, CT: Greenwood Press, 1987); and Wolfgang U. Eckart, *Medizin und Kolonialimperialismus: Deutschland 1884–1945* (München: Paderborn, 1997).

101. *Amtlicher Bericht Kolonial-Ausstellung,* 61.

102. Ibid., 49. A second outlet of the Kolonialhaus Bruno Antelmann was the cigar pavilion located near the restaurants of the Colonial Exhibition proper, which sold cigars made from New Guinea tobacco.

103. See the interior photographs in the *Amtlicher Bericht Kolonial-Ausstellung,* starting on p. 58.

104. When the Colonial Exhibition organizers awarded their prize medallions (determined separately from the main Industrial Exhibition), for instance, the judges granted the Oriental pavilion of Hoffmann & Tiede only a silver. Meanwhile, the grass-roofed hut of Bruno Antelmann's Kolonialhaus received an "Extraordinary Golden Medallion." *Amtlicher Bericht Kolonial-Ausstellung,* 360. One of the three judges was Ernst Vohsen, of the German Colonial Society and closely involved in the plan to create the Kolonialhaus—hardly an objective critic.

105. As attested by the lengthy planning lists of tropical commodities supplied to the Foreign Office. BA R1001/6332, docs. 178–204 (1895).

106. See the Heinrich Ad. Meyer firm's *Elfenbein-Bericht,* BA RKA 1001/6814.

107. See the descriptions and photos in the *Amtlicher Bericht Kolonial-Ausstellung,* 61–62. See also Holston, "'A Measure of the Nation,'" 36.

108. *Amtlicher Bericht Kolonial-Ausstellung,* 7.

109. *Illustrierter amtlicher Führer durch die Berliner Gewerbe-Ausstellung 1896* (Berlin), 156. Italics mine. On these reconstructed Native Villages, see especially Bruckner, "Tingle-Tangle," 158–185; Andrew Zimmerman, *Anthropology and Antihumanism in Imperial Germany* (Chicago: University of Chicago Press, 2001), 24–35; and the essays by Stefan Arnold, Roland Richter, and Harald Sippel in Debusmann and Riesz, *Kolonialausstellungen,* as well as Heyden and Zeller, *Kolonialmetropole Berlin,* 135–139.

110. Zimmerman, *Anthropology and Antihumanism,* 26–28.

111. *Amtlicher Bericht Kolonial-Ausstellung,* 2.

112. Ibid., 203–242. This lavishly illustrated coffee-table book was equal parts luxury guidebook, memento, and informational resource.

113. The German Colonial Society at the close of the exhibition in 1896 gave the number as "well over one million." DKZ 13:43 (1896): 342. The figure 2 million is later given in *Amtlicher Bericht Kolonial-Ausstellung,* 355. As a private enterprise, the Special Exhibition Cairo did not publish its expenses, income, or profits. The figure of 2 million visitors is given in Kühnemann, Fränkel, and Willner, *Berlin und seine Arbeit,* 873. The attendance for the whole of the Berlin Industrial Exhibition is given in Bruckner, "Tingle-Tangle," 221. Kaeselitz, *Die verhinderte Weltausstellung.*

114. "Still, the attempt to demonstrate the essence of colonialism *(Kolonialwesen),* in all of its diverse branches, to the German people, is in itself meritori-

ous, even when its implementation does not find the full success hoped for by German colonial enthusiasts *(Kolonialfreunden).*" *Amtlicher Bericht Kolonial-Ausstellung,* 1.

115. *Illustrierter Amtlicher Führer durch die Berliner Gewerbe-Ausstellung 1896* (Berlin: Verlag der Expedition des Amtlichen Führers, 1896), 33–34.

116. The drawing is by G. Theuerkauf. *Illustrirte Zeitung* no. 2765 (27 June 1896): 796–797. In other panoramic sketches, such as that in the conservative illustrated journal *Daheim,* one can make out the Native Village (and it is further tabbed "Kolonialaustellung"), but the handful of tiny huts pales in significance next to the fantastic cityscape of the miniature city Cairo. *Daheim* 32 (1896): 381.

117. Cf. *Illustrirte Zeitung* no. 2766 (1896): 14 and *Illustrirte Zeitung* no. 2770 (1896): 136.

118. "Uebersichtsplan zur schnellen Orientierung auf der Berliner Gewerbe-Ausstellung 1896," reproduced in Annemarie Lange, *Das Wilhelminische Berlin* (Berlin: Dietz, 1967), 80.

119. *Die Zeit,* 25 July 1896, reproduced in Frisby, *Georg Simmel in Wien,* 66.

120. Ibid.

121. In other pavilions, different themes took on this dual role. In the Machine Hall, for instance, displays of navalism—placing warships at the center of the technology displays—offered a dramatic spectacle that could lure visitors into the Hall; yet such spectacular militarism was legitimized by its educational role—it was simply describing the latest developments in engineering.

122. Bruckner, "Tingle-Tangle," 158.

123. Debusmann and Riesz, *Kolonialausstellungen.*

124. J. L. Sponsel, *Das Moderne Plakat* (Dresden: Gerhard Kühtmann, 1897), 273; Paul Ruben, *Die Reklame* (Berlin: Verlag für Sozialpolitik, 1914).

125. See Dirk Reinhardt, *Von der Reklame zum Marketing: Geschichte der Wirtschaftswerbung in Deutschland* (Berlin: Akademie, 1993), 53; for some of the satires, see Popitz et al., *Das frühe Plakat,* no. 634.

2. Impressions of Others

1. *Weser Zeitung* (31 May 1890), cited in Andreas Lüderwaldt, "Die Handels- und Kolonialausstellung von 1890," in *Bremen: Handelsstadt am Fluß,* ed. Hartmut Roder (Bremen: H. M. Hauschild, 1995), 37. People from India and Japan also became components of a few individual companies' displays. At Hamburg the year before, a "live Japanese" was on display among paper lanterns and storks of an exhibit of "oriental" wares. *Echo* no. 181 (4 August 1889), SAH 614 3/6 sig. 4.

2. *Officieller Katalog der Nordwestdeutschen Gewerbe- und Industrie-Ausstellung Bremen 1890* (Bremen: Rudolf Mosse, 1890), 218–219.

3. The *Illustrirte Zeitung* attained a subscribed circulation of 100,000 at its peak, but had many times that readership through borrowed copies. See Gideon Reuveni, "Reading Sites as Sights for Reading: The Sale of Newspapers in Germany before 1933: Bookshops in Railway Stations, Kiosks and Street Vendors," *Social History* 27, no. 3 (2002): 273–287.

4. On the sway of illustration vis-à-vis photography, see Gerry Beegan, *The Mass Image: A Social History of Photomechanical Reproduction in Victorian London* (New York: Palgrave Macmillan, 2008).

5. See Anne Dreesbach, *Gezähmte Wilde: Die Zurschaustellung "Exotischer" Menschen in Deutschland 1870–1940* (Frankfurt a. M.: Campus, 2005).

6. See James Caldwell's illustration of Mai ("Omai") in Cook's travelogue *A Voyage towards the South Pole, and Round the World,* vol. 1, 2nd ed. (London, 1777), 169, or in an 1838 painting by the English artist Theodore von Holst. See also Urs Bitterli, *Die "Wilden" und die "Zivilisierten"* (München: Beck, 1991), esp. 180–185.

7. Z. S. Strother, "Display of the Body Hottentot," in *Africans on Stage,* ed. Bernth Lindfors (Bloomington: Indiana University Press, 1999), 4–11. Jean Michel Massing, "The Image of Africa and the Iconography of Lip-Plated Africans in Pierre Desceliers's World Map of 1550," in *Black Africans in Renaissance Europe,* ed. T. F. Earle and K. J. P. Lowe (Cambridge: Cambridge University Press, 2005), 69, argues that "without visual evidence in front of them, artists could only adapt traditional formulae to match literary evidence." See also Michael Gaudio, *Engraving the Savage: the New World and Techniques of Civilization* (Minneapolis: University of Minnesota Press, 2008).

8. Christopher Steiner, "Travel Engravings and the Construction of the Primitive," in *Prehistories of the Future,* ed. Elazar Barkan and Ronald Bush (Stanford, CA: Stanford University Press, 1995), 225.

9. Cristelle Baskins and Lisa Rosenthal, eds., *Early Modern Visual Allegory: Embodying Meaning* (Burlington, VT: Ashgate, 2007).

10. See Hugh Honour, ed., *The Image of the Black in Western Art,* vol. 4 (Cambridge, MA: Harvard University Press, 1989). The three continents could also be associated with the three sons of Noah: Shem (Asia), Japheth (Europe), and Ham (Africa).

11. See Hugh Honour, *The New Golden Land: European Images of America from the Discoveries to the Present Time* (New York: Pantheon Books, 1975); Volker Harms, ed., *Andenken an den Kolonialismus* (Tübingen: Attempto, 1984).

12. See Jan P. Nederveen Pieterse, *White on Black: Images of Africa and Blacks in Western Popular Culture* (New Haven, CT: Yale University Press, 1992), 22; see also the examples in Roxanne Wheeler, *The Complexion of Race: Categories of Difference in Eighteenth-Century British Culture* (Philadelphia: University of Pennsylvania Press, 2000), 34 and 36.

13. The continental figures were accompanied by four figures representing the Winds. Regine Hrosch, *"Welttheile und Winde": Arthur Fitgers Gemälde im Haus Seefahrt zu Bremen: Eine Studie zur Kunst der Gründerzeit* (Bremen: Edition Temmen, 1996). When Fitger drew up the promotional poster for Bremen's exhibition in 1890, he centered the composition around Roland, Bremen's mythic protector and (in one perspective) allegorical representation of itself.

14. The second series produced by Liebig, printed in Paris in the mid-1870s, surveys Europe and the world by representing each land as a cherubic child adorned with a cultural prop, whether a turban (Egypt), a topknot (China), or a feathered headdress (America). See Bernhard Jussen, *Liebig's Sammelbilder* (DVD-ROM) (Berlin: Yorck Project, 2002), 76–87. The Liebig firm and its advertising cards are discussed further in Chapter 4. Compare also the chapter on "Explorers" in Joachim Zeller, *Bilderschule Der Herrenmenschen: Koloniale Reklamesammelbilder* (Berlin: Ch. Links, 2008), 25–34.

15. The *Pfennig-Magazin's* low price let it reach a circulation of 100,000, and it was a forerunner of the mass media. Yet its prints were of dubious quality and its success short lived. Hermann Diez, *Das Zeitungswesen* (Leipzig: B. G. Teubner, 1910), 57; Joachim Kirchner, *Das deutsche Zeitschriftwesen,* vol. 2 (Wiesbaden: Otto Harrassowitz, 1962), 140; Sibylle Obenaus, *Literarische und politische Zeitschriften 1830–1848* (Stuttgart: J. B. Metzlersche, 1986).

16. *Oxford English Dictionary,* 2nd ed. (1989).

17. Although the Tobacco Moor figure is almost always male, the figure's position of passive languor was historically coded as a "feminine" one. See Hugh Honour, *The European Vision of America* (Cleveland: Cleveland Museum of Art, 1975), esp. 112–122. Also relevant are Christina Ernst and Sabina Tischer, "Die Darstellung der Kolonialisierten in der europäischen Kunst," in *Andenken an den Kolonialismus,* ed. Volker Harms (Tübingen: Attempto, 1984); Karl-Heinz Kohl, *Entzauberter Blick: Das Bild vom Guten Wilden* (Berlin: Medusa, 1981); and Thomas Theye, ed., *Wir und die Wilden: Einblick in eine kannibalische Beziehung* (Reinbek: Rowohlt, 1985). On Dutch engravings of the New World, see Benjamin Schmidt, *Innocence Abroad: The Dutch Imagination and the New World, 1570–1670* (Cambridge: Cambridge University Press, 2001), esp. 130–138.

18. On "colonial goods," see Roman Sandgruber, "Genußmittel: Ihre reale und symbolische Bedeutung im neuzeitlichen Europa," *Jahrbuch für Wirtschafts Geschichte* 1 (1994); Roman Sandgruber, *Bittersüße Genüsse* (Wien: Hermann Böhlaus, 1986); Wolfgang Schivelbusch, *Tastes of Paradise: A Social History of Spices, Stimulants, and Intoxicants,* trans. David Jacobson (New York: Vintage, 1993); and the sketches in Gerhard Pfeisinger and Stefan Schennach, eds., *Kolonialwaren: Die Schaffung der ungleichen Welt* (Göttingen: Lamuv, 1989).

19. See Roxanne Wheeler's essay, "Colonial Exchanges," in *An Economy of Colour: Visual Culture and the Atlantic World, 1660–1830,* ed. Geoff Quilley and Kay Dian Kriz (New York: Manchester University Press, 2003).

20. An example of an "Indianer"-labeled Tobacco Moor is that of Anton Coblenz, Köln-Deutz, from before 1875 (but re-copyrighted), WZB (1895), 925, reg. no. 8088.

21. The very idea of the Moor in German culture had a great deal of flexibility. See Peter Martin, *Schwarze Teufel, edle Mohren* (Hamburg: Junius, 1993).

22. An example of a Tobacco Moor with blond hair is the re-registration by the Gebrüder Thorbecke (Osnabrück), WZB (1895), 1295, reg. no. 9976.

23. For slave-sale images, see Barbara E. Lacey, "Visual Images of Blacks in Early American Imprints," *William and Mary Quarterly* 53, no. 1 (1996), as well as Ellwood Parry, *The Image of the Indian and the Black Man in American Art* (New York: Braziller, 1974), particularly the 1769 classified on p. 45.

24. For instance, see Juliann Sivulka, *Soap, Sex, and Cigarettes: A Cultural History of American Advertising* (Belmont, CA: Wadsworth, 1998), 13; Parry, *Indian and Black in American Art,* 68.

25. Roxanne Wheeler suggests that slippage of representation between Indian and African figurations in painting—particularly the growing tendency to depict New World natives with "black" skin color—has a complex history inflected by the development of slavery as an economic and social system. Roxanne Wheeler, "Colonial Exchanges," in Quilley and Kriz, *Economy of Colour,* esp. 51–52.

26. See, for instance, the frontispiece of an eighteenth-century book on commerce, depicting an allegorical array of the four continents (Europe, Africa, Asia, America) in Nederveen Pieterse, *White on Black,* 22. On the social circles of tobacco consumption, see Matthew Hilton, *Smoking in British Popular Culture, 1800–2000* (Manchester, UK: Manchester University Press, 2000); and Woodruff D. Smith, *Consumption and the Making of Respectability: 1600–1800* (New York: Routledge, 2002).

27. This Tobacco Moor tableau overall is atypical in two regards: first, it depicts black figures as laboring, while the majority of Tobacco Moor figures were portrayed reclining or standing. Second, the feather or tobacco-leaf skirts tend to be more common than waist-cloths before the figure is reworked by advertisers in the 1890s.

28. L. B. "Die Hagenbeck'schen Singhalesen," *Die Gartenlaube* no. 34 (1884): 564.

29. A broad overview is Raymond Corbey, "Ethnographic Showcases, 1870–1930," in *The Decolonization of Imagination: Culture, Knowledge and Power,* ed. Jan Nederveen Pieterse and Bhikhu Parekh (London: Zed Books, 1995). See also especially Dreesbach, *Gezähmte Wilde;* Bernth Lindfors, *Africans on Stage*

(Bloomington: Indiana University Press, 1999); Sierra Bruckner, "The Tingle-Tangle of Modernity: Popular Anthropology and the Cultural Politics of Identity in Imperial Germany" (PhD diss., University of Iowa, 1999); and Alison Griffiths, *Wondrous Difference: Cinema, Anthropology, and Turn-of-the-Century Visual Culture* (New York: Columbia University Press, 2002).

30. See especially Bernth Lindfors, "Ethnological Show Business: Footlighting the Dark Continent," in *Freakery: Cultural Spectacles of the Extradordinary Body,* ed. Rosemarie Garland Thomson (New York: New York University Press, 1996); and Bernth Lindfors, "Charles Dickens and the Zulus," in Lindfors, *Africans on Stage.*

31. *Illustrated London News* (1853), 409.

32. The earliest "Zulu" show in Germany may have appeared in 1834. Hilke Thode-Arora, "Afrika-Völkerschauen in Deutschland," in *AfrikanerInnen in Deutschland und schwarze Deutsche,* ed. Marianne Bechhaus-Gerst and Reinhard Klein-Arendt (Munster: LIT, 2003); Dreesbach, *Gezähmte Wilde,* 37–38.

33. Honour, *The Black in Western Art,* 143. Compare also Meyerheim's *In der Tierbude,* in *Fremdkörper—Fremde Körper,* ed. Annemarie Hürlimann, Martin Roth, and Klaus Vogel (Ostfildern-Ruit: Hatje Cantz, 1999), 181.

34. Reinhard Oberschelp, ed., *Werbegraphik 1830–1870, aus niedersächsischen Zeitungen* (Hannover: Niedersächsische Landesbibliothek, 1986), 139. Two years later another notice for the show names the Zulu "Bamba Hongria"; p. 155.

35. Sierra Bruckner charts four types of *Völkerschau:* the anthropological monstrosity (small shows of one or two "atavistic" individuals in the 1870s and 1880s); the ethno-circus production (staging such fantastic spectacles as contortionism or acrobatics in the mid- and late 1880s); the choreographed "colonial village" (reproducing the ethnography of the colonial project in the late 1890s); and the panoramic ethnographic landscape (staging a panoramic survey of the performers' bodies, environment, and culture, pioneered by Hagenbeck). Bruckner, "Tingle-Tangle," 12, 252–282. Compare also the categorizations in Balthasar Staehelin, *Völkerschauen im Zoologischen Garten Basel* (Basel: Baseler Afrika Bibliographien, 1993).

36. Carl Hagenbeck, *Von Tieren und Menschen,* 11th ed. (Berlin: Vita, Deutsches Verlagshaus, 1909), 80. Much has been written about the legendary Hagenbeck; in addition to work by Anne Dreesbach, Nigel Rothfels, Sierra Bruckner, and Eric Ames, see also Hilke Thode-Arora, *Für fünfzig Pfennig um die Welt: Die Hagenbeckschen Völkerschauen* (Frankfurt a. M.: Campus, 1989); and Hilke Thode-Arora, "'Charakteristische Gestaltung des Volkslebens': Die Hagenbeckschen Südasien-, Orient- und Afrika-Völkerschau," in *Fremde Erfahrungen: Asiaten und Afrikaner in Deutschland, Österreich, und in der Schweiz,* ed. Gerhard Höpp (Berlin: Verlag Das Arabische Buch, 1996).

37. See the very useful appendix of *Völkerschau* in Bruckner, "Tingle-Tangle," 473–506; and Nigel T. Rothfels, *Savages and Beasts: The Birth of the Modern Zoo* (Baltimore: Johns Hopkins University Press, 2002), especially 88–89. On R. A. Cunningham, see especially Roslyn Poignant, *Professional Savages: Captive Lives and Western Spectacle* (New Haven, CT: Yale University Press, 2004).

38. Bruckner, "Tingle-Tangle," 242.

39. Eric Ames, "Where the Wild Things Are: Locating the Exotic in German Modernity" (PhD diss., University of California, Berkeley, 2000), chapter 1, esp. 32ff. On the travel implicit in Hagenbeck's constructed "panoramic ethnographic landscapes," see Bruckner, "Tingle-Tangle," 274–282; Rothfels, *Savages and Beasts,* 89, 91–92; Thode-Arora, *Für fünfzig Pfennig,* 140.

40. *Kleinen Presse* (16 July 1891), quoted in Viktoria Schmidt-Linsenhoff, Kurt Wettengl, and Almut Junker, eds., *Plakate 1880–1914* (Frankfurt a. M.: Historisches Museum Frankfurt am Main, 1986), 230.

41. Carl Hagenbeck, *Von Tieren und Menschen,* expanded edition (Berlin: Vita, 1909), 85; Rothfels, *Savages and Beasts,* 84. For 93,000, see Thode-Arora, *Für fünfzig Pfennig,* 169. I am skeptical of these numbers, as they derive from Hagenbeck's memoir and would not be the first wild exaggeration found therein.

42. Andrew Zimmerman, *Anthropology and Antihumanism in Imperial Germany* (Chicago: University of Chicago Press, 2001), 18–19; Bruckner, "Tingle-Tangle," 288.

43. Bruckner, "Tingle-Tangle," 242. More broadly, see also Sander Gilman, *Difference and Pathology: Stereotypes of Sexuality, Race, and Madness* (Ithaca, NY: Cornell University Press, 1985).

44. Sibylle Obenaus, *Literarische und politische Zeitschriften 1848–1880* (Stuttgart: J. B. Metzlersche, 1987), 22, 31–32, and 47–48. See also Kirsten Belgum, *Popularizing the Nation: Audience, Representation, and the Production of Identity in Die Gartenlaube, 1853–1900* (Lincoln: University of Nebraska Press, 1998).

45. Obenaus, *Zeitschriften 1848–1880,* 33.

46. For the masthead, see any issue of *Über Land und Meer (Over Land and Sea).* The masthead was actually registered as a trademark in 1908; see WZB (1908), reg. no. 104693. Magazines such as *Über Land und Meer* presaged the German colonial project by illustrating colonial fantasies of German domination in the Near East: see Antje Harnisch, "Der Harem in Familienblättern des 19. Jahrhunderts: Koloniale Phantasien und Nationale Identität," *German Life and Letters* 51, no. 3 (1998).

47. Schmidt-Linsenhoff, Wettengl, and Junker, *Plakate 1880–1914,* 229; Poignant, *Professional Savages,* 151.

48. See especially Dreesbach, *Gezähmte Wilde,* 110–181.

49. See Rothfels, *Savages and Beasts,* 96–103, and especially Bruckner, "Tingle-Tangle," 23, 456–471.

50. Rothfels, *Savages and Beasts,* quoting Hagenbeck (1908 ed.), 121. Translation is Rothfels's.

51. Peter Letkemann, "Das Berliner Panoptikum: Namer, Häuser und Schicksale," *Mitteilungen des Vereins für die Geschichte Berlins* 69 (1973); Poignant, *Professional Savages,* 128–141; Zimmerman, *Anthropology and Antihumanism,* 16–20, 173–174. Castan's had opened a "labyrinth" in Hamburg by 1889, according to a poster in Klaus Popitz et al., eds., *Das frühe Plakat in Europa und den USA: Band 3: Deutschland* (Berlin: Gebr. Mann, 1980), no. 3930. See also Pamela Pilbeam, *Madame Tussaud and the History of Waxworks* (London: Hambledon and London, 2003).

52. Klaus Gille, *125 Jahre zwischen Wachs und Wirklichkeit: Hamburgs Panoptikum und seine Geschichte* (Hamburg: P. Kivouvou, 2004), 20.

53. Stephan Oettermann, "Alles-Schau: Wachsfigurenkabinette und Panoptiken," in *Viel Vergnügen: Öffentliche Lustbarkeit im Ruhrgebiet der Jahrhundertwende,* ed. Lisa Kosok and Mathilde Jamin (Essen: Peter Pomp, 1992).

54. Andrea Stulman Dennett, *Weird and Wonderful: The Dime Museum in America* (New York: New York University Press, 1997). See also Poignant, *Professional Savages,* 98–105.

55. Zimmerman, *Anthropology and Antihumanism,* 18; Poignant, *Professional Savages,* 133.

56. Oettermann, "Alles-Schau," 36–54.

57. The black-and-white photos of these busts in Zimmerman, *Anthropology and Antihumanism,* 17, cannot convey the stark effect of the figures' bright red painted lips against the pitch black of their painted skin tone.

58. CMNL, Friedländer no. 1313.

59. Bruckner, "Tingle-Tangle," 82. It is likely that only replicas of the masks were sold.

60. Landesarchiv Berlin Kult 121, *Führer Durch Das Passage-Panopticum* (Berlin: 1905). See also *Straube's illustrierter Führer durch Berlin, Potsdam und Umgebung: Praktisches Reisehandbuch,* 18th ed. (Berlin: Geographisches Institut und Landkarten-Verlag, 1898), 65; and Oettermann, "Alles-Schau," 45.

61. The Cairo harem show of 1896 is seen in a drawing in Albert Kühnemann, *Groß Berlin: Bilder von der Ausstellungsstadt* (Berlin, 1896/1897), 245; that they were Tunisians is per Bruckner's appendix. Also in 1896 was the Lion-Man, a fire eater, and the Man with the Iron Mouth. Oettermann, "Alles-Schau," 45. The sign for the "Togo Negroes" is seen in a photograph in Karin Gaa and Bernd Krueger, *Das Kaiserpanorama* (Berlin: Berliner Festspiele, 1984), 7. The Togo Negro show poster depicts a placid colonial village with grass-roofed huts and a German flag; see Popitz et al., *Das frühe Plakat,* no. 4057; and CMNL, Friedländer no. 1652.

62. Schmidt-Linsenhoff, Wettengl, and Junker, *Plakate 1880–1914,* 89. The poster is incorrectly dated to 1882 in Carl-Albrecht Haenlein and Wolfgang

Till, eds., *Menschen—Tiere—Sensationen: Zirkusplakate 1880–1930* (Hannover: Kestner-Gesellschaft, 1978), no. 133, and to 1879 by CMNL (Friedländer no. 0296). In fact, this poster appeared just after 1892, datable through Casati's book publication and the timing of the trial and execution of Franz and Rosalie Schneider in 1892.

63. Reproduced respectively in Popitz et al., *Das frühe Plakat,* nos. 299, 3530, and 3982; Schmidt-Linsenhoff, Wettengl, and Junker, *Plakate 1880–1914,* no. 105; and CMNL, Friedländer no. 1313.

64. See Vanessa Schwartz, *Spectacular Realities: Early Mass Culture in Fin-de-Siècle Paris* (Berkeley: University of California Press, 1998).

65. Ruth Malhotra, *Manege frei: Artisten- und Circusplakaten von Adolph Friedländer* (Dortmund: Harenberg, 1979).

66. See CMNL, Friedländer nos. 0047, 0157, 0425, 0561. The given dates are uncertain; despite sequential numbering, early Friedländer posters remain problematic to date precisely. The cited dates are per Jaap Best, who provided the bulk of the CMNL collection. Alternative dating is seen in Popitz et al., *Das frühe Plakat,* 338. See also Stephan Oettermann and Jan Seffinga, *Adolph Friedländer Lithos: Ein Verzeichnis nach Nummern* (Gerolzhofen: Oettermann, 2002), and Schmidt-Linsenhoff, Wettengl, and Junker, *Plakate 1880–1914,* 24. The influence of American minstrel acts on German commercial visuality is discussed extensively in Chapter 5.

67. An extensive array of Friedländer posters (almost 500) are reproduced in Popitz et al., *Das frühe Plakat,* part 1, 337–361. In addition, the Jaap Best collection of the Circusmuseum in the Netherlands (circusmuseum.nl) has more than 3,400 different Friedländer designs.

68. Barnum's tour also initiated the German discourse of associating "circus-style" promotional tactics with America. See Eliot Shore, "Advertising as *Kulturkampf* in Berlin and Vienna," in *Advertising and the European City: Historical Perspectives,* ed. Clemens Wischermann and Eliot Shore (Aldershot, UK: Ashgate, 2000), 33. Shore sees this German view of Barnum's "Americanism" as largely rhetorical, in that practices were already incipient in Germany. I discuss the role of American modernity in the discourse and the practice of German advertising extensively in later chapters.

69. For the "Wild African Savages" of 1861, see Sivulka, *Soap, Sex, and Cigarettes,* 31. For Barnum's career in shows of "savages," see Poignant, *Professional Savages,* 77–89; and Robert Bogdan, *Freak Show: Presenting Human Oddities for Amusement and Profit* (Chicago: University of Chicago Press, 1988), 180–187.

70. Carl Hagenbeck, *Von Tieren und Menschen* (Berlin, 1909), 428–432.

71. Ibid., 428.

72. Schmidt-Linsenhoff, Wettengl, and Junker, *Plakate 1880–1914,* 21 and 225. On Barnum's influence on American advertising posters, see Donald Hen-

don and William Muhs, "Origin and Early Development of Outdoor Advertising in the United States," *Journal of Marketing History* 9, no. 1 (1986).

73. On Umlauff's see Eric Ames, *Carl Hagenbeck's Empire of Entertainments* (Seattle: University of Washington Press, 2009), 211–213; Alexander Honold and Klaus R. Scherpe, *Mit Deutschland um die Welt: Eine Kulturgeschichte des Fremden in der Kolonialzeit* (Stuttgart: J. B. Metzler, 2004), 152–162.

74. The photo is reproduced in Markus Schindlbeck, ed., *Die ethnographische Linse: Photographien aus dem Museum für Völkerkunde Berlin* (Berlin: Museum für Völkerkunde Berlin, 1989), 66. The three-dozen odd performers all sit or stand erect, posing stiffly for the camera, their elephants arrayed placidly behind them.

75. Bruckner, "Tingle-Tangle," 480.

76. Between 1900 and the First World War, the firm turned out another 8,000 designs. The firm's peak output occurred between 1900 and 1904, producing 2,000 posters in four years. Malhotra, *Manege frei,* 11–12.

77. Malhotra, *Manege frei,* 6.

78. See Henry John Drewal, "Mami Wata and Santa Marta: Imag(in)ing Selves and Others in Africa and the Americas," in *Images and Empires: Visuality in Colonial and Post-Colonial Africa,* ed. Paul S. Landau and Deborah Kaspin (Berkeley: University of California Press, 2002), 193–211.

79. See Popitz et al., *Das frühe Plakat,* nos. 3081 and 3919, respectively.

80. See the photograph in Schmidt-Linsenhoff, Wettengl, and Junker, *Plakate 1880–1914,* 12; for satirical cartoons, see Wischermann and Shore, *Advertising,* 14; and Dirk Reinhardt, *Von der Reklame zum Marketing: Geschichte der Wirtschaftswerbung in Deutschland* (Berlin: Akademie, 1993), 264.

81. Thode-Arora, *Für fünfzig Pfennig,* 47; and Thode-Arora, "Gestaltung des Volkslebens," 112.

82. See the poster for Hagenbeck's "Indien" show from 1895, with the text "Carl Hagenbeck's Indien, Berlin. Kauft Hagenbeck's Ceylon Thee. Direct bezogen von der Ceylon Tea Company. Unter dem Protectorate der Planters Association. Kandy Ceylon 1854," which includes prices of Orange Pekoe, Pekoe, and Pekoe Souchong. CMNL, Friedländer no. 1246; also in Popitz et al., *Das frühe Plakat,* no. 4050.

83. A Friedländer poster of the hot air balloon ride at Hamburg's 1889 exhibition, for instance, also served to advertise Kemmerich's beef bullion; while an 1896 poster for an acrobatic bicycle show, the Kaufmann Troupe, incorporated an plug for Continental Pneumatic tires. CMNL, Friedländer nos. 1305 and 1306; Popitz et al., *Das frühe Plakat,* no. 3919.

84. *Propaganda* 3, no. 1 (1899): 26; Johannes Lemcke ("P. Friesenhahn"), *Handbuch der Reklame* (Berlin: Brockhaus, 1901), 113.

85. See Henriette Väth-Hinz, *Odol: Reklame-Kunst um 1900* (Gießen: Anabas, 1985). Odol is still marketed today.

86. See the examples throughout Väth-Hinz, *Odol,* esp. 112; *Kolonie und Heimat* (1907); and *Süsserotts Illustrierte Kolonial Kalendar* (1912), 1.

87. See the photograph of Gumma in *Der Kurier,* 29 August 1896, reproduced in Schmidt-Linsenhoff, Wettengl, and Junker, *Plakate 1880–1914,* 235.

88. Heinrich Bloss and Max Bartels, *Das Weib in der Natur- und Völkerkunde,* 9th ed., vol. 1 (Leipzig: T. Grieben (L. Fernau), 1908), 8; Carl Stratz, *die Rassenschönheit des Weibes,* 2nd ed.(Stuttgart: F. Enke, 1902), 118. See also Stefan Goldmann, "Wilde in Europa," in Theye, *Wir und die Wilden,* 263.

89. For a useful list of *Völkerschauen* from which to extrapolate the frequency of a type of show, see the appendix of Bruckner, "Tingle-Tangle." For performances by Japanese, from mysterious Oriental princesses to dramatic charging of the "Japanese Guard Cavalry," see the collection at CMNL, esp. Friedländer nos. 2236 (1902), 2985 (1904), and 3602 (1906).

90. See the British Library's Evanion Collection, no. Evan.416.

91. A *Life of P. T. Barnum* text from the 1890s includes a chromolithograph of a parade of Ceylonese, including elephants and houdas. My thanks to Kathleen Maher, curator at the Barnum Museum in Bridgeport, Connecticut.

92. After the brig *Maria* was wrecked on a reef, several of the survivors who made it to shore (including the captain) were killed by Aborigines. In reprisal, punitive expeditions massacred several aboriginal settlements in the area.

93. See Hilke Thode-Arora, "'Blutrünstige Kannibalen' und 'wilde Weiber': Extrembeispiele für Klischees in der Völkerschau-Werbung," in *Schwarz Weissheiten: Vom Umgang mit fremden Menschen,* ed. Mamoun Fansa (Oldenburg: Isensee, 2001), 93–94.

94. Schmidt-Linsenhoff, Wettengl, and Junker, *Plakate 1880–1914,* 244–245, and Thode-Arora, "'Blutrünstige Kannibalen,'" 94, reproduce a composite image that shows this poster with a German-language overlay.

95. Reproduced in Schmidt-Linsenhoff, Wettengl, and Junker, *Plakate 1880–1914,* 228. See also Poignant, *Professional Savages,* 173.

96. Roslyn Poignant has adroitly reconstructed the show's footsteps and recounted interactions between the public, Berlin's scientific establishment, and the Australian aboriginal performers. There were originally nine performers; two died on the American tour, and by the end of the tour only three had survived. See Poignant, *Professional Savages,* 111–164; and also Bruckner, "Tingle-Tangle," 359–361.

97. Report from the annual meeting of the German Colonial Society, 1901, quoted in Sierra Bruckner, "Spectacles of (Human) Nature: Commercial Ethnography between Leisure, Learning, and *Schaulust,*" in *Objects of Culture: Ethnology and Ethnographic Museums in Imperial Germany,* ed. Glenn H. Penny (Chapel Hill: University of North Carolina Press, 2002), 26. The quotation continues, "The indigenous are dressed up so that they laugh at themselves and the

gullible spectator, they are taught dances that they never knew before, and thus they deceive the public and simultaneously become corrupted." Translation is Bruckner's.

98. From 1867 to 1884, six shows were of "Nubians." The years 1885 to 1889 saw thirty shows of sub-Saharan Africans and seven from North Africa. From 1900 to 1914, meanwhile, twenty-five shows were of sub-Saharan Africans and eight of North Africans, out of a total of fifty-four shows. See the appendix of Bruckner, "Tingle-Tangle," 473–506 (supplanting that in Thode-Arora, *Für fünfzig Pfennig*).

99. The Cameroon show is mentioned in Rothfels, *Savages and Beasts,* 126; Bruckner, "Tingle-Tangle," 482; and Dreesbach, *Gezähmte Wilde,* 59n117, 97, 124, and 272. Of course, the Native Villages of 1896 Berlin were also *Völkerschauen,* though differently staged.

100. See Elfi Bendikat, "The Berlin Conference in the German, French, and British Press," in *Bismarck, Europe, and Africa: The Berlin Africa Conference, 1884–1885 and the Onset of Partition,* ed. Stig Forster, Wolfgang J. Mommsen, and Ronald Robinson (Oxford: Oxford University Press, 1988).

101. These *Völkerschauen* are listed in the appendix of Bruckner, "Tingle-Tangle," 473–506, except Möllers's Sudanese Caravan, found in Thode-Arora, *Für fünfzig Pfennig,* 140. I have correlated them with headlines of colonial warfare.

102. The full quotation (from a critical colonialist) is "partly too sober, and partly too transparently deceptive." DKZ 17, no. 44 (1900): 500.

103. Bruckner, "Tingle-Tangle," 279, citing the show pamphlet *Das Amazon-Corps,* 1891. On the Amazon shows, see Bruckner, "Tingle-Tangle," 278–282; Rothfels, *Savages and Beasts,* 133–134; Schmidt-Linsenhoff, Wettengl, and Junker, *Plakate 1880–1914,* 251.

104. Poster for Umlauff's Weltmuseum in 1890 in Popitz et al., *Das frühe Plakat,* no. 290.

105. Malhotra, *Manege frei,* 61.

106. CMNL, Friedländer no. 1146. The poster includes copious text, with a description of the troupe (under chief warrioresses Marmona and Zamba), the program (including the "Holy War Dance of the Fetish-Idolater") and even lists the names/stage names and ages of the Africans. This poster is dated to 1894 by the Circusmuseum. A nearly identical poster was issued in 1902 with different costume colors and without the text.

107. Rothfels, *Savages and Beasts,* 134.

108. See the photograph of Gumma in *Der Kurier,* 29 August 1896, reproduced in Schmidt-Linsenhoff, Wettengl, and Junker, *Plakate 1880–1914,* 235.

109. Cf. Robert J. C. Young, *Colonial Desire: Hybridity in Theory, Culture and Race* (New York: Routledge, 1995); Ann Laura Stoler, "Carnal Knowledge and Imperial Power: Gender, Race and Morality in Colonial Asia," in *Gender at the*

Crossroads of Knowledge: Feminist Anthropology in the Postmodern Era, ed. Micaela di Leonardo (Berkeley: University of California Press, 1991); Anne McClintock, *Imperial Leather* (New York: Routledge, 1995); and many others. For the eroticization of the black female body, see especially Sander Gilman, *Sexuality: An Illustrated History* (New York: John Wiley & Sons, 1989); and Deborah Willis and Carla Williams, *The Black Female Body: A Photographic History* (Philadelphia: Temple University Press, 2002).

110. For the Frankfurt Zoo version, see Schmidt-Linsenhoff, Wettengl, and Junker, *Plakate 1880–1914,* 253, no. 378; for the Crystal Palace version, British Library's Evanion Collection, no. Evan.1060. Bernhardt's poster features a version of Gumma standing with her hips partially turned and one hand on her posterior; it is poorly drawn but to me seems reminiscent of the drawings of the "Hottentot Venus" (Sara Baartman) from eight decades earlier; compare Strother, "The Body Hottentot," esp. 28.

111. Bernard Mirabel, ed., *Negripub: L'Image des Noirs dans la publicite* (Paris: Somogy, 1987), 45; Griffiths, *Wondrous Difference,* 58. The greater ferocity evident in these French posters might be argued to stem from the fact that France fought Dahomey; yet the French forces in the actual conflict consisted primarily of African soldiers. Rather strangely, a number of Amazon posters from 1894 for the French bicylcle manufacturer Alfred Moyse & F. Hullier prominently feature bicycles; perhaps the show itself employed bicycles in the fashion of the *varieté,* and Moyse & Hullier were seeking to be topical. See Mirabel, *Negripub,* 47.

112. Dana Hale, *Races on Display: French Representations of Colonized Peoples, 1886–1940* (Bloomington: Indiana University Press, 2008); Brett Berliner, *Ambivalent Desire: The Exotic Black Other in Jazz-Age France* (Amherst: University of Massachusetts Press, 2002); Petrine Archer-Straw, *Negrophilia: Avant-Garde Paris and Black Culture in the 1920s* (New York: Thames & Hudson, 2000).

113. Lora Wildenthal, *German Women for Empire, 1884–1945* (Durham, NC: Duke University Press, 2001).

114. Harnisch, "Harem in Familienblättern."

115. Dreesbach, *Gezähmte Wilde,* 140–141; Jutta Engelhard and Peter Mesenhöller, *Bilder aus dem Paradies: Koloniale Fotographie Samoa 1875–1925* (Köln: Jonas, 1995); Schindlbeck, *Die ethnographische Linse.* Also useful is George Steinmetz, *The Devil's Handwriting: Precoloniality and the German Colonial State in Qingdao, Samoa, and Southwest Africa* (Chicago: University of Chicago Press, 2007).

116. See Schmidt-Linsenhoff, Wettengl, and Junker, *Plakate 1880–1914,* 254, no. 380; and also Thode-Arora, "'Blutrünstige Kannibalen,'" 94–95.

117. Schmidt-Linsenhoff, Wettengl, and Junker, *Plakate 1880–1914,* 254. However, Viktoria Schmidt-Linsenhoff reports that it was used for the 1899 show at the Moskauer Panoptikum in Frankfurt.

118. A colonial exhibition was part of the Deutsch-Nordische Handels- und Industrie-Ausstellung. Oliver Korn, *Hanseatische Gewerbeausstellungen im 19. Jahrhundert* (Opladen: Leske & Budrich, 1999) 169–170. See also DKZ 12 (1895): 260–261.

119. DKZ 17, no. 44 (1900): 500.

120. Hanns von Zobeltitz, "Von der Berliner Gewerbeausstellung," *Daheim* (1896): 401. On *Schaulust,* see Bruckner, "Spectacles of (Human) Nature," 151–155.

121. See especially Ames, *Carl Hagenbeck's Empire of Entertainments,* 98–102; Harald Sippel, "Rassismus, Protektionismus oder Humanität? Die Gesetzlichen Verbote der Anwerbung von 'Eingeborenen' zu Schaustellungszweck in den Deutschen Kolonien," in *Kolonialausstellungen—Begegnungen mit Afrika?* ed. Robert Debusmann and János Riesz (Frankfurt a. M.: Verlag für Interkulturelle Kommunikation, 1995), 43–63; Dreesbach, *Gezähmte Wilde;* Steinmetz, *Devil's Handwriting;* and Bruckner, "Tingle-Tangle," 375–424.

122. See especially Lora Wildenthal, "Race, Gender, and Citizenship in the German Colonial Empire," in *Tensions of Empire,* ed. Frederick Cooper and Ann Laura Stoler (Berkeley: University of California Press, 1997); Birthe Kundrus, *Moderne Imperialisten* (Köln: Böhlau, 2003); Pascal Grosse, *Kolonialismus, Eugenik und bürgerliche Gesellschaft in Deutschland 1850–1918* (Frankfurt a. M.: Campus, 2000).

123. Sudanese, Tunisians, and Moroccans performing at the Deutsche Armee, Marine, und Kolonial-Aussstellung left the exhibition enclosure (where they were contractually required to remain) to see the sights of the city. Most scandalously, they were joined in their revelry by a number of German women. Bruckner, "Spectacles of (Human) Nature," 144–151.

124. Gaetano Casati, *Zehn Jahre in Aequatoria und die Rückkehr mit Emin Pascha* (Bamberg: C. C. Buchner'schen, 1891).

125. The illustration appears in the English edition, *Ten Years in Equatoria and the Return with Emin Pasha,* trans. J. R. Clay (London: Frederick Warne & Co., 1891), on p. 103 of vol. 2, and in the French edition (1892) on p. 329.

126. *Illustrirte Zeitung* no. 2469 (1890): 427.

127. *Die Reklame* 4, no. 2 (1894): 33.

128. Bruckner, "Tingle-Tangle"; Poignant, *Professional Savages.*

129. For some of these stories of performers smoking, conversing fluently, and generally flummoxing Germans, see Alfred Lehmann, "Zietgenössische Bilder der ersten Völkerschauen," in *Von fremden Völkern und Kulturen: Beiträge zur Volkskunde: Hans Plischke zum 65. Geburtstag gewidment,* ed. Werner Lang (Düsseldorf: Drost, 1955). See also Thode-Arora, "Gestaltung des Volkslebens," 116.

3. Masters of the Modern Exotic

1. Rudolf Cronau, *Das Buch der Reklame: Geschichte, Wesen und Praxis der Reklame* (Ulm, 1887), sect. 1, 27. The first books on advertising in the German language were technically J. H. Wehle, *Die Reclame, Ihre Theorie und Praxis* (Vienna: A. Hartleben, 1880), and Josef Räber, *Die Gewerbliche Reklame* (Lucerne: Hermes, 1886). Writings on *Reklame,* moreover, appeared even earlier in journals; see esp. R. A. Fullerton, "A Prophet of Modern Advertising: Germany's Karl Knies," *Journal of Advertising* 27, no. 1 (1998). Nonetheless, Cronau's book was widely recognized as and cited as the first German handbook.

2. See Anandi Ramamurthy, *Imperial Persuaders: Images of Africa and Asia in British Advertising* (Manchester, UK: Manchester University Press, 2003), 39–42.

3. See *Illustrated London News* 91, no. 2520 (1885); Ramamurthy, *Imperial Persuaders;* Thomas Richards, *The Commodity Culture of Victorian England: Advertising and Spectacle, 1851–1914* (London: Verso, 1990), 122.

4. While many scholars have looked at this advertisement, it was in fact quite uncharacteristic for the *Illustrated London News* before 1887, not only for its imperial subject matter and dramatic pictorial style, but also for its size—a quarter page—and heavy ink usage. For a critical reevaluation of "the empire's" preeminence in British culture, see Bernard Porter, *The Absent-Minded Imperialists: Empire, Society, and Culture in Britain* (Oxford: Oxford University Press, 2004).

5. See Ramamurthy, *Imperial Persuaders;* Richards, *Commodity Culture;* and Timothy Burke, *Lifebuoy Men, Lux Women: Commodification, Consumption, and Cleanliness in Modern Zimbabwe* (Durham, NC: Duke University Press, 1996).

6. For the material connections, see Ramamurthy, *Imperial Persuaders,* 26–49; for gender constructions, see Anne McClintock, *Imperial Leather* (New York: Routledge, 1995), 207–231.

7. On the modernity of German colonialists, see especially Birthe Kundrus, *Moderne Imperialisten: Das Kaiserreich im Spiegel seiner Kolonien* (Köln: Böhlau, 2003). On the modernity of advertisers, see Pamela Swett, S. Jonathan Wiesen, and Jonathan Zatlin, eds., *Selling Modernity: Advertising in Twentieth-Century Germany* (Durham, NC: Duke University Press, 2007).

8. Christiane Lamberty, *Reklame in Deutschland 1890–1914: Wahrnehmung, Professionalisierung und Kritik der Wirtschaftswerbung* (Berlin: Duncker & Humblot, 2000), 225 and 234ff.

9. Fullerton, "Prophet of Advertising," esp. 53, 55, 60–63.

10. See Stanislaus Swierczewski, *Wider Schmutz und Schwindel im Inseratenwesen* (Leipzig: "Deutsche Kampf" Verlag, 1907), esp. 25–26, which rails against "obscene" ads for rubber gear and solicitations for prostitution.

11. Cf. Cronau, *Das Buch der Reklame,* 1 and 58; Ernst Growald, "Reklame-Nepper," *Die Reklame* 2 (1892): 105–118.

12. In 1865/1866 *Gartenlaube's* classified section was the inspiration of Rudolf Mosse, who went on to found one of the earliest classified brokerages *(Annonce Expedition)* in Berlin, from which he built the Mosse press empire.

13. Dirk Reinhardt, *Von der Reklame zum Marketing: Geschichte der Wirtschaftswerbung in Deutschland* (Berlin: Akademie, 1993), 197; and Kurt Koszyk, *Deutsche Presse,* vol. 6 (Berlin: Colloquium, 1966), 268–269. See also the statistics in Joachim Kirchner, *Das deutsche Zeitschriftwesen,* vol. 2 (Wiesbaden: Otto Harrassowitz, 1962), 425–430.

14. See *Fahrten im lande der Sioux* (Leipzig: T. O. Weigel, 1886); and *Amerika: Die Geschichte seiner Entdeckung von der ältesten bis auf die neuste Zeit* (Leipzig: Abel & Müller, 1892). Cronau was born in Solingen; he eventually immigrated to the United States just before the First World War, where he continued to write prodigiously.

15. See Cronau's illustration of the Massaua in *Die Gartenlaube* (1884), 217.

16. Cronau, *Das Buch der Reklame,* part III, 24. Cronau's *Fahrten im lande der Sioux (Travels in the Land of the Sioux)* was published the same year as the *Völkerschau* tour, in 1886.

17. Cronau, *Das Buch der Reklame,* part I, 1.

18. P. T. Barnum, *The Humbugs of the World: An Account of Humbugs, Delusions, Impositions, Quackeries, Deceits and Deceivers Generally, in All Ages* (New York: Carleton, 1866).

19. Cronau, *Das Buch der Reklame,* part I, 44.

20. Ibid., part I, 44–45. Theater productions of *Uncle Tom's Cabin* found enormously popularity in Germany after the 1850s; see Chapter 5.

21. On Barnum, see esp. Cronau, *Das Buch der Reklame,* part V, 1–8.

22. Cronau, *Das Buch der Reklame,* from his foreword.

23. *Scribner's Magazine* (later *Century Magazine*) 20, no. 4 (August 1880): 608.

24. Cronau, *Das Buch der Reklame,* part III, 27; part II, 27; part III, 22; and part IV, 4, respectively.

25. Ibid., part II, 15.

26. See Andrew Zimmerman, *Anthropology and Antihumanism in Imperial Germany* (Chicago: University of Chicago Press, 2001), 38–62; McClintock, *Imperial Leather,* 36–40.

27. Rudolf Cronau, *Im Wilden Westen: Eine Künstlerfahrt durch die Prairien und Felsengebirge der Union* (Braunschweig: O. Lobbecke, 1890), 54. The image itself, moreover, is clearly copied directly from George Catlin's 1835 painting on the Okipa Ritual of the Mandan (from which numerous engravings were made, and likely made their way to Germany and/or France).

28. See Cronau, *Das Buch der Reklame,* part I, 5; part II, 1; and passim.

29. Cf. Ratzel, *Völkerkunde* (1884); Cronau, *Das Buch der Reklame,* part II, 15; and Wilh. Fintel, *Tschaka der grosse Zulukönig* (1926), as reproduced in

Gottfried Mergner and Ansgar Häfner, *Der Afrikaner im deutschen Kinder- und Jugendbuch* (Oldenburg: Bibliotheks- und Informationssytem der Universität, 1985), 132.

30. Viktoria Schmidt-Linsenhoff, Kurt Wettengl, and Almut Junker, eds., *Plakate 1880–1914* (Frankfurt a. M.: Historisches Museum Frankfurt am Main, 1986), 230 and 246–247; Hilke Thode-Arora, *Für fünfzig Pfennig um die Welt: Die Hagenbeckschen Völkerschauen* (Frankfurt a. M.: Campus, 1989), 121.

31. *Mitteilungen des Vereins für Erdkunde zu Leipzig, 1883* (Leipzig: Duncker & Humblot, 1884).

32. Cronau, *Das Buch der Reklame,* part III, 24.

33. Ibid., part II, 9.

34. Ibid., part III, 3. Cf. Sierra Bruckner, "The Tingle-Tangle of Modernity: Popular Anthropology and the Cultural Politics of Identity in Imperial Germany" (PhD diss., University of Iowa, 1999), 484.

35. As recommended by J. J. Kaindl in his bibliography on advertising books in Paul Ruben, *Die Reklame,* vol. 1 (Berlin: Verlag für Sozialpolitik, 1914), 291.

36. See especially Peter Borscheid and Clemens Wischermann, eds., *Bilderwelt des Alltags: Werbung in der Konsumgesellschaft des 19. und 20. Jahrhunderts* (Stuttgart: Franz Steiner, 1995), and comparatively, Richard Ohmann, *Selling Culture: Magazines, Markets, and Class at the Turn of the Century* (New York: Verso, 1996).

37. Koszyk, *Deutsche Presse im 19 Jahrhundert, Teil II,* 271; and Volker Berghahn, *Imperial Germany, 1871–1914* (Providence: Berghahn Books, 1994), 186.

38. For a contemporary's overview of the various illustration technologies available, see Otto Krüger's technical handbook *Die Illustrationsverfahren: Eine vergleichende Behandlung der verschiedenen Reproduktionsarten, ihrer Vorteile, Nachteile, und Kosten* (Leipzig: F. A. Brockhaus, 1914). Enormously useful is Gerry Beegan, *The Mass Image: A Social History of Photomechanical Reproduction in Victorian London* (New York: Palgrave Macmillan, 2008).

39. Sibylle Obenaus, *Literarische und politische Zeitschriften 1848–1880* (Stuttgart: J. B. Metzlersche, 1987), 22; by 1905 the circulation of *Die Gartenlaube* had fallen to 100,000. The terms *Generalanzeiger, Massenpresse,* and *Geschäftspresse* all refer to this same general phenomenon, though each term highlights a different "face" of this new manner of media. A thorough overview of these terms can be found in Rudolf Stöber, *Deutsche Pressegeschichte. Einführung, Systematik, Glossar* (Konstanz: UVK Medien, 2000), esp. 231ff. See also Gideon Reuveni, *Reading Germany: Literature and Consumer Culture in Germany before 1933* (New York: Berghahn, 2006), 122–135; and Peter Fritzsche, *Reading Berlin 1900* (Cambridge, MA: Harvard University Press, 1996).

40. On bourgeois journals and German identity, see Kirsten Belgum, *Popularizing the Nation: Audience, Representation, and the Production of Identity in* Die Gartenlaube, *1853–1900* (Lincoln: University of Nebraska Press, 1998). As Peter Fritzsche argues, only the lowbrow metropolitan newspaper, appearing around 1900, attained a truly "national" reach. Fritzsche, *Reading Berlin,* 53.

41. See Hermann Diez, *Das Zeitungswesen* (Leipzig: Teubner, 1910), 102–104.

42. Gideon Reuveni, "Lesen und Konsum: Der Aufstieg der Konsumkultur in Presse und Werbung Deutschlands bis 1933," *Archiv fur Sozialgeschichte* 41 (2001); Fritzsche, *Reading Berlin,* 73. The first issue of the *Lokal-Anzeiger* was even distributed gratis.

43. Koszyk, *Deutsche Presse,* 272; Stöber, *Deutsche Pressegeschichte,* 231–237.

44. *Mitteilung über Insertionsmittel (Beilage zur "Propaganda")* 1, no. 5 (February 1898): 72.

45. On branding in Germany, see especially Holme Friebe's essay in Pamela E. Swett, S. Jonathan Wiesen, and Jonathan R. Zatlin, eds., *Selling Modernity: Advertising in Twentieth-Century Germany* (Durham, NC: Duke University Press, 2007), 78–101; on *Markenartikel,* see Lamberty, *Reklame,* 109–122; Jürgen Schwarz, *Bildannoncen aus der Jahrhundertwende* (Frankfurt a. M.: Kunstgeschichtliches Institut der Johann Wolfgang Goethe-Universität, 1990), 18–29; Reinhardt, *Reklame zum Marketing,* 24–31; and Michael Weisser, *Annoncen aus der Jahrhundertwende 1896–1926* (Hannover: Schlütersche, 1982).

46. This was the first *Bildreklame*—according to advertising lore, at least. Reinhardt, *Reklame zum Marketing,* 206, citing Erwin Paneth in 1927. On the standardized woodcuts that peppered textual classifieds, see Peter Borscheid, "Am Anfang war das Wort: Die Wirtschaftswerbung beginnt mit der Zeitungsannonce," in Borscheid and Wischermann, *Bilderwelt des Alltags,* 35–36.

47. Schwarz, *Bildannoncen,* 10. See also Stefan Haas, "Die neue Welt der Bilder: Werbung und visuelle Kultur der Moderne," in Borscheid and Wischermann, *Bilderwelt des Alltags,* 64–77.

48. Eugen Leitherer and Hans Wichmann, eds., *Reiz und Hülle: Gestaltete Warenverpackungen des 19. und 20. Jahrhunderts* (Stuttgart: Birkhäuser, 1987).

49. Cronau, *Das Buch der Reklame,* 53.

50. The literature on posters is immense; a starting point is Jeremy Aynsley, *Graphic Design in Germany, 1890–1945* (Berkeley: University of California Press, 2000).

51. See Lamberty, *Reklame,* 166–224. Also of interest is Dorle Weyers and Christoph Köck, *Die Eroberung der Welt: Sammelbilder Vermitteln Zeitalter* (Detmold: Westfälisches Freilichtmuseum Detmold, 1992); Christa Pieske, *Das ABC des Luxuspapiers: Herstellung, Verarbeitung und Gebrauch* (Berlin: Staatliche Museen Preußischer Kulturbesitz Museum für Deutsche Volkskunde, 1983); and Lotte

Maier, *Reklame-Schau: Plakatkunst en miniature: Ausstellungs-, Reklame- und Propagandamarken von 1896 bis 1939 aus der Sammlung Hans König* (Dortmund: Harenberg, 1984).

52. Stefan Haas, "Visual Discourse and the Metropolis: Mental Models of Cities and the Emergence of Commercial Advertising," in *Advertising and the European City: Historical Perspectives,* ed. Clemens Wischermann and Eliot Shore (Aldershot, UK: Ashgate, 2000), 54–78.

53. The earliest documented *Annoncen* bureau in Germany is that of Ferdinand Haasenstein, in Hamburg in 1855 —fifty years after similar agencies had appeared in England. One of the earliest and most successful of these *Annoncen* agencies was that of Rudolf Mosse, founded in 1867.

54. The first advertising bureau within a German firm was that in Hoff in 1870. Lamberty, *Reklame,* 225 and 234–247. Major brand-name manufacturers that set up their own advertising bureaus between 1900 and 1908 included Wagner (Pelikan ink), Kaffee HAG (coffee), Zeiss (optics), and Dr. Oetker (baking powder). Reinhardt, *Reklame zum Marketing,* 28.

55. The *Neue Mittelstand* is often juxtaposed with the "old" bourgeoisie of industrialists *(Wirtschaftsbürgertum)* and educated elites *(Bildungsbürgertum).* The "old" *Mittelstand,* meanwhile, included artisans and shopkeepers. See Geoffrey Cocks and Konrad Jarausch, eds., *German Professions, 1800–1950* (Oxford: Oxford University Press, 1990); Jürgen Kocka, *Industrial Culture and Bourgeois Society* (New York, 1999), esp. 192–207 and 255–274; and Heike Franz, "Betriebswirte in Deutschland 1900–1930: 'Bürger' oder 'Professionals'?" in *Wege zur Geschichte des Bürgertums: Vierzehn Beiträge,* ed. Klaus Tenfelde and Hans Ulrich Wehler (Göttingen: Vandenhoeck & Ruprecht, 1994), 249–272.

56. The trade journals researched include (with initial year of publication): *Die Reklame* (1891); *Die Geschäftspraxis* (1895); *Propaganda* (1898); *Organisation* (1898); *Goldener Boden* (1900); *Moderne Reklame* (1902); *Zeitschrift für Moderne Reklame* (1904); *Jentsch Reklame-Brief* (1907); *Das Kontor* (1907); *Das Moderne Geschäft* (1908); *Mitteilungen des Vereins Deutscher Reklamefachleute* (1910); *Monographien Deutscher Reklamekünstler* (1911); *Siedels Reklame* (1913); and *Das Plakat* (1913). Some of these had very short publication runs.

57. See also Lamberty, *Reklame,* 247–263.

58. F. Kretzschmar, "Pyschologie der Reklame," *Die Reklame* 3, no. 1 (1893): 1.

59. *Die Reklame* 4, no. 2 (1894): 33.

60. Most thoroughly in Schwarz, *Bildannoncen,* 38–40, 54–63; and also to some degree in Reinhardt, *Reklame zum Marketing,* 387–396, and Hanna Gagel, "Studien zur Motivgeschichte des deutschen Plakats 1900–1914" (PhD diss., Freie Universität-Berlin, 1971).

61. "The poster-ad has been termed the art gallery of the *Volk.*" Dr. Jur. Ludwid Lindner, "Warenanpreisungen an Läden," in Ruben, *Die Reklame,* vol. 1, 119. Numerous contemporaries commented on this idea of posters as art. Even a cartoon from the *Fliegende Blätter* of 1893 shows a clever German urbanite scrimping on museum admission by leading his country-bumpkin relatives to a wall of ad posters, and telling them it is the art exhibit. Reproduced in Wischermann and Shore, *Advertising,* 14. Connections between "art" and *Bildung* are discussed in Lamberty, *Reklame,* 321–377. See also Schwarz, *Bildannoncen,* 54–63; and Martin Henatsch, *Die Entstehung des Plakates: Eine rezeptionsästhetische Untersuchung* (Hildesheim: Georg Olms, 1994), 64–76.

62. A number of Ernst Growald's essays in Ruben, *Die Reklame,* for instance, point to such a tense and almost confrontational relationship in Germany between the advertising expert and his stubborn businessmen clients.

63. Reinhardt, *Reklame zum Marketing,* 45.

64. Alexander Schmidt, *Reisen in die Moderne: Der Amerika-Diskurs des deutschen Bürgertums vor dem Ersten Weltkrieg im europäischen Vergleich* (Berlin: Akademie, 1997).

65. See August Marahrens, "Der Theorie und Praxis der Annonce und Reclame," *Archiv für Buchdruckerkunst und verwandte Geschäftszweige* 11 (1874): 160; and Eliot Shore's essay in Wischermann and Shore, *Advertising.*

66. See, for instance, Philipp Berges, "Reklamewissenschafliche Spaziergang durch Amerika," *Die Reklame* 4 (1894): 2. J. L. Sponsel's *Das Moderne Plakat* (Dresden: Gerhard Kühtmann, 1897) presented a gallery of worthy French, English, American, Belgian, and even Japanese advertising posters, although the first three predominate.

67. Walter von Zur Westen's *Reklamekunst* (Leipzig: Velhagen & Klasing, 1903) reproduces more posters from France than from any other nation (commenting that most German posters are not yet worthy of reproduction or emulation), yet he holds the French posters up as evidence of artistic worth, not of advertising acumen. Sponsel's *Das Moderne Plakat* similarly reproduces countless French posters, but again as artistic rather than commercial successes.

68. Ludwig Hohlwein, the most renowned of all German graphic artists, studied in both Paris and London before designing his first poster in 1898. Klaus Popitz et al., eds., *Das frühe Plakat in Europa und den USA: Band 3: Deutschland* (Berlin: Gebr. Mann, 1980), 119. More broadly, see Schmidt, *Reisen in die Moderne.* Victoria de Grazia's discussion of visiting America to acquire expertise reveals the durability of this trope, which was quite venerable by the time of her study in the 1930s; see Victoria De Grazia, *Irresistible Empire: America's Advance through Twentieth-Century Europe* (Cambridge, MA: Harvard University Press, 2005).

69. See Kevin Repp, "Marketing, Modernity and 'the German People's Soul,'" in Swett, Wiesen, and Zatlin, *Selling Modernity,* 26–51.

70. Lamberty, *Reklame,* 383–391. German ad writers admired the social status of the advertising industry in America; Ernst Growald wrote that "the American businessman demands that the advertisement be effective, that it fulfill its goal," and lamented that "the German businessman demands that it please him." Growald, "Amerikanische und Deutsche Reklame," in Ruben, *Die Reklame,* vol. 1, 59.

71. Ramamurthy, *Imperial Persuaders,* 26–49.

72. See Cronau, *Das Buch der Reklame,* part I, 88–89, and part IV, 56–57.

73. See *Die Reklame* 6, no. 2 (1896); and "Die schönen Künste im Dienst der englischen Propaganda," *Propaganda* 1, no. 9 (1898): 527–534.

74. *Propaganda* 1, no. 7 (1898): 390.

75. *Die Reklame* 7, no. 16 (1897): 243.

76. See Martin Behrend, "Cigaretten- und Tabak-Plakate," *Propaganda* 1, no. 8 (1898): 395. For British tobacco advertising, see Matthew Hilton, *Smoking in British Popular Culture, 1800–2000: Perfect Pleasures* (Manchester, UK: Manchester University Press, 2000), 83–160.

77. "Englische Tabaksreklame," *Propaganda* 2, no. 12 (1899): 399.

78. See Chapter 5.

79. Several hundred of the firm's posters from before 1914 are in Popitz et al., *Das Frühe Plakat.*

80. Jörg Meißner, ed., *Strategien der Werbekunst von 1850–1933* (Berlin: Deutsches Historisches Museum, 2004).

81. "Komme den Deutschen nicht amerikanisch, sonst kommt es ihnen spanisch vor." Ernst Growald, *Der Plakat-Spiegel: Erfahrungssätze für Plakat-Künstler und Besteller* (Berlin: Kampffmeyer'scher Zeitungs-Verlag Dr. Otto L. Saloman, 1904). Growald also wrote articles for *Die Reklame* as early as 1893.

82. Repp, "Marketing, Modernity and 'the German People's Soul.'"

83. Growald, *Der Plakat-Spiegel,* 77.

84. Popitz et al., *Das frühe Plakat,* no. 2842. The poster is based on a provocatively staged photograph that appears in Hagenbeck's book, but the poster designer chose to stress even more the posed affinity between black and simian. Hagenbeck, *Von Tieren und Menschen* (Berlin: Vita, deutsches Verlagshaus, 1909), 408. Compare to the 1908 Circus Busch poster for Zizi, the "controversial wonder of nature," a half-ape, half-man; CMNL, Friedländer no. 4621.

85. Cronau juxtaposes the historical role of the European herald with the log drummers of "isolated Negro-hordes of Africa" and then tacks on "for instance, the Cameroonians." Cronau, *Das Buch der Reklame,* part I, 5. The Maasai are referenced in part II, 2ff., and part IV, 1ff.

86. On the changing relationship of German anthropology to the German colonial project after 1885, see Zimmerman, *Anthropology and Antihumanism;*

Woodruff D. Smith, "Anthropology and German Colonialism," in *Germans in the Tropics: Essays in German Colonial History,* ed. Arthur J. Knoll and Lewis H. Gann (Westport, CT: Greenwood Press, 1987); and Manfred Gothsch, *Die deutsche Völkerkunde und ihr Verhältnis zum Kolonialismus: 1870 bis 1975* (Baden-Baden: Nomos, 1983). For medicine, see Wolfgang U. Eckart, *Medizin und Kolonialimperialismus: Deutschland 1884–1945* (München: Paderborn, 1997). On the larger continuities between ethnography (writ large) and colonial policy, see George Steinmetz, *The Devil's Handwriting* (Chicago: University of Chicago Press, 2007).

87. Roger Chickering, *We Men Who Feel Most German: A Cultural Study of the Pan-German League, 1886–1914* (Boston: Allen & Unwin, 1984).

88. The Colonial Society has been called elitist, particularly in the way its leaders were connected to the bureaucracy, the military, and Reichstag; see Richard V. Pierard, "The German Colonial Society," in Knoll and Gann, *Germans in the Tropics.* See also Geoff Eley, *Reshaping the German Right: Radical Nationalism and Political Change after Bismarck* (Ann Arbor: University of Michigan Press, 1990), 119–122; and Chickering, *Men Who Feel Most German,* 316. Local chapters could look somewhat different: see Ulrich S. Soenius, *Koloniale Begeisterung im Rheinland wahrend des Kaiserreichs* (Köln: Rheinisch-Westfalisches Wirtschaftsarchiv zu Koln, 1992).

89. These lectures could be travel accounts by explorers or aristocratic big-game hunters; academic reports on the field of tropical hygiene, ethnography, or geography; or overviews of the colonial economy. Many scholars have echoed the Colonial Society's own description of these events as "agitation" or "propaganda," though recognizing (in contrast to the colonialists themselves) that the audiences for such talks came largely from within the ranks of the already converted.

90. See David Ciarlo, "Consuming Race, Envisioning Empire: Colonialism and German Mass Culture, 1887–1914" (PhD diss., University of Wisconsin, Madison, 2003), 320–333. Evenings featuring military or travel themes seemed more likely to be described as "well attended" or "popular"; see DKZ (1889): 80 and 159.

91. The *Kolonialheim* came out of the Berlin chapter, with support from the national leadership; the more academically minded chapter of Berlin-Charlottenburg, however, refused to chip in for it, insisting that *their* chapter was "not a 'colonial *club*,' but a colonial *association* (Verein)." DKZ 14, no. 16 (1897): 45. See the critique in DKZ 13, no. 2 (1896): 13, and the defense in *Jahresbericht der Deutschen Kolonialgesellchaft 1895* (1896): 48, 298, and 356. In 1897 the *Kolonialheim* was incorporated as a financial consortium with its own board of directors. Originally located in Potsdamerstrasse, it moved to Schellingstrasse in 1901.

92. DKZ 14, no. 19 (1897): 183–184.

93. See BA R1001/6691, "Mitteilungen aus der Abteilung Berlin der DKG" (January 1898): 7.

94. A 1901 article on the Colonial Home suggests that one might even run into His Highness, Duke Johann Albrecht, who "often" drop by" the Colonial Home, "to the delight of the membership." Any individuals dedicated to the goals of colonialism were welcome at the Colonial Home, the article concludes. DKZ 18, no. 4 (1901): 33.

95. DKZ 13, no. 9 (1896): 68. This rhetorical position had become a refrain in Colonial Society discourse: the desired project—in this case, a glorified clubhouse—would be defended in advance by its "informational" or "agitational" value in bringing the colonial idea into "wide circles of the German public." After the project was completed, its success was lauded effusively using the precise terminology of the initial proposal.

96. The Kassel chapter, for instance, keen to capitalize on the "excitement" over Berlin's meeting place, proudly reported that it, too, had founded a Colonial Home; a private clubroom for the members of the local chapter in a first-rate local wine restaurant. This clubroom was adorned with ethnographic objects, pelts of exotic animals, and tasteful paintings of colonial landscapes and wildlife. DKZ 18, no. 2 (1901): 14.

97. Maximilian Brose, ed., *Repertorium der Deutsch-Kolonialen Litteratur: 1884–1890* (Berlin: Georg Winckelmann, 1891), iii. Brose was the librarian of the Colonial Society. This bibliography of "colonial" books, after a mere five years as an empire (1885–1890), already stretched to over 100 pages, with each page averaging more than twenty entries.

98. Of course, these 200 periodicals include more than just Colonial Society publications (although it had some hand in many of them), for it includes missionary society and official government periodicals, and academic geography and linguistic newsletters. See Peter Junge, *Bibliographie deutscher Kolonialzeitschriften,* vol. 3 (Bremen: Übersee-museum Bremen, 1985).

99. In 1902, 4,872 men, 1,034 women, and 1,617 children who were "white" (i.e., of European origin—at least for the adults) were in the German colonies in Africa and the Pacific. Heinrich Schnee, *Deutsches Koloniallexicon,* vol. 1 (Leipzig: Quelle & Meyer, 1920), 196. The massive German military commitment to the Southwest African War after 1904 changed the population proportions considerably.

100. DKZ (1889): 191.

101. See the response of the *Colonial News* to a critique of its prose style. A. Seidel, "Die Deutsche Kolonial-Zeitung: Einiges darüber, was sie kann und was sie nicht kann" (1899): 150–151.

102. Nonetheless, it was read in libraries; see John Phillip Short, "Everyman's Colonial Library: Imperialism and Working-Class Readers in Leipzig, 1890–1914," *German History* 21, no. 4 (2003).

103. See BA R8023/911, "Ausschussberichte von 1897," no. 15 (25 May 1897).

104. DKZ (1896): 9.

105. Ibid.; *Illustrierte Beilage* no. 16, pl. 149.

106. The venerable Berlin firm E. S. Mittler & Sons printed a large portion of colonialist works, particularly those sanctioned by the state. See E. S. Mittler & Sohn, *Königliche Hofbuchhandlung und Hofbuchdruckerei: Berlin. Zum 3. März 1914 Dem Gedenktage Ihres 125 Jahre Bestehens, Zugleich Ein Rückblick Auf Ihre Verlagstätigkeit Während Der Letzten 25 Jahre* (Berlin, 1914). Dietrich Reimer was owned by Ernst Vohsen, imperial consul and member of the executive committee of the German Colonial Society. Other specialized firms like Gustav Fischer (Jena) or Carl Heymanns (Berlin) issued colonialist literature, and very occasionally, so too did the printing giants like Brockhaus (Leipzig) or even Rudolf Mosse (Berlin).

107. For instance, in 1896 Rudolf Fitzner, the editor of *Aus allen Weltteilen,* appealed to the executive committee of the society for a subsidy of his book, the *German Colonial Handbook*. He proposed that the society purchase a specific number of copies at a reduced rate, which would then be given to Colonial Society chapters. The society's executive committee agreed to the arrangement, with half of the cost of the "free" copies covered by central funds, and the other half coming from the chapters themselves. Soon after, a review of the book appeared in *Westermann's* calling the handbook "indispensable." BA R8023/911, "Ausschussberichte von 1896," no. 19 (29 September). See also *Westermann's* 81, no. 486 (1897): 806. The topic of subventions was carefully avoided in public discussions of the Colonial Society, but was occasionally broached by would-be competitors, such as the unaffiliated *Kolonial Zeitschrift* (1901). The *Colonial News* responded to the attack with sarcastic denial, feigned innocence, and nationalistic rhetoric. DKZ 18, no. 41 (1901): 405.

108. Gustav Meinecke, *Die Deutschen Kolonien in Wort und Bild* (Leipzig: J. J. Weber, 1901).

109. For a vivid example in Britain, see the before-and-after shot in James Ryan, *Picturing Empire: Photography and the Visualization of the British Empire* (London: Reaktion, 1997), 220.

110. *Archiv für Geschichte des Buchwesens*, vol. 24 (Frankfurt a. M.: Buchhändler-Vereinigung, 1983), 1979.

111. *Deutschland und seine Kolonien im Jahre 1896: Amtliche Bericht über die erste deutsche Kolonial-Ausstellung* (Berlin: Dietrich Reimer/Ernst Vohsen, 1897), 9. See also DKZ (1896): 125; and Präger, *Kolonialgesellschaft* (Berlin: Dietrich Reimer (Ernst Vohsen), 1908), 119.

112. Cf. Hermann von Wissmann, *Meine zweite Durchquerung Äquatorial-Afrikas vom Congo zum Zambesi während der Jahre 1886 und 1887* (Frankfurt a. M.: Trowitzsch & Sohn, 1891); Curt von Morgen, *Durch Kamerun von Süd nach Nord Reisen und Forschungen im Hinterlande 1889 bis 1891* (Leipzig: Brockhaus, 1893).

His paintings and illustrations saturate the book by Ottomar Beta, *Das Buch von unseren Kolonien* (Leipzig: Ferdinand Hirt und Sohn, 1902), which went through at least 7 editions (1902–1908).

113. As per an advertisement in Emil Sembritzki, *Der Kolonialfreund: Kritischer Führer Durch Die Volkstümlich Deutsche Kolonial-Literature* (Berlin: "Kolonie und Heimat" Verlag GmbH, 1912), 171. One of his early illustration collections was Rudolf Hellgrewe, *Aus Deutsch-Ost-Afrika: Wanderbilder* (Berlin: T. Zenkers, 1888).

114. To 36,000. Pierard, "Colonial Society," 25.

115. Colonial Society members drew on their social networks to recruit "suitable" new members. See DKZ (1898): 339.

4. Packaged Exoticism and Colonial Rule

Epigraph: *Die Reklame* 4, no. 2 (20 February 1894): 31. From the essay "Reklame und Plakat-Kunst" by Professor Ferdinand Luthmer (1842–1921), the director of Frankfurt's *Kunstgewerbeschule* after 1879.

1. Broader arguments about the manifestation, prevalence, and historical trajectory of images are based on an array of sources, but especially upon patterns seen in the Trademark Registration Rolls (WZB); see the discussion of sources in the Introduction.

2. See DHM AK 94/516.1039.

3. Karen Pinkus, *Bodily Regimes: Italian Advertising under Fascism* (Minneapolis: University of Minnesota Press, 1995), 11–16.

4. For Cuban chromolithography, see Narciso Menocal, *Cuban Cigar Labels: The Tobacco Industry in Cuba and Florida: Its Golden Age in Lithography and Architecture* (Coral Gables, FL: Cuban National Heritage, 1995), esp. 37. For other tins, see Ulrich Feuerhorst and Holger Steinle, *Die Bunte Verführung: Zur Geschichte der Bleckreklame* (Berlin: Silberstreif, 1985).

5. Tobacco, of course, was not produced in Egypt. Nestor Giancalis, originally from Greece, arrived in Suez in 1864, and by the 1870s he was a major cigarette manufacturer and exporter to European and American markets. Cigarettes, long said to have made their way to Europe via the Crimean conflict, may rather have found their way into European taste by means of British officers stationed in Egypt; Lord Kitchner later helped to popularize them. Relli Shechter, "Selling Luxury: The Rise of the Egyptian Cigarette and the Transformation of the Egyptian Tobacco Market, 1850–1914," *International Journal of Middle East Studies* 35, no. 1 (2003).

6. Shechter, "Selling Luxury," 60. The low cost of the cigarette due to inexpensive Egyptian labor played a role in the cigarette's early success.

7. Synthetic dye, elephant caravan in India, by AG Farbwerke vorm. Meister Lucius & Brüning, Höchst a. M., WZB (1902): 839, reg. no. 56054; synthetic dye, camel scene, Samuel Fr. Holzkapfel Grub b. Coburg, WZB (1895): 768, reg. no. 7296 (re-registr. from 1881). Bayer aniline, tiger hunt in India, AG Farbenfabriken F. Bayer & Co., Elberfeld, WZB (1895): 768, reg. no. 7229.

8. A large number of illustrations relating to India were trademarked by AGFA. See, for instance, WZB (1901): 99–103, reg. nos. 47281–47532. Many of these images were collectible cards; since AGFA regularly trademarked them for many different product categories, it is difficult to determine if such illustrations of India, Tibet, and other exotic locales were use for photographic supplies or for textile dyes.

9. In addition to Shechter, "Selling Luxury," see also Sander Gilman and Zhou Xun, eds., *Smoke: A Global History of Smoking* (London: Reaktion, 2004). For Germany specifically, see Michael Weisser, *Cigaretten-Reclame: Über die Kunst Blauen Dunst zu Verkaufen* (Münster: E. Coppenrath, 1980); and Magdalene Moeller, *Plakate für den blauen Dunst: Reklame für Zigarren und Zigaretten 1880–1940* (Dortmund: Harenberg, 1983).

10. Tino Jacobs and Sandra Schürmann, "Rauchsignale: Struktureller Wandel und Visuelle Strategien auf dem deutschen Zigarettenmarkt im 20. Jahrhundert," *WerkstattGeschichte* 16, no. 45 (2007).

11. See "Der Siegeszug der Zigarette," *Berliner Kolonialwaren-Zeitung* 7, no. 30 (27 July 1913): 559; E. E. H. Schmidt, "Tabak und Reklame," *Das Kontor* (January–December 1916).

12. *Die Reklame* 4, no. 2 (1894): 31. Luthmer's insistence on the allure of the female image includes non-orientalist enticements as well, urging the use of images of women in ball costume or sport clothes.

13. The phrase "continent most in fashion" comes from the introduction to the African Hall at Bremen's 1890 Commercial Exhibition. *Officieller Katalog der Handels-Ausstellung* (Bremen: Max Nössler's Buchdruckerei, 1890), 128: "Afrika, der gegenwärtige Modeerdteil, der seit mehreren Jahrenzehnten die allgemeine Aufmerksamkeit unausgesetzt in Spannung erhalten hat, bietet für die wirtschaftliche Entwickelung nicht gerade die günstigsten Voraussetzung dar."

14. On the relationship of ethnography to policy, see George Steinmetz, *The Devil's Handwriting: Precoloniality and the German Colonial State in Qingdao, Samoa, and Southwest Africa* (Chicago: University of Chicago Press, 2007).

15. Martin Kitchen, *The Political Economy of Germany, 1815–1914* (London: Croom Helm, 1978).

16. On the *Tabakmohr*/Blackamoor more broadly, see Jan P. Nederveen Pieterse, *White on Black: Images of Africa and Blacks in Western Popular Culture* (New

Haven, CT: Yale University Press, 1992), 189–192; and David Dabydeen, *Hogarth's Blacks: Images of Blacks in Eighteenth Century English Art* (Kingston-upon-Thames, UK: Dangaroo Press, 1985). For examples of Tobacco Moor statuettes, see Hermann Pollig, ed., *Exotische Welten: Europäische Phantasien* (Stuttgart: Insitut für Auslandsbeziehungen,1987), 189; Mamoun Fansa, ed., *Schwarz Weissheiten: Vom Umgang mit fremden Menschen* (Oldenburg: Isensee, 2001), 80; Roman Sandgruber and Harry Kühnel, *Genuss & Kunst: Kaffee, Tee, Schokolade, Tabak, Cola* (Innsbruck: Athesia-Tyrolia Druck, 1994), 107; and Ellwood Parry, *The Image of the Indian and the Black Man in American Art* (New York: Braziller, 1974), 68–70.

17. Georg Brongers, *Nicotiana Tabacum: The History of Tobacco and Tobacco Smoking in the Netherlands* (Amsterdam: Bechts, 1964), 125.

18. Cf. Nederveen Pieterse, *White on Black,* 22, where a frontispiece includes a Tobacco Moor figure. On social patterns of tobacco consumption, see Matthew Hilton, *Smoking in British Popular Culture, 1800–2000: Perfect Pleasures* (Manchester, UK: Manchester University Press, 2000); and Woodruff D. Smith, *Consumption and the Making of Respectability: 1600–1800* (New York: Routledge, 2002).

19. See, for instance, the eighteenth-century labels from Cologne appended in August Boerner, *Kölner Tabakhandel und Tabakgewerbe 1628–1910* (Essen: Baedeker, 1912), or those from the 1840s in Deutscher Verein für Buchwesen und Schrifttum, ed., *Alte Tabakzeichen* (Berlin: Widder Verlag, 1924).

20. Elias Erasmus, foreword to Deutscher Verein für Buchwesen und Schrifttum, *Alte Tabakzeichen.*

21. Susanne Zantop, *Colonial Fantasies: Conquest, Family, and Nation in Precolonial Germany, 1770–1870* (Durham, NC: Duke University Press, 1997).

22. See E. E. Hermann Schmidt, ed., *Tabak und Reklame: Eine Artikel-Serie: Erscheinen in Der Zeitschrift "Das Kontor," 1916* (Berlin: Verlag "Das Kontor," 1916): esp. 32ff, 93ff; Joseph Feinhals (the Cologne cigarette firm), *Der Tabak in Kunst und Kultur* (Köln, 1911); and Eduard Maria Schranka, *Tabak-Anekdoten: Ein historisches Braunbuch* (Köln, 1914). *Alte Tabakzeichen* (cited in note 20 above) took labels from the collection of the Garbaty firm.

23. See, for instance, the detailed Tobacco Moor and African native ads for Anker tobacco, A. H. Thorbeck & Co., Mannheim, WZB (1898): 203, reg. no. 29017 and 561, no. 31408.

24. "W. T.," "Korea!" *Die Reklame* 4, no. 10 (1894): 233. The "bygone war(s)" to which he refers is almost certainly the Franco-Prussian War of 1870–1871, which saw a surge of German public interest fed by telegraph reports. The writer's nostalgia for such battle maps hints at a larger wistfulness, missing the thrill of being at war.

25. Bülow's speech on *Weltpolitik* before the Reichstag, on December 6, 1897, was particularly welcomed by the Pan-German League, founded in 1890 as a vehement denunciation of the "colonial sell-out" of the Heligoland-Zanzibar treaty.

26. *Die Unseren in Kiautschau* could translate as "that which is ours in Kiautschau"; the spelling, Kiaut-schau, might be a pun. See Viktoria Schmidt-Linsenhoff, Kurt Wettengl, and Almut Junker, eds., *Plakate 1880–1914* (Frankfurt a. M.: Historisches Museum Frankfurt am Main, 1986), 53, no. 31.

27. The "China in Berlin" poster, which features a Chinese mandarin caricature with elongated ears, a long drooping mustache and beard, and long pointed fingernails at the end of spindly fingers, quickly became famous. See Johannes Lemcke ("P. Friesenhahn"), *Handbuch der Reklame* (Berlin, 1901), 9; *Modern Reklame* 1, no. 1 (1902): 9.

28. See Robert Lebeck and Manfred Schütte, eds., *Propagandapostkarten I: 80 Bildpostkarten aus den Jahren 1898–1929* (Dortmund: Harenberg, 1978), nos. 7 and 8; and DHM DO 77/33 I.

29. See Lebeck and Schütte, *Propagandapostkarten I,* nos. 7 and 8. See also DHM PK 96/280 and PK 96/522.

30. The firm of Dr. Eysler & Co., for instance, sold a cliché with a friendly-looking German sailor reclining atop a Chinese fortification, casually smoking his pipe. The postcard included the following ditty: "Fritz sitz vergnügt in Kiaotschau, Und denkt an seine Lieben; entfloh'n ist der Chinesen Schaar—Nur Einer ist geblieben!" Dr. Eysler & Co., reprinted in *Propaganda* (1899): 250. One of two "priced-for-mass-consumption" postcards by the Hamburg firm Wasmuth & Co. was a rough sketch of German marines pulling a cannon directly out of the sea as the Chinese flee in terror; the editor's caption describes it as droll. *Propaganda* 2, no. 10 (1899): 329 and 331.

31. *Propaganda* 2, no. 6 (1899): 193. The details of the scene seem a bit odd, however; the white-uniformed soldier appears almost Japanese, for instance, and the camel is out of place. This illustration may in fact have been crafted with some other context in mind and only hastily pressed into "colonial" service in the heat of the moment. When it appeared in *Fliegende Blätter* in 1898, it was expressly captioned: "Transport of Goods to Kiautschou." *Fliegende Blätter* 109, no. 2579 (1898). See also Stefanie Wolter, *Die Vermarktung des Fremden* (Frankfurt a. M.: Campus, 2005), 63.

32. Kiautschou Liquor, C. A. Krammisch, Halle, WZB (1899): 615, reg. no. 38376: the ad features a caricature of a Chinese man, with slanted eyes, long mustache, braids, and dragon-embroidered robes. Kiaotschau Gebäck, W. Hromadka & Jäger, Plauen-Dresden, WZB (1898): 276, reg. no. 29642: the label offers a smorgasbord of Far Eastern imagery, including a portly mandarin in mustache and robes, and a woman holding a fan, wearing a kimono. Prinz Heinrich

Kiao-Tchau Thee, Martin Becker & Co., Frankfurt a. M., WZB (1898): 708, reg. no. 31984; and Kia King cigars, Otto Beyer Cigarren-Versandhaus Germania, Strassburg, WZB (1898): 931, reg. no. 33479. One unusual ad shows a German sailor varnishing a floor, with paint cans held by a Chinese man; see Hannoverische Zündholz-Co AG, WZB (1898): 341, reg. no. 30625. The nationwide brand Marco Polo Tea issued a twelve-card collectible series of "Pictures from Kiaotschau," showing such placid scenes as a Chinese son with his father, who carries a giant Marco Polo tea canister.

33. The packaging features an illustration of a stylized Chinese man carrying an umbrella and smoking a cigarette. DHM AK 94/516.544. On the history of the German Kolonialhaus–Bruno Antelmann, see Ulrich van der Heyden and Joachim Zeller, *Kolonialmetropole Berlin: Eine Spurensuche* (Berlin: Quintessenz, 2002), 85, and David Ciarlo, "Consuming Race, Envisioning Empire: Colonialism and German Mass Culture, 1887–1914" (PhD diss., University of Wisconsin, Madison, 2003), chapter 5.

34. "Wortzeichen 'Kiaotschau' [*sic*]," *Propaganda* 2, no. 6 (1899): 206.

35. Otto Sehrndt, "Deutsches Volk trinkt Deutschen Thee!" Berlin, WZB (1900): 1075, reg. no. 46706.

36. "Ein Sieger" (postmarked 1900) from DHM PK 96/278; "Seeman's Liebe" (after 1898), in Jürgen Petschull and Thomas Höpker, *Der Wahn vom Weltreich: Die Geschichte der deutschen Kolonien* (Hamburg: Gruner, 1984), 29.

37. Joachim Zeller, *Bilderschule der Herrenmenschen: Koloniale Reklamesammelbilder* (Berlin: Ch. Links, 2008), 128–135.

38. See the DHM PK 97/271 and 274, PK 96/277, 278, and AK 97/276.

39. "Excelsior Pneumatic in Asia." The Hannoverian rubber company issued these travel-themed postcard ads for their bicycle tires around 1900; their "Excelsior Pneumatic in Australien" card shows native aboriginals, armed with spears and bows, hunting kangaroos while riding bicycles. See Robert Lebeck, *Das Zweirad: Postkarten aus alter Zeit* (Dortmund: Harenberg, 1981), 123. This firm was often at the vanguard of developments in colonialist and racist advertisements.

40. Landesarchiv Berlin Kult 121, *Führer durch das Passage-Panopticum* (Berlin, 1905).

41. For the postcard, see Zeller, *Bilderschule der Herrenmenschen,* 133.

42. "BlueJackets to the Front!" *Illustrated London News* 84, no. 2344 (1884): color supplement. Many library copies of the *Illustrated London News* are missing this illustration, for it was printed to be cut out and used as wall decoration. Röchling painted this for the Kaiser, according to one popular art magazine. *Die Kunst für Alle* 17 (1902), 333.

43. Founded in 1898 by industrial elites, the Navy League had 269,000 members by 1900 and thereby quickly became the largest of all the nationalist groups, far outstripping the Colonial Society. By 1907 the total rose to over

900,000, when corporate memberships were included. See especially Geoff Eley, "Reshaping the Right: Radical Nationalism and the German Navy League, 1898–1908," *Historical Journal* 21, no. 2 (1978): 327–354; and Martin Loiperdinger, "The Beginnings of German Film Propaganda: The Navy League as Traveling Exhibitor, 1901–1907," *Historical Journal of Film, Radio and Television* 22, no. 3 (2002): 305–313. On navalism as theater, see Jan Rüger, *The Great Naval Game: Britain and Germany in the Age of Empire* (Cambridge: Cambridge University Press, 2007), chapter 3. On navalism outside of the Navy League, see Erik Grimmer-Solem, "Imperialist Socialism of the Chair: Gustav Schmoller and German Weltpolitik, 1897–1905," in *Wilhelminism and Its Legacies: German Modernities, Imperialism, and the Meanings of Reform, 1890–1930,* ed. Geoff Eley and James Retallack (New York: Berghahn Books, 2004).

44. "Nationale Propaganda," *Propaganda* 3, no. 4 (1900): 105. Italics mine.

45. For the cigar fleet, see "Vorschläge," *Propaganda* 3, no. 6 (1900): 206. Rober Exner later editorialized that "the recent events in China—the murder of emissaries, the massacre of foreigners—supplies the best proof that a strong battle fleet is vital for the security of maritime commerce. It is therefore welcome that the German Reichstag approved a renewed expansion of the fleet." *Propaganda* 3, no. 10 (1900): 350.

46. See the trade card "S. M. armored cruiser *Prince Bismarck* holds gunnery exercises off the Chinese coast," in Robert Lebeck, ed., *Reklame-Postkarten* (Dortmund: Harenberg Kommunikation, 1978), no. 17. Liebig's "Deutschland Übersee" Series 458/1 (1900) is reproduced in Bernhard Jussen, *Liebig's Sammelbilder* (DVD-ROM) (Berlin: Yorck Project, 2002). The margarine giant Jurgens and Prinzen's version of the same theme is more aggressive looking; and other naval-themed postcards relating to Kiautschou are in Petschull and Höpker, *Der Wahn vom Weltreich,* 29, and Zeller, *Bilderschule der Herrenmenschen,* 44 and 97.

47. For instance, the Liebig Co.'s "Deutschland Übersee" series (no. 458) freely interchanges illustrations of cruiser squadrons, native troop garrisons, a gunboat, a village scene, and "natives" in ethnographic and/or racial profile views. The two themes, cruisers and natives, were treated as equivalent, visually speaking.

48. Zeller, *Bilderschule der Herrenmenschen,* 44.

49. The commercialization of the Boxer engagement itself continued on for a few years after hostilities had ceased. See, for instance, the amateurish drawing for "Chinakämpfer" cigarettes, Carl Warmann & Co, Bünde, WZB (1904): 317, reg. no. 66474, which shows a German marine, with sheathed sword and doffing his pith helmet, returning home in a rowboat, under a massive flag.

50. *Propaganda* 3, no. 6 (1900): 206. The author is Exner, who earlier recommended warships built from cigars.

51. Ulrich van der Heyden, "Politisches Kalkül oder doppeltes Spiel? Die koloniale Propaganda als Teil der offiziellen Haltung Deutschlands im Vorfeld des songennanten Burenkrieges von 1899 bis 1902," in *Studien zur Geschichte des*

deutschen Kolonialismus in Afrika: Festschrift zum 60. Geburtstag von Peter Sebald, ed. Peter Heine and Ulrich van der Heyden (Pfaffenweiler: Centaurus Verlagsgesellschaft, 1995).

52. See Heyden, "Politisches Kalkül oder doppeltes Spiel?" 320–322.

53. For the former, see Heyden, "Politisches Kalkül oder doppeltes Spiel?" and also Ulrich Kroll, *Die international Buren-Agitation, 1899–1902* (Münster: Regensberg, 1973), esp. 67–81. For the latter, see Roger Chickering, *We Men Who Feel Most German: A Cultural Study of the Pan-German League, 1886–1914* (Boston: Allen & Unwin, 1984), 64–65. Chickering points out that fifty new chapters of the Pan-Germans appeared during the Boer War.

54. Peter Fritzsche, *Reading Berlin 1900* (Cambridge, MA: Harvard University Press, 1996).

55. *Die Reklame* spoke of a "famine" in the paper supply in Britain, caused by the hunger for news of "the African war," with the circulation of the *Daily Mail* as almost doubling, from 620,000 to 1,052,000. "Krieg und Papier," *Die Reklame* 10, no. 5 (1900): 52. For British advertising and the Anglo-Boer War, see Thomas Richards, *The Commodity Culture of Victorian England: Advertising and Spectacle 1851–1914* (London: Verso, 1990), 148–167.

56. Klaus Popitz et al., eds., *Das frühe Plakat in Europa und den USA: Band 3: Deutschland* (Berlin: Gebr. Mann, 1980), no. 1632.

57. Alfred von Müller authored *Der Krieg in Süd-Afrika 1899/1900* (Berlin, 1900), *Die Wirren in China,* and, a few years earlier, *Der Krieg zwischen China und Japan 1894/95.* These books were divided into self-contained sections, presumably to sell serially. *Der Krieg in Süd-Afrika* was filled with maps and orders of battle, and received rave reviews from the colonial establishment (the *Deutsches Kolonialblatt* and the *Deutsches Offizierblatt*) but also from mass dailies like the *Berlin Lokal-Anzeiger.* It went through at least four editions in 1900 alone.

58. Frederick Rompel, *Siegen oder Sterben: Die Helden des Burenkriegs* (Stuttgart: Anton Hoffmann, 1901).

59. Ottmar Zieher in Munich issued an array of postcards (drawn by Arthur Thiele) in 1899 caricaturing the British and portraying the Boer as a popular folk hero; others followed suit. See Lebeck and Schütte, *Propagandapostkarten;* see also DHM DO 60/631, DO 60/357, DO 60/357-2, PK 96/202, 203, 204, and 205.

60. CMNL, Friedländer nos. 1683, 1946, and 2173, respectively.

61. Caricature from Neurüppin satirized early German colonial warfare (and the Africans) as early as 1888; Gesine Krüger, *Kriegsbewaltigung und Geschichtsbewusstsein: Realität, Deutung und Verarbeitung des Deutschen Kolonialkriegs in Namibia 1904 bis 1907* (Gottingen: Vandenhoeck & Ruprecht, 1999). The chocolate manufacturer Hildebrand issued a series of collectible trading cards circa 1900 that celebrated Wissmann's military triumphs in the late 1880s; see Detlaf Bald

et al., *Die Liebe zum Imperium: Deutschlands dunkle Vergangenheit in Afrika* (Bremen: Überseemuseum, 1978), 140; and for West Africa, F. Ad Richter cards in Otto Hahn, *Reklame—Reklame—Reklame* (Rudolstadt: Spielhaus Richtersche Villa Rudolstadt e.V., 1996), 86. See also Zeller, *Bilderschule der Herrenmenschen,* 209.

62. "Buren-Siegeskuchen" by the Karl Franz Welker bakery, Glauschau, WZB (1900): 527, reg. no. 44113; and "Burenkäse" by the Molkereigenossenschaft Stargard GmbH, Stargard, WZB (1901): 591, reg. no. 49417. See also the images for *Buren-Hölzer* (Boer matches), L. Kiesel, Essen-Ruhr, WZB (1901): 748, reg. no. 50191; Heil den Buren brand liquor, August Stengert, St. Johann, WZB (1901): 215, reg. no. 47731 and 1024, reg. no. 51705, reproduced in David Ciarlo, "Rasse konsumieren: Von der exotischen zur kolonialen Imagination in der Bildreklame des Wilhelminischen Kaiserreichs," in *Phantasiereiche: Der deutsche Kolonialismus in kulturgeschichtlicher Perspektive,* ed. Birthe Kundrus (New York: Campus, 2003), 162; "Boer cigarettes" by G. Koch, Metz, WZB (1904): 704, reg. no. 67874. "Buren" was also trademarked for rubber; see Josef Reithoffer's Söhne, Berlin, WZB (1902): 550, reg. no. 54604. Schicht soap also issued Boer advertising postcards. Imagery of the Boer in German commercial culture continued for a decade or more; see Burenblut (an alcohol-free drink), Alban Grohmann, Chemnitz, WZB (1905): 40, reg. no. 75142; Böer-Käse by Georg Böer, Posen, WZB (1912): 590, reg. no. 155680. The product is a play on the cheese maker's name—Böer—but it still deploys the bearded Boer with bush hat and rifle.

63. See Heyden, "Politisches Kalkül oder doppeltes Spiel?" 316.

64. Heinrich c. Nebels, "Absatz in Südafrika," *Propaganda* 4, no. 3 (1901): 51–52.

65. Ulrich van der Heyden, "Die Kolonial- und Transvaal Austellung in Berlin," in *Fremde Erfahrungen: Asiaten und Afrikaner in Deutschland, Österreich, und in der Schweiz bis 1945,* ed. Gerhard Höpp (Berlin: Das Arabische Buch, 1996). For the exhibition poster, see CMNL, Friedländer no. 0992.

66. On the interchangeability of cowboys and Indians with Africans and pioneers, see Jeff Bowersox, "Raising Germans in the Age of Empire: Education and the Modern Colonial Imagination in Germany, 1871–1914" (PhD diss., University of Toronto, 2008).

67. Robert Exner, *Moderne Schaufenster-Reklame* (Berlin: Verlag der Robert Exner Kommand-Ges., 1896), 80.

68. In 1895 the value of tobacco exports from all German colonies totaled only 276,903 marks, or roughly one-third of 1 percent of all German tobacco imports. Walther Hoffmann, *Das Wachstum der deutschen Wirtschaft seit der Mitte des 19. Jahrhunderts* (Berlin: Springer, 1965), 526 and 654. In Africa, tobacco cultivation was seriously attempted only in German East Africa, where quantities fluctuated but remained very, very small.

69. See Klaus Bade, *Friedrich Fabri und der Imperialismus in der Bismarckzeit* (Freiburg: Atlantis, 1975), 340, 343, 385, and 432.

70. The first *Deutscher Kolonial-Kalender,* ed. Gustav Meinecke (Berlin: Verlag für Sprach- und Handelswissenschaft—Dr. P. Langenscheidt, 1889), for instance, made almost a fetish out of highlighting the dates of these *Flaggenhissungen* in Bagida, Lome, Bimbia, Klein-Batanga, and so forth. For an example of the ubiquitous illustrations of this ritual in German colonialist literature, see the engraving in Gustav Meinecke, *Die Deutschen Kolonien in Wort und Bild* (Leipzig: J. J. Weber, 1899), 27. The scene remained an icon for German colonialists, reproduced on trading cards (see Zeller, *Bilderschule der Herrenmenschen*, 207) all the way down to the cigarette trading cards of the late 1930s—for instance, in the ubiquitous album *Deutschlands Kolonien: Ein Bildwerk vom Kampf um deutschen Lebensraum* (1938), 41 (examples available in many museum collections, including in the MEK).

71. Carl Peters, *Die deutsche Emin-Pascha Expedition: Von Dr. Carl Peters: Mit 32 vollbildern und 66 textabbildungen von Rudolf Hellgrewe in Berlin, dem porträt des verfassers nach Franz von Lenbach und einer Karte in Farbendruck* (Munich: Oldenbourg, 1891).

72. Landesarchiv Berlin, Rep 250, Acc 332, C5582.

73. See the famous photograph of the Askari, reproduced in Uwe Timm, *Deutsche Kolonien* (Munich: AutorenEdition, 1981), 55. The Askari image, in turn, inspired a series of Fürstenberg beer ads in the 1960s; see Jörg Becker, "Reklame als Vehikel von Kolonialismus und Ausbeutung," *tendenzen* 86 (1973): 60.

74. On the Askari, see Sandra Mass, *Weisse Helden schwarze Krieger: Zur Geschichte kolonialer Maennlichkeit in Deutschland 1918–64* (Cologne: Böhlau, 2006); Stefanie Michels, *Schwarze Deutsche Kolonialsoldaten: Mehrdeutige Repräsentationsräume und früher Kosmopolitismus in Afrika* (Bielefeld: Transcript, 2009); Thomas Morlang, *Askari und Fitafita: "Farbige" Söldner in den deutschen Kolonie* (Berlin: Ch. Links, 2008); and Michelle Moyd, "Becoming Askari: African Soldiers and Everyday Colonialism in German East Africa, 1850–1918" (PhD diss., Cornell University, 2008).

75. On the discourse of romanticized colonialism as a "marriage" in German literature, see Zantop, *Colonial Fantasies.*

76. Though "German" was ubiquitous as an adjectival modifier around 1900 (e.g., Echt Deutscher Kaffee), it rarely received the added stress of having its own subordinate clause until just before the start of the First World War.

77. The tricolor was used by the North German Confederation and became the flag of the German merchant marine after 1871. It was only officially adopted as the imperial flag in 1892, the same time as the war flag.

78. Ciarlo, "Rasse konsumieren," 160.

79. For instance, an identical image without the designation of "Schutztruppe" was used two years later in a margarine ad by the Westfälisches Margarine Werk GmbH, Bielefeld, WZB (1900): 227, reg. no. 42520, although it is unclear whether this was with the Flensburger Brewery's consent.

80. See WZB (1901): 500, reg. no. 49000; and 595, reg. no. 49523.

81. Held argues that ads directed at German colonists were less likely to deploy romanticized notions of the natives in their imagery because they had actual contact with natives. This may very well be true, though is not supported by his source base, namely *Kolonie und Heimat,* with a readership mostly in Germany. Thomas Held, "Kolonialismus und Werbung," in *Andenken an den Kolonialismus,* ed. Volker Harms (Tübingen: Attempto, 1984).

82. Ciarlo, "Consuming Race, Envisioning Empire," chapter 5.

83. The Liebig Company also produced the lower-end Oxo brand bouillon, still popular today. At its peak, the Liebig Extract of Meat Company employed 5,000 people and slaughtered 2,000 cattle a day in the Uruguayan factory. See Detlef Lorenz, *Reklamekunst um 1900: Künstlerlexikon für Sammelbilder* (Berlin: Reimer, 2000), 17–18. See also Detlev Lorenz, *Liebigbilder: Große Welt in Kleinformat,* vol. 3 (Berlin: Freunde des Museums für Deutsche Volkskunde, 1980).

84. Some date the first Liebig series to 1872. The Stollwerck company, however, actually issued a series of image cards as early as 1860. Dorle Weyers and Christoph Köck, *Die Eroberung der Welt: Sammelbilder vermitteln Zeitalter* (Detmold: Westfälisches Freilichtmuseum Detmold, 1992), 10.

85. "Von den Liebig-Bildern," *Die Reklame* 10, no. 4 (1900): 35.

86. Ibid.; Weyers and Köck, *Eroberung der Welt.* For a thematic guide to *Sammelbilder,* see the appendix of Erhard Ciolina and Evamaria Ciolina, *Garantirt Aecht: Das Reklame-Sammelbild als Spiegel der Zeit* (Munich: Marketing und Wirtschaft Verlag, 1988).

87. These different needs for each manner of advertisement were recapitulated in the first theoretical treatise of advertising practice, Viktor Mataja, *Die Reklame: Eine Untersuchung über Ankündigungswesen und Werbetätigkeit im Geschäftsleben* (Leipzig: Duncker & Humblot, 1910).

88. Accordions, harmonicas, and other portable instruments were often sold to German settlers as well as sailors, and accordion advertisements were often replete with images of the colonizing mission. Cf. G. A. Dörsel, Brunndöbra, WZB (1904): 60, reg. no. 65398; Fa. Böhm, Untersachsenberg, WZB (1910): 2465, reg. no. 137927; and after the war, Fa. Hutmeinel-Otto Meinel, Klingenthal-Hut, WZB (1923): 1491, reg. no. 303061.

89. Zeller, *Bilderschule der Herrenmenschen,* 31.

90. David Steensma, "Congo Red: Out of Africa?" *Archives of Pathology and Laboratory Medicine* 125, no. 2 (February 2001).

91. See, for instance, the cigar label for A. C. Brauer in Kiel; Schranka, *Tabak-Anekdoten,* 148.

92. Cf. August Hene, Lippstadt, WZB (1897): 365, reg. no. 22955, and Gebrüder Grenzhaeuser, Trier, WZB (1899): 897, reg. no. 39956.

93. On colonialist discourses of labor, see Jürgen Zimmerer, *Deutsche Herrschaft über Afrikaner: Staatlicher Machtanspruch und Wirklichkeit im kolonialen Namibia* (Munster: LIT, 2004); and Sebastian Conrad, *Globalisierung und Nation im deutschen Kaiserreich* (Munich: Beck, 2006).

94. "Der junge Künstler muss entweder weitgehende Konzessionen an den herrschenden Geschmack machen, oder er muss auf den Verkauf seiner Werke verzichten," *Propaganda* 2, no. 10 (1898): 488.

95. Peter Martin, *Schwarze Teufel, edle Mohren: Afrikaner in Bewußtsein und Geschichte der Deutschen* (Hamburg: Junius, 1993); Nederveen Pieterse, *White on Black.*

96. The manufacture of chicory coffee in Germany stretched back at least to the 1760s; the firm of Heinrich Franks made this product as early as 1828 in Vaihingen, before moving to Ludwigsburg to take advantage of the rail lines in 1870 (at which point the firm had 300 employees). The firm's original trademark, the Vaihinger lion, is thought to be the oldest known trademark in the German food industry; the trademark later changed to a coffee mill. Before the First World War the firm had twenty-seven factories in eleven countries and eventually gained control over many rival companies and brands, from Linde's to Kathreiner Kneipp Malzkaffee to Caro. It is today owned by Nestlé.

97. The instantaneous "veracity" of vision has often been discussed; see particularly Paul Messaris, *Visual Persuasion: The Role of Images in Advertising* (London: Sage, 1997), and Charles Forceville, *Pictorial Metaphor in Advertising* (London: Routledge, 1996).

98. See, for instance, Figure 6.15. This was an increasingly prevalent pictorial device after 1890; my thanks to Volker Langbehn for first pointing out to me the visual and/or racial implications of a black child on a black-and-white floor.

99. Puhonny was from Baden-Baden; he attended art school at Karlsruhe and was also a noted humorist. Curt Büsch, in his handbook *Von Der Reklame Des Kaufmanns* (Hamburg: Gebrüder Lüdeking, 1909), 144–146, reproduces this ad of Ivo Puhonny's along with two others (of pyramids and palm trees) and ranks Puhonny among the most important poster artists. Puhonny also crafted many images for *Sammelbilder* and *Reklamemarken.*

100. Two of the most popular themes of early German advertising from the 1880s and 1890s (and earlier in Britain and the United States) were of children (meeting the gaze of the viewer, seemingly asking to be cared for by means of the advertised product, à la Ruger chocolate ads), and women (gazing in awed

appreciation at the product, clearly eager to secure it for their own home, à la Maggi bouillon).

101. See Michael Adas, *Machines as the Measure of Men: Science, Technology, and Ideologies of Western Dominance* (Ithaca, NY: Cornell University Press, 1989). See also Richards, *Commodity Culture,* 119–146, on this discourse in Stanley's writings.

102. Cf. Richards, *Commodity Culture,* 141.

103. See particularly Bradley Naranch, "'Colonized Body,' 'Oriental Machine': Debating Race, Railroads, and the Politics of Reconstruction in Germany and East Africa, 1906–1910," *Central European History* 33, no. 3 (2000), as well as Zimmerer, *Deutsche Herrschaft,* and Conrad, *Globalisierung.* For this discourse in the 1880s, see Michael Schubert, *Der schwarze Fremde: Das Bild des Schwarzafrikaners in der parlamentarischen und publizistischen Kolonialdiscussion in Deutschland von den 1870er bis in die 1930erJahre* (Stuttgart: Franz Steiner, 2003), 65–189.

104. Held, "Kolonialismus und Werbung." The diminutive black Moor, Karen Pinkus argues, is a "figure of no resistance." Pinkus, *Bodily Regimes,* 69.

105. A parallel strategy to elevate the commodity by juxtaposing a figure can be seen in the development of an automaton, the "Funny Little Man," derived from caricature, that appeared in German advertising after 1912. Virginia Smith, *The Funny Little Man: The Biography of a Graphic Image* (New York: Van Nostrand Reinhold, 1993).

5. Featuring Race

1. Even at the fin de siècle, most advertising continued to draw on elaborate decorative motifs or else staged scenes that suggested brief, homily-laden storylines. The shift in advertising from the story to the icon is part of the story of the emerging *Sachplakat.* Jürgen Schwarz, *Bildannoncen aus der Jahrhundertwende: Studien zur künstlerischen Reklamegestaltung in Deutschland zwischen 1896 und 1914* (Frankfurt a. M.: Kunstgeschichtliches Institut der Johann Wolfgang Goethe-Universität, 1990); Jörg Meißner, ed., *Strategien der Werbekunst von 1850–1933* (Berlin: Deutsches Historisches Museum, 2004).

2. The literature on the popularization of race science is immense; particularly relevant here are George Mosse, *Toward the Final Solution: A History of European Racism* (New York: Howard Fertig, 1978); Pascal Grosse, *Kolonialismus, Eugenik und bürgerliche Gesellschaft in Deutschland 1850–1918* (Frankfurt a. M.: Campus, 2000); Andrew Zimmerman, *Anthropology and Antihumanism in Imperial Germany* (Chicago: University of Chicago Press, 2001); Paul Weindling, *Health, Race, and German Politics between National Unification and Nazism, 1870–1945* (Cambridge: Cambridge University Press, 1989); and Richard T. Gray, *About*

Face: German Physiognomic Thought from Lavater to Auschwitz (Detroit: Wayne State University Press, 2004).

3. Minstrelsy was the most widely viewed theater in the United States in the second half of the nineteenth century. Joseph Boskin, *Sambo: The Rise & Demise of an American Jester* (Oxford: Oxford University Press, 1986), 65–94; Eric Lott, *Love and Theft: Blackface Minstrelsy and the American Working Class* (New York: Oxford University Press, 1993).

4. The minstrel craze in 1880s Paris is recounted in Petrine Archer-Straw, *Negrophilia: Avant-Garde Paris and Black Culture in the 1920s* (New York: Thames & Hudson, 2000), 40–44.

5. See Robert Toll, *Blacking Up: The Minstrel Show in Nineteenth-Century America* (New York: Oxford University Press, 1974), 202, 206, 212.

6. As related in Brander Matthews, "The Rise and Fall of Negro Minstrelsy," *Scribner's Magazine* 57, no. 6 (1915): 751–758. Also cited in Hugh Honour, ed., *The Image of the Black in Western Art,* vol. 4 (Cambridge, MA: Harvard University Press, 1989), part 2, 64. For the history of Haverly's show, see Toll, *Blacking Up,* 145–152.

7. Honour, *The Black in Western Art,* part 2, 61 and 64.

8. See particularly Sarah Meer, *Uncle Tom Mania: Slavery, Minstrelsy, and Transatlantic Culture in the 1850s* (Athens: University of Georgia Press, 2005), chapters 2, 5, 6.

9. Ibid., 149–150.

10. Dale Cockrel, *Demons of Disorder: Early Blackface Minstrels and their World* (Cambridge: Cambridge University Press, 1997), 32–33.

11. Christopher Steiner, "Travel Engravings and the Construction of the Primitive," in *Prehistories of the Future,* ed. Elazar Barkan and Ronald Bush (Stanford, CA: Stanford University Press, 1995).

12. The original lithography shows a young black boy in tattered rags, huddling up close to a stove for warmth; his facial features reveal the influence of minstrel caricature, namely exaggerated white lips. For Fairland's versions, see Honour, *The Black in Western Art,* part 2, 60. For the German version, see Christa Pieske, *Bürgerliches Wandbild, 1840–1920: Populäre Druckgraphik aus Deutschland, Frankreich und England* (Göttingen: E. Goltze, 1975), 51. For minstrel engravings and sheet-music illustrations from the 1820s and 1840s, see Guy C. McElroy, *Facing History: The Black Image in American Art, 1710–1940* (Washington, DC: Bedford Arts, 1990), xvi–xvii, 26.

13. Toll, *Blacking Up,* 220–227. See also Karen Sotiropoulos, *Staging Race: Black Performers in Turn of the Century America* (Cambridge, MA: Harvard University Press, 2006).

14. See CMNL, Friedländer nos. 0047, 0157, 0425, 0561. The given dates are uncertain; despite sequential numbering, it is difficult to date early Friedländer posters precisely.

15. Cf. Fantoches Theater & Miniatur Circus (1887), CMNL, Friedländer no. 0699, and many others.

16. See "A morning in Afrika. Executed by the renowned Jack Barett Troupe. American Burlesque Pantomime," probably from 1891; CMNL, Friedländer no. 0941. American minstrelsy produced countless iterations of a seated, banjo-playing minstrel with one raised shoe, however, so Bouchy's model might lay elsewhere.

17. *Propaganda* 3, no. 10 (1900): 340–341. Italics mine.

18. Heike Paul, "The German Reception of Harriet Beecher Stowe's *Uncle Tom's Cabin,*" in *Amerikanische Populärkultur in Deutschland,* ed. Heike Paul and Katja Kanzler (Leipzig: Leipziger Universitätsverlag, 2002). The first German edition of *Onkel Tom's Hütte* appeared in 1852 and immediately proved hugely popular, inspiring countless theater productions. Even a Bauhaus housing project built in 1920s Berlin was named after the novel, and remains the name of an S-bahn station today.

19. See James H. Dormon, "Shaping the Popular Image of Post-Reconstruction American Blacks: The 'Coon Song' Phenomenon of the Gilded Age," *American Quarterly* 40, no. 4 (1988); Astrid Eichstedt and Bernd Polster, *Wie die Wilden: Tänze auf der Höhe ihrer Zeit* (Berlin: Rotbuch, 1985), 14–16.

20. Carl Schultzik, Rybnik, WZB (1914): 491, reg. no. 187351. Rybnik was at that time a part of Germany. I have not found evidence that this brand of biscuits actually appeared on the German market, however.

21. See Astrid Kusser's intriguing essay "Cakewalking the Anarchy of Empire around 1900," in *German Colonialism, Visual Culture, and Modern Memory,* ed. Volker M. Langbehn (New York: Routledge, 2010), 87–104.

22. A poster of Kummer's ad can be found in Viktoria Schmidt-Linsenhoff, Kurt Wettengl, and Almut Junker, eds., *Plakate 1880–1914* (Frankfurt a. M.: Historisches Museum Frankfurt am Main, 1986), 431, no. 602.

23. The closest in terms of style and detail to Kummer's that I have seen is the Art Nouveau poster "Le Vrai Cake Walk au Nouveau Cirque" by Franz Laskoff (originally from Poland), probably drawn before 1901 (when he left Paris for Milan). For American cakewalk music cover illustrations, see various internet collections, including www.ragtimepiano.ca/rags/cakewalk.htm. On the cakewalk in Germany, see Michael Budds, *Jazz & the Germans: Essays on the Influence of "Hot" American Idioms on the 20th-Century German Music* (Hillsdale, NY: Pendragon Press, 2002).

24. The poster is for the Altvater Bar, by Joseph Witzel. See Deutsches Historisches Museum, *Reklame: Produktwerbung im Plakat 1890 bis 1918* (DVD-ROM) (Berlin: Directmedia, 2005), 311.

25. The literature on the image of blacks in American culture is understandably massive, given the key role that race played and continues to play in the construction of American identities. A starting point is Jessie Carney Smith,

ed., *Images of Blacks in American Culture: A Reference Guide to Information Sources* (Westport, CT: Greenwood Press, 1988). See also Kenneth Goings, *Mammy and Uncle Mose: Black Collectables and American Stereotyping* (Bloomington: Indiana University Press, 1994), 32–33; M. M. Manring, *Slave in a Box: The Strange Career of Aunt Jemima* (Charlottesville: University Press of Virginia, 1998). The scope of racial advertising can be glimpsed in museum and collectors' catalogs: see Larry Vincent Buster, *The Art and History of Black Memorabilia* (New York: Clarkson Potter, 2000); Douglas Congdon-Martin, *Images in Black: 150 Years of Black Collectables* (West Chester, PA: Schiffer, 1990); and a multitude of online museum and collectors' sites.

26. See especially Goings, *Black Collectables,* 11–15; Jo-Ann Morgan, "Mammy the Huckster: Selling the Old South for the New Century," *American Art* 9, no. 1 (1995); Marily Maness Mehaffy, "Advertising Race/Racing Advertising: The Feminine Consumer(-Nation), 1876–1900," *Signs* 23, no. 1 (1997): 135.

27. Despite the discourse of American's advertising precociousness, the chronologies of advertising technology and technique, on close examination, seem fairly consistent on both sides of the Atlantic. One clear difference, however, seems to be the greater social prestige enjoyed by American advertisers in the early years. Pamela Walker Laird, *Advertising Progress: American Business and the Rise of Consumer Marketing* (Baltimore: Johns Hopkins University Press, 1998); Ellen Gruber Garvey, *The Adman in the Parlor: Magazines and the Gendering of Consumer Culture, 1880s to 1910s* (Oxford: Oxford University Press, 1996); T. Jackson Lears, *Fables of Abundance: A Cultural History of Advertising in America* (New York: Basic Books, 1994); Susan Strasser, *Satisfaction Guaranteed: The Making of the American Mass Market* (New York: Pantheon Books, 1989); Richard Ohmann, *Selling Culture: Magazines, Markets, and Class at the Turn of the Century* (New York: Verso, 1996).

28. Luthmer, "Reklame und Plakat-Kunst," *Die Reklame* 4 (1894): 31. Italics mine. Note the use of *Mohr* rather than *Neger.*

29. For three examples, see shoe polish ads by: A. Jacquot & Cie., Stettin, a maker of cleaning supplies (including Lederfett), WZB (1897): 104, reg. no. 21692; W. Rödiger i. F. Kluge & Co., Madgeburg WZB (1897): 306, reg. no. 22998; and Frederick Peart, Bermingham, vertr. Max Meyer, Erfurt, WZB (1901): 459, reg. no. 49152.

30. Christiane Lamberty, *Reklame in Deutschland 1890–1914: Wahrnehmung, Professionalisierung und Kritik der Wirtschaftswerbung* (Berlin: Duncker & Humblot, 2000); Dirk Reinhardt, *Von der Reklame zum Marketing: Geschichte der Wirtschaftswerbung in Deutschland* (Berlin: Akademie, 1993).

31. For a reproduction of this, see Michael Scholz-Hänsel, ed., *Das Exotische Plakat* (Stuttgart: Institut für Auslandsbeziehungen/Staatsgalerie Stuttgart,

1987), 67. Reithoffer was also a pioneer in colonialist imagery (see Chapter 4); it was an Austrian firm (first Vienna, then Steyr) but advertised extensively in Germany to German audiences.

32. The Seeger firm was founded in 1885 and was an exhibitor at the 1896 Industrial Exhibition in Berlin.

33. Florian's illustration of the two black boys, rather surprisingly for 1910, was not overly racialized, although there is great emphasis on their shiny white teeth. See Chemische Werke Florian & Co., Berlin, WZB (1910): 1837, reg. no. 134281; a color version of this packaging can be found in the collection of the DHM, AK 94/516.516. For Komasept, see the reproduction in Scholz-Hänsel, *Das Exotische Plakat,* 68.

34. *Die Reklame* (1895): 398.

35. See Pelikan's paper wrapper, DHM, AK 94/516.1004. The Wagner firm had earlier deployed chromolithographed tin posters in a *Jugendstil* style; Theo Matejko's famous Pelikan poster with a cherub carrying the old-style Pelikan ink bottle to a reclining New Woman is quite artistic.

36. Further description and discussion of each of these motifs or "types" in a larger European and American context can be found in Jan P. Nederveen Pieterse, *White on Black: Images of Africa and Blacks in Western Popular Culture* (New Haven, CT: Yale University Press, 1992), especially 152–156 and 188–200. On the iconology of black figures in America, see Joseph Boskin, "Sambo and Other Male Images," in Smith, *Images of Blacks,* 257–272. See also Honour, *The Black in Western Art,* part 2, 57–64.

37. The N. K. Fairbank Co., Chicago (vertr by patent-anwalt), WZB (1901): 950, reg. no. 51022.

38. Johnson & Johnson, New Brunswick, vertr. Weber, Hamburg, WZB (1914): 648, reg. no. 188573.

39. J. S. Staedtler, WZB (1896): 362, reg. no. 14089. The firm was founded in 1835, but the Staedtler name can be linked to *Bleiweißsteftmacher* all the way back to 1662. See also "Congo," Johann Faber, Nürnberg, WZB (1895): 808, reg. no. 7444.

40. Saxony was the center of German concertina and bandonion (miniature accordion) manufacturing for the domestic and the export markets. As early as 1862 there were twenty concertina and accordion factories in the environs of Klingenthal.

41. For example, the Württbürgische Harmonikafabrik Ch. Weitz (in Trossingen) trademarked an ad poster for "The 20th Century Harmonicas" in 1904; this image included an array of "ethnicities"—including American "blacks" and African "natives"—clustered around the instrument. WZB (1904): 1271, reg. no. 70816. The Böhm company trademarked the Globophone brand featuring its logo on a banner held by an American Indian, Uncle Sam, an African native,

and a top hat–wearing European. F. A. Böhm, Untersachsenberg, WZB (1907): 700, reg. no. 96396.

42. See the *Mitteilungen des Vereins Deutscher Reklamfachleute* no. 33 (1912): 5–6, and the conclusion of this book.

43. See, for instance, Peter Jelavich, *Berlin Cabaret* (Cambridge, MA: Harvard University Press, 1993), 174–175.

44. See Robert Darnton, *The Great Cat Massacre and Other Episodes in French Cultural History* (New York: Basic Books, 1984), 9–74; and especially Maria Tatar, *The Hard Facts of the Grimms' Fairy Tales* (Princeton, NJ: Princeton University Press, 2003).

45. Anthony Smith has written extensively on the "myth-symbol complexes" of *ethnie* as the origins of nations. Anthony D. Smith, *Ethnic Origins of Nations* (New York: Blackwell, 1987). Yet this all too readily glosses over how inchoate and heterogeneous such myth-symbol complexes were in the age before print media and later visual mass media mapped out those myth-symbols that were (or were not) part of the "national" heritage.

46. Cf. "Wer behielte die Lust einen Mohren zu waschen?" Goethe, letter 20, 251. Cited under the idiomatic usage of "einen Mohren waschen" in J. Grimm and W. Grimm, *Deutsches Wörterbuch,* vol. 13 (Leipzig: Hirzel, 1922), 2239.

47. Jeremiah 13:23, "Can the Ethiopian change his skin, or the leopard his spots? Then may you also do good, who are accustomed to do evil." See Lutz Röhrich, *Das Große Lexikon Der Sprichwörtlichen Redensarten* (Freiburg: Herder, 1992), 1040–1041.

48. Jean Michel Massing, "From Greek Proverb to Soap Advert: Washing the Ethiopian," *Journal of the Warburg and Courtauld Institutes* 58 (1995): 182–183. See also Nederveen Pieterse, *White on Black,* 195–198.

49. Massing, "From Greek Proverb to Soap Advert." On "black" and "white" more broadly, see Honour, *The Black in Western Art;* Nederveen Pieterse, *White on Black,* 24–29. For Germany, see Peter Martin, *Schwarze Teufel, edle Mohren: Afrikaner in Bewußtsein und Geschichte der Deutschen* (Hamburg: Junius, 1993), esp. 19–27.

50. See Nederveen Pieterse, *White on Black,* 195–199; Bernard Mirabel, ed., *Negripub: L'Image des Noirs dans la publicite* (Paris: Somogy, 1987), 92–103; and Anne McClintock, *Imperial Leather: Race, Gender, and Sexuality in the Colonial Contest* (New York: Routledge, 1995), 207–231. For the story of this theme transformed in colonial Africa, see Timothy Burke, *Lifebuoy Men, Lux Women: Commodification, Consumption, and Cleanliness in Modern Zimbabwe* (Durham, NC: Duke University Press, 1996); and Dana Hale, *Races on Display: French Representations of Colonized Peoples, 1886–1940* (Bloomington: Indiana University Press, 2008).

51. The secret to the mechanism is that there are three different lead Moors—a black figure cast as leaping in, a black figure cast as standing, and a whitened Moor figure cast as standing—and, in a manner reminiscent of German clock-tower figurines, they rotate in and out of the scene, one after the other. "Die Mohrenwäsche, ein hervorragendes Schaufensterstück," *Die Reklame* 7 (1897): 195.

52. Ribot continued to issue *Sammelbilder* up through 1907. Evamaria Ciolina, "Reklamesammelbilder," paper presented at the Bild und Text: Internationale Konferenz des Komitees für ethnologische Bildforschung in der Société internationale pour Ethnologie et Folklore (SIEF), Innsbruck, 1993; Volker Langbehn, "Greetings from Africa," in *Genocide, War and Memory: German Colonialism and National Identity,* ed. Michael Perraudin and Jürgen Zimmerer (New York: Routledge, 2009).

53. For British and French examples, see McClintock, *Imperial Leather;* Archer-Straw, *Negrophilia,* 37; Brett Berliner, *Ambivalent Desire: The Exotic Black Other in Jazz-Age France* (Amherst: University of Massachusetts Press, 2002), 150–155.

54. Viktor Mataja, *Die Reklame: Eine Untersuchung über Ankündigungswesen und Werbetätigkeit im Geschäftsleben* (Leipzig: Duncker & Humblot, 1910), 55.

55. Edward Lucie-Smith, *The Art of Caricature* (Ithaca, NY: Cornell University Press, 1981), 7.

56. Especially the work of Johann Caspar Lavater, *Physiognomische Fragmente zur Beförderung der Menschenkenntniss und Menschenliebe* (1775–1778). See also Gray, *About Face,* and Sander Gilman, "Lavater, Lichtenberg, and the Physiognomy of the Black," in Sander L. Gilman, *On Blackness without Blacks: Essays on the Image of the Black in Germany* (Boston: G. K. Hall, 1982), 49–56.

57. Judith Wechsler, *A Human Comedy: Physiognomy and Caricature in 19th Century Paris* (Chicago: University of Chicago Press, 1982), 7. See Elizabeth C. Childs, *Daumier and Exoticism: Satirizing the French and the Foreign* (New York: Peter Lang, 2004).

58. Ann Robertson discusses the role of caricature in the accelerated mass communication of modern life, making a distinction between the "discursive symbolism" of speech and the written word, and the non-discursive "presentative symbolism" of the image. Ann Robertson, *Karikatur im Kontext: Zur Entwicklung der sozialdemokratischen illustrierten satirischen Zeitschrift "Der Wahre Jacob"* (Frankfurt a. M.: Peter Lang, 1992).

59. Werner Hofmann, *Daumier und Deutschland* (Munich: Deutscher Kunstverlag, 2004).

60. Robertson, *Karikatur im Kontext,* 323. The development of the satirical magazine over the course of the nineteenth century (including the gradual reduction of text in favor of illustrations, the growing centrality of advertising, the

role of printing technology, and so forth) is discussed in Robertson, *Karikatur im Kontext,* 68–107; and Ann Taylor Allen, *Satire and Society in Wilhelmine Germany: Kladderadatsch and Simplicissimus 1890–1914* (Lexington: University Press of Kentucky, 1984).

61. Walter Arndt, ed., *The Genius of Wilhelm Busch* (Berkeley: University of California Press, 1982), 212.

62. *The Dictionary of Art,* vol. 5 (New York: Grove, 1996), 291.

63. Busch's earlier picture story "Die Rache des Elefanten" involves similar depictions of Africans and is discussed in Klaus Barthel, "Negerstereotypen und karikierende Darstellungen," in *Andenken an den Kolonialismus,* ed. Volker Harms (Tübingen: Attempto, 1984), 127–128. Busch's original sketches in partial color can be observed in Wilhelm Busch, *Fipps der Affe: Faksimiliedruck* (Hamburg: Rütten & Loening, 1960).

64. The Busch couplet is "Kleider sind dort wenig Sitte, / Höchstens trägt man einen Hut / Und ein Schurtzfell um die Mitte; / Man ist schwarz und damit gut." For Busch it is a moment of relativism, for Behr, a disparagement. H. F. von Behr, *Kriegsbilder aus dem Araberaufstand in Deutsch-Ostafrika* (Leipzig: Brockhaus, 1891), 80.

65. Busch's portrayal of blacks can be usefully viewed in the light of the more developed scholarly discussions of his depictions of Jews. Walter Arndt points out that, while the caricatures in Busch's *Plisch und Plum* provided a "striking model for the yid of the Nazi gutter press," Busch's talent lay in exaggerating endemic "nasty-genteel anti-Semitism ad absurdum by dragging it shamelessly into the open and seeming to indulge in it." Arndt, *The Genius of Wilhelm Busch,* 4.

66. David Kunzle, "Busch Abroad: How a German Caricaturist Willy Nilly Helped Launch the New Cheap Comic Magazines in Britain and the United States," *Victorian Periodicals Review* 25, no. 3 (1992): 101.

67. These stories showed the Africans of Cameroon as childish and inept, and the illustrations caricatured African facial features. At the same time, the political subtext to these broadsheets used the colonial context to savagely satirize *Prussians* as obsessive about regimentation and self-defeating in their arrogance. See Astrid Frevert, Gisela Rautenstrauch, and Matthias Rickling, "Kolonialismus und Darstellungen aus den Kolonien," in *Neuruppiner Bilderbogen,* ed. Stefan Brakensiek, Regina Krull, and Irina Rockel (Bielefeld: Verlag für Regionalgeschichte, 1993).

68. Gottfried Mergner and Ansgar Häfner, *Der Afrikaner im deutschen Kinder- und Jugendbuch* (Oldenburg: Bibliotheks- und Informationssytem der Universität, 1985), esp. 146–147; and Albert Schug, *Die Bilderwelt im Kinderbuch; Kinder- und Jugendbücher aus fünf Jahrhunderten* (Köln: Stadt Köln, 1988), 93–95. See also Brigitta Benzing, "Bombi und Bimba: Zum Afrika-Bild in deutschsprachigen

Kinder- und Jugendbüchern," in *Die Menschen sind arm weil sie arm sind: Die Dritte Welt im Spiegel von Kinder- und Jugendbüchern,* ed. Jörg Becker and Charlotte Oberfeld (Frankfurt a. M.: Haag und Herchen, 1978).

69. F. H. Benary and C. W. Allers, *Aus Kamerun: Ein Bilderbuch für kleine und große Kinder* (Munich: Braun & Schneider, 1885). I translate "Negerlein" in the harsher meaning ("niggers") primarily as it drew from the English-language song "Ten Little Niggers" written by Frank Green in 1869. Green, in turn, was rewriting Septimus Winner's 1868 minstrel show song "Ten Little Injuns"; this version likely was performed in Germany by the troupe Cristy's Minstrels. See *The Oxford Dictionary of Nursery Rhymes,* ed. Iona and Peter Opie (Oxford: Oxford University Press, 1997), 386–388; and also Inge Künkler-Kehr, "Der immerwährende Tod der 'Zehn kleinen Negerlein,'" in Mergner and Häfner, *Afrikaner im Jugendbuch,* 146ff; and Smith, *Images of Blacks,* 194–195.

70. *Simplicissimus* in 1905 printed 90,000–100,000 copies, while *Jugend* circulated 62,000. Robertson, *Karikatur im Kontext,* 327. This remained only one-tenth of the circulation of the *Berliner Illustrirte Zeitung,* however.

71. The humor magazines' role as purveyors of the newest ads is discussed extensively in Schwarz, *Bildannoncen,* esp. 67–76. Indeed, the distinctive decorative style in art and advertising right at the turn of the twentieth century, *Jugendstil,* takes its name from the Munich magazine.

72. Anita Kühnel, *Julius Klinger: Plakatkunstler und Zeichner* (Berlin: Gebr. Mann, 1997). Many of Klinger's advertising posters before 1914 are in Klaus Popitz et al., eds., *Das frühe Plakat in Europa und den USA: Band 3: Deutschland* (Berlin: Gebr. Mann, 1980), nos. 1628–1811.

73. Timothy W. Hiles, *Thomas Theodor Heine: Fin-de-Siècle Munich and the Origins of Simplicissimus* (New York: Peter Lang, 1996). For Heine's advertising posters, see his section in Popitz et al., *Das frühe Plakat,* 110–111 and nos. 1209–1229.

74. The image of an African boy carrying an umbrella, pulled from Heinrich Hoffmann's popular *Strewwelpeter* (1845), for instance, was an oft-used theme by advertisers; see the umbrella ad for E. Ohlischläger & Co., Biersen, WZB (1900): 508, reg. no. 43917.

75. Rudolf Cronau, *Das Buch der Reklame: Geschichte, Wesen und Praxis der Reklame* (Ulm: Kommissionsverlag der Wohler'schen Buchhandlung, 1887), 3.

76. Ibid., 24.

77. F. Luthmer, "Reklame und Plakat-kunst," *Die Reklame* 4 (1894): 32.

78. "Wie man in Deutschland annonciert," *Die Reklame* 5 (1895): 335. "Ebenfalls humoristisch und auf dem mit Recht so sehr beliebten Gebiete der modernsten Afrikakultur bewegt sich die Kitt-Reklame . . . Der Löwe, der zum großen Genuß einiger Kaffern seinen Schwanz an dem Baum festgeklebt hat, wird gewiß Spaß machen und sich einprägen."

79. Hermann Niebour, *Warenzeichen-Humor: Scherzhafte Darstellungen aus der deutschen Zeichenrolle* (Berlin: P. Stankiewicz Buchdruckerei, 1916).

80. "Aber sie sind und bleiben auf einer niedrigen Stufe, und wo sich einer erhebt und mit dem Europäer gleich werden will, wird er zur Karikatur." From the *Deutsch-Ostafrikanische Zeitung* (1907), cited in Peter Schmitt-Egner, *Kolonialismus und Faschismus* (Lollar: Achenbach, 1975), 99.

6. Racial Imperium

Epigraph: Ernst Growald, *Der Plakatspiegel: Erfahrungssätze für Plakat-Künstler und Besteller* (Berlin: Kampffmeyer'scher Zeitungs-Verlag, 1904).

1. See Paul Messaris, *Visual Persuasion: The Role of Images in Advertising* (London: Sage, 1997).

2. In addition to the discussion of the iconography of "washing the Ethiopian" in the previous chapter, and Jean Michel Massing, "From Greek Proverb to Soap Advert: Washing the Ethiopian," *Journal of the Warburg and Courtauld Institutes* 58 (1995), see also Kelley Anne Graham, "Advertising in Britain, 1880–1914: Soap Advertising and the Socialization of Cleanliness" (PhD diss., Temple University, 1994); and Vincent Vinikas, *Soft Soap, Hard Sell: American Hygiene in an Age of Advertisement* (Ames: Iowa State University Press, 1992).

3. See also Anandi Ramamurthy, *Imperial Persuaders* (Manchester, UK: Manchester University Press, 2003), 24–62.

4. For Lever's advertising, see Adam MacQueen, *The King of Sunlight: How William Lever Cleaned Up the World* (New York: Bantam, 2004), esp. 39–86; for the company's multinational structure after the 1920s, see D. K. Fieldhouse, *Unilever Overseas: The Anatomy of a Multinational 1895–1965* (Stanford, CA: Hoover Institution Press, 1978). For Lever's advertising in Rhodesia, see Timothy Burke, *Lifebuoy Men, Lux Women: Commodification, Consumption, and Cleanliness in Modern Zimbabwe* (Durham, NC: Duke University Press, 1996), esp. 93–99.

5. Michael Schubert, *Der schwarze Fremde: Das Bild des Schwarzafrikaners in der parlamentarischen und publizistischen Kolonialdiscussion in Deutschland von den 1870er bis in die 1930er Jahre* (Stuttgart: Franz Steiner, 2003); Mihran Dabag, Horst Gründer, and Uwe K. Ketelsen, eds., *Kolonialismus, Kolonialdiskurs und Genozid* (Munich: Wilhelm Fink, 2004); Roger Fletcher, *Revisionism and Empire: Socialist Imperialism in Germany, 1897–1914* (London: G. Allen & Unwin, 1984).

6. Helmut Walser Smith, "The Talk of Genocide, the Rhetoric of Miscegenation: Notes on Debates in the German Reichstag Concerning Southwest Africa, 1904–1914," in *The Imperialist Imagination: German Colonialism and Its Legacy*, ed. Sara Friedrichsmeyer, Sara Lennox, and Susanne Zantop (Ann Arbor:

University of Michigan Press, 1999); George Steinmetz, "'The Devil's Handwriting': Precolonial Discourse, Ethnographic Acuity, and Cross-Identification in German Colonialism," *Comparative Studies in Society and History* 45, no. 1 (2003).

7. The Herero took to arms for a number of reasons. Many Herero were forced into unwilling wage labor for the white colonists after a rinderpest epidemic in the late 1890s wiped out their cattle. Unscrupulous white traders had taken advantage of the crisis to sell goods on credit, then recovered the debts by seizing Herero property. Finally, the planning of a reservation system for the Herero in 1902 and 1903—the "solution" to the post-1893 wave of German settlers and companies encroaching on Herero farming lands—threatened to displace the power of Herero chiefs. In the larger view, however, the increasingly virulent racism of the German settlers toward the indigenous people was the underlying source of the uprising, as even the German colonial administrators of the time recognized. See Jürgen Zimmerer, *Deutsche Herrschaft über Afrikaner: Staatlicher Machtanspruch und Wirklichkeit im kolonialen Namibia* (Munster: LIT, 2004); Gesine Krüger, *Kriegsbewaltigung und Geschichtsbewusstsein: Realität, Deutung und Verarbeitung des Deutschen Kolonialkriegs in Namibia 1904 bis 1907* (Gottingen: Vandenhoeck & Ruprecht, 1999); and Jan-Bart Gewald, *Herero Heroes: A Socio-Political History of the Herero of Namibia, 1890–1923* (Athens: Ohio University Press, 1999), esp. 142–191. Gewald also argues the war was sparked by overanxious German junior officers. For military culture's role in the genocide, see Isabel Hull, *Absolute Destruction: Military Culture and the Practices of War in Imperial Germany* (Ithaca, NY: Cornell University Press, 2005), 5–90.

8. Hull, *Absolute Destruction,* 10–11.

9. The exact population of the Herero peoples before the uprising is unknown. See Hull, *Absolute Destruction,* 88–90; Krüger, *Kriegsbewaltigung und Geschichtsbewusstsein,* 62–68; Helmut Bley, *South-West Africa under German Rule, 1894–1914,* trans. Hugh Ridley (London: Heinemann, 1971), 150, 163.

10. See Joachim Zeller and Jürgen Zimmerer, eds., *Völkermord in Deutch-Südwestafrika: Der Kolonialkrieg (1904–1908) in Namibia und seine Folgen* (Berlin: Christoph Links, 2003), 52–63. Birthe Kundrus draws apt distinctions between this mass murder and the Holocaust, and therefore sees (along with Gesine Krüger) the term "*Völkermord*" as more appropriate than "*Genozid.*" Birthe Kundrus, "Von den Herero zum Holocaust?" *Mittelweg 36* 14, no. 4 (2005); see also Krüger, *Kriegsbewaltigung und Geschichtsbewusstsein,* 62–68.

11. Zeller and Zimmerer, *Völkermord,* 146; Bley, *South-West Africa under German Rule, 1894–1914,* 165.

12. Hull traces the genocide in South-West Africa instead back to a German military culture that increasingly insisted on "total" solutions to military problems. Hull, *Absolute Destruction,* 3, 330–333. This useful argument is well

grounded but downplays the pervasive imprint of racist discourse on not just military policy, but also civilian reaction to it. See Pascal Grosse, *Kolonialismus, Eugenik und bürgerliche Gesellschaft in Deutschland 1850–1918* (Frankfurt a. M.: Campus, 2000); Fatima El-Tayeb, *Schwarze Deutsche: Der Diskurs um "Rasse" und nationale Identität 1890–1933* (Frankfurt a. M.: Campus, 2001), 76–83. However, German soldiers' view of Africans, revealed in memoirs and diaries, show a complicated mixture of respect, racism, and "ethnographic interest." Krüger, *Kriegsbewaltigung und Geschichtsbewusstsein,* 84ff.

13. Andreas Heinrich Bühler, *Der Namaaufstand gegen die deutsche Kolonialherrschaft in Namibia von 1904–1913* (Frankfurt a. M.: IKO, 2003). See also Horst Drechsler, *"Let Us Die Fighting": The Struggle of the Herero and Nama against German Imperialism (1884–1915)* (London: Zed Press, 1980); and Hull, *Absolute Destruction,* 67–69, 85–90.

14. Hull, *Absolute Destruction,* 157.

15. The political crisis and rallying of the procolonial bloc are discussed in Ulrich van der Heyden, "Der 'Hottentottenwahlen' von 1907," in Zeller and Zimmerer, *Völkermord,* 86–96; Stig Forster, Wolfgang J. Mommsen, and Ronald Robinson, eds., *Bismarck, Europe, and Africa: The Berlin Africa Conference, 1884–1885 and the Onset of Partition* (Oxford: Oxford University Press, 1988); Lora Wildenthal, *German Women for Empire, 1884–1945* (Durham, NC: Duke University Press, 2001); and Ulrich S. Soenius, *Koloniale Begeisterung im Rheinland wahrend des Kaiserreichs* (Köln: Rheinisch-Westfalisches Wirtschaftsarchiv zu Koln, 1992).

16. Kenneth Holston, "'A Measure of the Nation': Politics, Colonial Enthusiasm and Education in Germany, 1896–1933" (PhD diss., University of Pennsylvania, 1996), 194. See also Woodruff D. Smith, *The German Colonial Empire* (Chapel Hill: University of North Carolina Press, 1978), 183–191; and Brehl and van der Heyden's essays in Zeller and Zimmerer, *Völkermord,* 86–102.

17. From this election, the SPD took away the lesson that it was risky to oppose war fever—a "lesson" that likely contributed to their support for war in 1914. See van der Heyden in Zeller and Zimmerer, *Völkermord,* 97–104.

18. Carl Hagenbeck, *Von Tieren und Menschen,* 11th ed. (Berlin, 1909). See also Eric Ames, "Where the Wild Things Are: Locating the Exotic in German Modernity" (PhD diss., University of California, Berkeley, 2000), 6.

19. F. Reddaway & Co. (Hamburg), WZB (1907): 2253, reg. no. 102005.

20. *Simplicissimus* 9, vol. 6 (1904).

21. Even the stridently anticolonialist *Der Wahre Jacob* and *Süddeutsche Postillon* defined the oppressed Africans by their black skin, bulging lips, and frizzy hair. See also Edward Graham Norris and Arnold Beuke, "Kolonialkrieg und Karikatur in Deutschland: Die Aufstände der Herero und der Nama und die Zeichnungen der deutschen satirischen Zeitschriften," in *Studien zur Geschichte*

des deutschen Kolonialismus in Afrika: Festschrift zum 60. Geburtstag von Peter Sebald, ed. Peter Heine and Ulrich van der Heyden (Pfaffenweiler: Centaurus Verlagsgesellschaft, 1995).

22. On the panorama, see the appendix of *Schilder, Bilder, Moritaten: Sonderschau des Museums für Volkskunde im Pergamonmuseum* (Berlin: Staatliche Museen zu Berlin, 1987).

23. For *Bilderbogen,* the caricatured buffoonery of colonial natives in the late 1880s gave way to scenes of heroic German soldiers fighting hordes of tough and merciless Africans. See Astrid Frevert, Gisela Rautenstrauch, and Matthias Rickling, "Kolonialismus und Darstellungen aus den Kolonien," in *Neuruppiner Bilderbogen: Ein Massenmedium des 19. Jahrhunderts,* ed. Stefan Brakensiek, Regina Krull, and Irina Rockel (Bielefeld: Verlag für Regionalgeschichte, 1993); Theodor Kohlmann, *Neuruppiner Bilderbogen* (Berlin: Museum für Deutsche Volkskunde, 1981).

24. Joachim Zeller, *Bilderschule der Herrenmenschen: Koloniale Reklamesammelbilder* (Berlin: Ch. Links, 2008), 137.

25. See the bibliographic category "war narratives" in Emil Sembritzki's *Der Kolonialfreund: Kritischer Führer durch die volkstümlich Deutsche Kolonialliterture* (Berlin: "Kolonie und Heimat" Verlag, 1912). The illustrated magazine *Colony and Home in Words and Pictures (Kolonie und Heimat),* begun in 1907, drew its staff from returned settlers and soldiers who had served in the South-West African war. Wildenthal, *German Women for Empire,* 146.

26. See Medardus Brehl, " 'Das Drama spielte sich auf der dunklen Bühne des Sandfeldes ab': Die Vernichtung der Herero und Nama in der deutschen (Popülar-) Literatur," in Zeller and Zimmerer, *Völkermord,* 86–96. *Colony and Home* eventually served as the organ of the Women's League *(Frauenbund)* of the German Colonial Society, which paid for its page at a discounted rate.

27. See, for instance, Zeller, *Bilderschule,* esp. 183 and 136–147.

28. Friedrich Lange, *Deutsch-Südwest-Afrika. Kriegs- und Friedensbilder* (Windhoek: Franz Rohloff, 1907); *Kreuz und quer durch Deutsch-Süd-West-Afrika: Eine Sammlung von 100 der schönsten Ansichten* (Hamburg: Spenker, ca. 1905).

29. David Ciarlo, "Picturing Genocide in German Consumer Culture, 1904–1910," in *German Colonialism and National Identity,* ed. Michael Perraudin and Jürgen Zimmerer (New York: Routledge, 2010).

30. Meister was a very successful writer of youth literature in the *Kaiserreich,* writing on themes such as pirates, the Boer War (1900), the Germans in China (1900), and the South Seas (1902). See the cover for *Muhérero riKárera (Beware, Herero),* reproduced in Brehl, " 'Das Drama spielte sich auf der dunklen Bühne des Sandfeldes ab,' " 89.

31. David Spurr, *The Rhetoric of Empire: Colonial Discourse in Journalism, Travel Writing, and Imperial Administration* (Durham, NC: Duke University Press,

1993); Patrick Brantlinger, *Rule of Darkness: British Literature and Imperialism, 1830–1914* (Ithaca, NY: Cornell University Press, 1988).

32. Hottentot cigarettes, Simon & Lehmann, Mannheim, WZB (1907): 2429, reg. no. 102865. "Nama," Nahrungsmittel-Versand-Gesellchaft GmbH, Madgeburg, WZB (1911): 327, reg. no. 139961 and WZB (1913): 944, reg. no. 173322.

33. See, for instance, Stanislaus Swierczewski, *Wider Schmutz und Schwindel im Inseratenwesen* (Leipzig: "Deutsche Kampf" Verlag, 1907). Swierczewski and others railed against classified ads for thinly disguised erotic books. One such book, often advertised, was Carl Heinrich Stratz, *Die Rassenschönheit des Weibes* (Stuttgart: F. Enke, 1901), which went through twenty-two editions between 1901 and 1941 alone and featured hundreds of photographs of nude women, displayed for racial edification. On erotic ethnographic photographs, see Jutta Engelhard and Peter Mesenhöller, *Bilder aus dem Paradies: Koloniale Fotographie Samoa 1875–1925* (Köln: Jonas, 1995); Michael Wiener, *Ikonographie des Wilden: Menschen-Bilder in Ethnographie und Photographie zwischen 1850 und 1918* (Munich: Trickster, 1990). More broadly, see Elazar Barkan and Ronald Bush, eds., *Prehistories of the Future: The Primitivist Project and the Culture of Modernism* (Stanford, CA: Stanford University Press, 1995), esp. 86–94; Raymond Corbey, "Alterity: The Colonial Nude," *Critique of Anthropology* 8, no. 3 (1988); and "porno-tropics" as a trope in Anne McClintock, *Imperial Leather: Race, Gender, and Sexuality in the Colonial Contest* (New York: Routledge, 1995).

34. On censorship, see Robin Lenman, "Control of the Visual Image in Imperial Germany," in *Zensur und Kultur/Censorship and Culture,* ed. John McCarthy and Werner von der Ohe (Tübingen: Max Niemeyer, 1995); and Lynn Abrams, "From Control to Commercialization: The Triumph of Mass Entertainment in Germany, 1900–1925?" *German History* 8 (1990).

35. On the increasing vitriol of racist rhetoric after 1904, see particularly Smith, "Talk of Genocide," and Jürgen Zimmerer and Joachim Zeller, *Genocide in German South-West Africa: The Colonial War of 1904–1908 and Its Aftermath,* trans. E. J. Neather (Monmouth, Wales: Merlin Press, 2007).

36. For Britain, see Beth Fowkes Tobin, *Picturing Imperial Power: Colonial Subjects in Eighteenth-Century Painting* (Durham, NC: Duke University Press, 1999). For Germany, see Peter Martin, *Schwarze Teufel, edle Mohren: Afrikaner in Bewußtsein und Geschichte der Deutschen* (Hamburg: Junius, 1993), esp. 100–112. The classic survey is Hugh Honour, ed., *The Image of the Black in Western Art,* vol. 4 (Cambridge, MA: Harvard University Press, 1989).

37. For the "reflective" approach, see David Dabydeen, *Hogarth's Blacks: Images of Blacks in Eighteenth Century English Art* (Kingston-upon-Thames, UK: Dangaroo Press, 1985), 17–40; for the symbolic, see Michael D. Harris, *Colored Pictures: Race and Visual Representation* (Chapel Hill: University of North Caro-

lina Press, 2003), 126–134; Jan P. Nederveen Pieterse, *White on Black: Images of Africa and Blacks in Western Popular Culture* (New Haven, CT: Yale University Press, 1992), 159.

38. See Karen Pinkus, *Bodily Regimes: Italian Advertising under Fascism* (Minneapolis: University of Minnesota Press, 1995), 15–16. See also the discussions in Thomas Richards, *The Commodity Culture of Victorian England: Advertising and Spectacle 1851–1914* (London: Verso, 1990), esp. 8–16; and Burke, *Lifebuoy Men, Lux Women,* 5–12.

39. Tengelmann has 180,000 employees and annual sales of 26 billion euros, and includes subsidiary chains such as Kaiser's, A&P, OBI, and Plus.

40. WZB (1898): 913, reg. no. 33633.

41. The Czech graphic artist Alfons Mucha inspired many imitators in German advertising: see Fernand Schultz-Wettel's ad for Otto Ring's Syndetikon glue in Deutsches Historisches Museum, *Reklame: Produktwerbung im Plakat 1890 bis 1918* (DVD-ROM) (Berlin: Directmedia, 2005).

42. See Stuart Hall, "Encoding, Decoding," in *The Cultural Studies Reader,* ed. Simon During (London: Routledge, 1999).

43. One of these, a trademark for "Cameroon Rubber for dental use" in 1910, deploys the bust of a black man with lips that are only slightly emphasized; it would be ordinary for 1900, yet was a striking anomaly by 1910. See Geo. Poulson, Hamburg, WZB (1910): 28, reg. no. 124505.

44. Anita Kühnel, *Julius Klinger: Plakatkunstler und Zeichner* (Berlin: Gebr. Mann, 1997). After the First World War broke out Klinger moved back to Vienna, where he designed war-loan posters; he continued to work in Vienna in the 1920s and 1930s, designing the ads for Tabu cigarette papers, most notably. Klinger was of Jewish descent and faced persecution by the National Socialists; he was deported east in 1942 and likely murdered that same year.

45. Eduard Palm, Berlin, WZB (1911): 2722, reg. no. 152615. All of the scholarly literature echoes Wember's claim that the Palm poster was crafted in 1906, although such a long delay before registration is extraordinarily unusual; images were usually registered right before they were publicly circulated.

46. See Ruben, *Die Reklame,* vol. 1, 56; *Das Plakat* 8 (1917).

47. *Mitteilungen des Vereins Deutscher Reklamfachleute* (1913): 63.

48. See Martin Henatsch, *Die Entstehung des Plakates: Eine rezeptionsästhetische Untersuchung* (Hildesheim: Georg Olms, 1994), 73; Paul Wember, *Die Jugend der Plakate, 1887–1917* (Krefeld: Scherpe, 1961), 470; Michael Scholz-Hänsel, ed., *Das Exotische Plakat* (Stuttgart: Institut für Auslandsbeziehungen/Staatsgalerie Stuttgart, 1987), 44; and many others. Henatsch calls the black native a smoking "Mohr."

49. Scholz-Hänsel, *Exotische Plakat,* 70. Another example is the three Moor figures appearing on an Erhardt jewelers *Reklamemark.* MEK no. 33 Q 2027

no. 2, 14. The corpus of Klinger's expansive prewar ad work for Hollerbaum & Schmidt is surveyed in Klaus Popitz et al., eds., *Das frühe Plakat in Europa und den USA: Band 3: Deutschland* (Berlin: Gebr. Mann, 1980), nos. 1628–1811.

50. Hanna Gagel, "Studien zur Motivgeschichte des deutschen Plakats 1900–1914" (PhD diss., Freie Universität-Berlin, 1971), 63.

51. J. B. Maier's black-dandy poster advertised Poröse Tricot-Leibwäsche. Hans Heinz Moor, *Reklame Lexicon: Neue Ideen für moderne Reklame: Vorschläge, Ratschläge, Anregung und Tricks zur unmittelbar praktischen Verwertung unterstützt durch Beispiele und Muster: Keine theoretische Schrift sondern verwertbare Praxis!* (Leipzig, Phönix, 1908), 158. Maier's illustration was captioned by the advertising writer as a "model poster"; it was also reproduced four years later in the journal *Das Plakat* (1913).

52. The basic stylistic elements of Hohlwein's Marco Polo tea ad were drawn from the Beggarstaff Brothers' 1895 event poster, "A trip to China town" (see Suckale-Redlefsen, *Plakate in München,* 75), but the "black" facial features are Hohlwein's addition. More than a decade later Hohlwein's illustration for Riquet tea, designed in 1924, blended elements of his Marco Polo and Café Odeon designs. See the reproduction in Scholz-Hänsel, *Exotische Plakat,* 65. For a survey of Hohlwein's prewar work, see Popitz et al., *Das frühe Plakat,* nos. 1315–1485.

53. Gude Suckale-Redlefsen, ed., *Plakate in München, 1840–1940* (München: Stadtmuseum, 1975), 74; and Hermann Pollig, ed., *Exotische Welten: Europäische Phantasien* (Stuttgart: Edition Cantz, 1987), 226.

54. An Austrian poster for the Schindler liquor manufacturer in Innsbruck, for instance, copies the tableau figure for figure, though with far less skill; the Schindler poster black serving boy's lips are neon red. Deutsches Historisches Museum, *Reklame* (DVD-ROM). Franz Laskoff's 1914 ad poster for Costina's Coffee (drafted in Milan) clearly draws on Hohlwein's work as well.

55. Kunstgewerbemuseum Zürich, ed., *Ferdinand Hodler und das schwiezer Künstlerplakat, 1890–1920* (Zurich: Kunstgewerbemuseum der Stadt Zürich, 1983), 20. See the lower right of the lower photograph.

56. Italics mine. Ernst Growald, "Die Repräsentation des Geschäfts," in Ruben, *Die Reklame,* 115. "Ähnliche Erfolge hatten die Plakate für Steinway und Palm, die die alten nichtssageden Firmenzeichen rasch verdrängten. . . . Dieses rasch Verdrängen der alten Signets beweist, daß unpopuläre Zeichen vollkommen wertlos sind. Die hier abgebildeten Beispiele zeigen auch, wie Firmenzeichen beschaffen sein müssen, damit sie populär werden können."

57. *Propaganda* (1898): 488. "Nicht der *persönliche* Geschmack des Inserenten soll maßgebend sein, vielmehr der Eindruck, den das Inserat beim Publikum machen soll, also die *Absicht,* das Publikum für sich zu gewinnen!" Ruben, *Die Reklame,* 229. Italics in original.

58. For Hohlwein, see MEK 33 Q 1236/82, 36.

59. Lamberty discusses the history of the *Reklamemark,* likely originating in 1894, first as a commemoration for exhibitions. The fervor to collect them rose to a mania in the first decade of the twentieth century, largely subsiding by 1914. Christiane Lamberty, *Reklame in Deutschland 1890–1914* (Berlin: Duncker & Humblot, 2000), 175–176. See also Lotte Maier, *Reklame-Schau: Plakatkunst en Miniature: Ausstellungs-, Reklame- und Propagandamarken von 1896 bis 1939* (Dortmund: Harenberg, 1984); Bernhard Reichel, ed., *Bitte bitte kleb' mich: Werbemarken als Spiegel der Stadt- und Regionalgeschichte* (Frankfurt a. M.: Institut für Stadtgeschichte, 1998); and Christa Pieske, *Das ABC des Luxuspapiers: Herstellung, Verarbeitung und Gebrauch* (Berlin: Staatliche Museen Preußischer Kulturbesitz Museum für Deutsche Volkskunde, 1983).

60. See Höllandische Margarine-Werke Jurgens & Prinzen, WZB (1909): 1870, reg. no. 121870.

61. The following relies heavily upon Lamberty, *Reklame,* 406–429. See also Stefan Haas's insightful "Psychologen, Künstler, Ökonomen: Das Selbstverständnis der Werbetriebenden zwischen fin de siecle und Nachkriegzeit," in *Bilderwelt des Alltags,* ed. Peter Borscheid and Clemens Wischermann (Stuttgart: Franz Steiner, 1995), 78–89.

62. Bernhard Wities, "Das Wirkungsprinzip der Reklame: Eine psychologische Studie," in *Zeitschrift für Philosophie und philosophische Kritik* 128 (1906): 138–154. Cited in Lamberty, *Reklame,* 407.

63. Lamberty, *Reklame,* 408. The French edition of Le Bon's book initially appeared in 1895.

64. M. Picard, "Zur Psychologie der Reklame," *Zeitschrift für Handelswissenschaft und Handelspraxis* (1913): 42–43, quoted in Lamberty, *Reklame,* 409–410. As Lamberty cogently argues, this discourse was highly gendered, with "the masses" as feminine (irrational and susceptible to suggestion) and the advertiser as the penetrating masculine.

65. Alongside appeals to sympathy or antipathy, humor, curiosity, and so forth. From the chapter "Experimente über die Wirkung der Anzeigen," in Hugo Münsterberg, *Psychologie und Wirtschaftsleben* (Leipzig: Johann Abrosius Barth, 1912), 152 and 153.

66. For example, see Herbert Schindler, ed., *Monographie des Plakats: Entwicklung Stil Design* (Munich: Süddeutscher, 1972), 122; Gagel, "Studien zur Motivgeschichte," 73.

67. See Stephen Eskilson, *Graphic Design: A New History* (New Haven, CT: Yale University Press, 2007); Steven Heller and Louise Fili, *German Modern: Graphic Design from Wilhelm to Weimar* (San Francisco: Chronicle Books, 1998); and Leslie Cabarga, *Progressive German Graphics, 1900–1937* (San Francisco: Chronicle Books, 1994); Jeremy Aynsley, *Graphic Design in Germany, 1890–1945* (Berkeley: University

of California Press, 2000). Aynsley focuses on individual artists (such as Fritz Helmut Ehmcke, Peter Behrens, and Lucian Bernhard) but situates them within the cultural context of advertising. For the larger implications of *Sachlichkeit,* see Frank Trommler, "The Creation of a Culture of *Sachlichkeit,*" in *Society, Culture, and the State in Germany, 1870–1930,* ed. Geoff Eley (Ann Arbor: University of Michigan Press, 1996), 465–485.

Conclusion

1. I have not come across a single overt or recognizably anti-Semitic illustration in my extensive research through the trademark rolls. I do not mean to suggest that anti-Semitic caricature was absent from the *Kaiserreich,* but it does seem to have been mostly confined to a very few specific sites, such as spa postcards, or propaganda postcards printed by the small Anti-Semite Peoples Party. See those in Helm Gold and Georg Heuberger, eds., *Abgestempelt: Judenfeindliche Postkarten* (Frankfurt a. M.: Umschau/Braus, 1999).

2. Some art historians and cultural historians remind us that, no matter how vibrant the small avant-garde before 1914, Germans tastes and norms seem to have remained generally conservative. See Wolfgang Mommsen, *Bürgerliche Kultur und künstlerische Avantgarde: Kultur und Politik im deutschen Kaiserreich, 1870 bis 1918* (Berlin: Propyläen, 1994); Peter Jelavich, "Literature and the Arts," in *Imperial Germany: A Historiographical Companion,* ed. Roger Chickering (Westport, CT: Greenwood Press, 1996). Matthew Jefferies complicates this schema but does not essentially challenge it; Matthew Jefferies, *Imperial Culture in Germany, 1871–1918* (New York: Palgrave, 2003).

3. Dada brand hair conditioner was produced after 1906 by the Bergmann firm and provided the likely eponym for the infamous avant-garde movement. The Bergmann company, with factories in Radebeul, Tetschen (in Austria-Hungary), and Zurich, was a large soap manufacturer at the cutting edge of modern advertising in Germany. Long before its Dada brand, the Bergmann company also produced *Steckenpferd* (Hobby Horse) brand soap—notable for its use of colonial and racial advertising imagery (see Figure 6.13). "Dada" is colloquial French for "hobby horse"; and the brand name was taken up by a soon-to-be-infamous avant-garde Zurich cabaret act in 1916. Hans Bolliger, Guido Magnaguagno, and Raimund Meyer, *Dada in Zürich* (Zürich: Arche, 1985), 85.

4. Soenke Neitzel, *Kriegsausbruch: Deutschlands Weg in die Katastrophe 1900–1914* (Munich: Pendo, 2002); Mark Hewitson, *Germany and the Causes of the First World War* (New York: Berg, 2004).

5. Ann Laura Stoler, *Race and the Education of Desire: Foucault's History of Sexuality and the Colonial Order of Things* (Durham, NC: Duke University Press, 1995).

6. On reactions to the Morocco crisis, see Woodruff D. Smith, *The Ideological Origins of Nazi Imperialism* (New York: Oxford University Press, 1986); Roger Chickering, *We Men Who Feel Most German: A Cultural Study of the Pan-German League, 1886–1914* (Boston: Allen & Unwin, 1984); James Retallack, *The German Right, 1860–1920: Political Limits of the Authoritarian Imagination* (Toronto: University of Toronto Press, 2006); and Geoff Eley, *Reshaping the German Right: Radical Nationalism and Political Change after Bismarck* (Ann Arbor: University of Michigan Press, 1990). On the failure of efforts to make Samoa a colony in 1875–1880, see Paul Kennedy, *The Samoan Tangle: A Study in Anglo-German-American Relations, 1878–1900* (Dublin: Irish University Press, 1974).

7. On Nivea advertising during the Third Reich, see Uta Poiger, "Beauty, Business and German International Relations," *Werkstatt Geschichte* 45 (2007): 53–71.

8. *Mitteilungen des Vereins Deutscher Reklamfachleute* no. 33 (1912): 5–6.

9. Sachs continued, "In this way the roots of a new racial construction emerges; we are quite justified in talking about a distinct 'American' race, whose features are sharply defined and not just by differences of speech and outward appearances." *Mitteilungen des Vereins Deutscher Reklamfachleute* no. 33 (1912): 5–6.

10. Hellmut Rademacher and René Grohnert, *Kunst! Kommerz! Visionen! Deutsche Plakate 1888–1933* (Berlin: Deutsches Historisches Museum, 1992).

11. See Peter Jelavich, *Berlin Cabaret* (Cambridge, MA: Harvard University Press, 1993), 174–175.

12. For the former, see George Mosse, *Toward the Final Solution: A History of European Racism* (New York: Howard Fertig, 1978), and Pascal Grosse, *Kolonialismus, Eugenik und bürgerliche Gesellschaft in Deutschland 1850–1918* (Frankfurt a. M.: Campus, 2000); for the latter, see Peter Walkenhorst, *Nation—Volk—Rasse: Radikaler Nationalismus Im Deutschen Kaiserreich 1890–1914* (Göttingen: Vandenhoeck & Ruprecht, 2007); and Chickering, *We Men Who Feel Most German.*

13. Cf. Fritz Fischer, *War of Illusions: German Policies from 1911 to 1914,* trans. Marian Jackson (London: Chatto and Windus, 1975). Fischer concentrates upon the illusions and delusions of political leadership, not of the public. The insight that the processes of mass culture transformed traditional political practices in the 1920s emerges in Walter Benjamin's brief reflections on the aestheticization of politics and the rise of fascism; this has been intriguingly reworked by Susan Buck-Morss, "Aesthetics and Anesthetics: Walter Benjamin's Artwork Essay Reconsidered," *October* 62 (Fall 1992).

14. Jeffrey Verhey, *The Spirit of 1914: Militarism, Myth and Mobilization in Germany* (Cambridge: Cambridge University Press, 2000).

15. David Welch, *Germany, Propaganda, and Total War, 1914–1918* (New Brunswick, NJ: Rutgers University Press, 2000); Peter Paret, Paul Paret, and

Beth Lewis, eds., *Persuasive Images* (Princeton, NJ: Princeton University Press, 1992).

16. Matthew Stibbe, *German Anglophobia and the Great War, 1914–1918* (Cambridge: Cambridge University Press, 2001), 38–44, 52–59, 181; see also Christian Koller, "Feind—Bilder: Rassen- und Geschlechterstereotype in der Kolonialtruppendiskussion Deutschlands und Frankreichs, 1914–1923," in *Heimat—Front: Militaer und Geschlechterverhaeltnisse im Zeitalter der Weltkriege,* ed. Karen Hagemann and Stefanie Schueler-Springorum (Frankfurt a. M.: Campus, 2002). Some propaganda examples are in Mamoun Fansa, ed., *Schwarz Weissheiten: Vom Umgang mit fremden Menschen* (Oldenburg: Isensee, 2001), 151. Britain's and France's use of colonial troops became a hot topic in the German press, entirely out of proportion to the military role or strategic implications of these forces. Christian Koller, *"Von Wilden aller Rassen niedergemetzelt": Die Diskussion um die Verwendung von Kolonialtruppen in Europa zwischen Rassimus, Kolonial- und Militärpolitik (1914–1930)* (Stuttgart: Steiner, 2001).

17. Andrew D. Evans, "Capturing Race: Anthropology and Photography in German and Austrian Prisoner-of-War Camps During World War I," in *Colonialist Photography: Imag(in)ing Race and Place,* ed. Eleanor M. Hight and Gary D. Sampson (New York: Routledge, 2002). See also the propaganda tract by O. Stiehl, *Unsere Feinde: 96 Charakterköpfe aus deutschen Kriegsgefangenenlagen* (Stuttgart: Verlag Julius Hoffmann, 1916).

18. For the history of the propaganda campaign, see particularly Sandra Mass, *Weisse Helden schwarze Krieger: Zur Geschichte kolonialer Maennlichkeit in Deutschland 1918–64* (Cologne: Böhlau, 2006); Christian Koller, "Die 'Schwarze Schmach': afrikanische Besatzsungssoldaten und Rassismus in den zwanziger Jahren," in *AfrikanerInnen in Deutschland und schwarze Deutsche: Geschichte und Gegenwart,* ed. Marianne Bechhaus-Gerst and Reinhard Klein-Arendt (Munster: LIT, 2003); Gisela Lebzelter, "Die 'Schwarze Schmach': Vorurteile-Propaganda-Mythos," *Geschichte und Gesellschaft* 11 (1985); and "Blacks, Germans, and the Politics of Imperial Imagination, 1920–60," in *The Imperialist Imagination: German Colonialism and Its Legacy,* ed. Sara Friedrichsmeyer, Sara Lennox, and Susanne Zantop (Ann Arbor: University of Michigan Press, 1999), 205–229.

19. For instance, one propaganda medallion features an African in profile with a sloped forehead, massive lips, and an earring in a distended earlobe, wearing a French helmet; on the reverse of the medallion a young nude white woman is tied to a massive black phallus also "wearing" a French helmet. See Iris Wigger, "'Schwarze Schmach' und 'weiße Frau': Über die Logic rassisticher Rhetorik," in Fansa, *Schwarz Weissheiten,* 150–156. In another illustration a gigantic African figure with huge white lips, nude except for a French helmet, presses two armfuls of young, nude white women to his groin; see Annemarie Hürli-

mann, Martin Roth, and Klaus Vogel, eds., *Fremdkörper—Fremde Körper: Von unvermeidlichen Kontakten und widerstreitenden Gefühlen* (Ostfildern-Ruit: Hatje Cantz, 1999), 197. A poster promoting a film against the "Black Horror" shows a racialized black African with large lips, sloped face, and an earring, looking furtive and animalistic as he grabs the hair of a screaming white woman with a partially torn shirt. See Gerhard Höpp, ed., *Fremde Erfahrungen: Asiaten und Afrikaner in Deutschland, Österreich, und in der Schweiz bis 1945* (Berlin: Das Arabische Buch, 1996), 204. See also the files of such propaganda collected by the Colonial Office; BA 8023/536. One organization distributing this propaganda in 1922 actually charged for it: 2 marks for every ten copies. The prices did not include postage. BA 8023/536, doc 4.

20. Such as with Nessim cigarettes; DHM AK 94/516.1131.

21. Cf. "Nationalstolz" by the Neutzer Margarine Werk GmbH (Neutz a.R.) and "Nationalstolz" by the cigar manufacturer Halle & Bensinger (Mannheim). WZB (1915): 176, reg. no. 201559, and 885, reg. no. 204548, respectively. The orientalist Berlin cigarette giant of Garbáty (Rosenthal) registered the trademark Garbáty Feldgrau (Garbáty Field Gray); field gray was both the color of the German Army uniforms and a slang term for a soldier. WZB (1914): 3000, reg. no. 200170. "Deutschland Über Alles Margarine" was by the Margarinenwerk Berolina GmbH, Berlin, WZB (1916): 371, reg. no. 209496. Artillery and submarines were popular, too; see Juwel's U-Boote cigarettes by the manufacturer Julius Geck, Dresden, WZB (1917): 582, reg. no. 216953. See also Dirk Reinhardt, *Von der Reklame zum Marketing: Geschichte der Wirtschaftswerbung in Deutschland* (Berlin: Akademie, 1993), 416–422.

22. Fa. Julius Staege, Berlin, WZB (1914): 1130, reg. no. 190215, and WZB (1903): 547, reg. no. 59291. For Staege coffee tins, see DHM ak 94/516.5829 and ak 94/516.598. For the poster, see Klaus Popitz et al., eds., *Das frühe Plakat in Europa und den USA: Band 3: Deutschland* (Berlin: Gebr. Mann, 1980), no. 2146.

23. Sarotti Chokoladen- & Cacao-Industrie AG, Berlin, WZB (1919): 295, reg. no. 229674. The date that Sarotti AG submitted the trademark was 27 August 1918; the yearlong delay in processing was by then usual, since manpower was moved from the *Patentamt* into areas crucial to the war effort. For a sympathetic history of Sarotti's icon, see Rita Gudermann and Bernhard Wulff, *Der Sarotti-Mohr: Die bewegte Geschichte einer Werbefigur* (Berlin: Ch. Links, 2004).

24. Mass, *Weisse Helden;* Susanne Zantop, "Colonial Legends; Postcolonial Legacies," in *A User's Guide to German Cultural Studies,* ed. Scott Denham, Irene Kacandes, and Jonathan Peropoulos (Ann Arbor: University of Michigan Press, 1997).

25. The *German Colonial News,* like most organizational newsletters, appended an "honor roll" during the war—a growing list of its members killed on the eastern and western fronts.

26. Post-1918 colonialist organizations included such colonial veterans' groups as the *Kolonialkriegerbund* and even a colonialist youth society, the Colonial Scouts *(Kolonialpfadfinder)*. See Wolfe Schmokel, *Dream of Empire: German Colonialism, 1919–1945* (New Haven, CT: Yale University Press, 1964), 1–45. In the cultural arena, see particularly Mass, *Weisse Helden;* Eric Ames, Marcia Klotz, and Lora Wildenthal, eds., *Germany's Colonial Pasts* (Lincoln: University of Nebraska Press, 2005); and Christian Rogowski's essay in Birthe Kundrus, ed., *Phantasiereiche: Der deutsche Kolonialismus in kulturgeschichtlicher Perspektive* (New York: Campus, 2003).

27. Former German colonial officials redirected their careers to the realm of publication; the former governer Heinrich Schnee published a three-volume tome, *Deutsches Kolonial-lexicon* (Leipzig: Quelle & Meyer, 1920); Major Kurd Schwabe and Dr. Paul Leutwein "reworked" and published a new two-volume edition of *Die Deutschen Kolonien (Jubiläumsausgabe)* (Berlin: Carl Weller, 1926), among countless examples.

28. See Jared Poley, *Decolonization in Germany: Weimar Narratives of Colonial Loss and Foreign Occupation* (Bern: Peter Lang, 2005); Joachim Warmbold, *Germania in Africa: Germany's Colonial Literature* (New York: Lang, 1989), 105ff. A Deutsche Kolonien cigarette series was printed by the Cigaretten-Bilderdienst Dresden AG in the 1930s for many cigarette brands. The text framing from the 1936 album published to hold the cards was penned by old colonialists. On film, see Jörg Schöning, ed., *Triviale Tropen: Exotische Reise- un Abenteuerfilme aus Deutschland, 1919–1939* (Munich: edition text & kritik, 1997); Wolfgang Kabatek, *Imagerie des Anderen im Weimarer Kino* (Bielefeld: Transcript, 2003); Assenka Oksiloff, *Picturing the Primitive: Visual Culture, Ethnography, and Early German Cinema* (New York: Palgrave, 2001); and Wolfgang Struck's essay in *Phantasiereiche: Der Deutsche Kolonialismus in Kulturgeschichtlicher Perspektive*, ed. Birthe Kundrus (New York: Campus, 2003).

29. A Nuremberg antenna manufacturer crafted an ad showing two racialized African cannibals ingeniously using their spears to hold up an antenna to listen to a German violinist who plays into a radio transmitter across the ocean. *Die Deutsche Reklame-Industrie* (Berlin: Verband Deutscher Reklamefachleute Verlag, 1925), 104.

30. The literature on Baker is immense; starting points are Carole Sweeney, *From Fetish to Subject: Race, Modernism, and Primitivism, 1919–1935* (Westport, CT: Praeger, 2004); Petrine Archer-Straw, *Negrophilia: Avant-Garde Paris and Black Culture in the 1920s* (New York: Thames & Hudson, 2000); and Nancy Nenno, "Femininity, the Primitive, and Modern Urban Space: Josephine Baker in Berlin," in *Women in the Metropolis,* ed. Katharina von Ankum (Berkeley: University of California Press, 1997).

31. See the illustration in Jelavich, *Berlin Cabaret,* 173.

32. Michael Budds, ed., *Jazz & the Germans: Essays on the Influence Of "Hot" American Idioms on the 20th-Century German Music* (Hillsdale, NY: Pendragon Press, 2002), 11.

33. It is a critique of fashion. Edith Gräfin Salburg, "Die Entsittlichung der Frau durch die jüdische Mode," *Völkische Beobachter* (18 June 1927), cited in Irene Guenther, *Nazi Chic? Fashioning Women in the Third Reich* (Oxford: Berg, 2004), 76.

34. Guenther, *Nazi Chic?* 72.

35. Jan P. Nederveen Pieterse, *White on Black: Images of Africa and Blacks in Western Popular Culture* (New Haven, CT: Yale University Press, 1992), 144. See especially Birgit Haehnel, "'The Black Jew': An Afterimage of German Colonialism," in *German Colonialism, Visual Culture, and Modern Memory*, ed. Volker Langbehn (New York: Routledge, 2010), 240–241.

36. See particularly Kristin Kopp, "Constructing Racial Difference in Colonial Poland," and Pascal Grosse, "What Does German Colonialism Have to Do with National Socialism? A Conceptual Framework," both in Ames, Klotz, and Wildenthal, *Colonial Pasts,* as well as Jürgen Zimmerer, "The Birth of the *Ostland* Out of the Spirit of Colonialism: A Postcolonial Perspective on the Nazi Policy of Conquest and Extermination," *Patterns of Prejudice* 39, no. 2 (2005). For a critique of drawing a straight line from colonialism to Nazism, see Birthe Kundrus, "Kontinuitäten, Parallelen, Rezeptionen: Überlegungen zur 'Kolonialisierung' des Nationalsozialismus," *WerkstattGeschichte* 43 (2006).

37. See, for instance, Gerhard Paul, *Aufstand der Bilder: NS Propaganda vor 1933* (Bonn: Dietz, 1990).

38. See Haehnel "'The Black Jew,'" 239–269.

39. In the Kaloderma tableau, a diminutive black boy figure holds up a mirror to a muscled white man in khaki, who calmly shaves. Nederveen Pieterse, *White on Black,* 88; see also Christian Schneegass, ed., *Ludwig Hohlwein: Plakate der Jahre 1906–1940 aus der Graphischen Sammlung, Staatsgalerie Stuttgart* (Stuttgart: Staatsgalerie, 1985), 303, 345, 347. The poster for Zeiss, featuring a white safari hunter looking into the distance, with a slightly racialized African behind him, pointing over his shoulder, can be found in Bernard Mirabel, *Negripub* (Paris: Somogy, 1987), 50.

40. Photos of the blackface Sarotti Moor in malls today are easily found online. One specific photo from 2001 is in *Hanse-Schmack* (Bremen, 2001), 13, with the caption "Der 'Sarotti-Mohr' war zu Besuch in der Galeria Kaufhof und ließ aus seinem Brunne flüssige Schokolade fließen. Auf ähnliche Aktionen dürfen die Kunden in Zukunft gespannt sein." The persistence of racial imagery of blacks in contemporary German consumer culture is highlighted by a plethora of books, including Rosemarie K. Lester, *"Trivialneger": Das Bild des Schwarzen im westdeutschen Illustriertenroman,* vol. 124 (Stuttgart: Hans-Dieter Heinz, 1982);

Helmut Fritz, "Negerköpfe, Mohrenküsse: Der Wilde im Alltag," in *Wir und Die Wilden: Einblick in eine kannibalische Beziehung,* ed. Thomas Theye (Reinbek: Rowohlt, 1985); Marie Lorbeer and Beate Wild, eds., *Menschen Fresser Neger Küsse: Das Bild vom Fremden im deutschen Alltag* (Berlin: Elefanten, 1991); Hermann Pollig, ed., *Exotische Welten: Europäische Phantasien* (Stuttgart: Edition Cantz, 1987); and Regina Riepe and Gerd Riepe, *Du Schwarz—ich weiss: Bilder und Texte gegen den alltäglichen Rassismus* (Wuppertal: Hammer, 1992).

INDEX

Note: Page numbers in *italics* indicate figures. Brand names are listed under the category of ware or product.

Harvard University Press is a member of Green Press Initiative (greenpressinitiative.org), a nonprofit organization working to help publishers and printers increase their use of recycled paper and decrease their use of fiber derived from endangered forests. This book was printed on recycled paper containing 30% post-consumer waste and processed chlorine free.